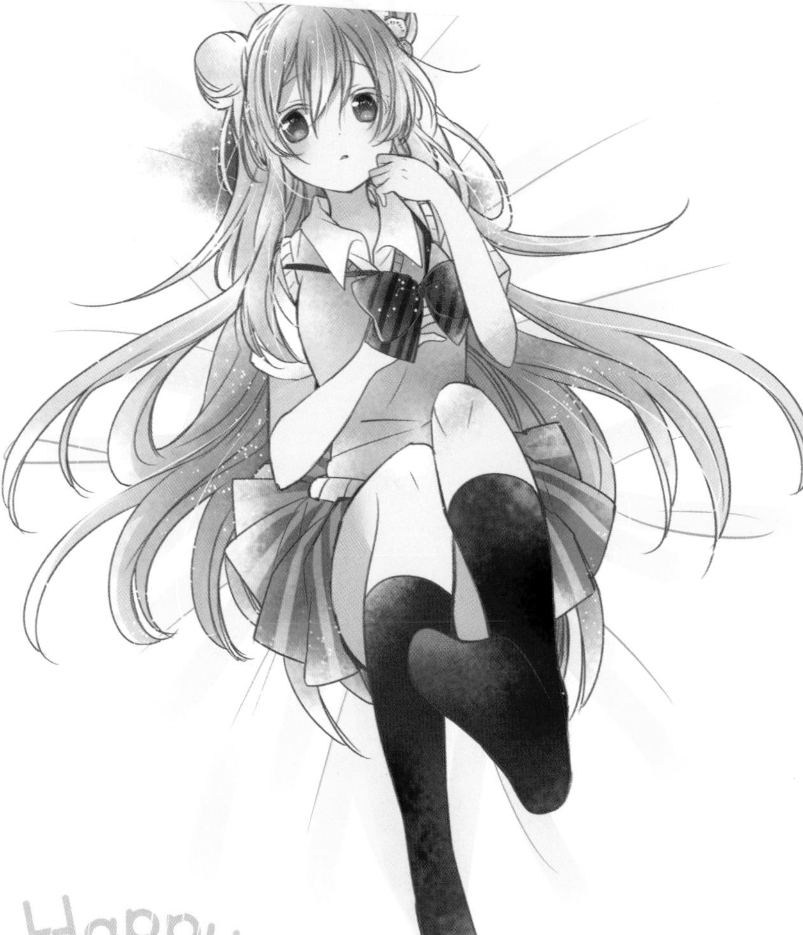

Happy Sugar Life 5

Tomiyaki Kagisora

Happy Sugar Life

Tomiyaki Kagisora

Lifelog ★

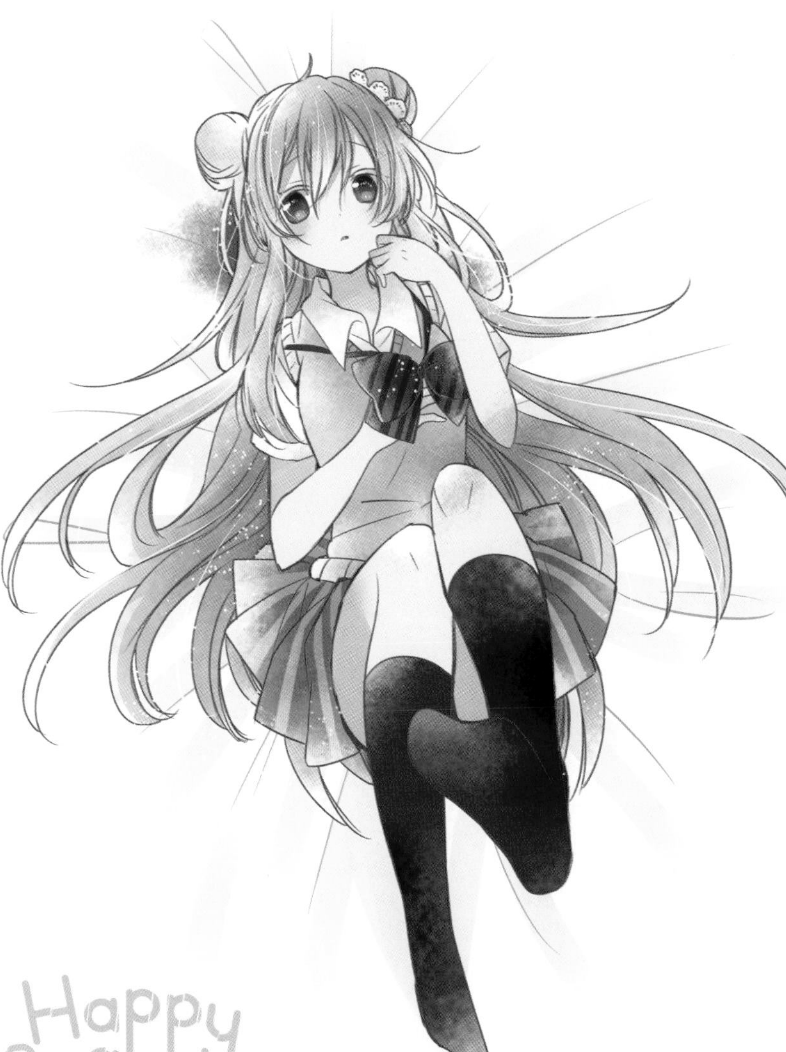

Happy Sugar Life 5

Tomiyaki Kagisora

Happy Sugar Life

Tomiyaki Kagisora

Lifelog ★

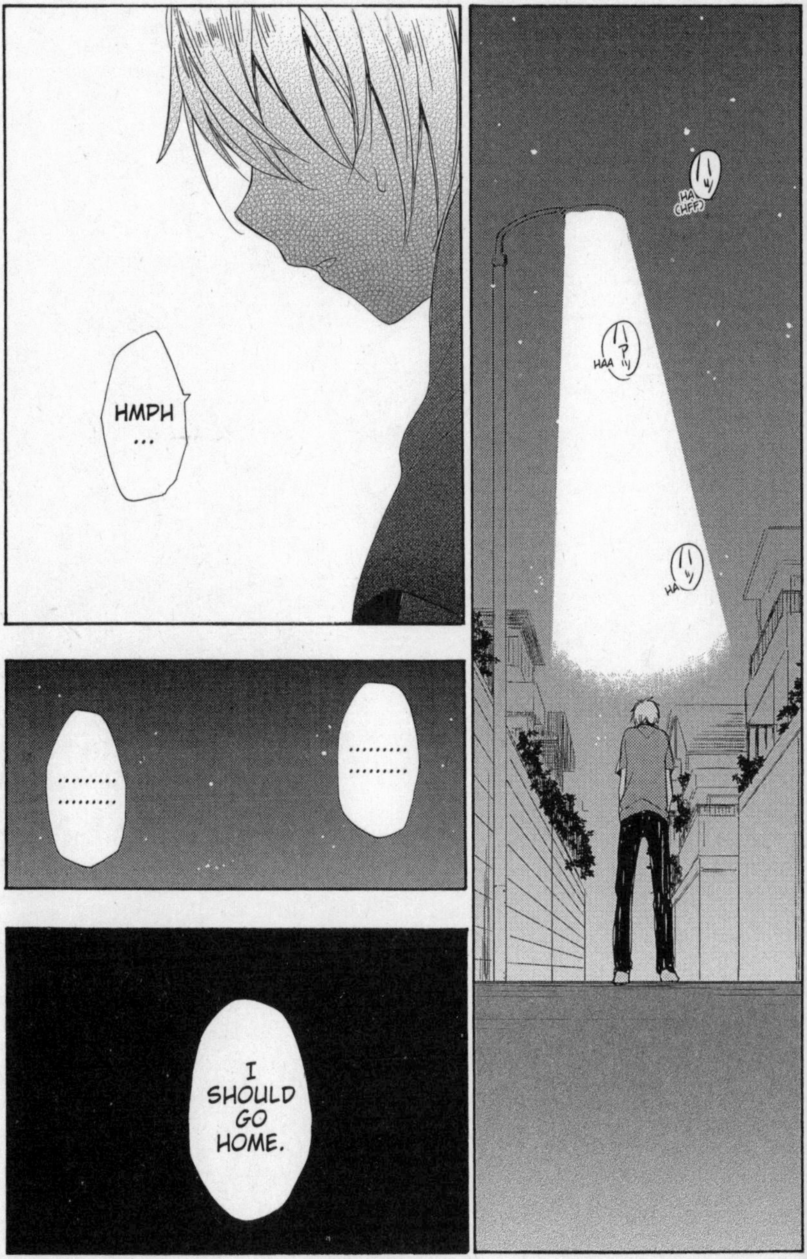

HA (HFF)
HAA
HA
HMPH ...
....
....
I SHOULD GO HOME.

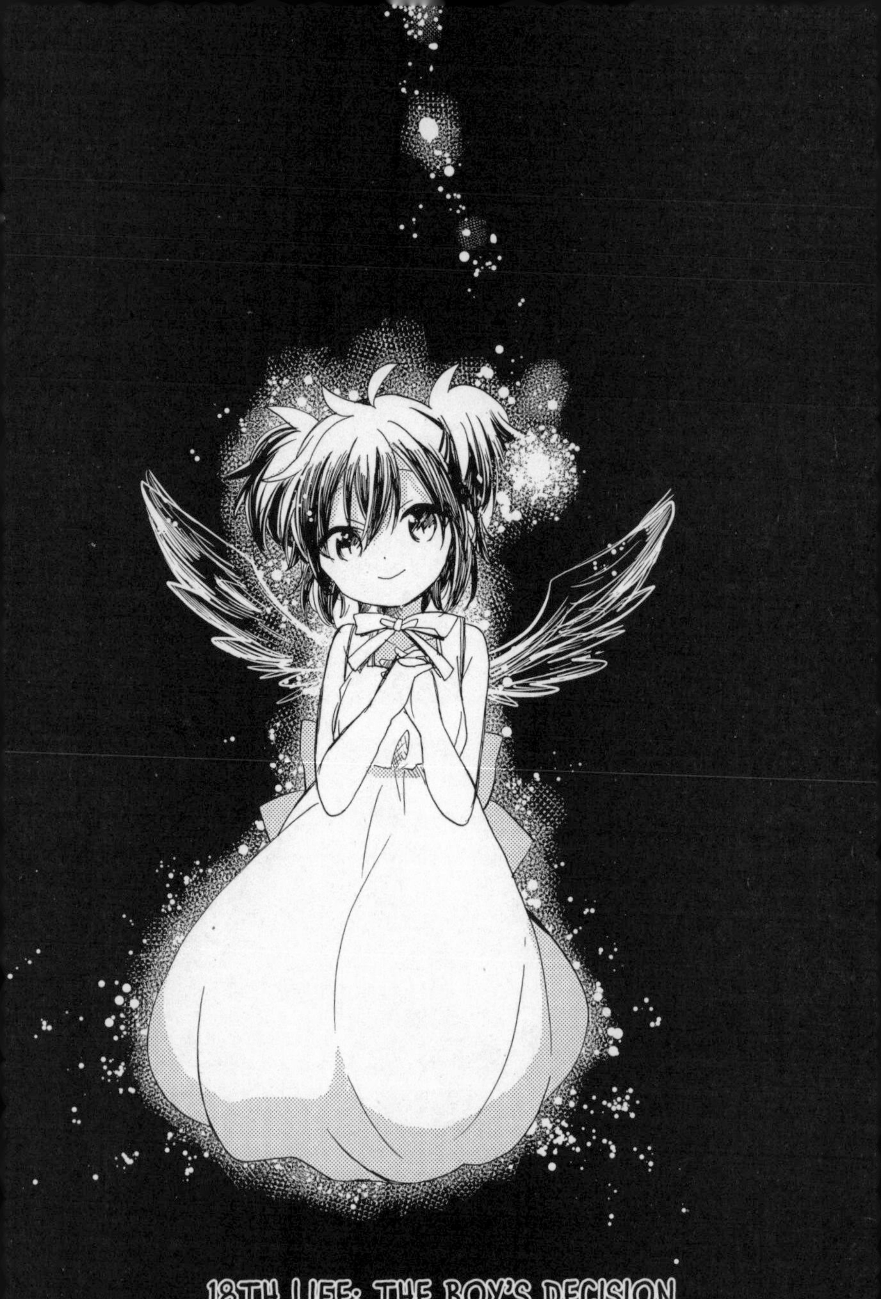

18th Life: The Boy's Decision

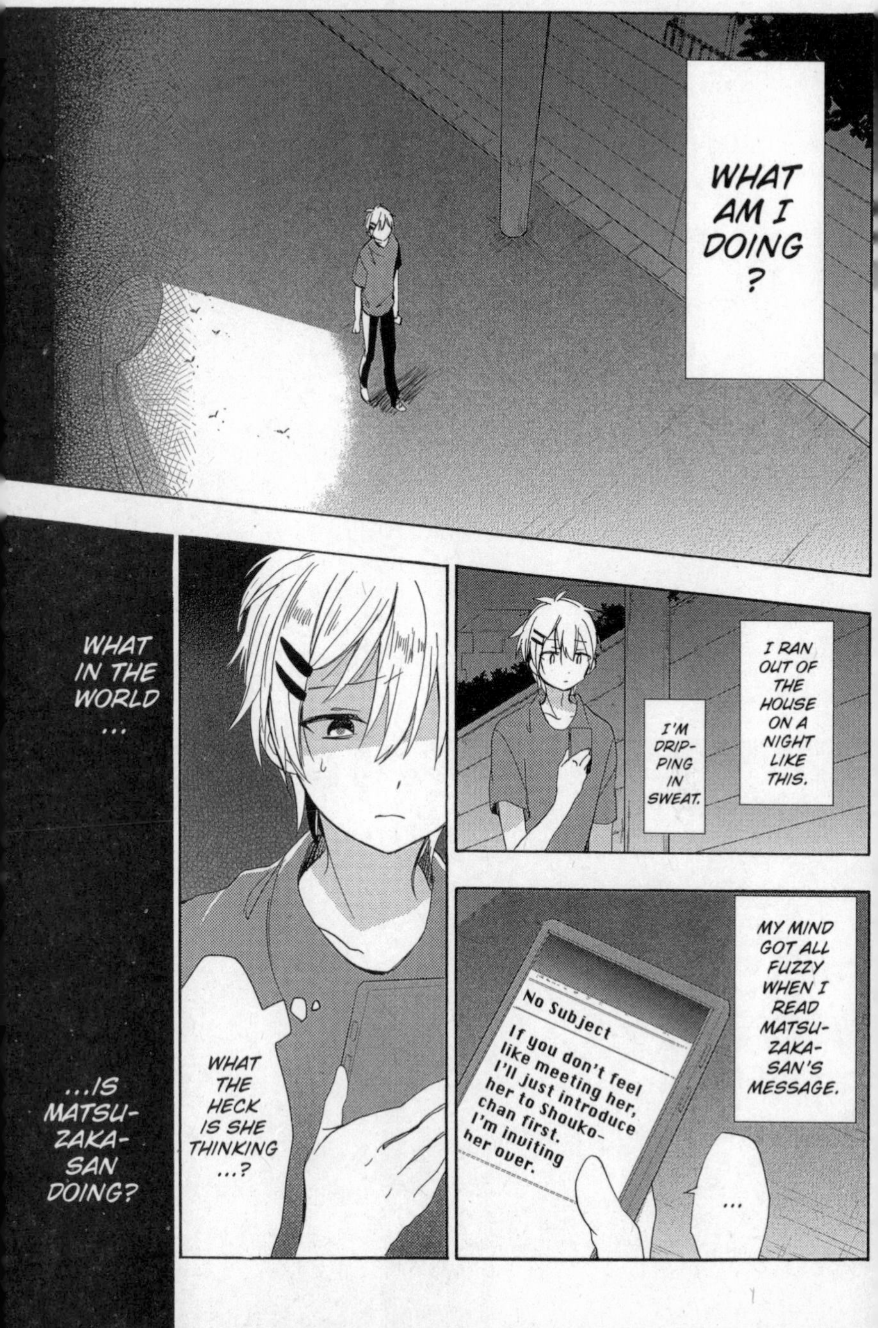
WHAT AM I DOING?
I RAN OUT OF THE HOUSE ON A NIGHT LIKE THIS.
I'M DRIPPING IN SWEAT.
MY MIND GOT ALL FUZZY WHEN I READ MATSUZAKA-SAN'S MESSAGE.
No Subject
If you don't feel like meeting her, I'll just introduce her to Shouko-chan first. I'm inviting her over.
...
WHAT IN THE WORLD...
WHAT THE HECK IS SHE THINKING...?
...IS MATSUZAKA-SAN DOING?

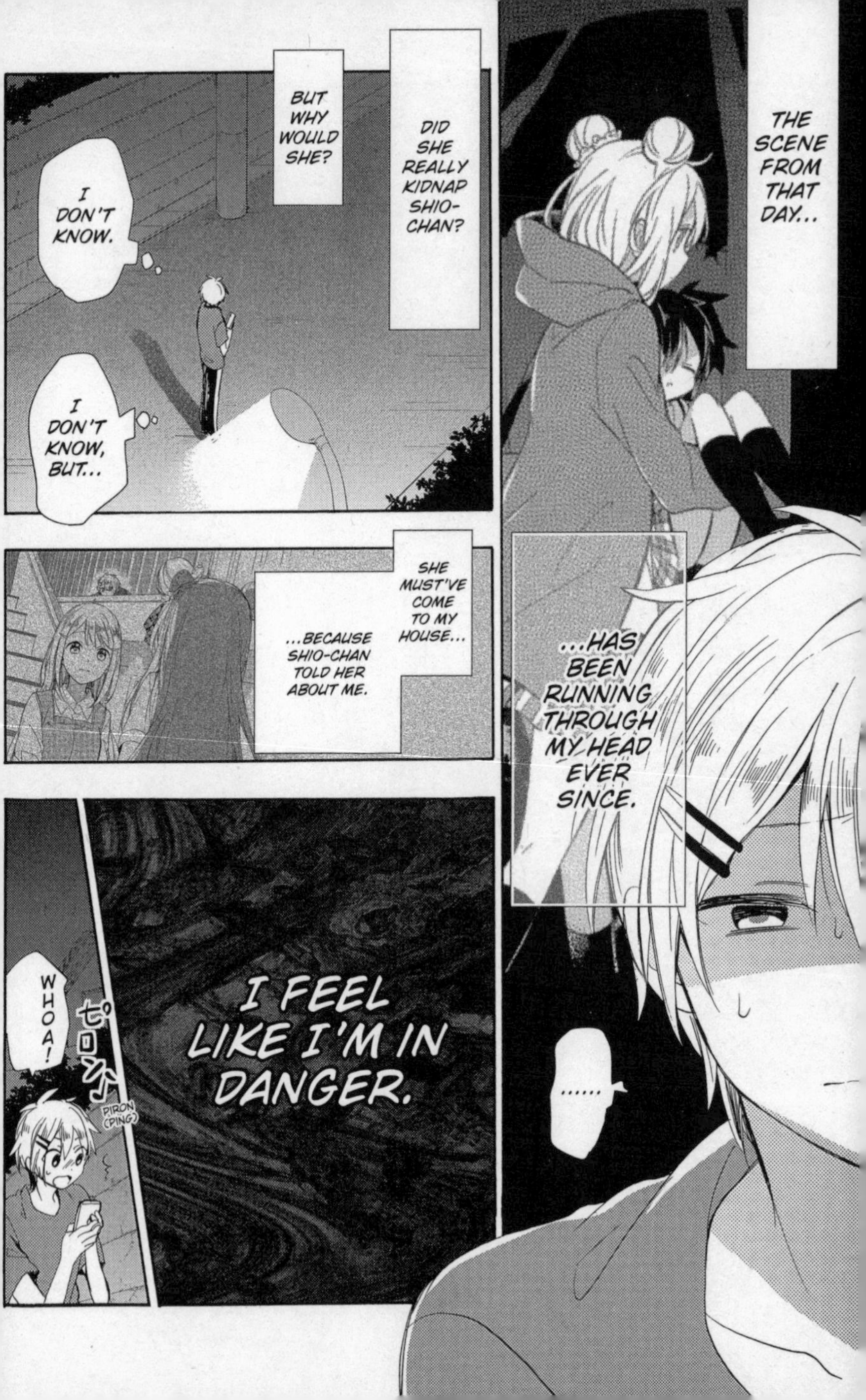
THE SCENE FROM THAT DAY...
...HAS BEEN RUNNING THROUGH MY HEAD EVER SINCE.
......
DID SHE REALLY KIDNAP SHIO-CHAN?
BUT WHY WOULD SHE?
I DON'T KNOW.
I DON'T KNOW, BUT...
SHE MUST'VE COME TO MY HOUSE...
...BECAUSE SHIO-CHAN TOLD HER ABOUT ME.
I FEEL LIKE I'M IN DANGER.
ピロン
PIRON (PING)
WHOA!

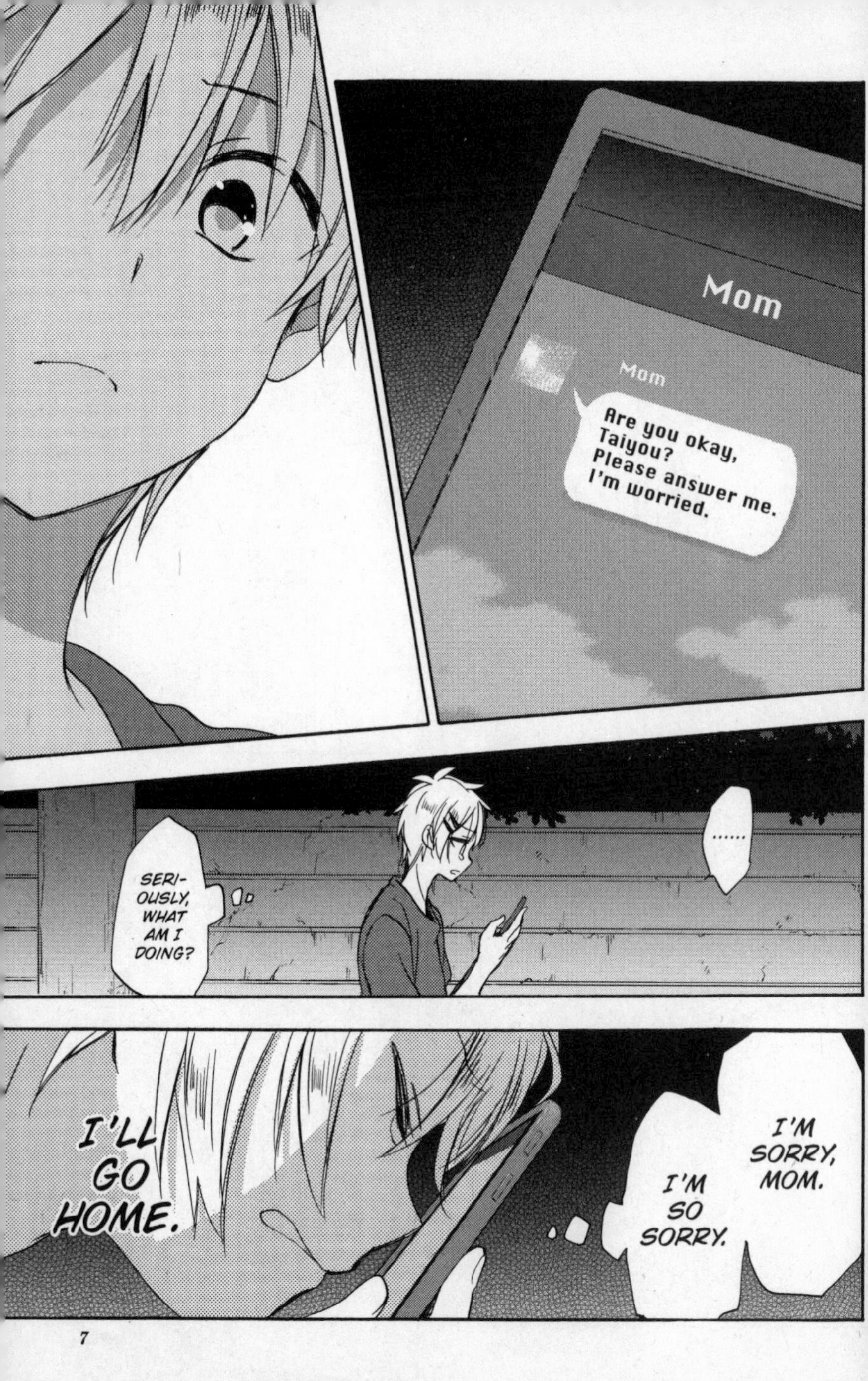
Mom
Mom
Are you okay, Taiyou? Please answer me. I'm worried.
......
SERIOUSLY, WHAT AM I DOING?
I'M SORRY, MOM.
I'M SO SORRY.
I'LL GO HOME.

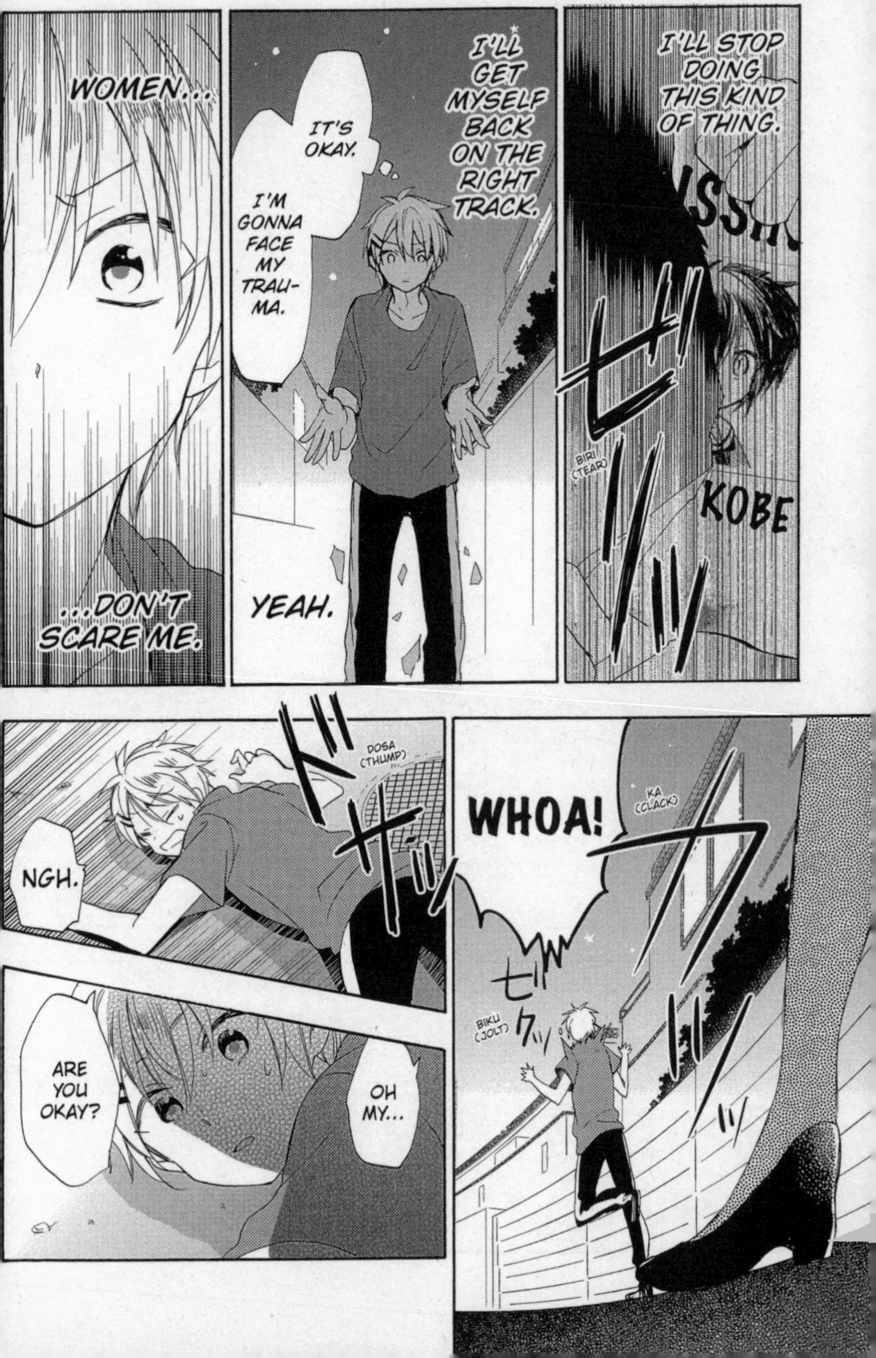
I'LL STOP DOING THIS KIND OF THING.
BIRI (TEAR)
KOBE
I'LL GET MYSELF BACK ON THE RIGHT TRACK.
IT'S OKAY.
I'M GONNA FACE MY TRAU-MA.
YEAH.
WOMEN...
...DON'T SCARE ME.
KA (CLACK)
WHOA!
BIKU (JOLT)
DOSA (THUMP)
NGH.
OH MY...
ARE YOU OKAY?

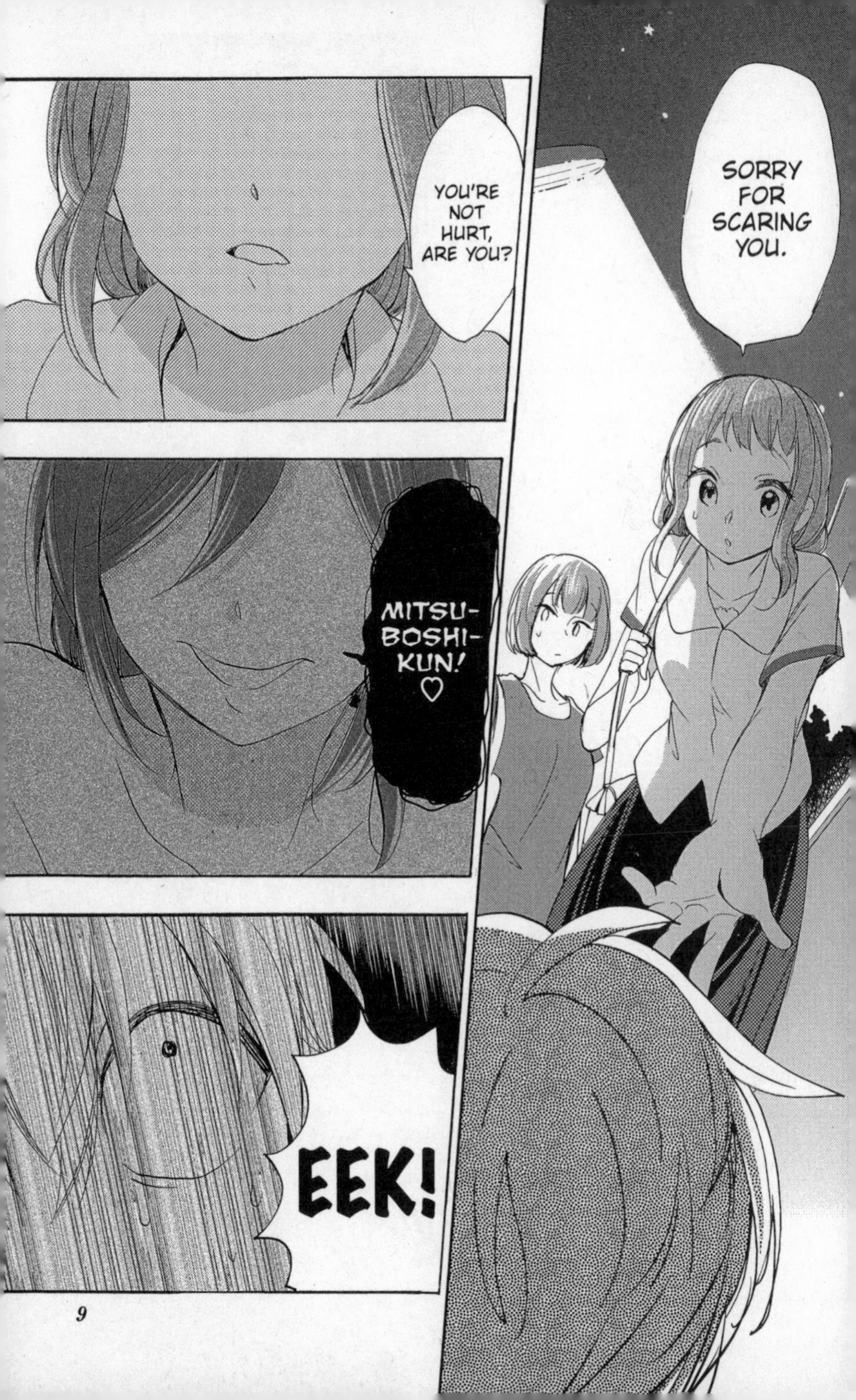
SORRY FOR SCARING YOU.
YOU'RE NOT HURT, ARE YOU?
MITSU-BOSHI-KUN! ♡
EEK!

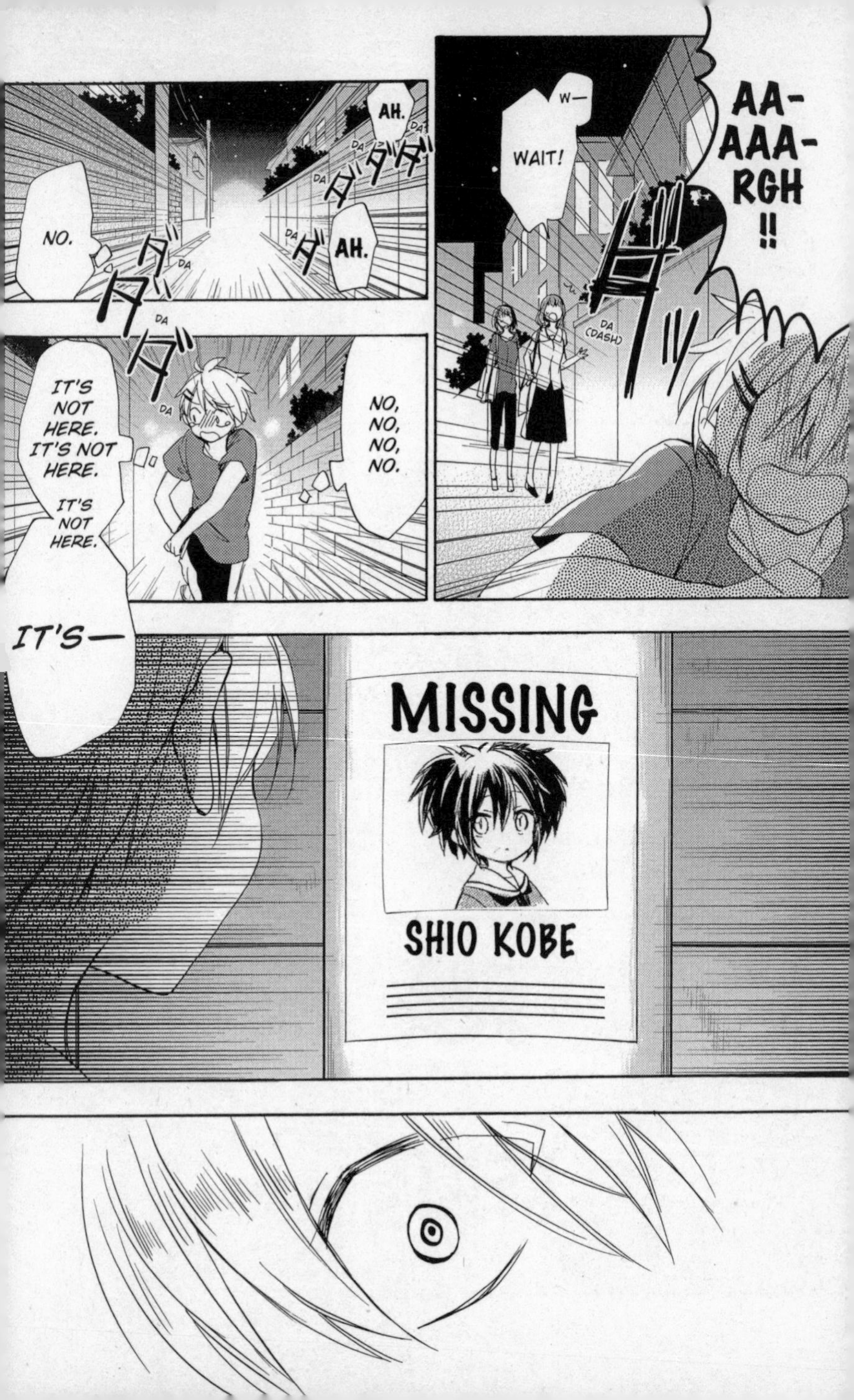
AA-AAAA-RGH!!
W—
WAIT!
DA (DASH)
AH.
DA DA
AH.
NO.
NO, NO, NO, NO.
IT'S NOT HERE. IT'S NOT HERE.
IT'S NOT HERE.
IT'S—
MISSING
SHIO KOBE

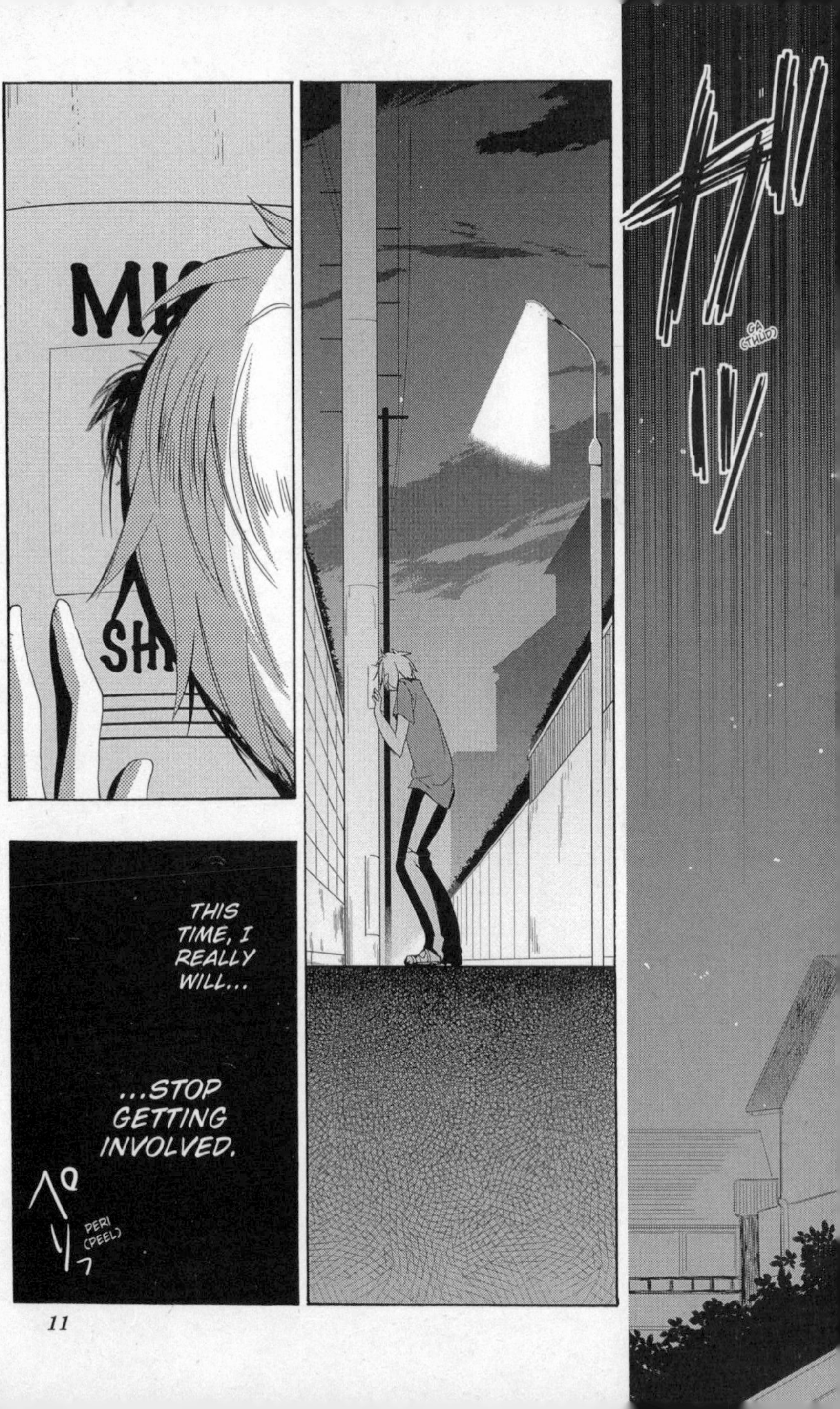
GA (THUD)
THIS TIME, I REALLY WILL...
...STOP GETTING INVOLVED.
PERI (PEEL)

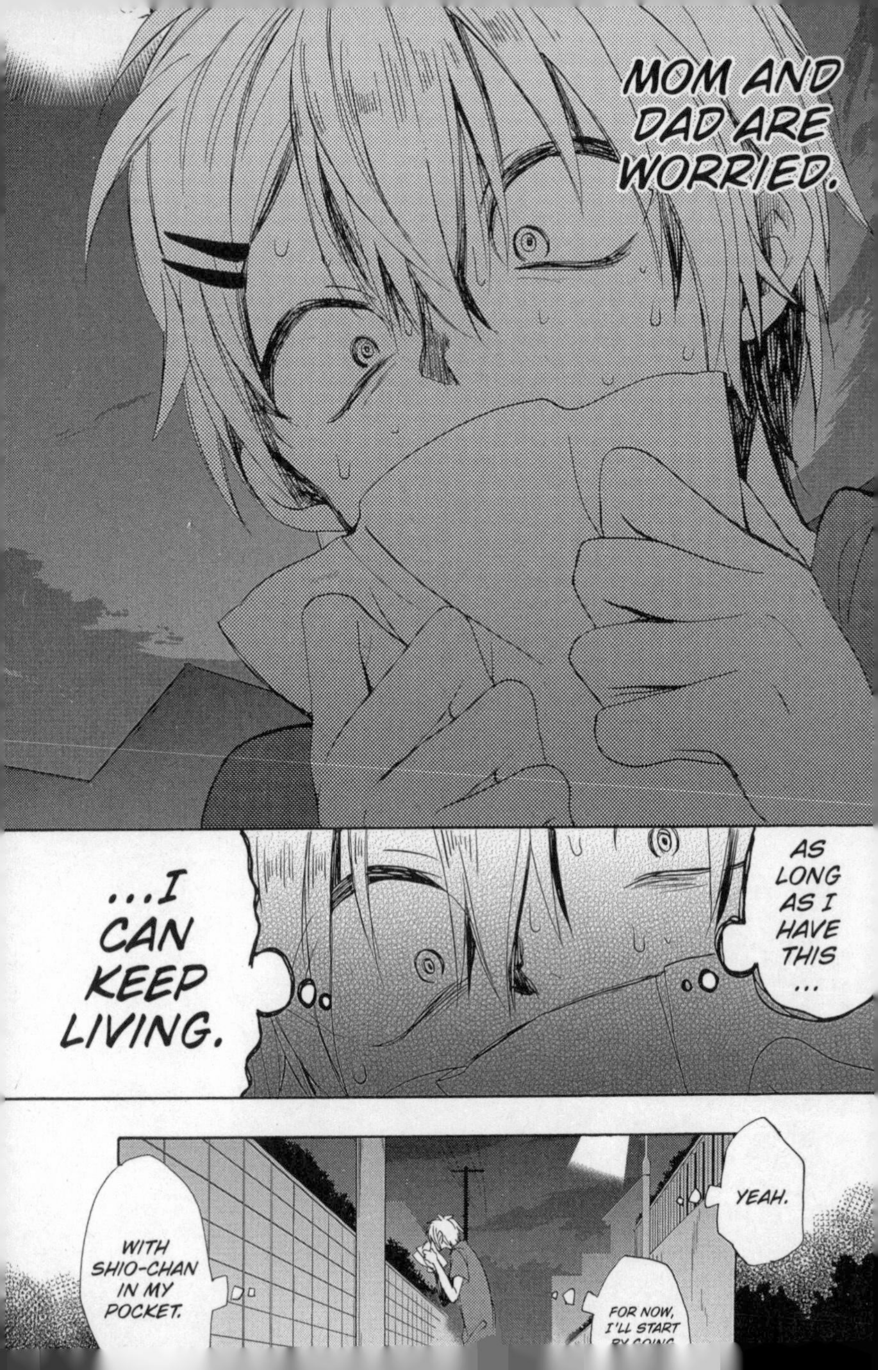
MOM AND DAD ARE WORRIED.
AS LONG AS I HAVE THIS...
...I CAN KEEP LIVING.
YEAH.
FOR NOW, I'LL START
WITH SHIO-CHAN IN MY POCKET.

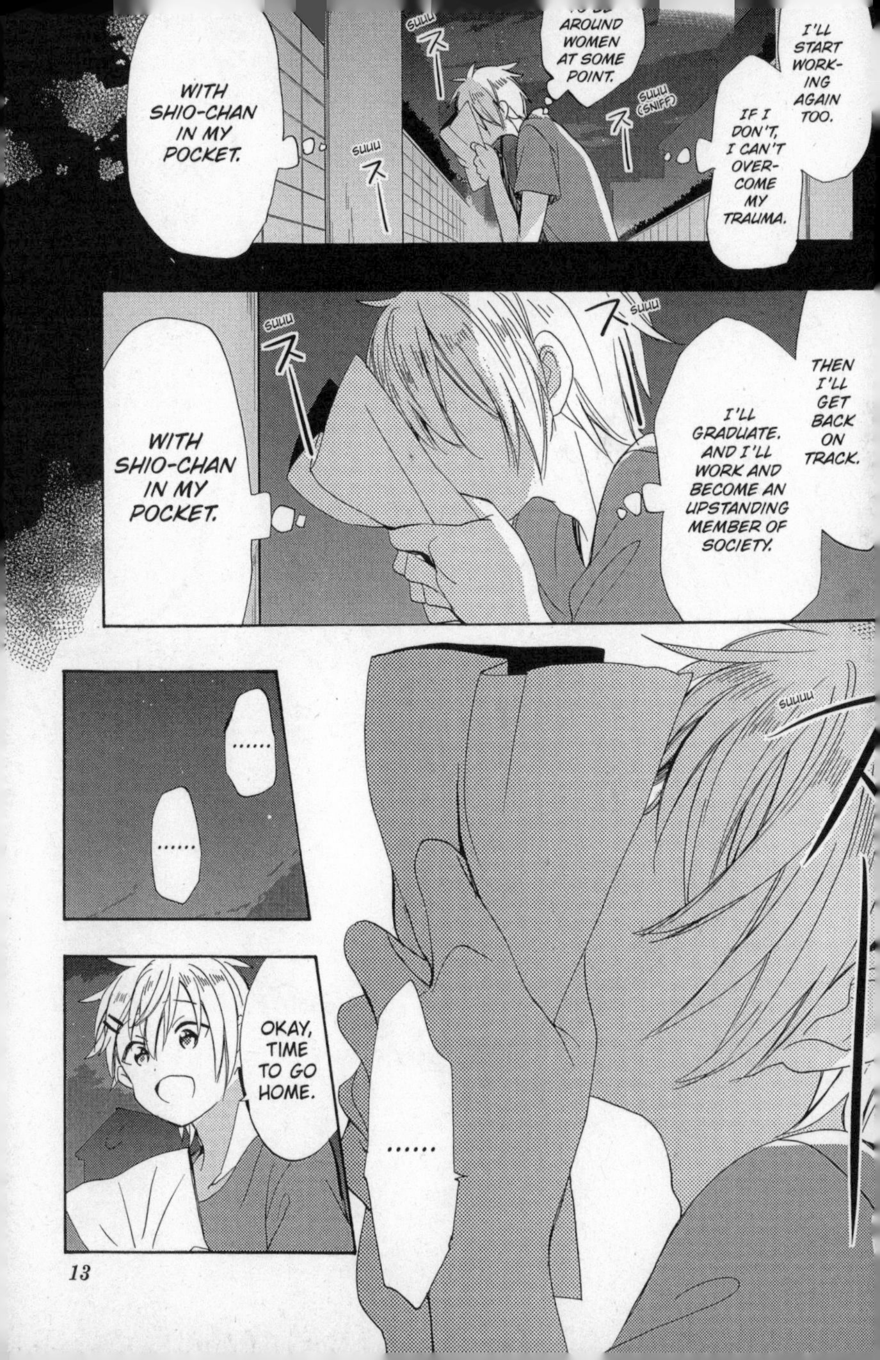
I'LL START WORKING AGAIN TOO.
IF I DON'T, I CAN'T OVERCOME MY TRAUMA.
AROUND WOMEN AT SOME POINT.
SUUU (SNIFF)
SUUU
SUUU
WITH SHIO-CHAN IN MY POCKET.
THEN I'LL GET BACK ON TRACK.
I'LL GRADUATE. AND I'LL WORK AND BECOME AN UPSTANDING MEMBER OF SOCIETY.
SUUU
SUUU
WITH SHIO-CHAN IN MY POCKET.
SUUUU
......
......
......
OKAY, TIME TO GO HOME.

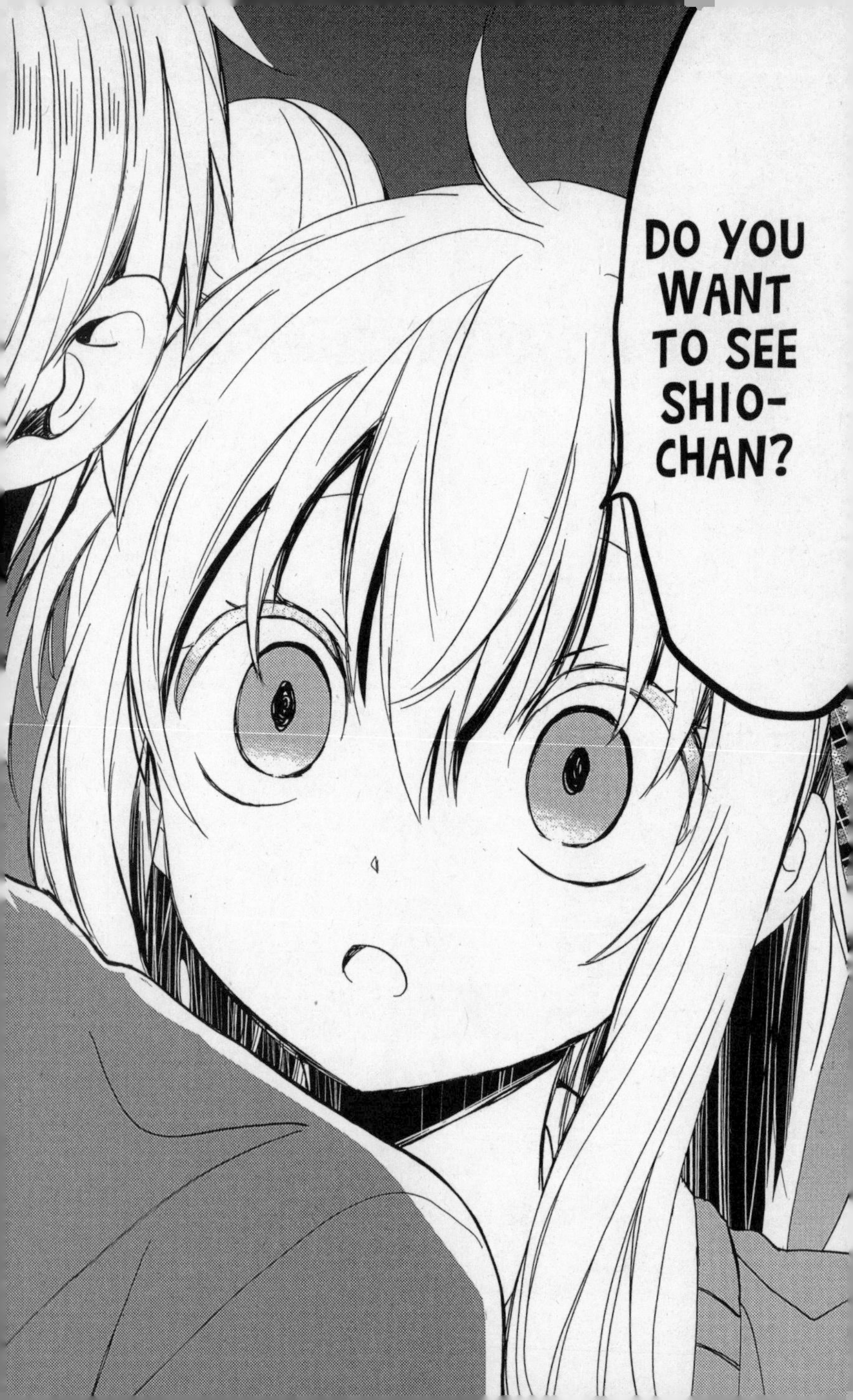
DO YOU WANT TO SEE SHIO-CHAN?

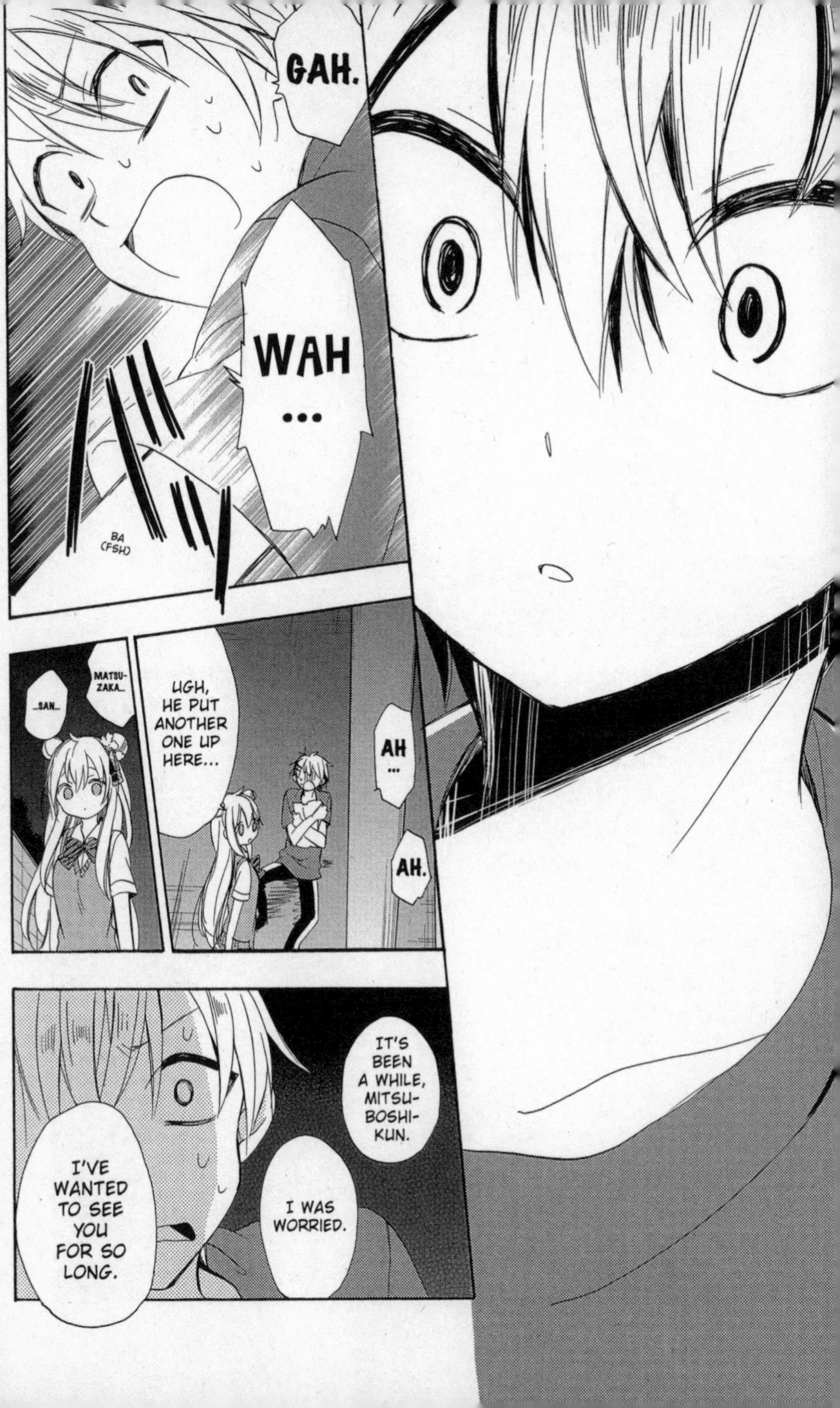
AH...
AH.
GAH.
WAH...
BA (FSH)
UGH, HE PUT ANOTHER ONE UP HERE...
MATSUZAKA...
...SAN...
IT'S BEEN A WHILE, MITSUBOSHI-KUN.
I WAS WORRIED.
I'VE WANTED TO SEE YOU FOR SO LONG.

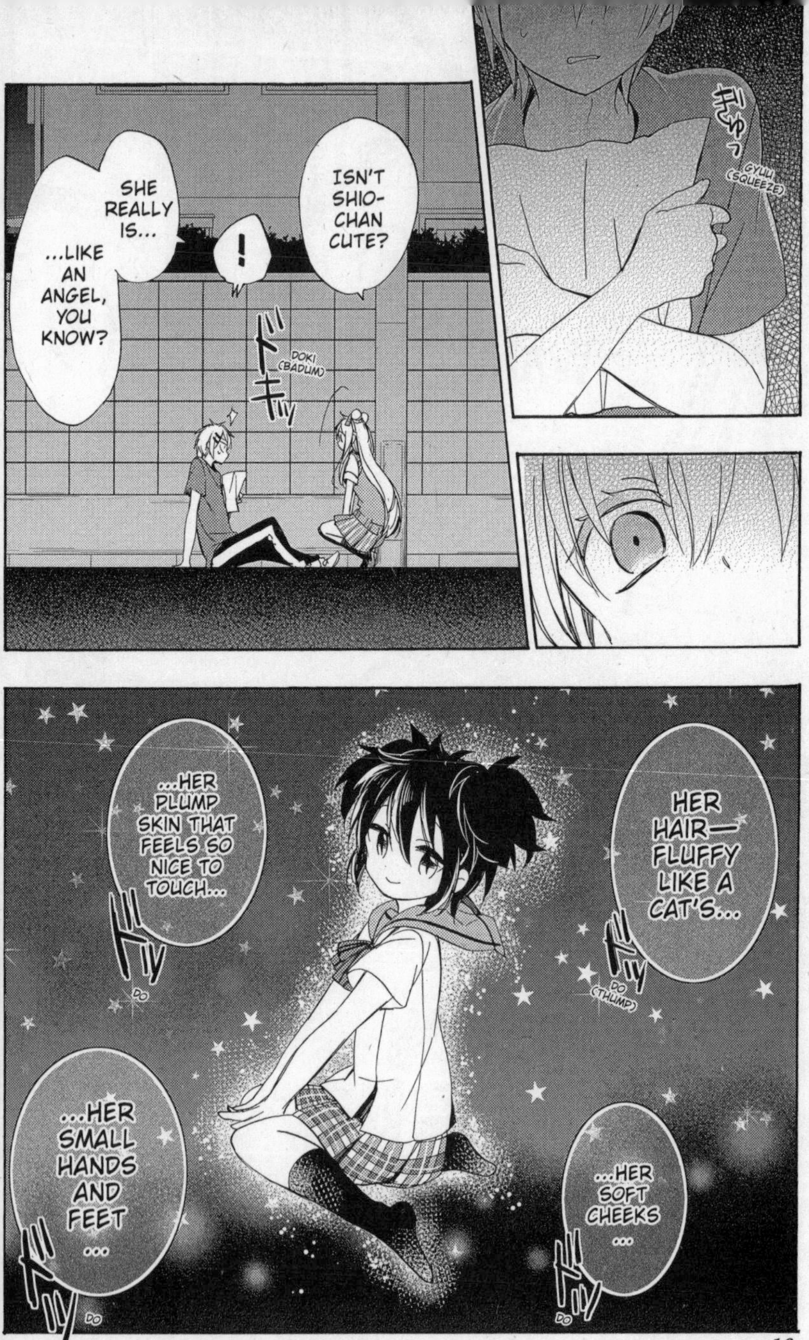
GYUU (SQUEEZE)
ISN'T SHIO-CHAN CUTE?
!
DOKI (BADUM)
SHE REALLY IS...
...LIKE AN ANGEL, YOU KNOW?
HER HAIR—FLUFFY LIKE A CAT'S...
DO (THUMP)
...HER PLUMP SKIN THAT FEELS SO NICE TO TOUCH...
DO
...HER SOFT CHEEKS...
DO
...HER SMALL HANDS AND FEET...
DO

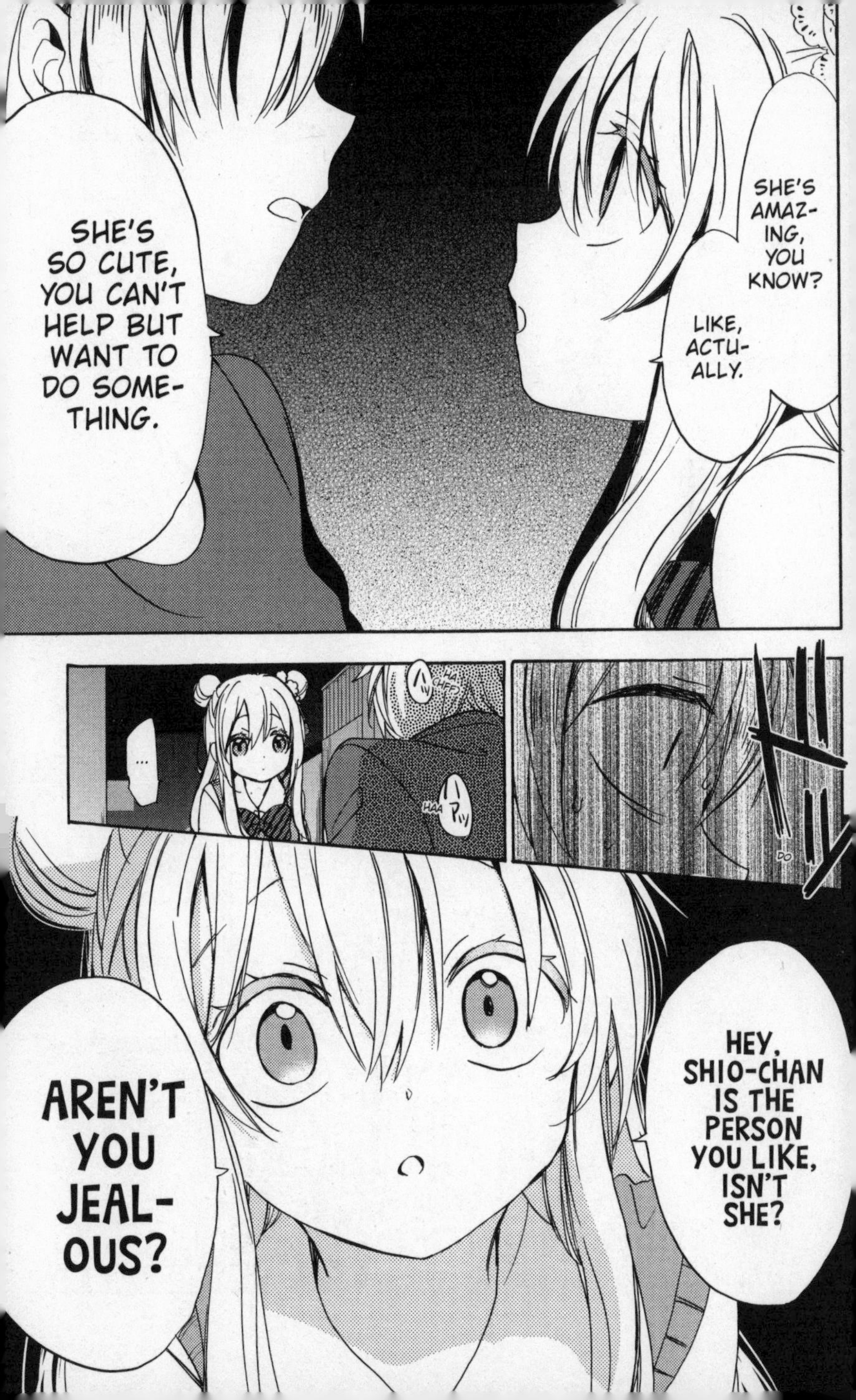
SHE'S AMAZ-ING, YOU KNOW?
LIKE, ACTU-ALLY.
SHE'S SO CUTE, YOU CAN'T HELP BUT WANT TO DO SOME-THING.
ド
DO
ハッ
HA CHFF?
ハァッ
HAA
...
HEY, SHIO-CHAN IS THE PERSON YOU LIKE, ISN'T SHE?
AREN'T YOU JEAL-OUS?

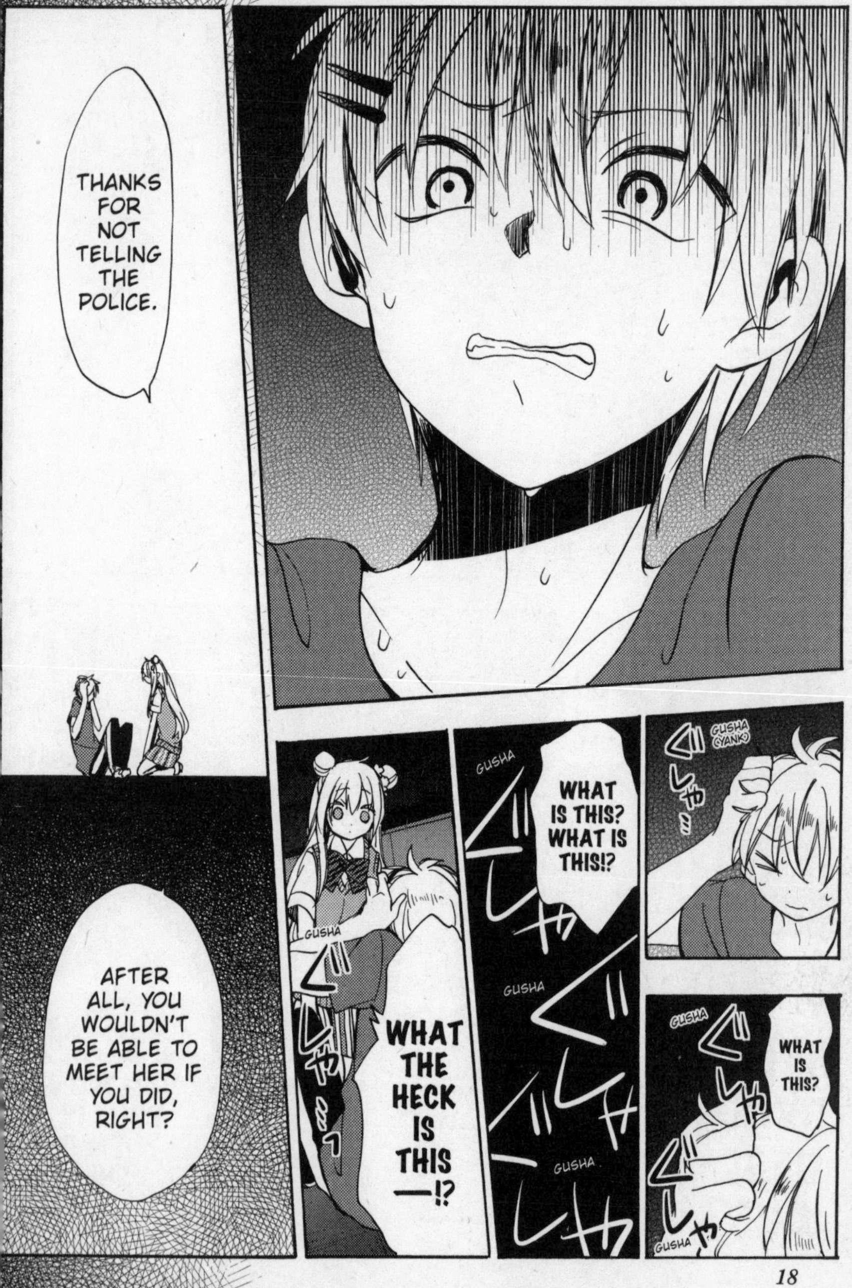
GUSHA (YANK)
GUSHA
WHAT IS THIS?
GUSHA
GUSHA
WHAT IS THIS? WHAT IS THIS!?
GUSHA
GUSHA
GUSHA
WHAT THE HECK IS THIS—!?
THANKS FOR NOT TELLING THE POLICE.
AFTER ALL, YOU WOULDN'T BE ABLE TO MEET HER IF YOU DID, RIGHT?

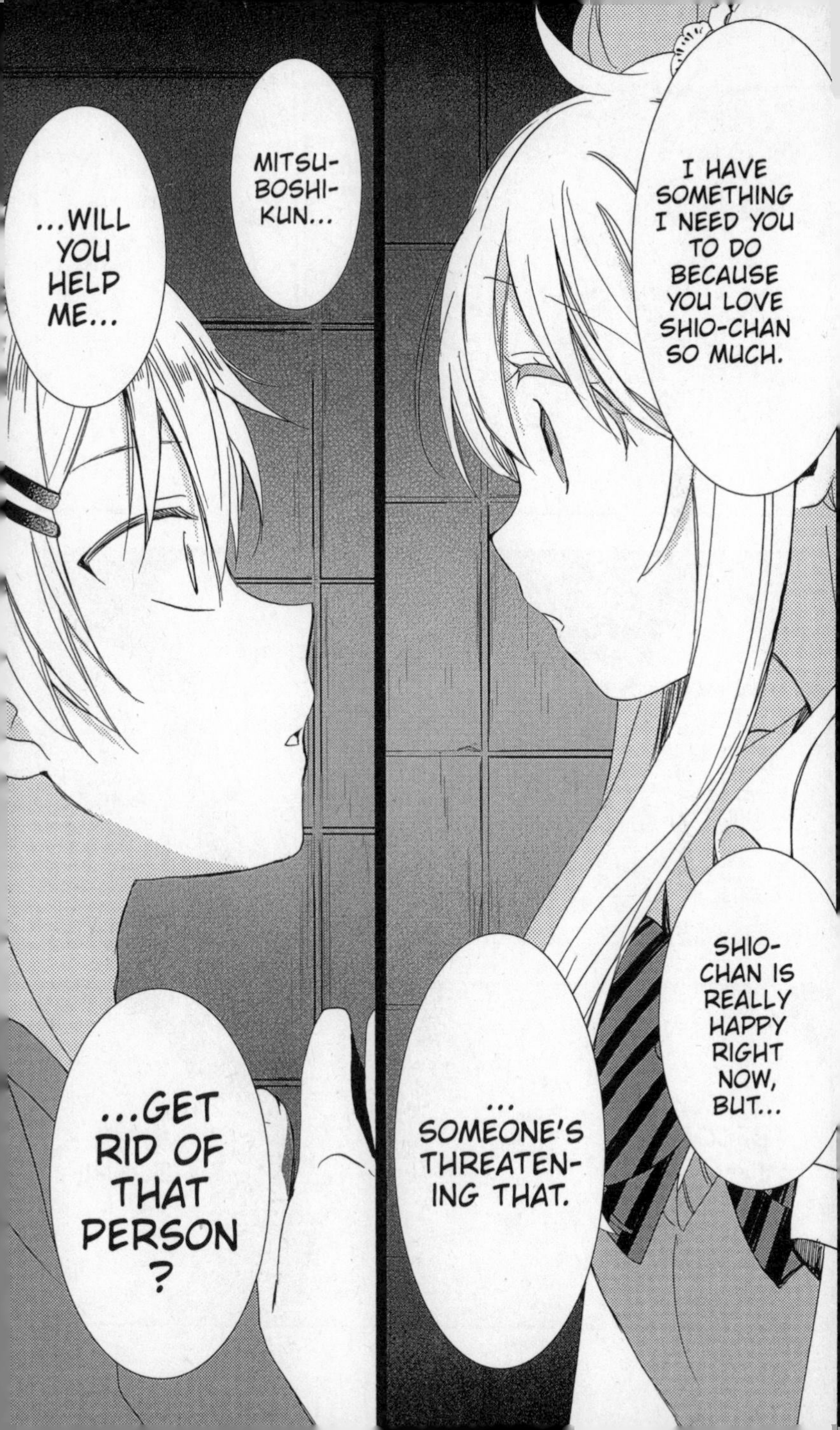
I HAVE SOMETHING I NEED YOU TO DO BECAUSE YOU LOVE SHIO-CHAN SO MUCH.
SHIO-CHAN IS REALLY HAPPY RIGHT NOW, BUT...
...SOMEONE'S THREATEN-ING THAT.
MITSU-BOSHI-KUN...
...WILL YOU HELP ME...
...GET RID OF THAT PERSON?

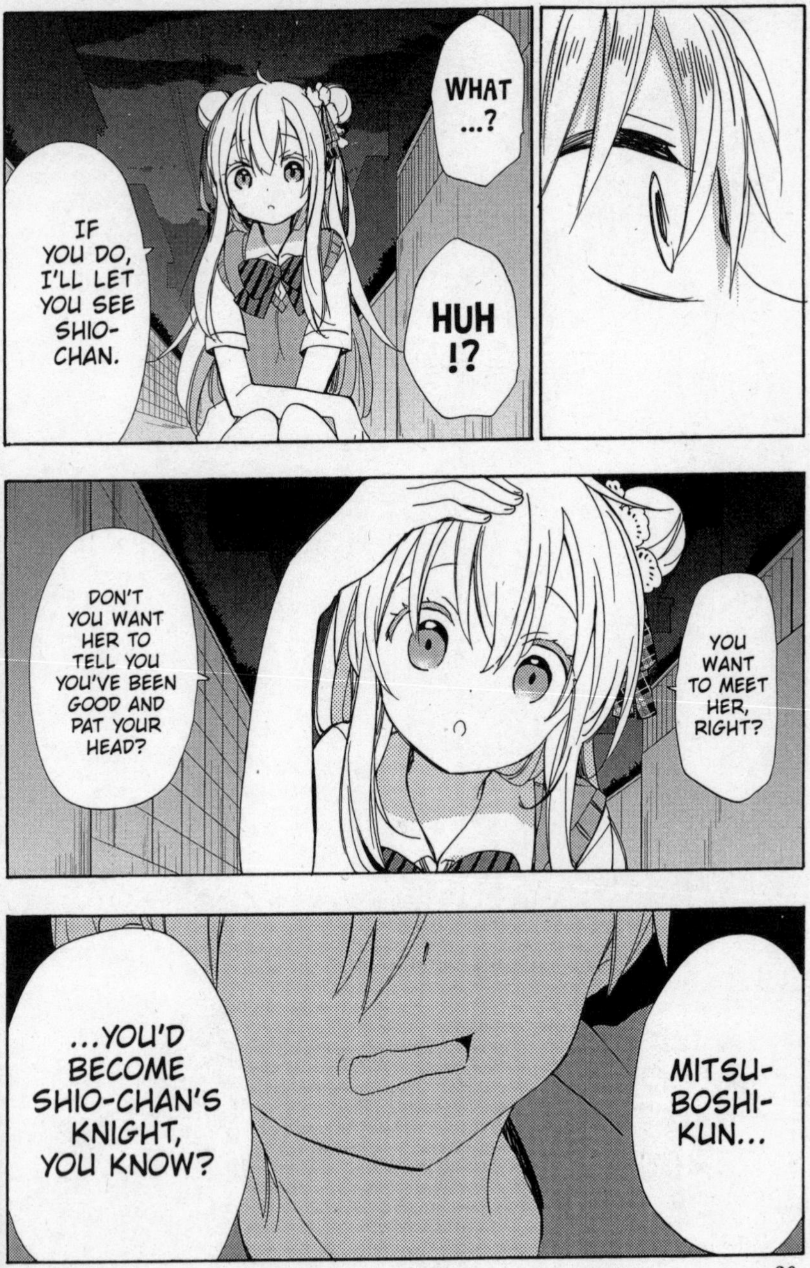
WHAT ...?
HUH !?
IF YOU DO, I'LL LET YOU SEE SHIO-CHAN.
YOU WANT TO MEET HER, RIGHT?
DON'T YOU WANT HER TO TELL YOU YOU'VE BEEN GOOD AND PAT YOUR HEAD?
MITSU-BOSHI-KUN...
...YOU'D BECOME SHIO-CHAN'S KNIGHT, YOU KNOW?

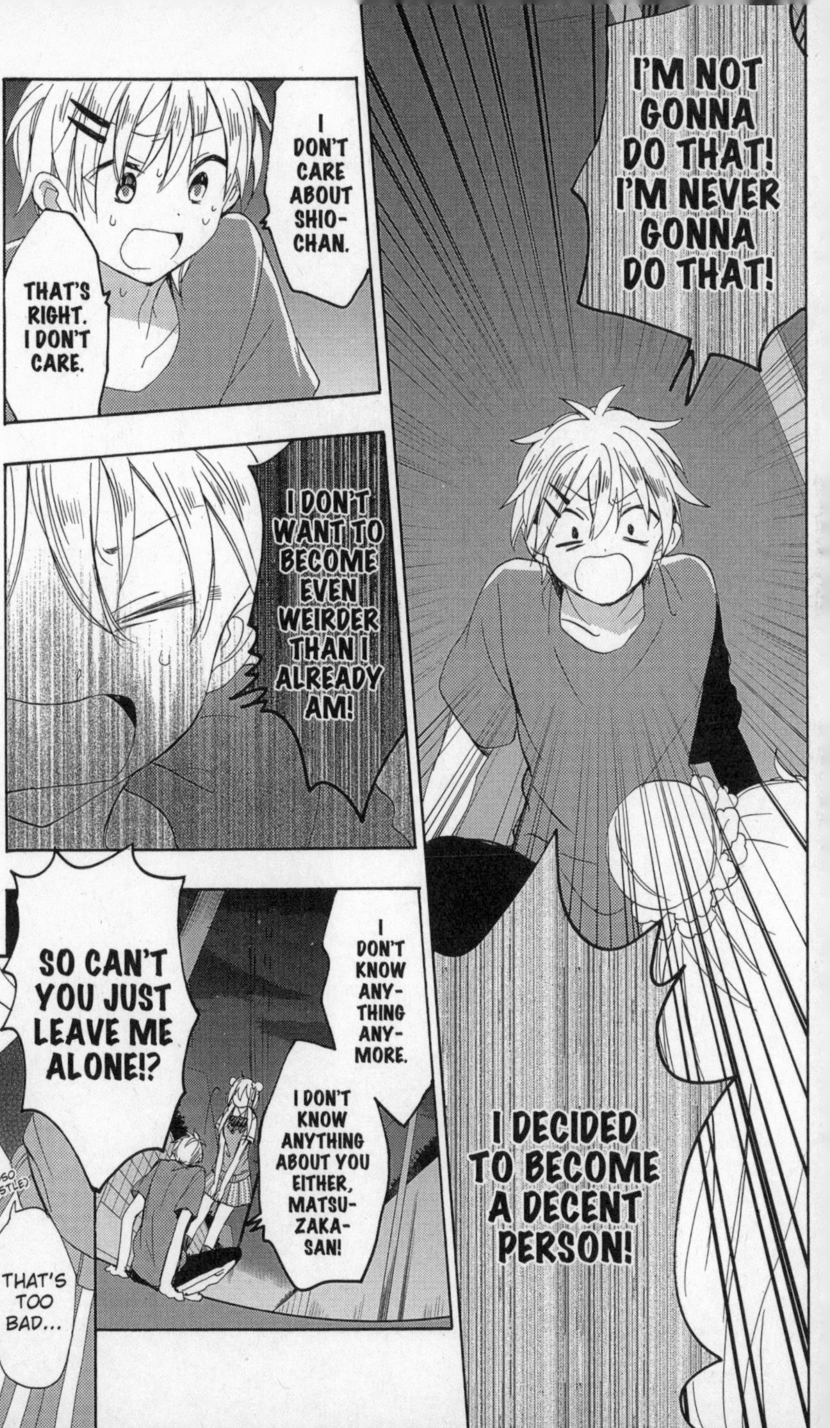
I'M NOT GONNA DO THAT! I'M NEVER GONNA DO THAT!
I DECIDED TO BECOME A DECENT PERSON!
I DON'T CARE ABOUT SHIO-CHAN.
THAT'S RIGHT. I DON'T CARE.
I DON'T WANT TO BECOME EVEN WEIRDER THAN I ALREADY AM!
I DON'T KNOW ANYTHING ANYMORE.
SO CAN'T YOU JUST LEAVE ME ALONE!?
I DON'T KNOW ANYTHING ABOUT YOU EITHER, MATSUZAKA-SAN!
GOSO (RUSTLE)
THAT'S TOO BAD...

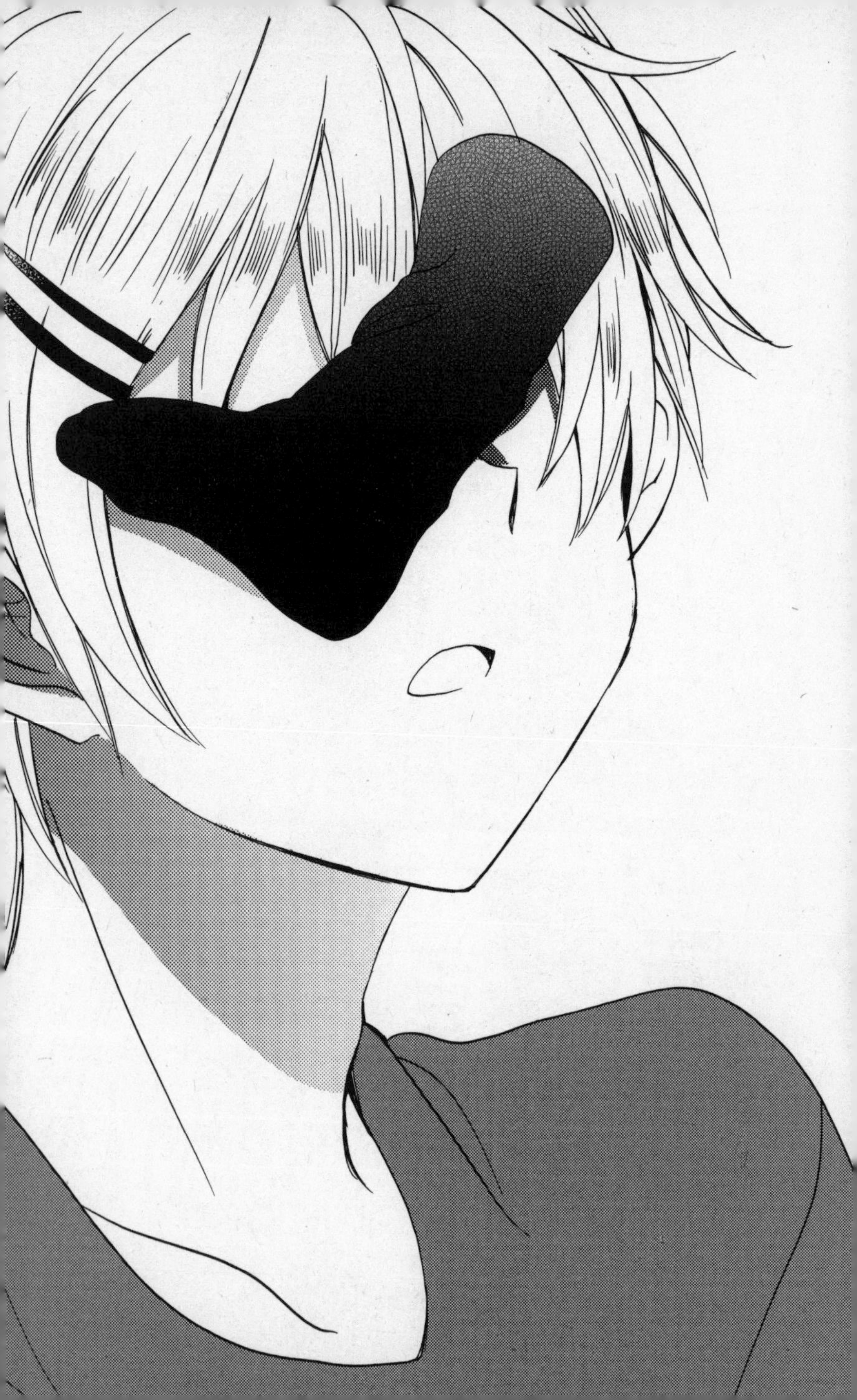

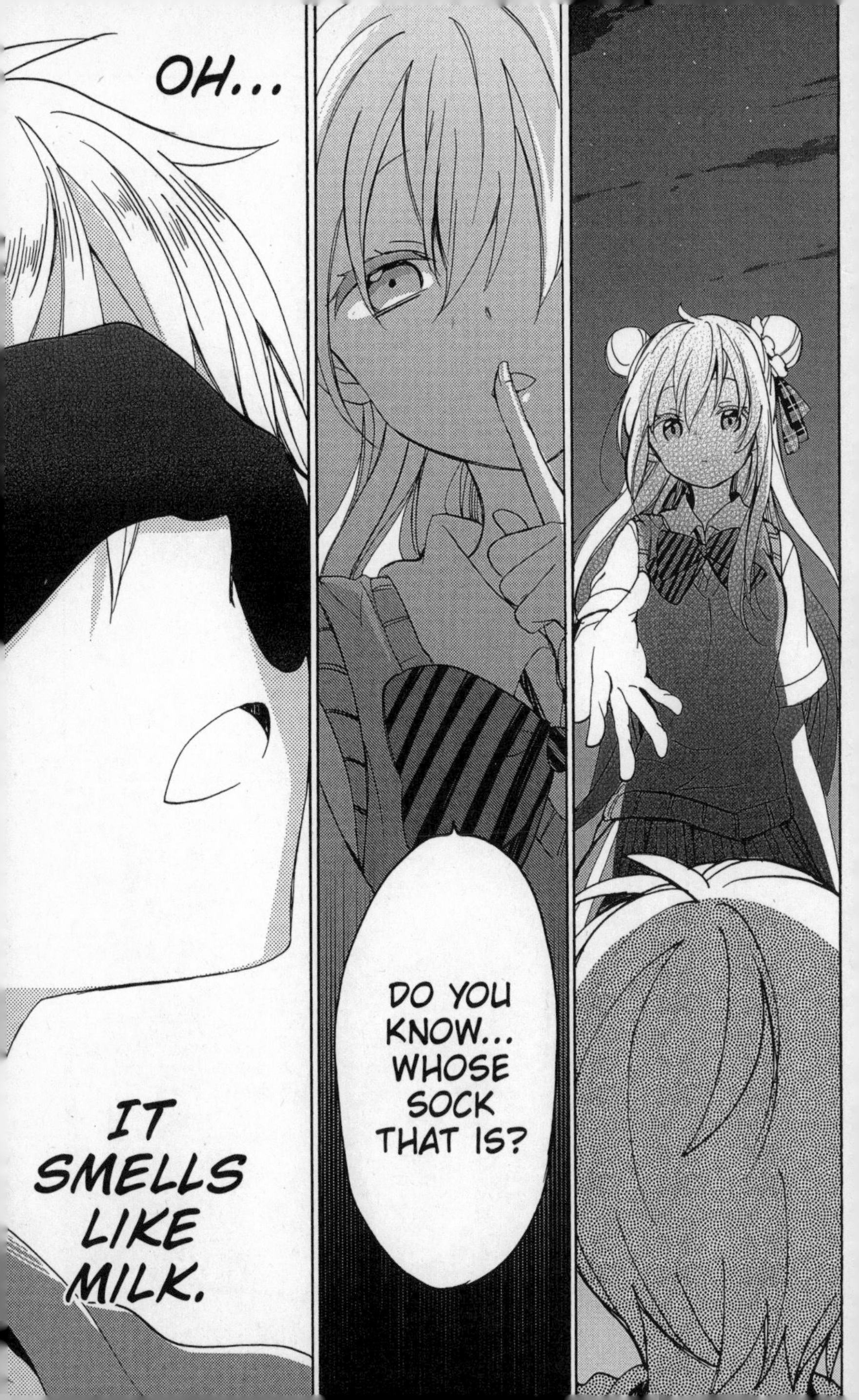
DO YOU KNOW... WHOSE SOCK THAT IS?
OH...
IT SMELLS LIKE MILK.

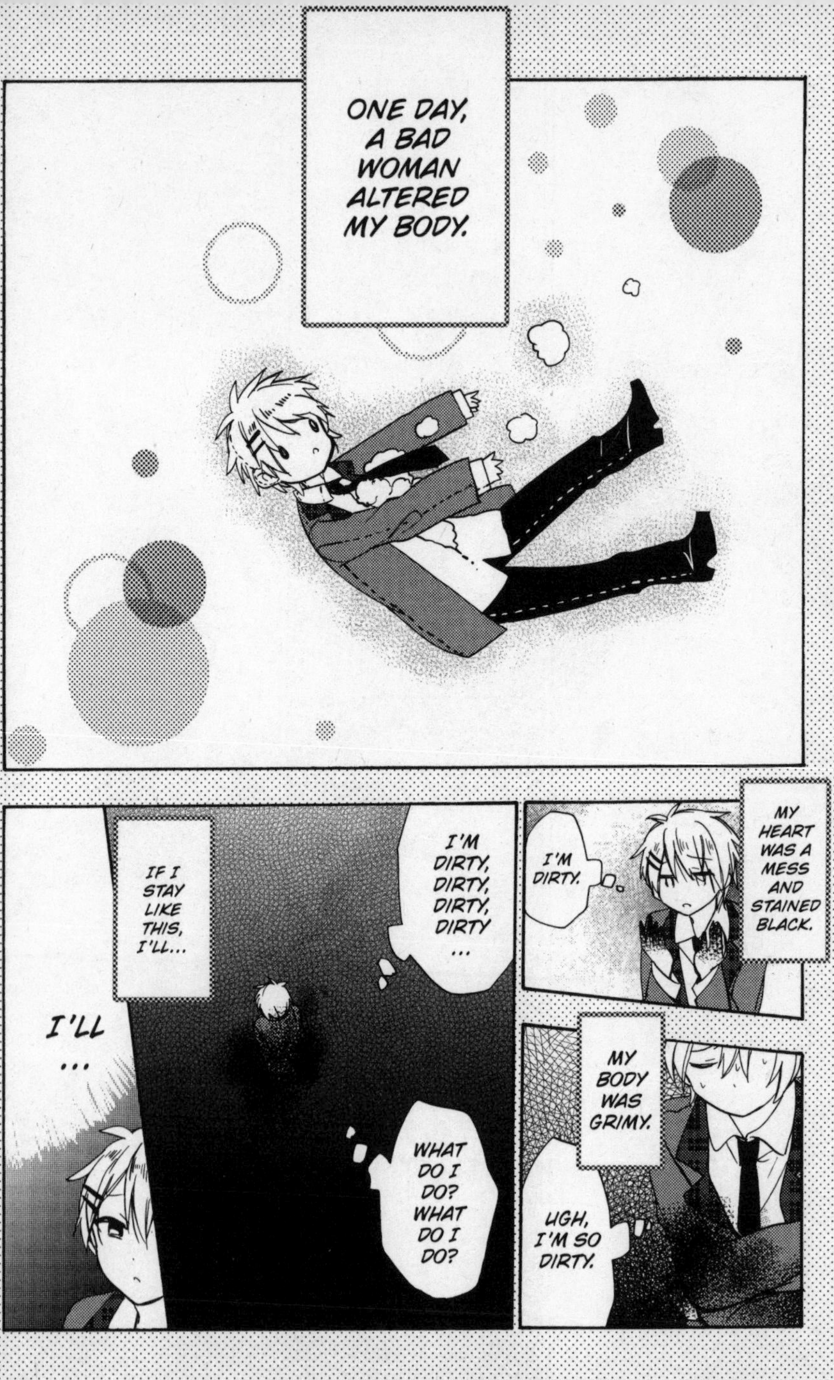
ONE DAY, A BAD WOMAN ALTERED MY BODY.
MY HEART WAS A MESS AND STAINED BLACK.
I'M DIRTY.
MY BODY WAS GRIMY.
UGH, I'M SO DIRTY.
I'M DIRTY, DIRTY, DIRTY, DIRTY...
IF I STAY LIKE THIS, I'LL...
WHAT DO I DO? WHAT DO I DO?
I'LL...

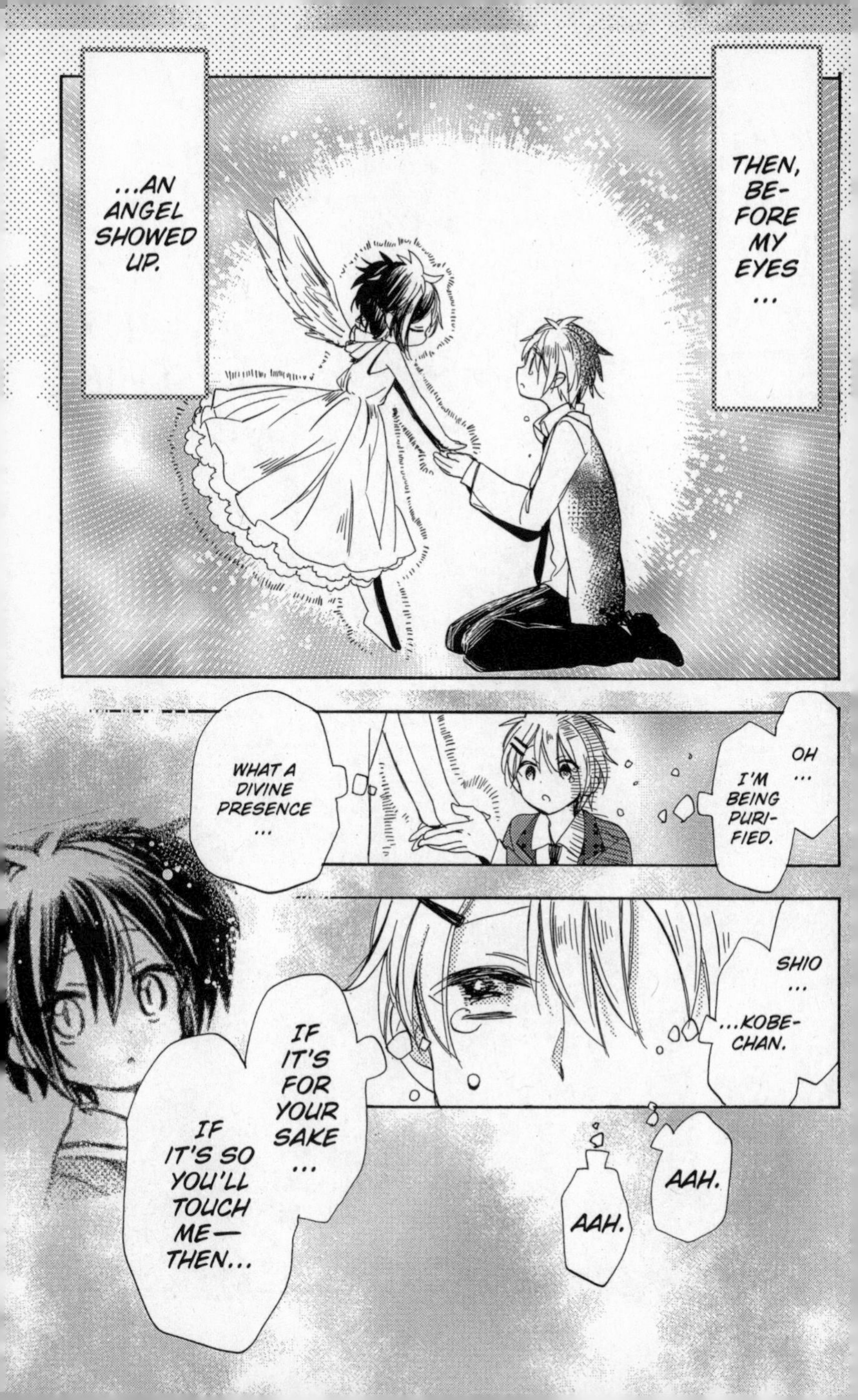

THEN, BE-FORE MY EYES...
...AN ANGEL SHOWED UP.
OH... I'M BEING PURI-FIED.
WHAT A DIVINE PRESENCE...
SHIO... ...KOBE-CHAN.
AAH.
AAH.
IF IT'S FOR YOUR SAKE...
IF IT'S SO YOU'LL TOUCH ME—THEN...

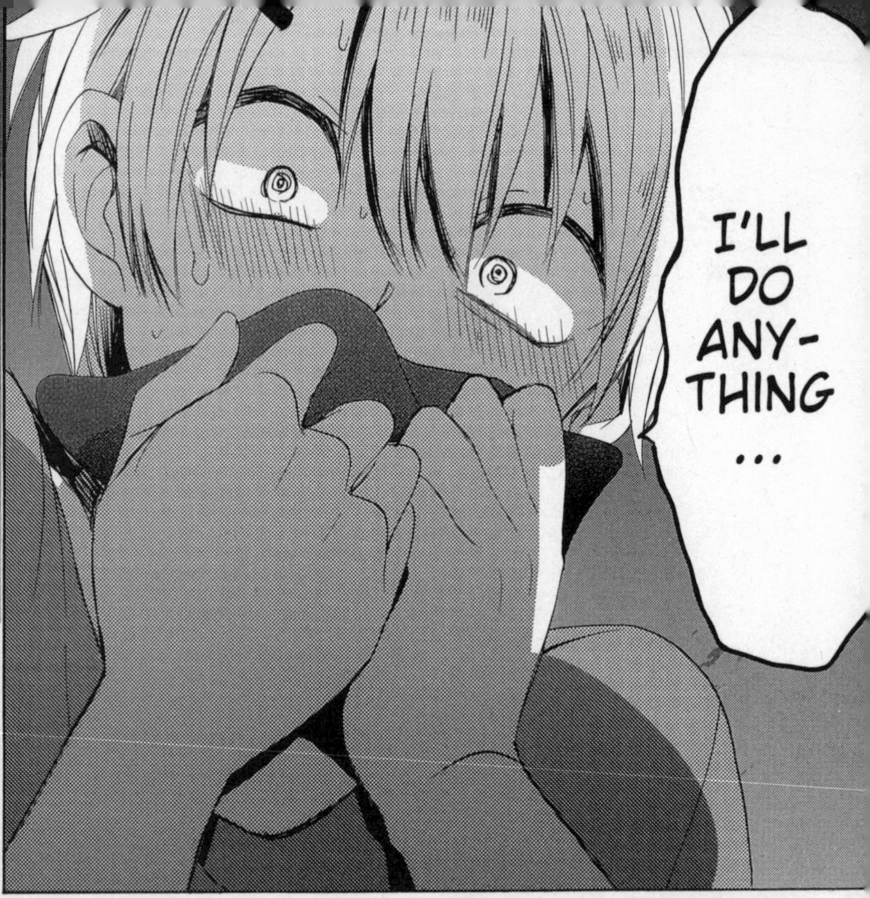
I'LL DO ANY-THING ...
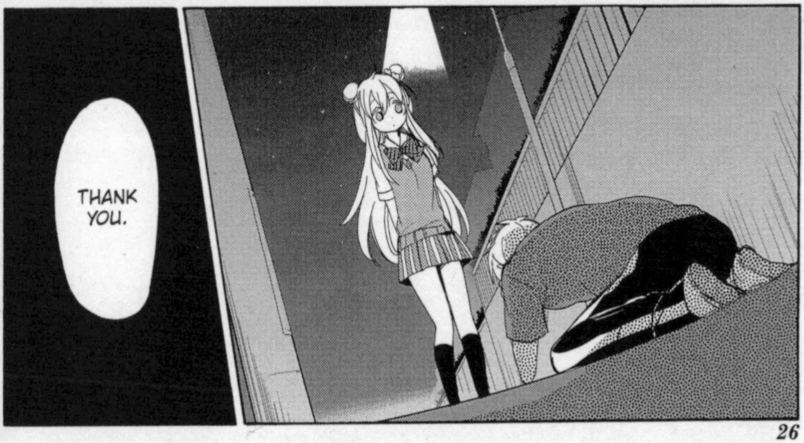
THANK YOU.

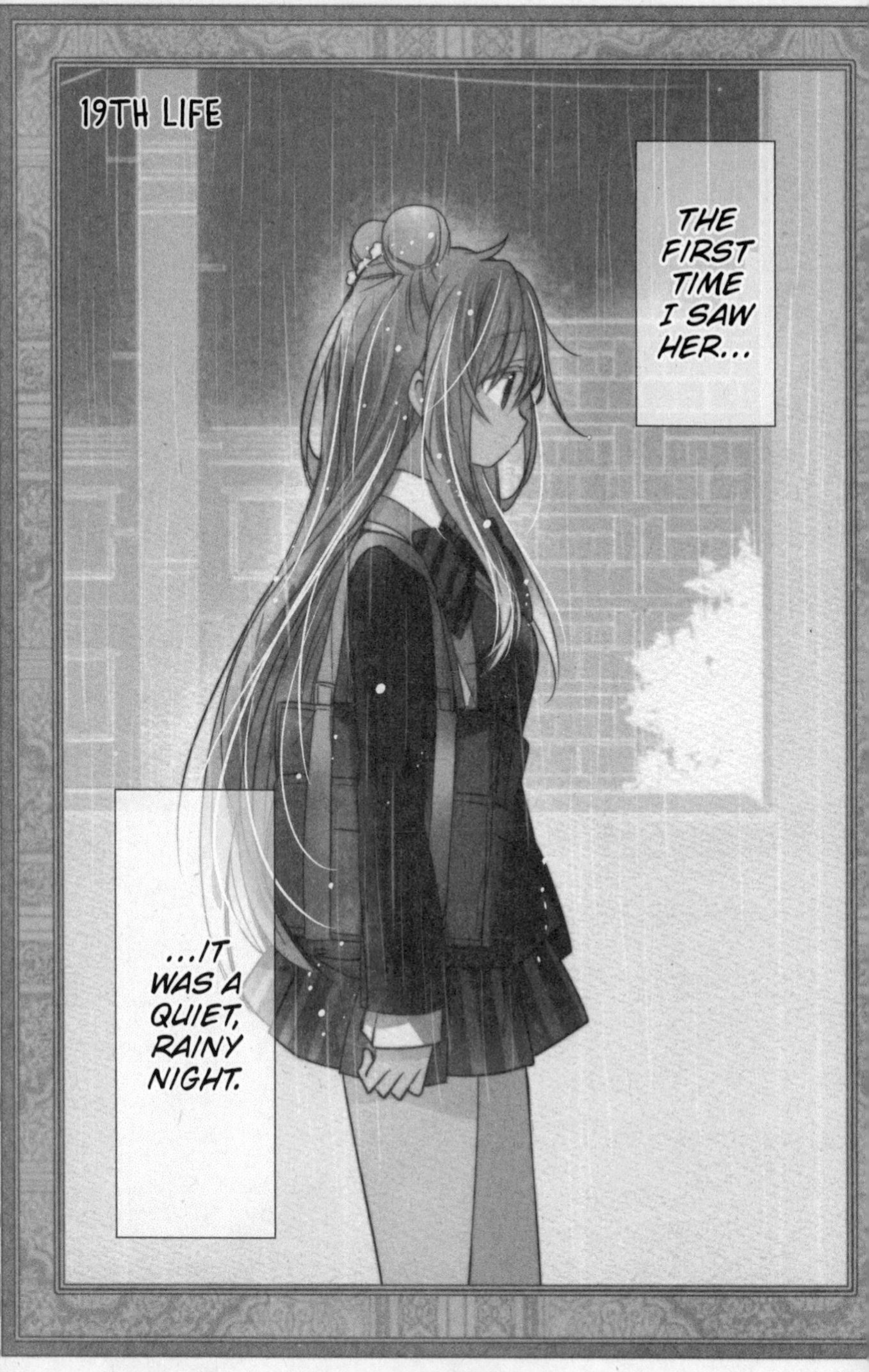
19TH LIFE
THE FIRST TIME I SAW HER...
...IT WAS A QUIET, RAINY NIGHT.

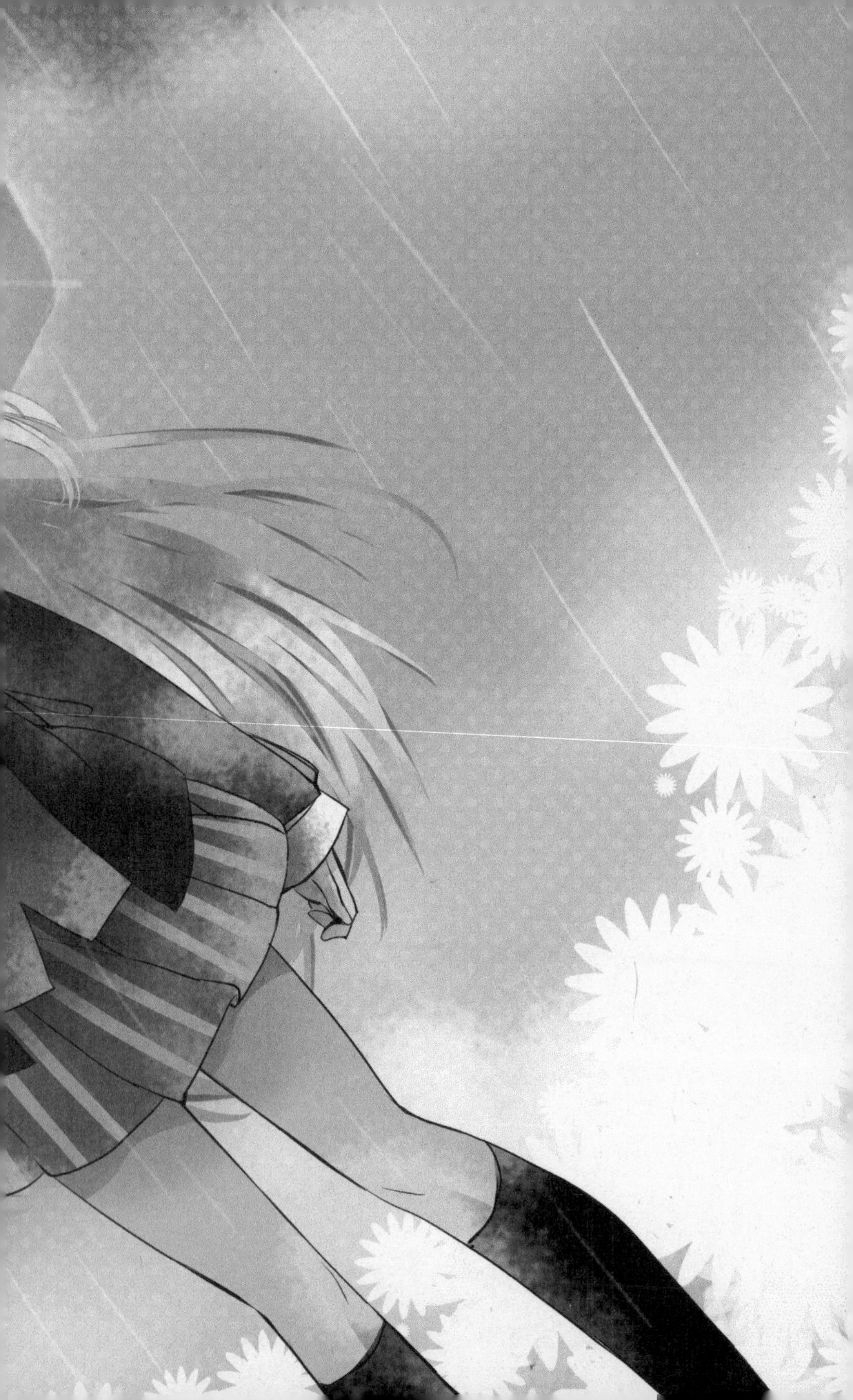

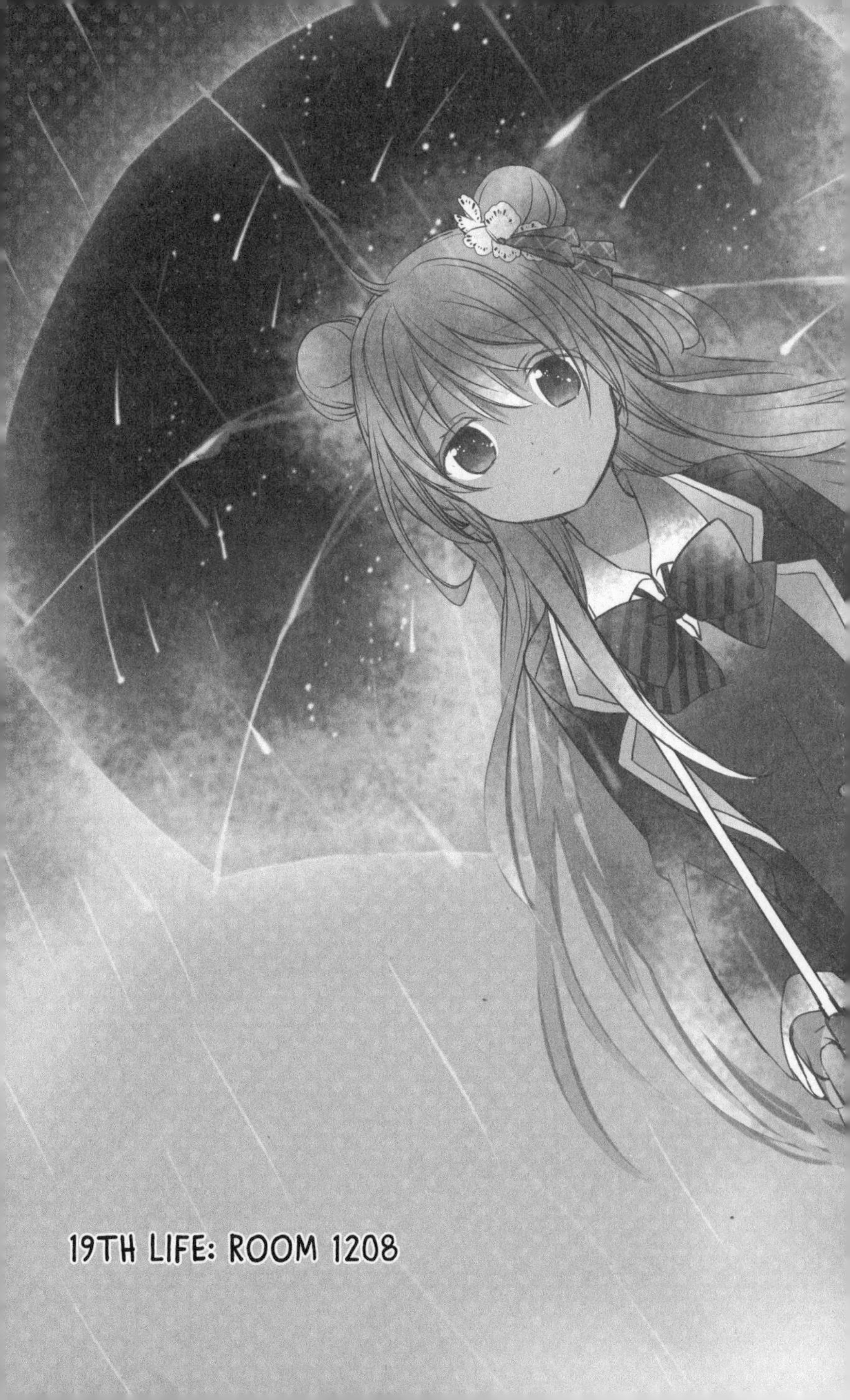

19TH LIFE: ROOM 1208

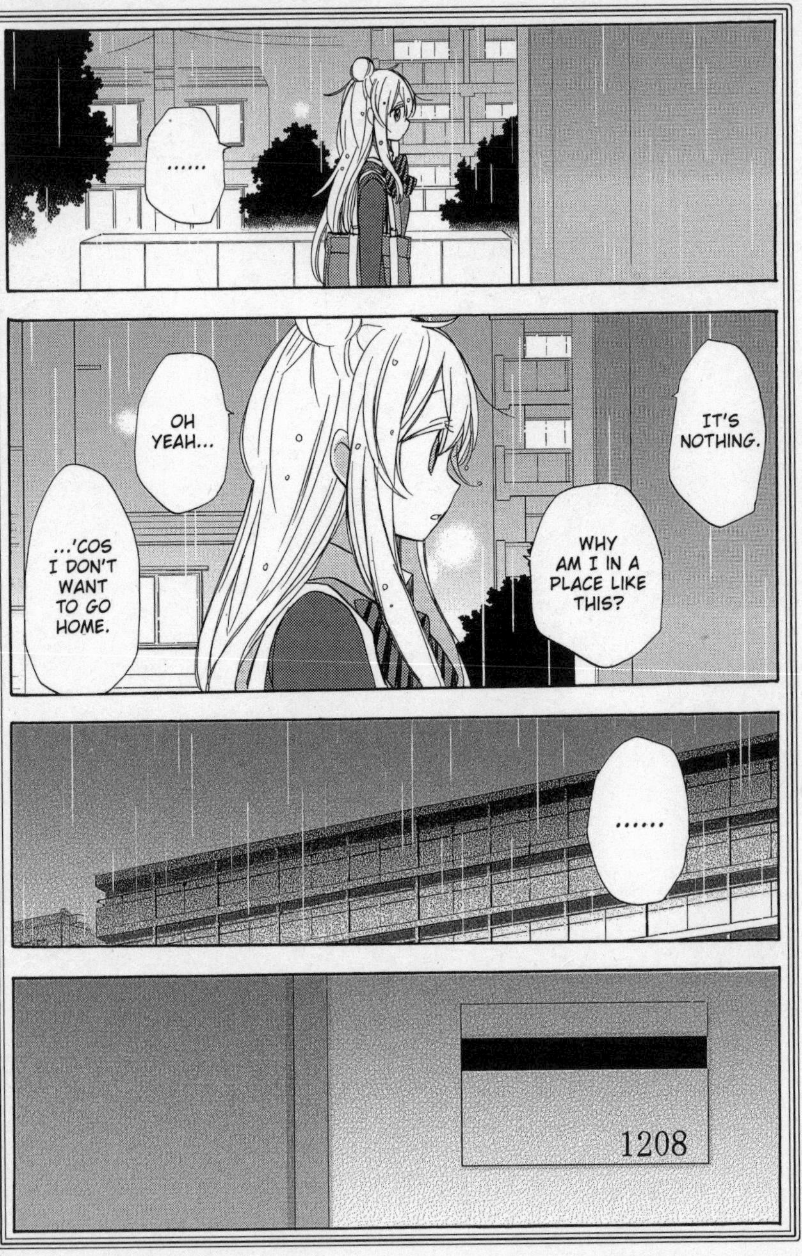
......
IT'S NOTHING.
WHY AM I IN A PLACE LIKE THIS?
OH YEAH...
...'COS I DON'T WANT TO GO HOME.
......
1208

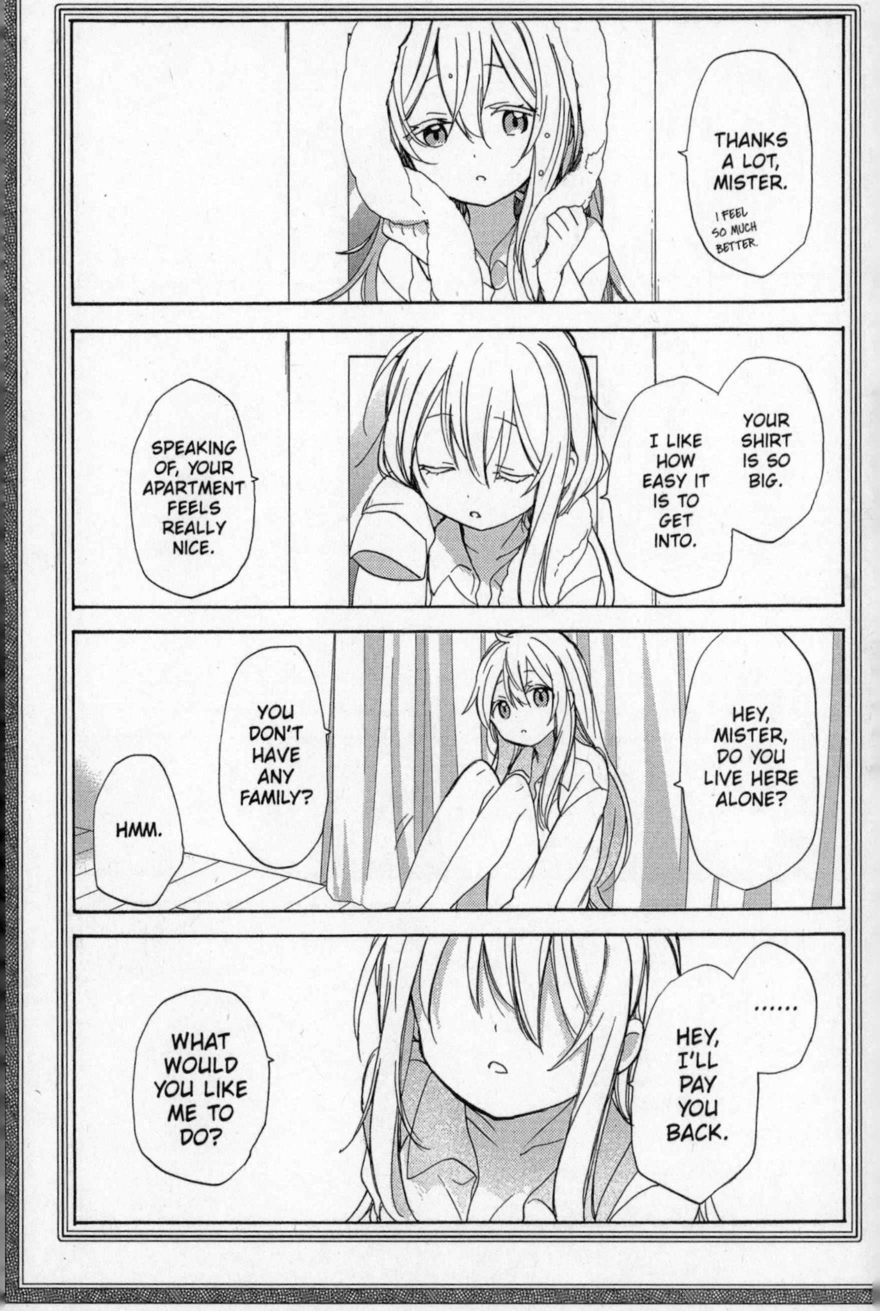
THANKS A LOT, MISTER.
I FEEL SO MUCH BETTER.
YOUR SHIRT IS SO BIG.
I LIKE HOW EASY IT IS TO GET INTO.
SPEAKING OF, YOUR APARTMENT FEELS REALLY NICE.
HEY, MISTER, DO YOU LIVE HERE ALONE?
YOU DON'T HAVE ANY FAMILY?
HMM.
......
HEY, I'LL PAY YOU BACK.
WHAT WOULD YOU LIKE ME TO DO?

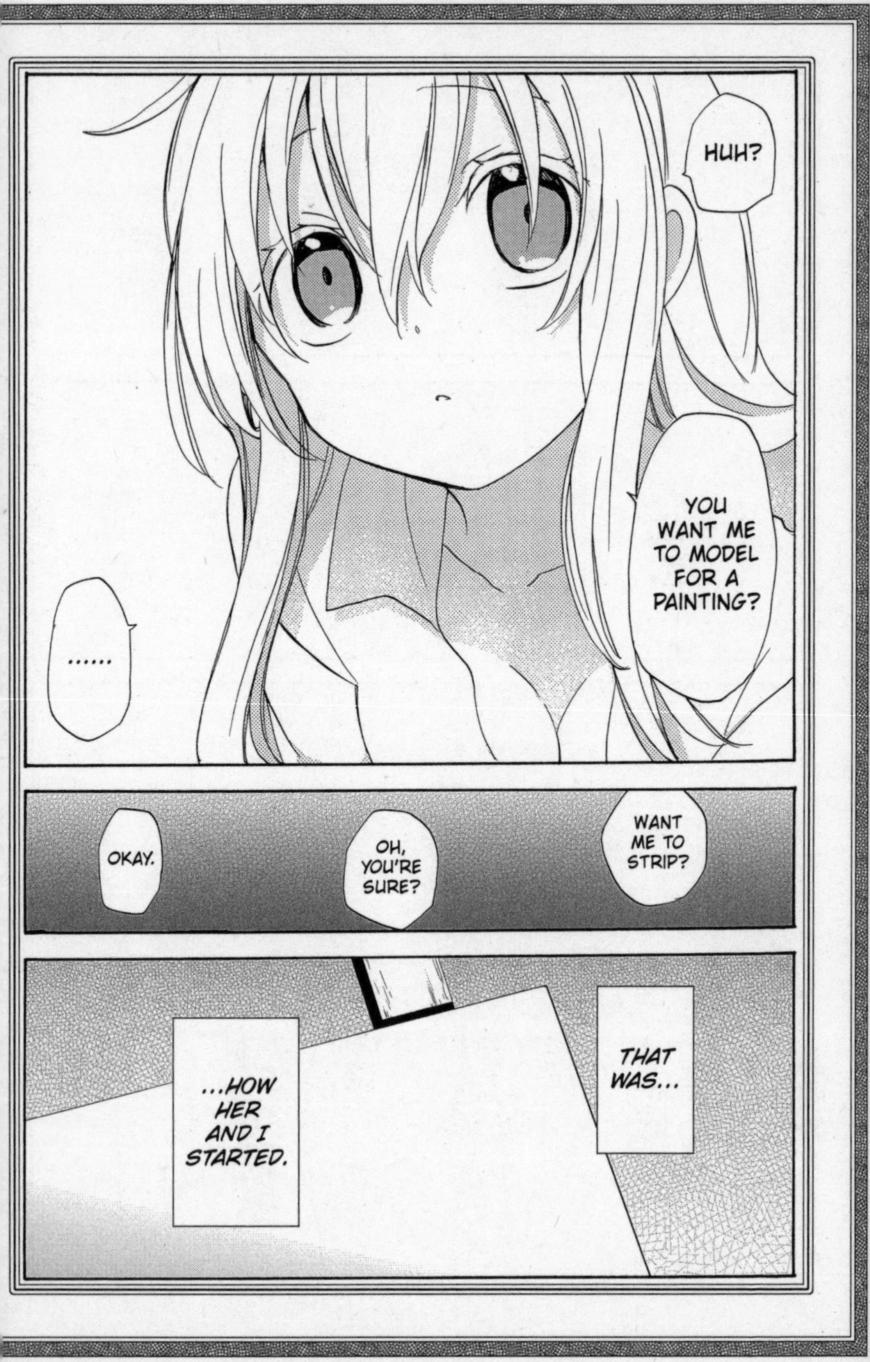
HUH?
YOU WANT ME TO MODEL FOR A PAINTING?
......
WANT ME TO STRIP?
OH, YOU'RE SURE?
OKAY.
THAT WAS...
...HOW HER AND I STARTED.

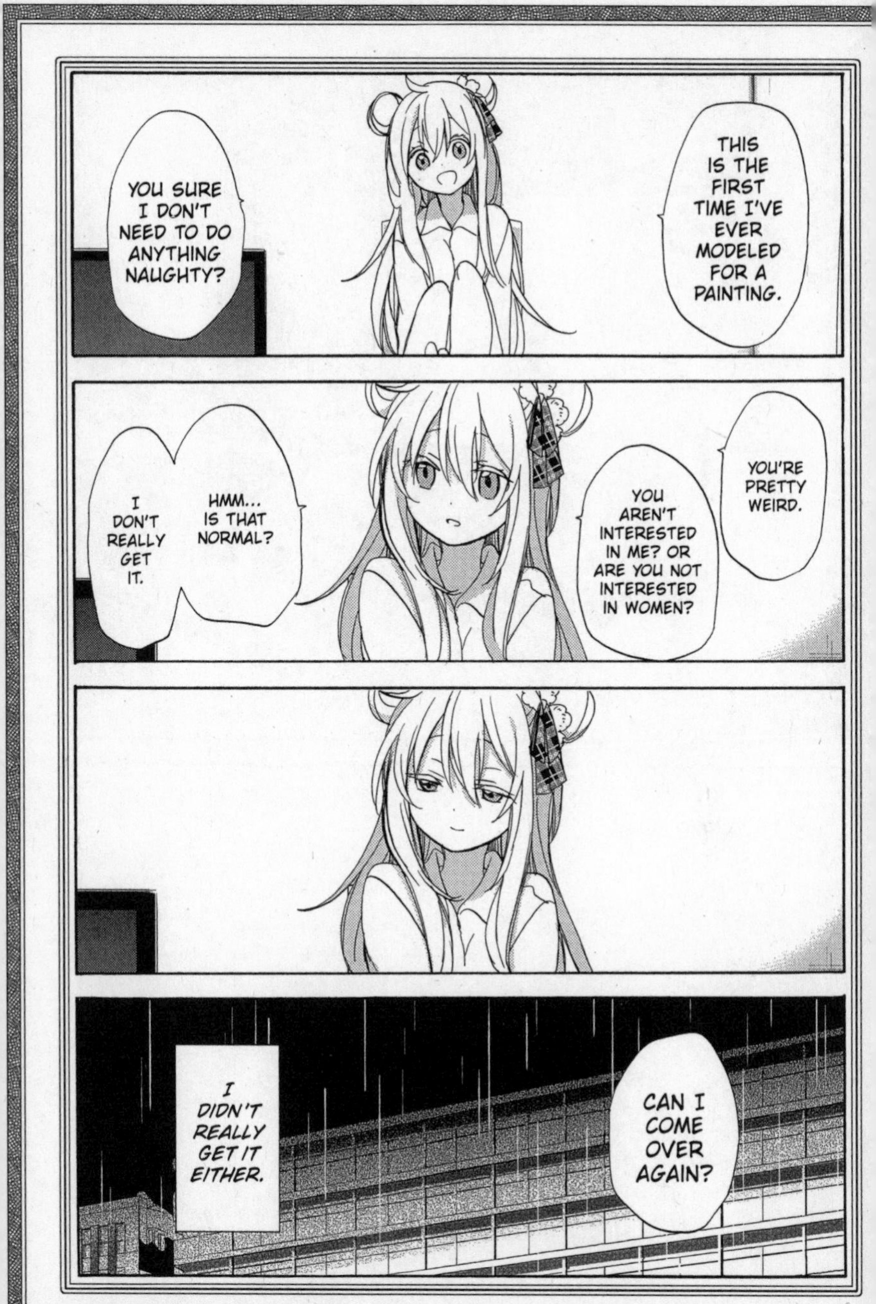
THIS IS THE FIRST TIME I'VE EVER MODELED FOR A PAINTING.
YOU SURE I DON'T NEED TO DO ANYTHING NAUGHTY?
YOU'RE PRETTY WEIRD.
YOU AREN'T INTERESTED IN ME? OR ARE YOU NOT INTERESTED IN WOMEN?
HMM... IS THAT NORMAL?
I DON'T REALLY GET IT.
CAN I COME OVER AGAIN?
I DIDN'T REALLY GET IT EITHER.

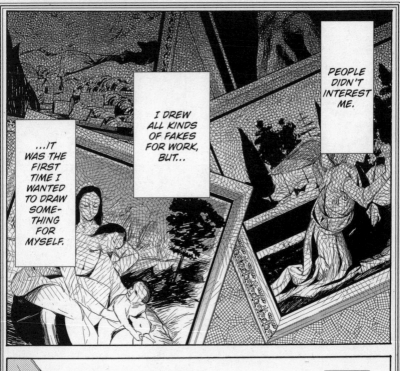

PEOPLE DIDN'T INTEREST ME.
I DREW ALL KINDS OF FAKES FOR WORK, BUT...
...IT WAS THE FIRST TIME I WANTED TO DRAW SOME-THING FOR MYSELF.
I DIDN'T KNOW WHY, BUT...
...I FELT LIKE I NEEDED TO DRAW HER NOW.
THERE WAS SOMETHING EPHEMERAL ABOUT HER, LIKE THE RIPPLES ON A WATER'S SURFACE.

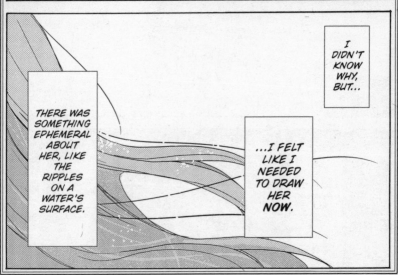

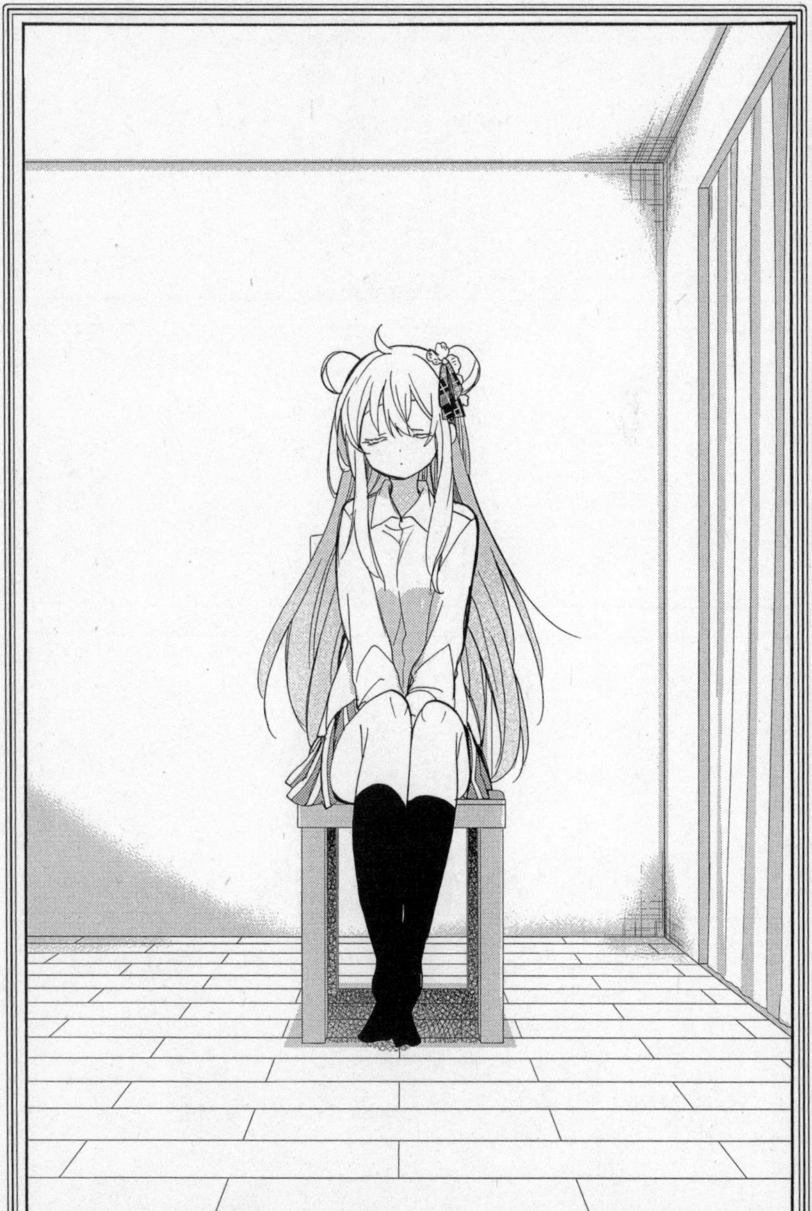

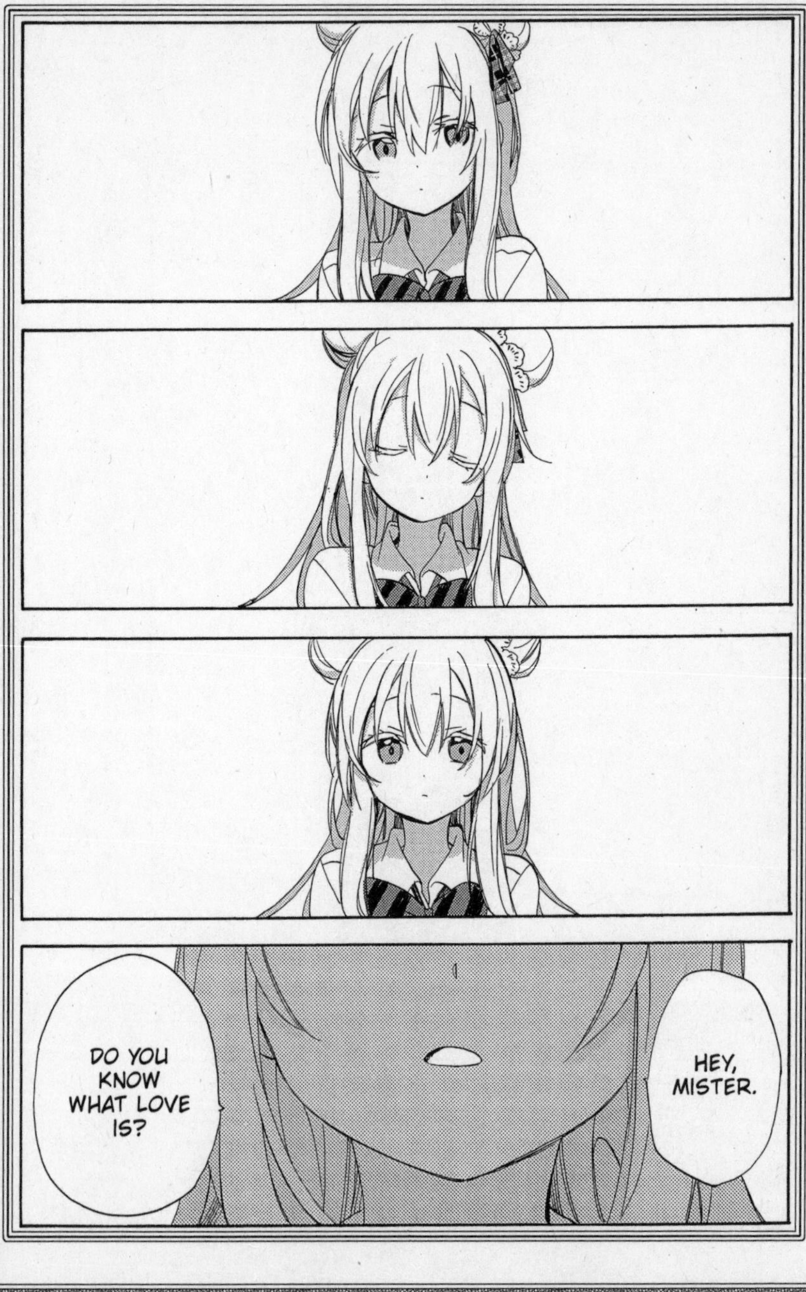
HEY, MISTER.
DO YOU KNOW WHAT LOVE IS?

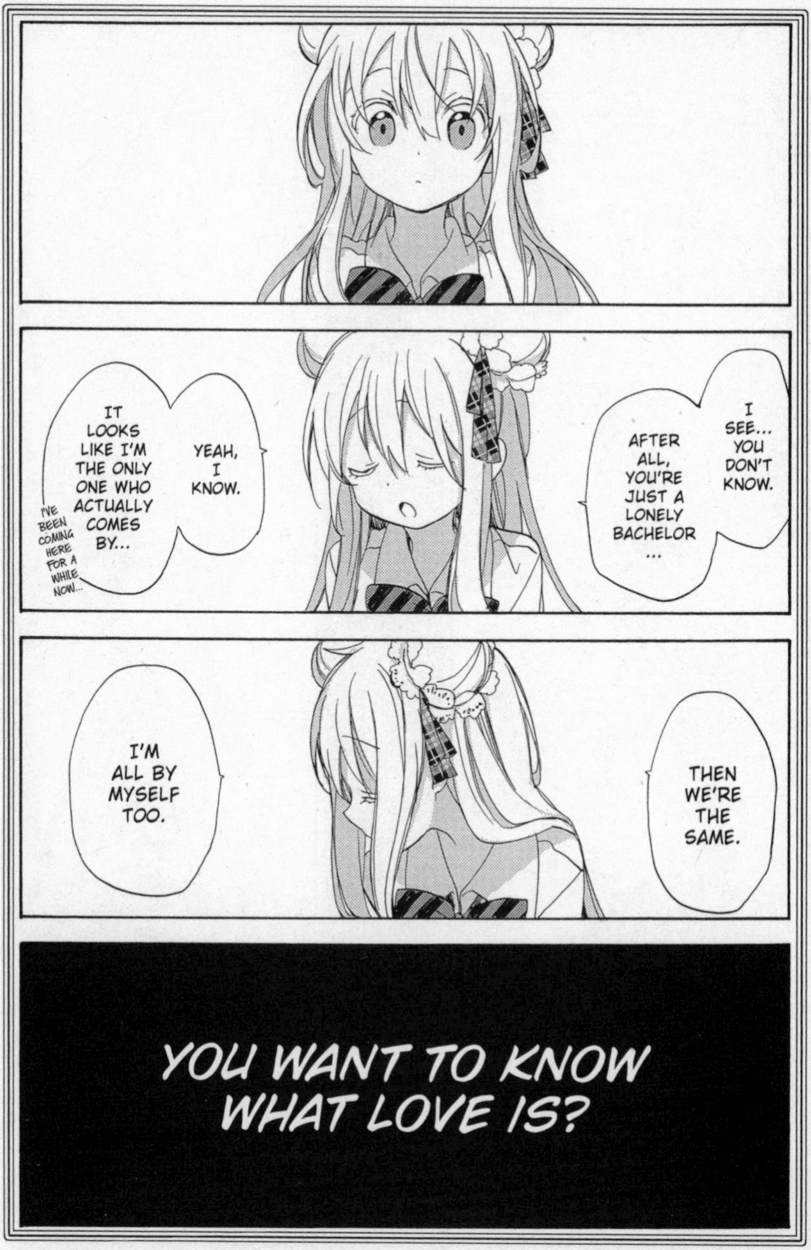
I SEE... YOU DON'T KNOW.
AFTER ALL, YOU'RE JUST A LONELY BACHELOR...
YEAH, I KNOW.
IT LOOKS LIKE I'M THE ONLY ONE WHO ACTUALLY COMES BY...
I'VE BEEN COMING HERE FOR A WHILE NOW...
THEN WE'RE THE SAME.
I'M ALL BY MYSELF TOO.
YOU WANT TO KNOW WHAT LOVE IS?

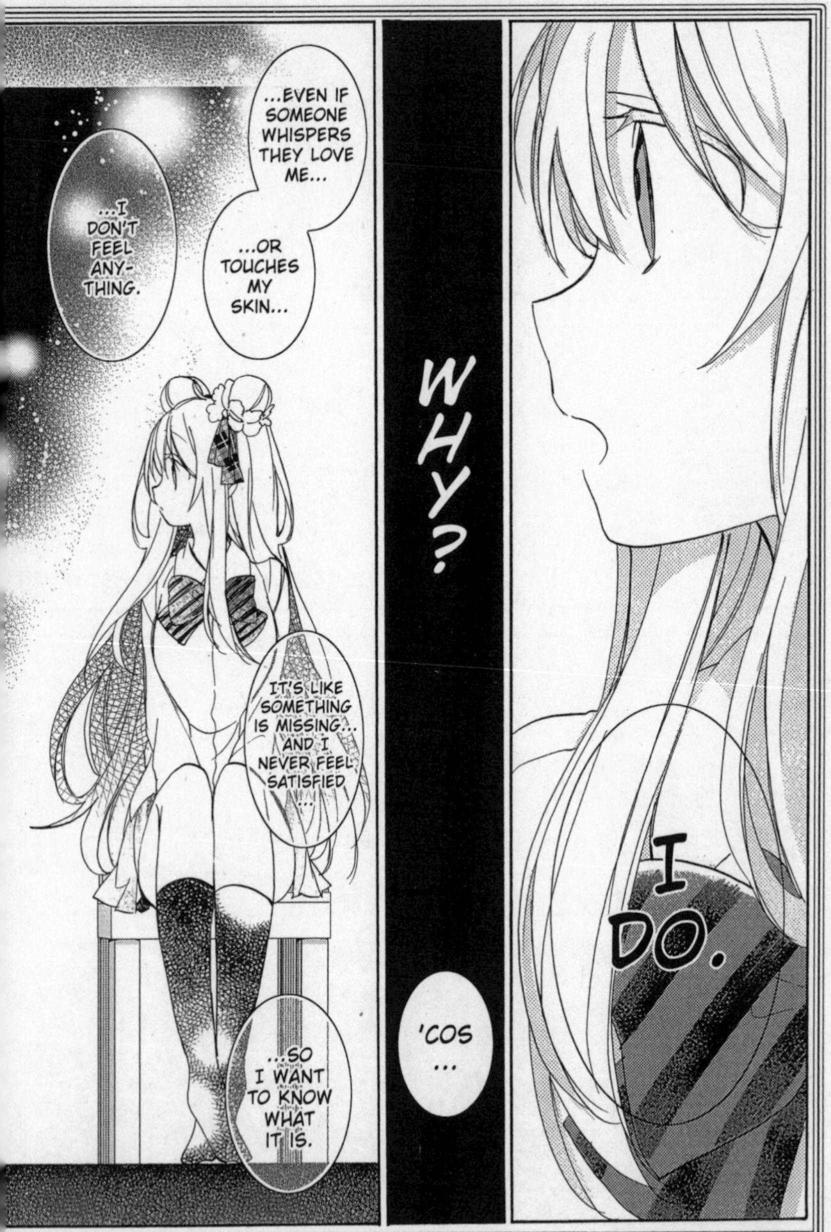
...EVEN IF SOMEONE WHISPERS THEY LOVE ME...
...OR TOUCHES MY SKIN...
...I DON'T FEEL ANY-THING.
IT'S LIKE SOMETHING IS MISSING... AND I NEVER FEEL SATISFIED ...
...SO I WANT TO KNOW WHAT IT IS.
WHY?
'COS ...
I DO.

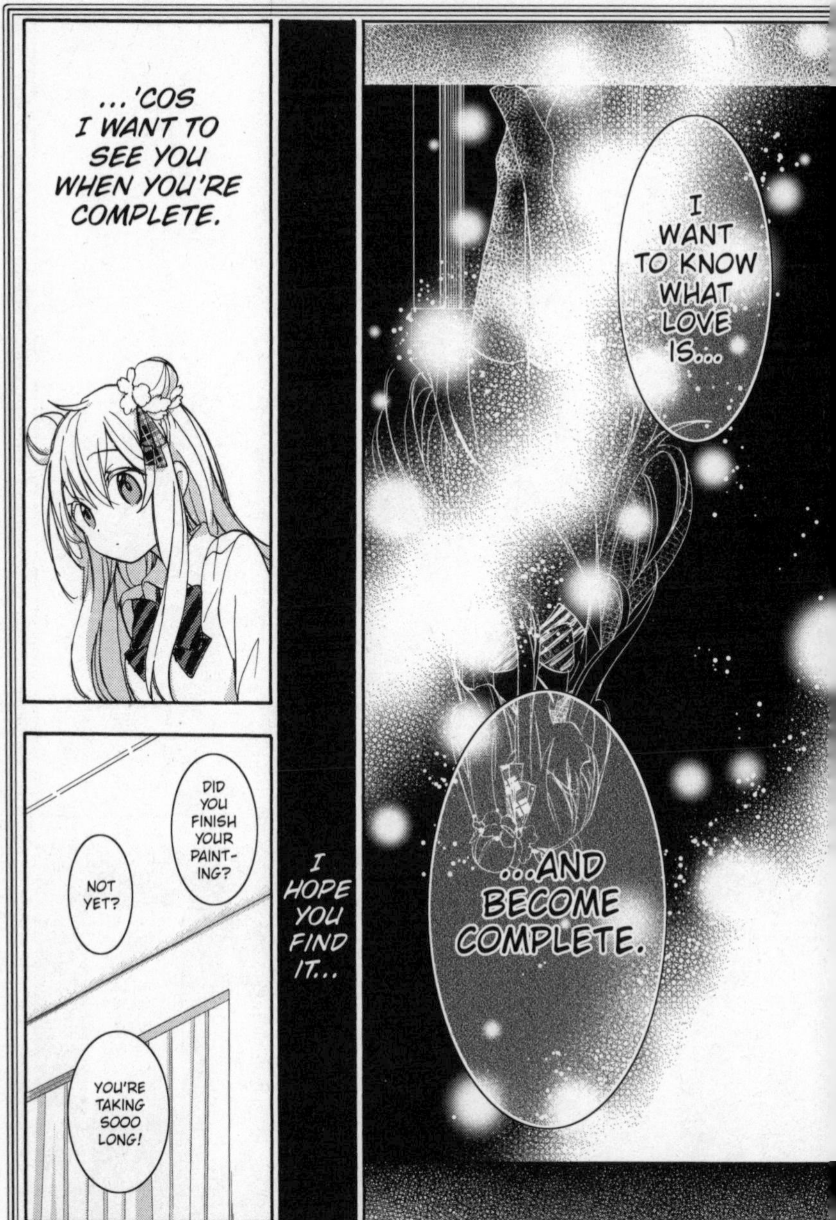

I WANT TO KNOW WHAT LOVE IS...
...AND BECOME COMPLETE.
I HOPE YOU FIND IT...
...'COS I WANT TO SEE YOU WHEN YOU'RE COMPLETE.
DID YOU FINISH YOUR PAINTING?
NOT YET?
YOU'RE TAKING SOOO LONG!

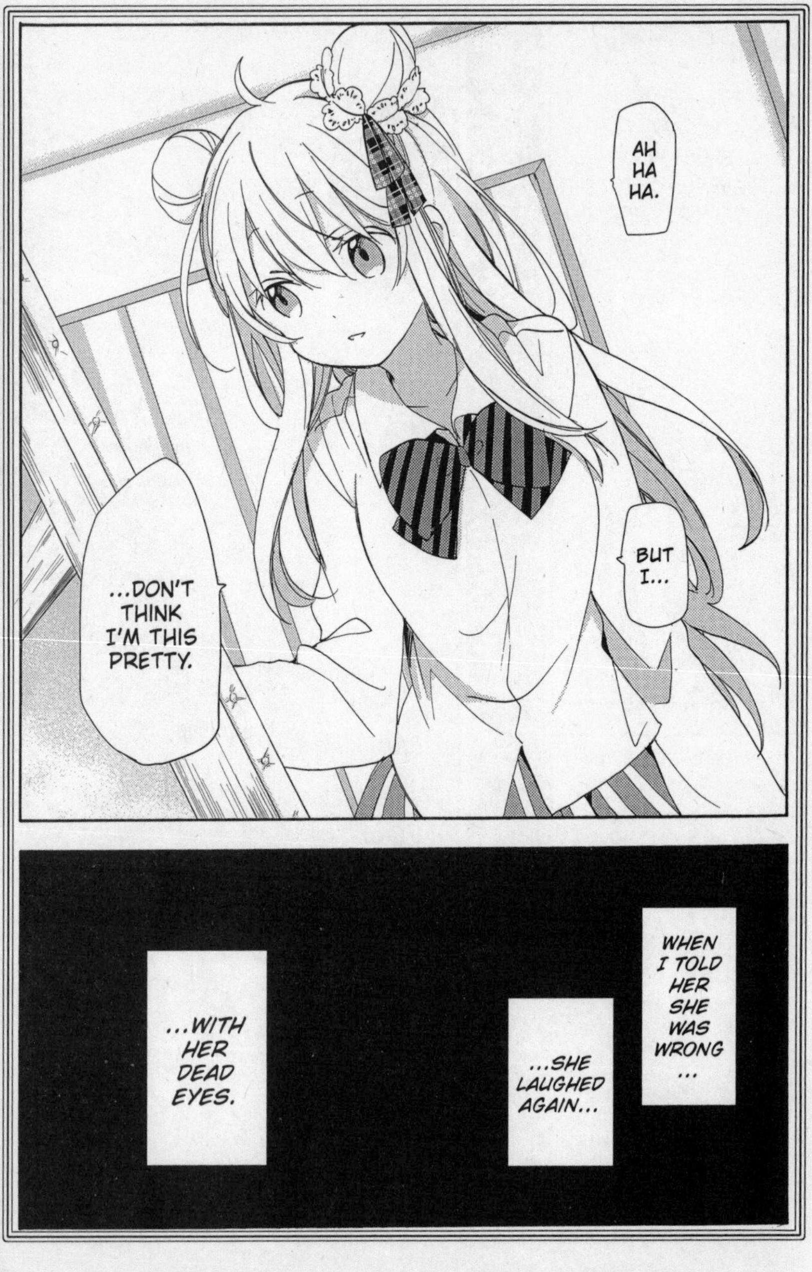
AH HA HA.
BUT I...
...DON'T THINK I'M THIS PRETTY.
WHEN I TOLD HER SHE WAS WRONG...
...SHE LAUGHED AGAIN...
...WITH HER DEAD EYES.

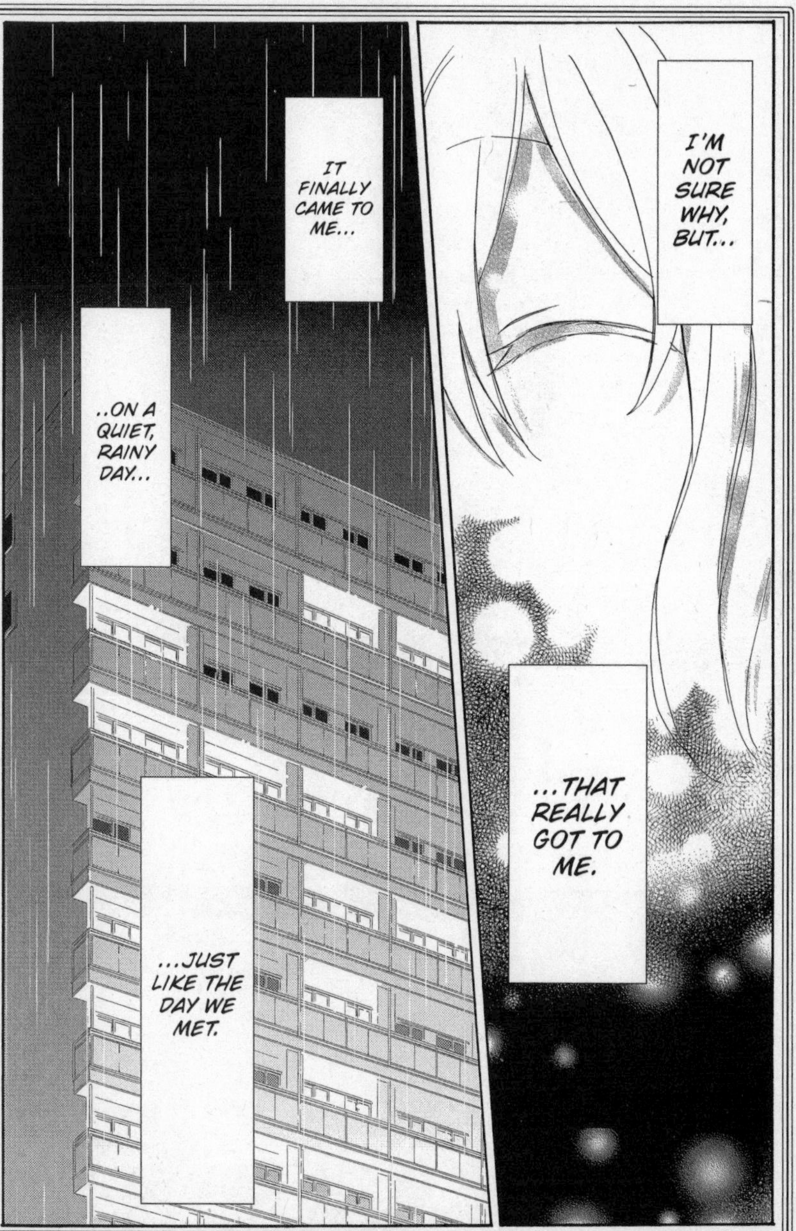
I'M NOT SURE WHY, BUT...
...THAT REALLY GOT TO ME.
IT FINALLY CAME TO ME...
..ON A QUIET, RAINY DAY...
...JUST LIKE THE DAY WE MET.

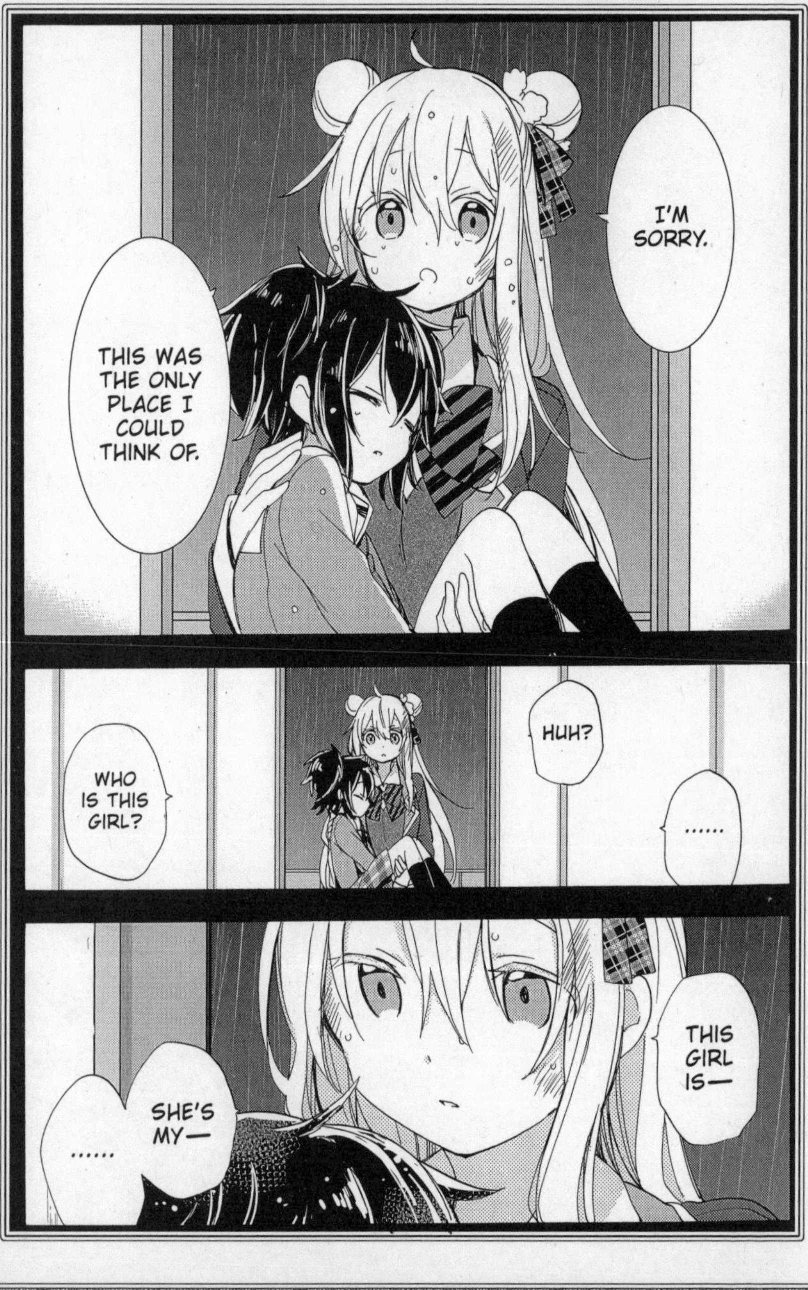
I'M SORRY.
THIS WAS THE ONLY PLACE I COULD THINK OF.
HUH?
......
WHO IS THIS GIRL?
THIS GIRL IS—
SHE'S MY—
......

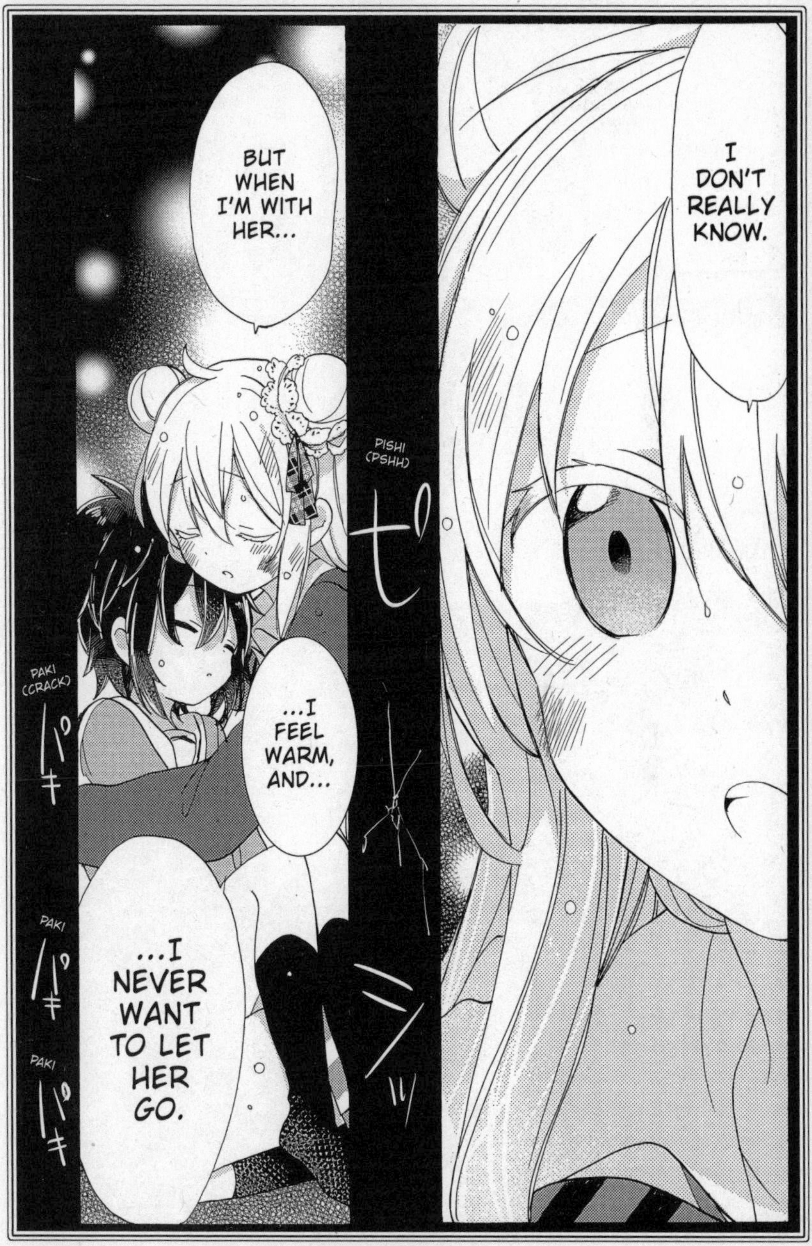
I DON'T REALLY KNOW.
PISHI (PSHH)
BUT WHEN I'M WITH HER...
...I FEEL WARM, AND...
PAKI (CRACK)
...I NEVER WANT TO LET HER GO.
PAKI
PAKI

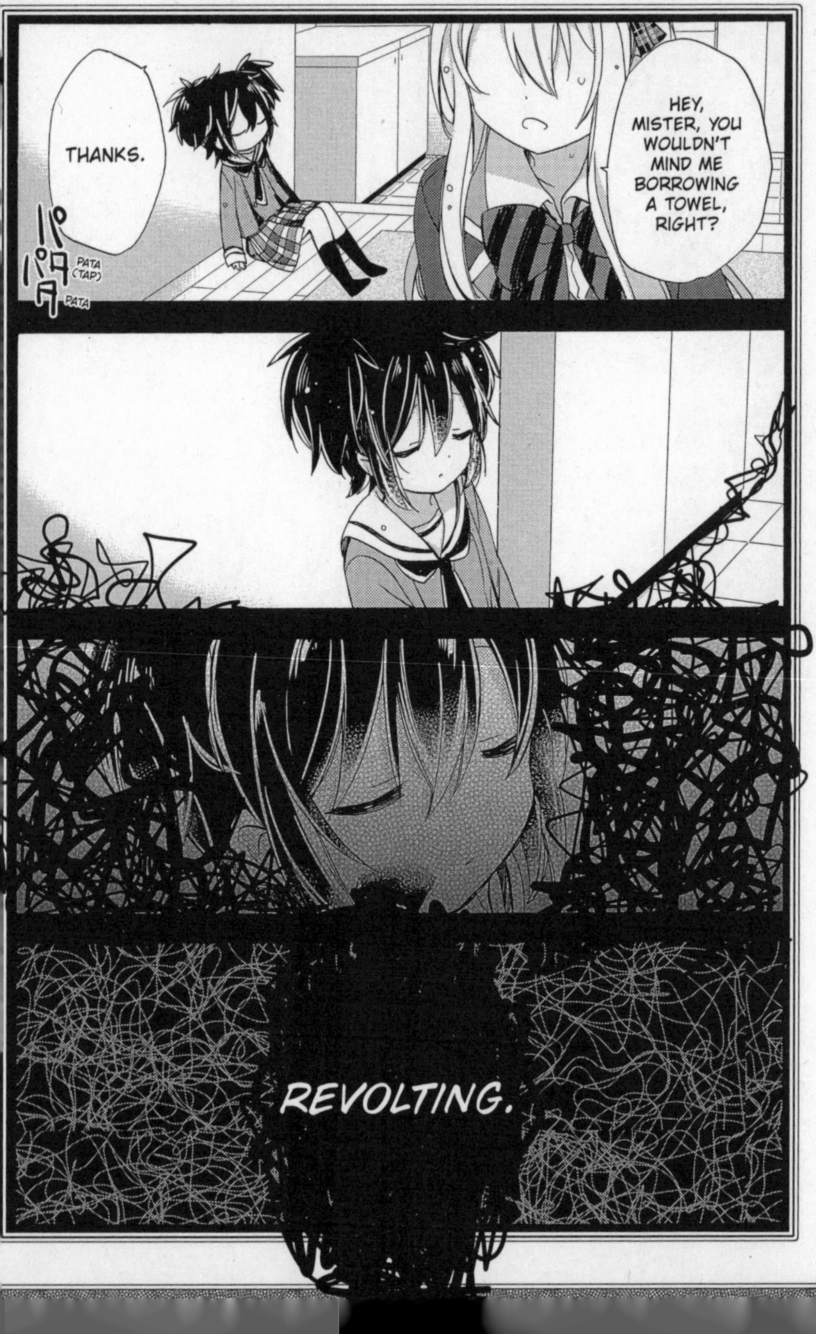
HEY, MISTER, YOU WOULDN'T MIND ME BORROWING A TOWEL, RIGHT?
THANKS.
パタ PATA (TAP)
パタ PATA
REVOLTING.

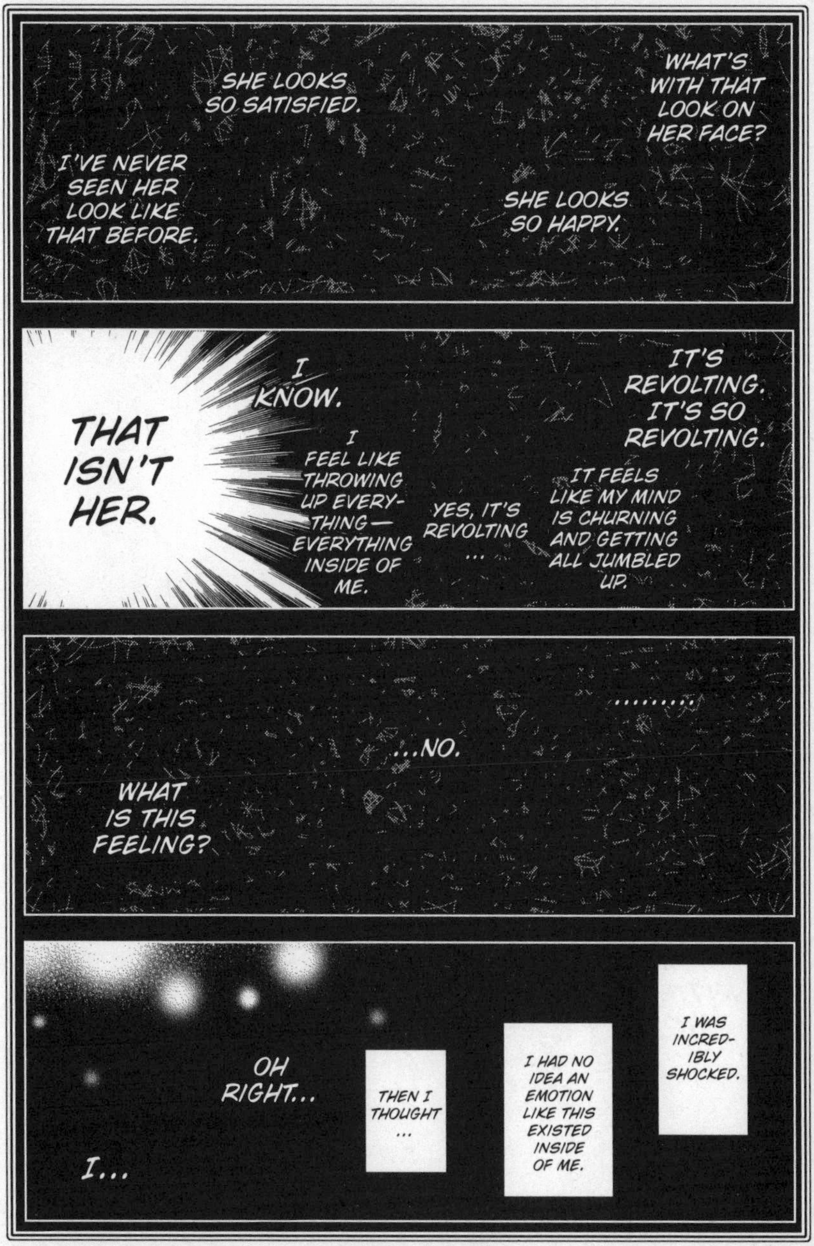
WHAT'S WITH THAT LOOK ON HER FACE?
SHE LOOKS SO HAPPY.
SHE LOOKS SO SATISFIED.
I'VE NEVER SEEN HER LOOK LIKE THAT BEFORE.
IT'S REVOLTING. IT'S SO REVOLTING.
IT FEELS LIKE MY MIND IS CHURNING AND GETTING ALL JUMBLED UP.
YES, IT'S REVOLTING...
I KNOW.
I FEEL LIKE THROWING UP EVERY-THING—EVERYTHING INSIDE OF ME.
THAT ISN'T HER.
....
...NO.
WHAT IS THIS FEELING?
I WAS INCRED-IBLY SHOCKED.
I HAD NO IDEA AN EMOTION LIKE THIS EXISTED INSIDE OF ME.
THEN I THOUGHT...
OH RIGHT...
I...

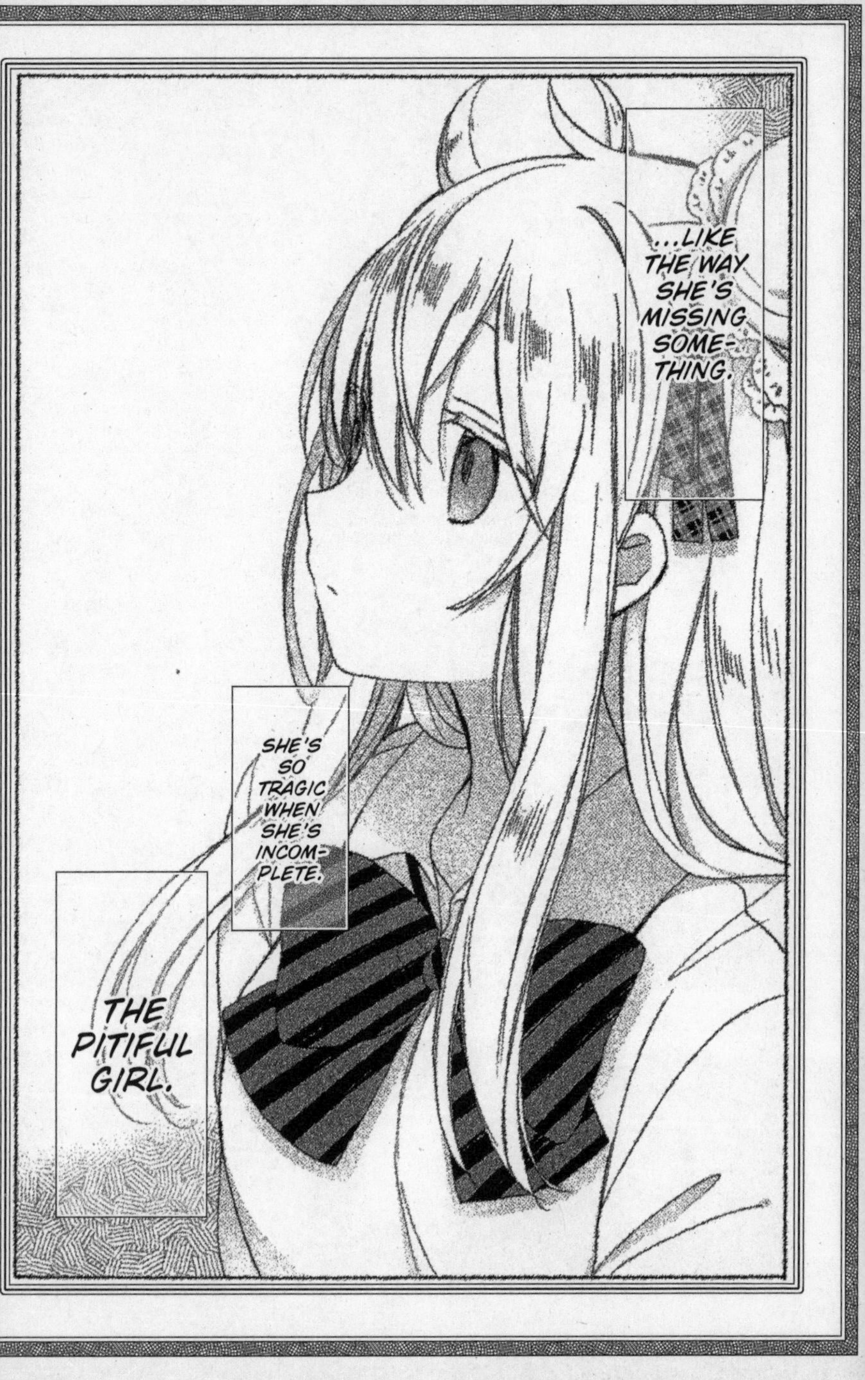
...LIKE THE WAY SHE'S MISSING SOME-THING.
SHE'S SO TRAGIC WHEN SHE'S INCOM-PLETE.
THE PITIFUL GIRL.

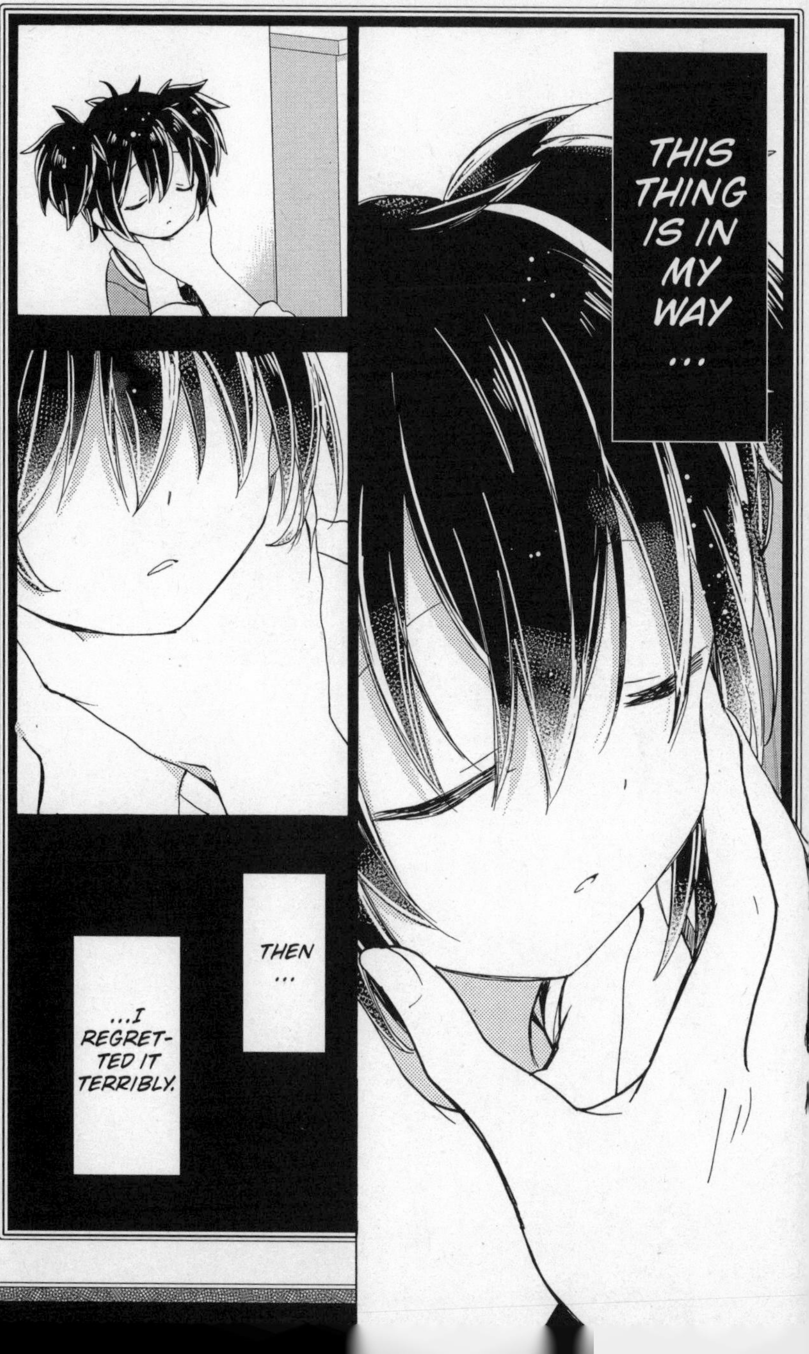
THIS THING IS IN MY WAY...
THEN...
...I REGRET-TED IT TERRIBLY.

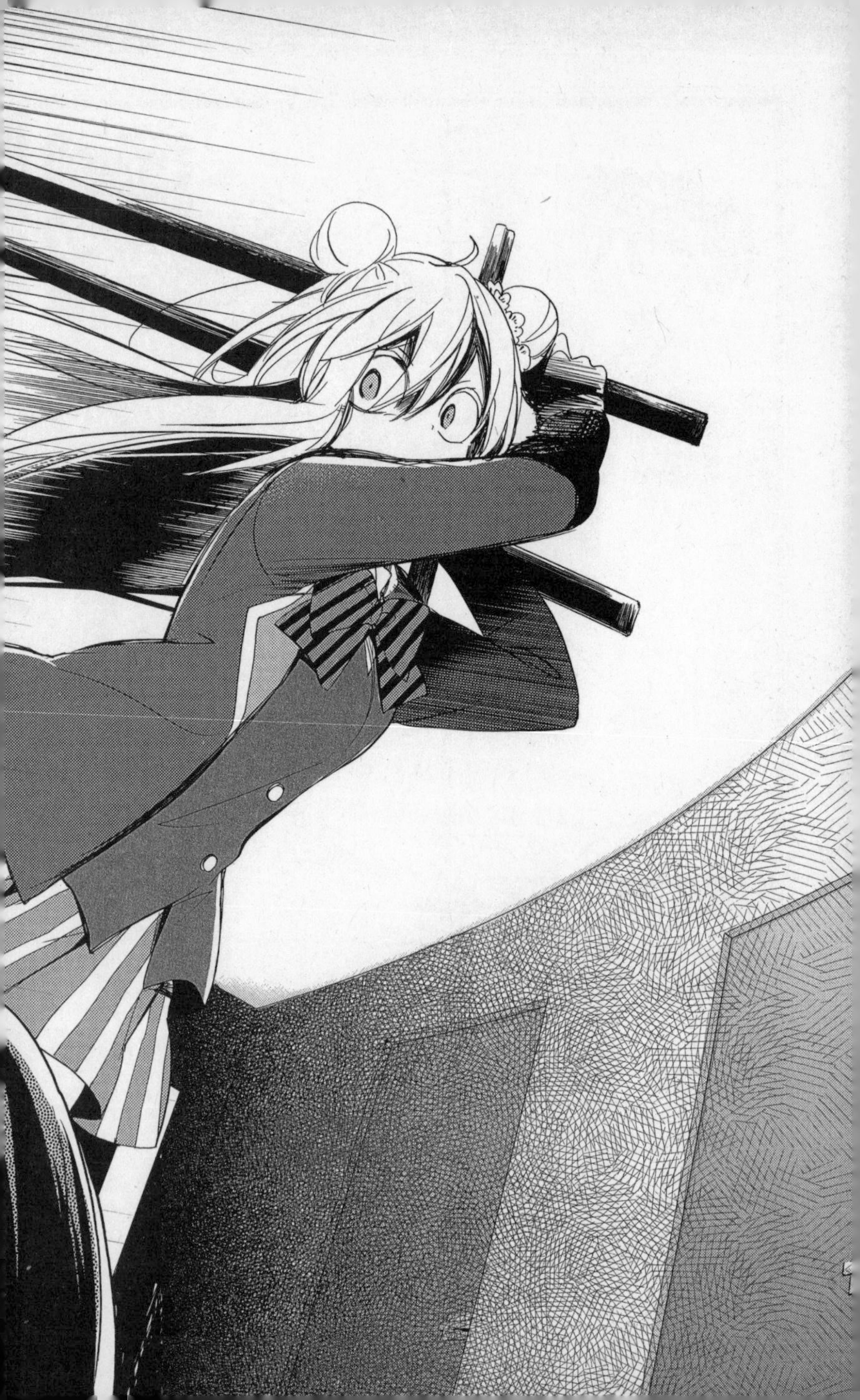

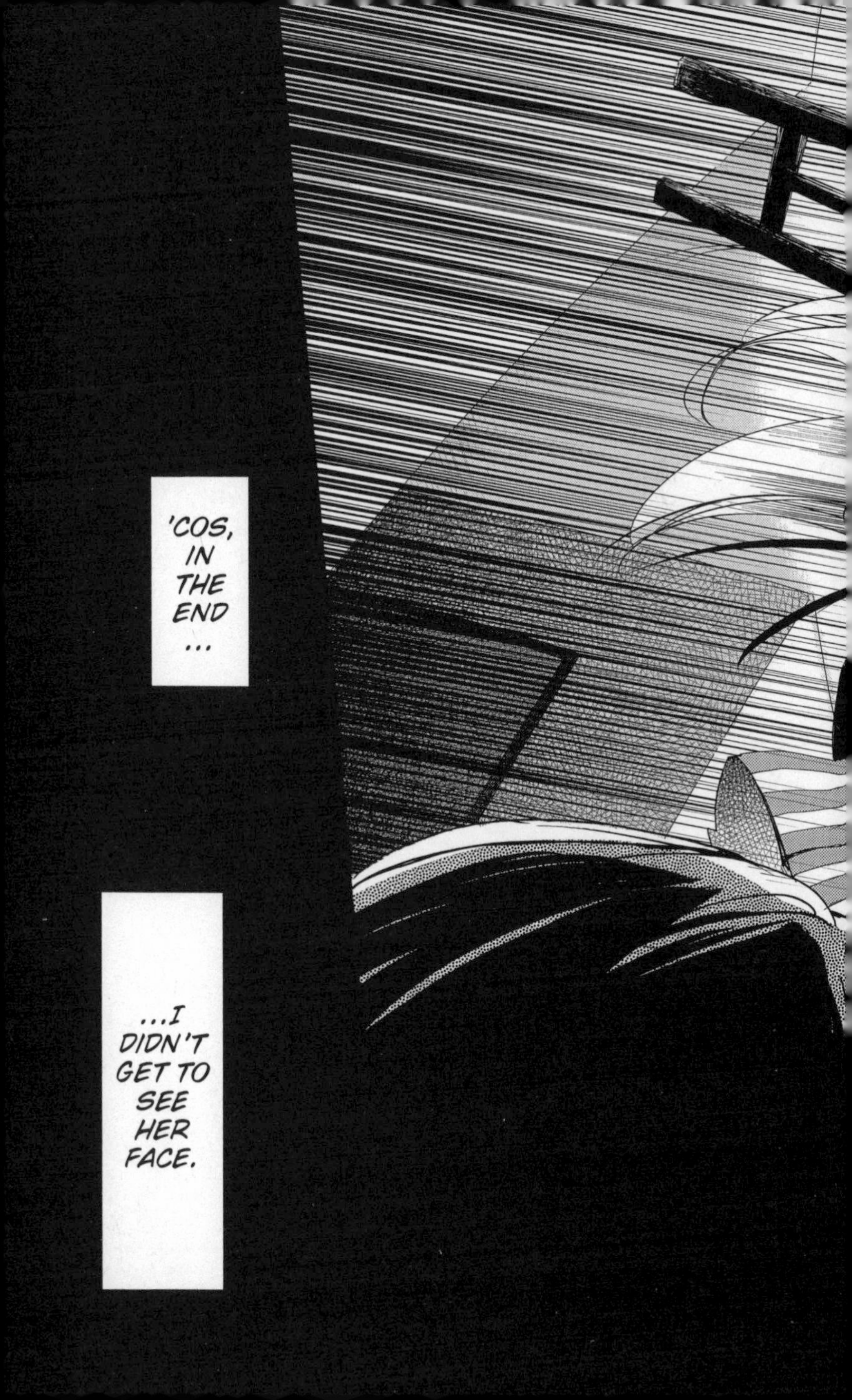
'COS, IN THE END ...
...I DIDN'T GET TO SEE HER FACE.

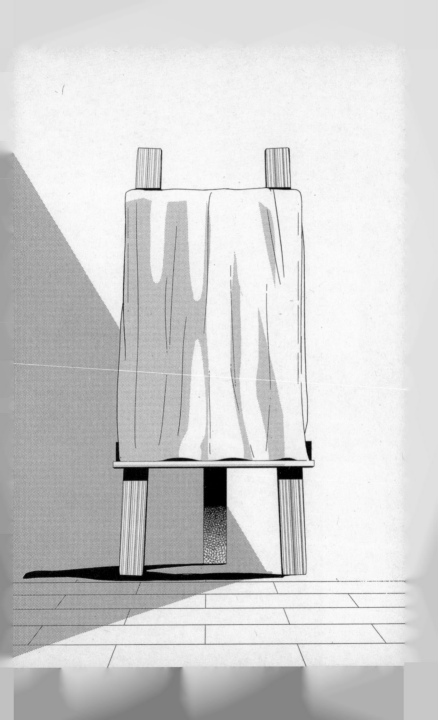

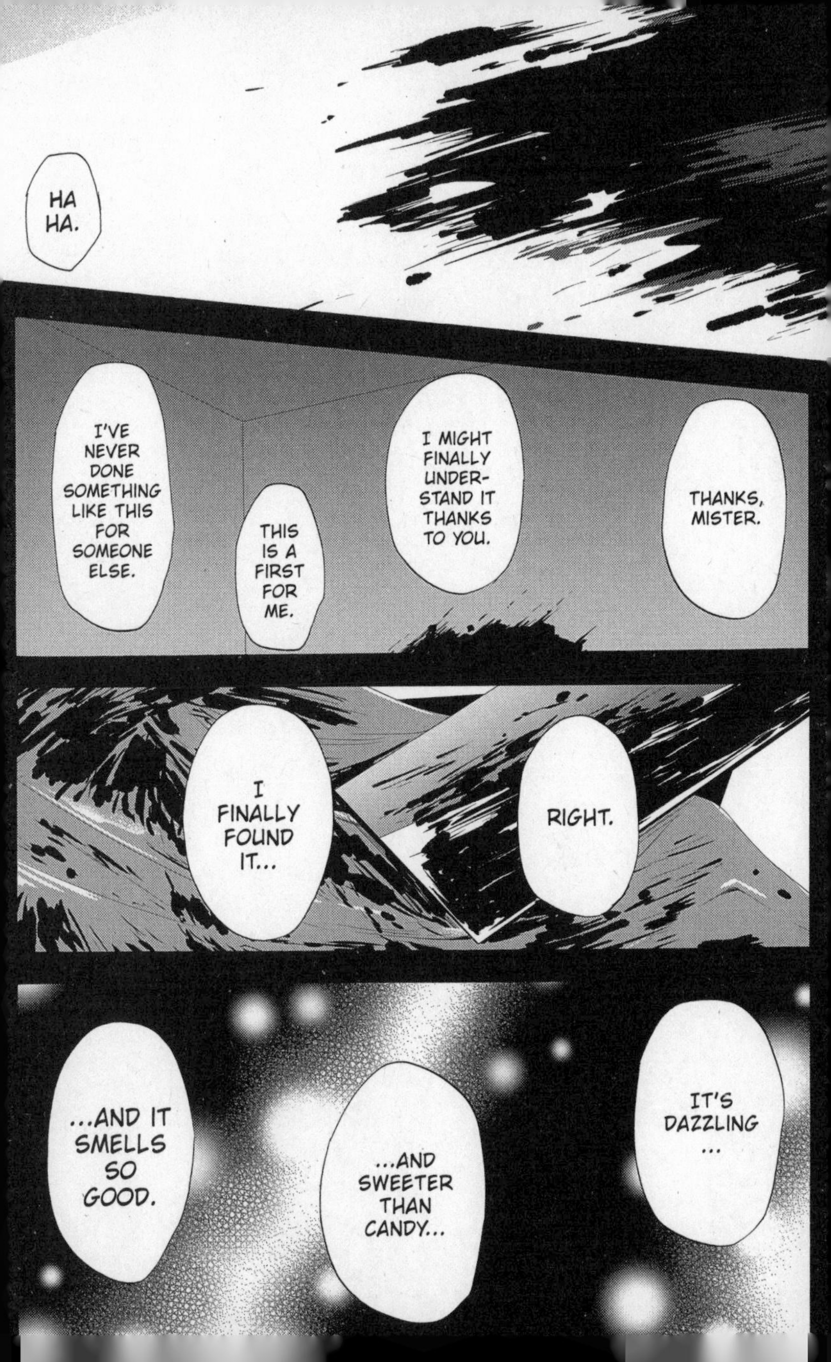
HA HA.
THANKS, MISTER.
I MIGHT FINALLY UNDER-STAND IT THANKS TO YOU.
THIS IS A FIRST FOR ME.
I'VE NEVER DONE SOMETHING LIKE THIS FOR SOMEONE ELSE.
RIGHT.
I FINALLY FOUND IT...
IT'S DAZZLING...
...AND SWEETER THAN CANDY...
...AND IT SMELLS SO GOOD.

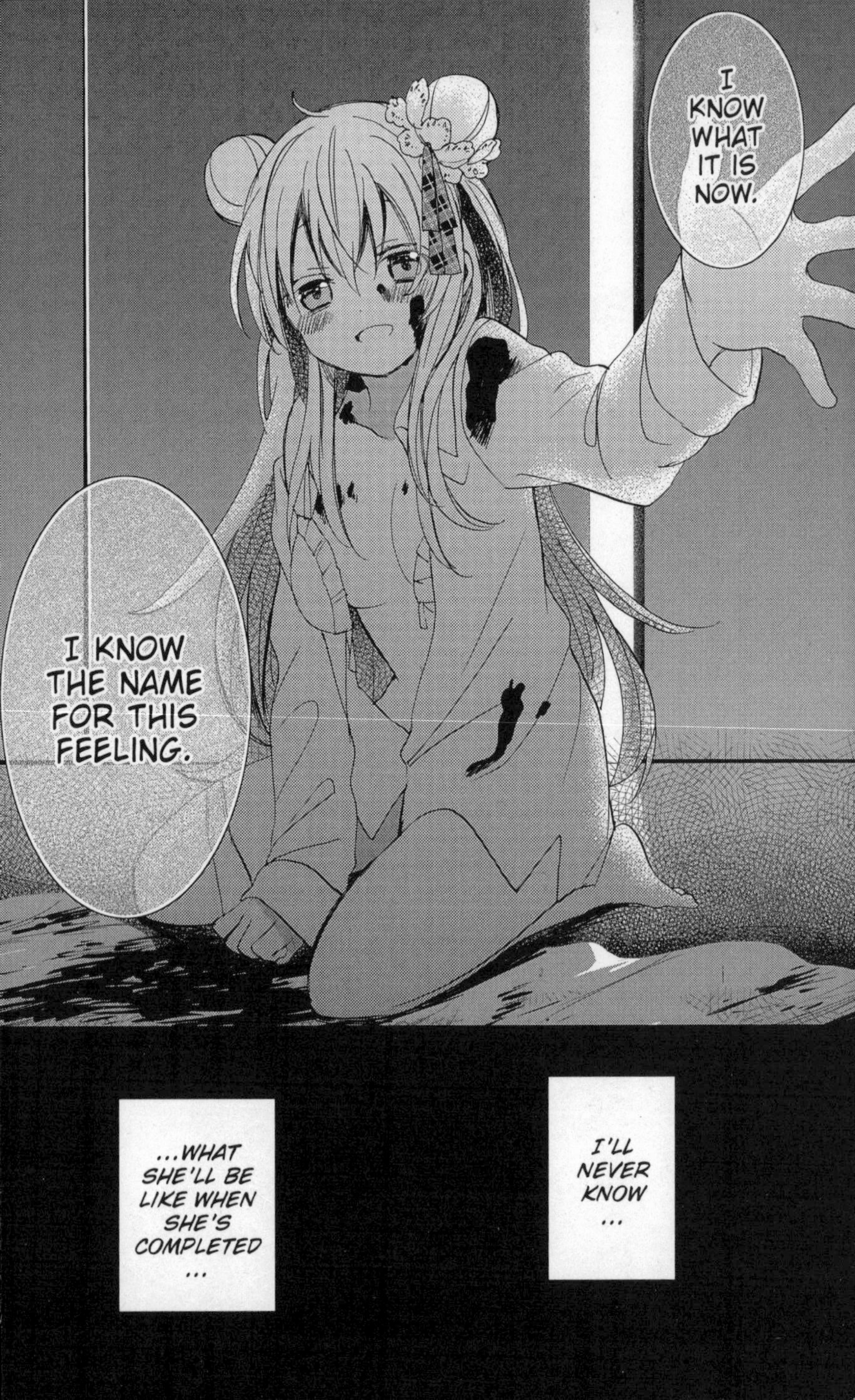
I KNOW WHAT IT IS NOW.
I KNOW THE NAME FOR THIS FEELING.
I'LL NEVER KNOW ...
...WHAT SHE'LL BE LIKE WHEN SHE'S COMPLETED ...

Happy
Sugar
Life

**Happy
Sugar
Life**

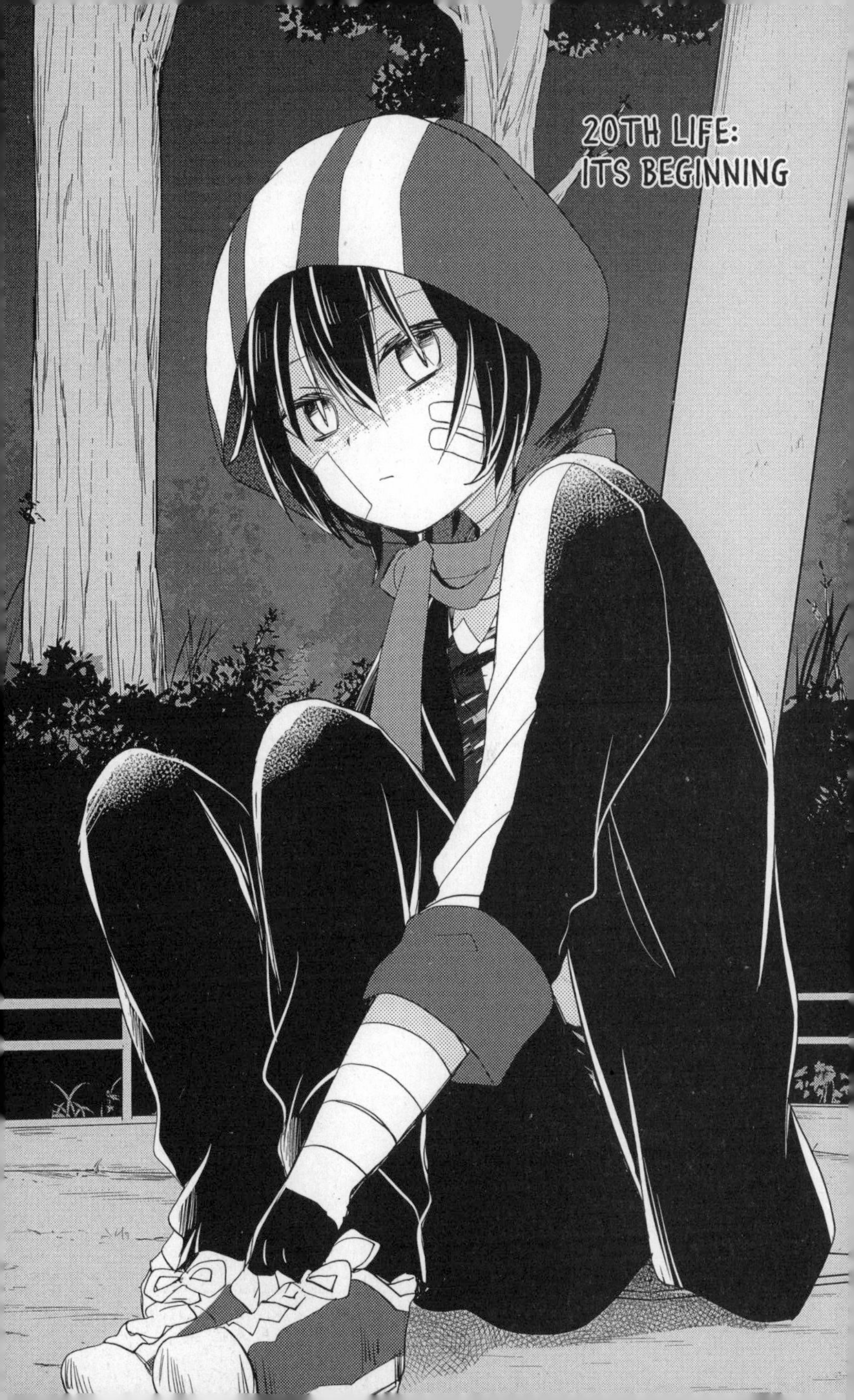
20TH LIFE:
ITS BEGINNING

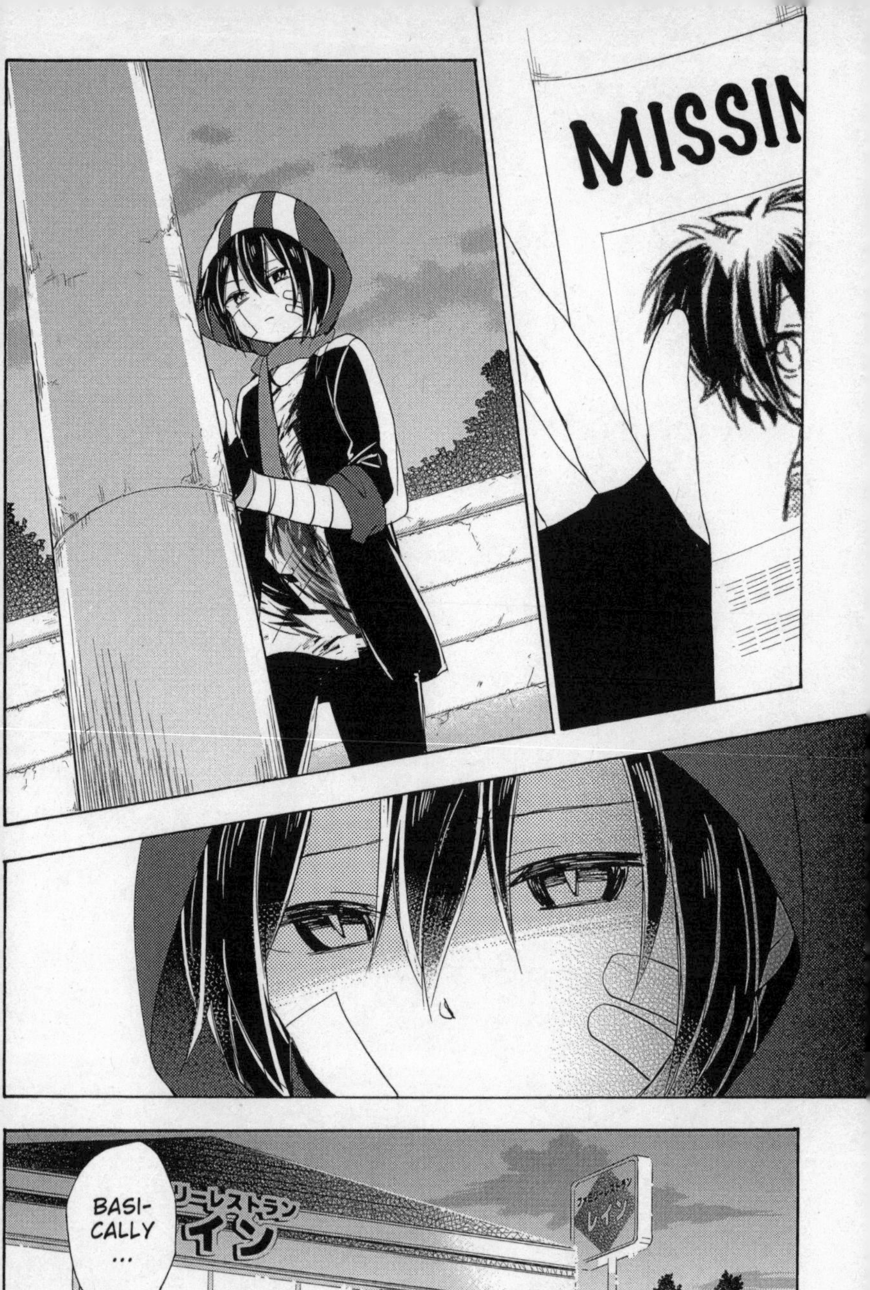
MISSIN
リーレストラン
イン
BASI-CALLY ...

SIGNS: FAMILY RESTAURANT LANE

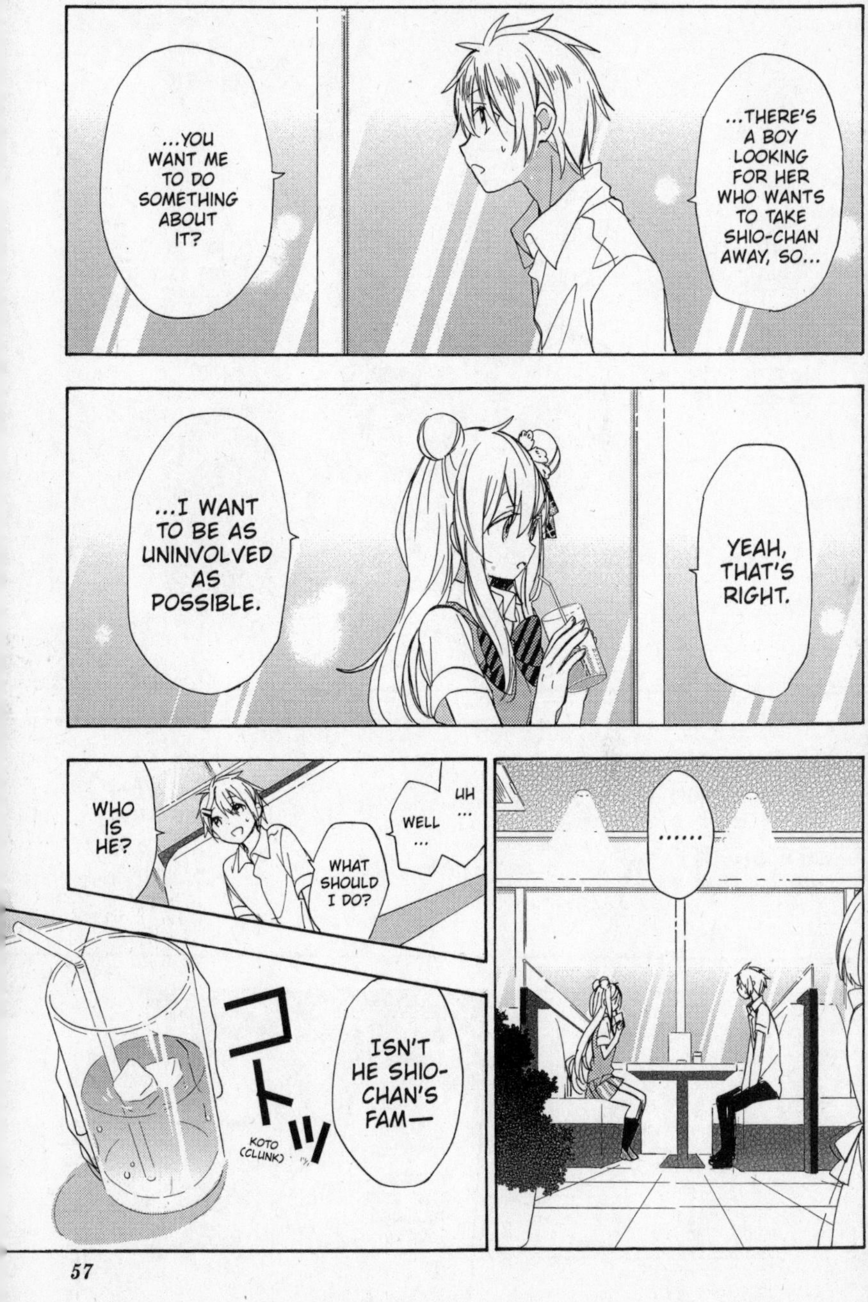
...THERE'S A BOY LOOKING FOR HER WHO WANTS TO TAKE SHIO-CHAN AWAY, SO...
...YOU WANT ME TO DO SOMETHING ABOUT IT?
YEAH, THAT'S RIGHT.
...I WANT TO BE AS UNINVOLVED AS POSSIBLE.
......
UH ...
WELL ...
WHAT SHOULD I DO?
WHO IS HE?
ISN'T HE SHIO-CHAN'S FAM—
KOTO (CLUNK)

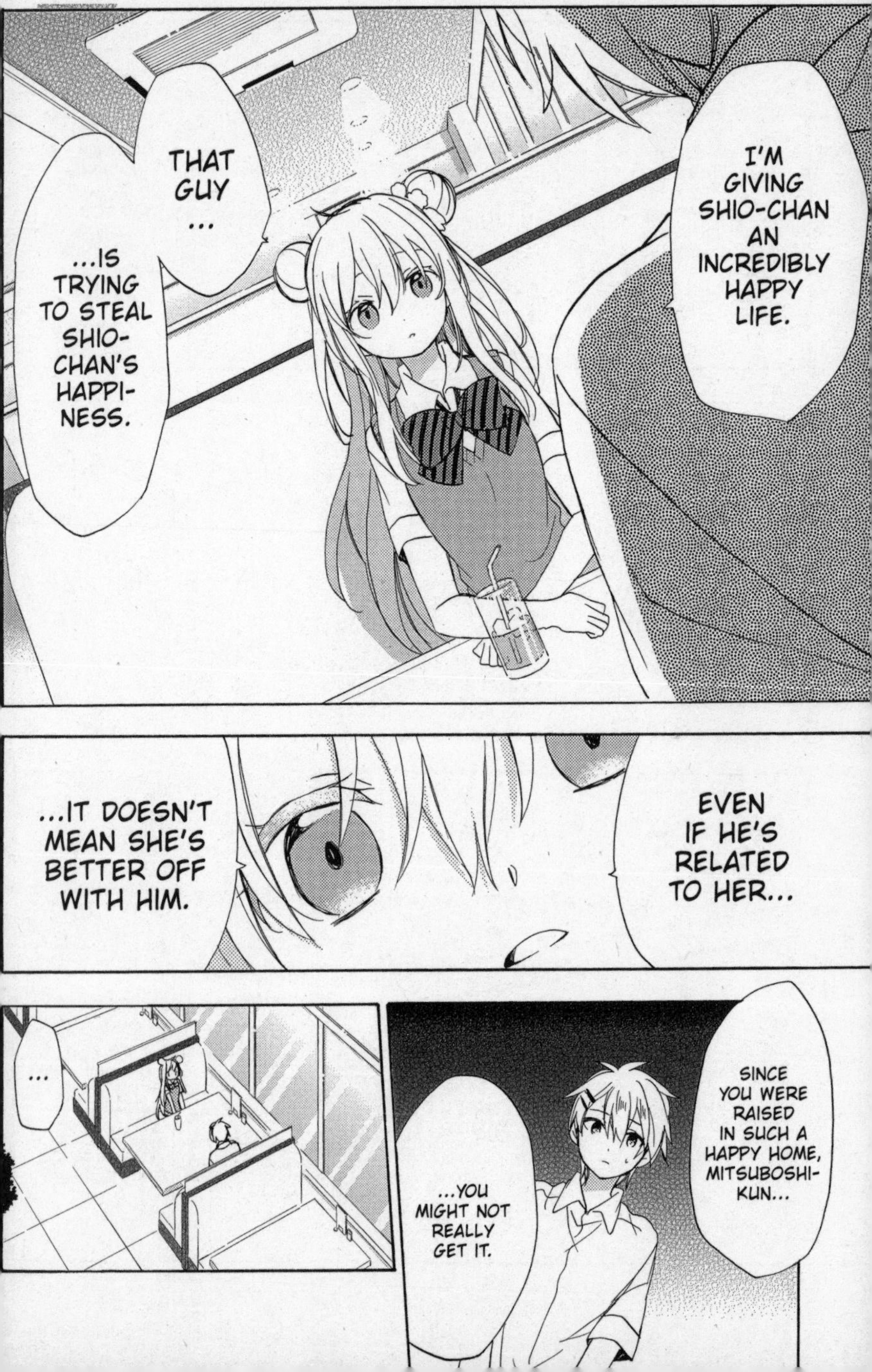
I'M GIVING SHIO-CHAN AN INCREDIBLY HAPPY LIFE.
THAT GUY ...
...IS TRYING TO STEAL SHIO-CHAN'S HAPPINESS.
EVEN IF HE'S RELATED TO HER...
...IT DOESN'T MEAN SHE'S BETTER OFF WITH HIM.
SINCE YOU WERE RAISED IN SUCH A HAPPY HOME, MITSUBOSHI-KUN...
...YOU MIGHT NOT REALLY GET IT.
...

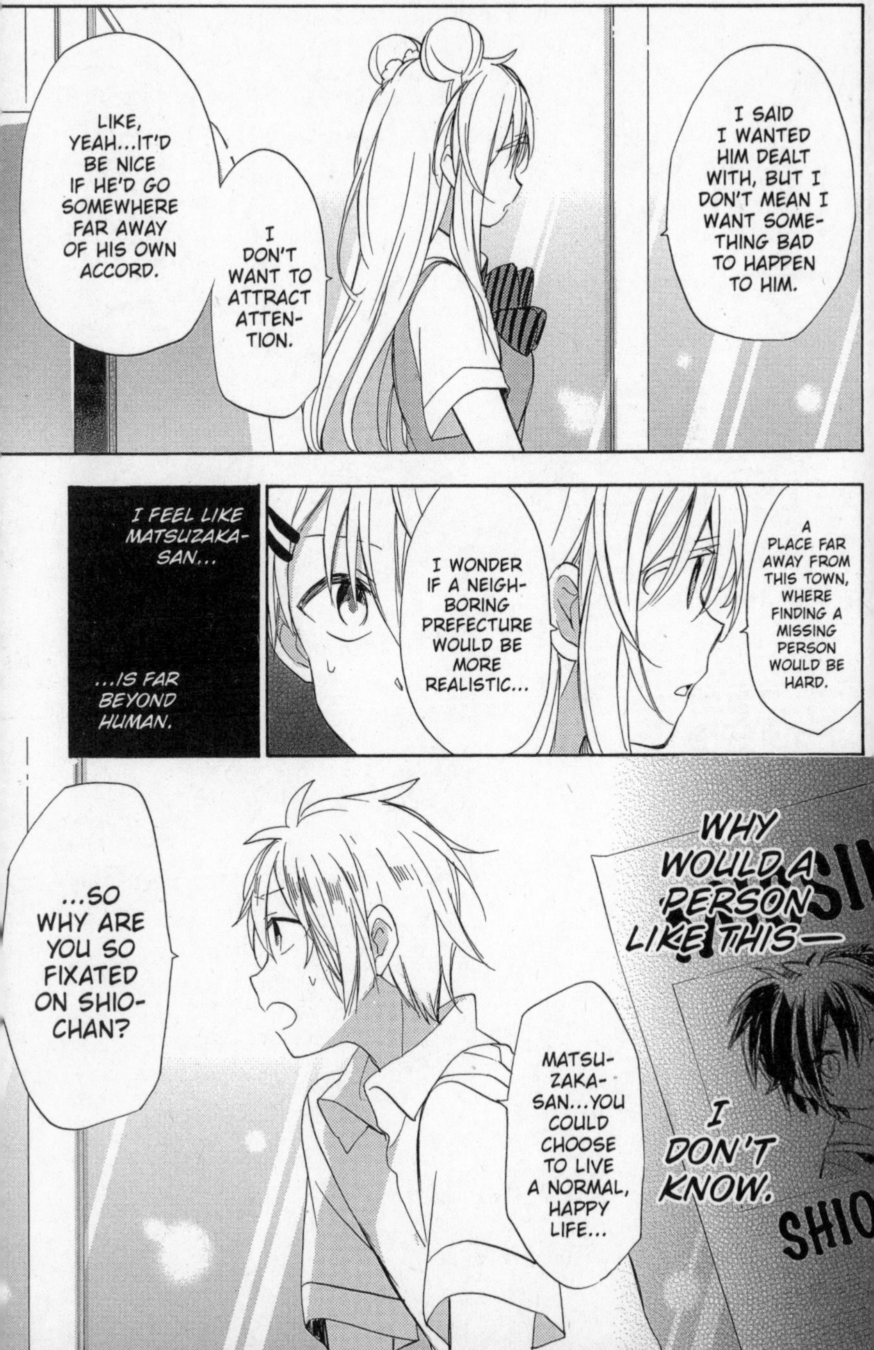
I SAID I WANTED HIM DEALT WITH, BUT I DON'T MEAN I WANT SOMETHING BAD TO HAPPEN TO HIM.
I DON'T WANT TO ATTRACT ATTENTION.
LIKE, YEAH...IT'D BE NICE IF HE'D GO SOMEWHERE FAR AWAY OF HIS OWN ACCORD.
A PLACE FAR AWAY FROM THIS TOWN, WHERE FINDING A MISSING PERSON WOULD BE HARD.
I WONDER IF A NEIGHBORING PREFECTURE WOULD BE MORE REALISTIC...
I FEEL LIKE MATSUZAKA-SAN...
...IS FAR BEYOND HUMAN.
WHY WOULD A PERSON LIKE THIS—
I DON'T KNOW.
MATSUZAKA-SAN...YOU COULD CHOOSE TO LIVE A NORMAL, HAPPY LIFE...
...SO WHY ARE YOU SO FIXATED ON SHIO-CHAN?

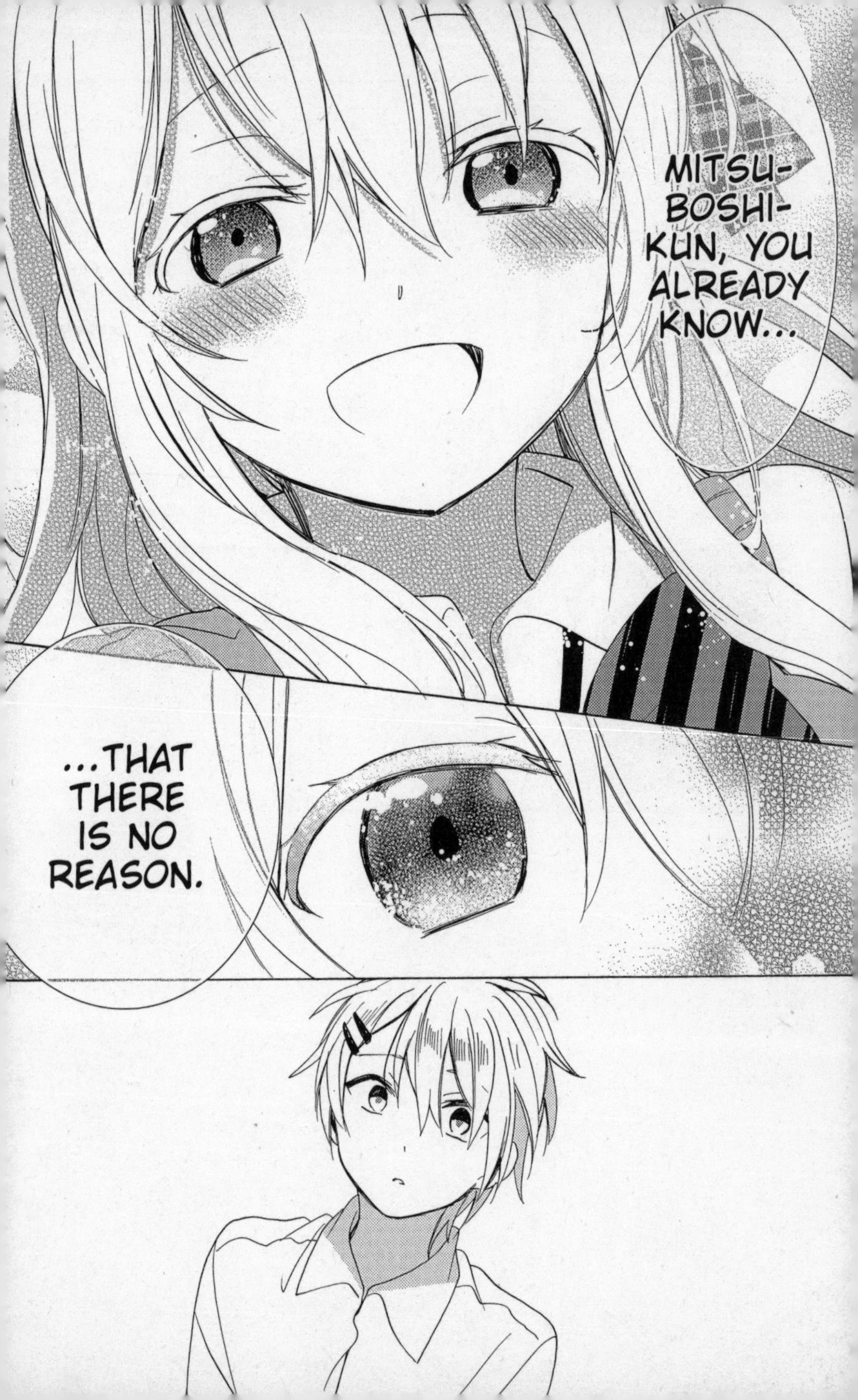
MITSU-BOSHI-KUN, YOU ALREADY KNOW...
...THAT THERE IS NO REASON.

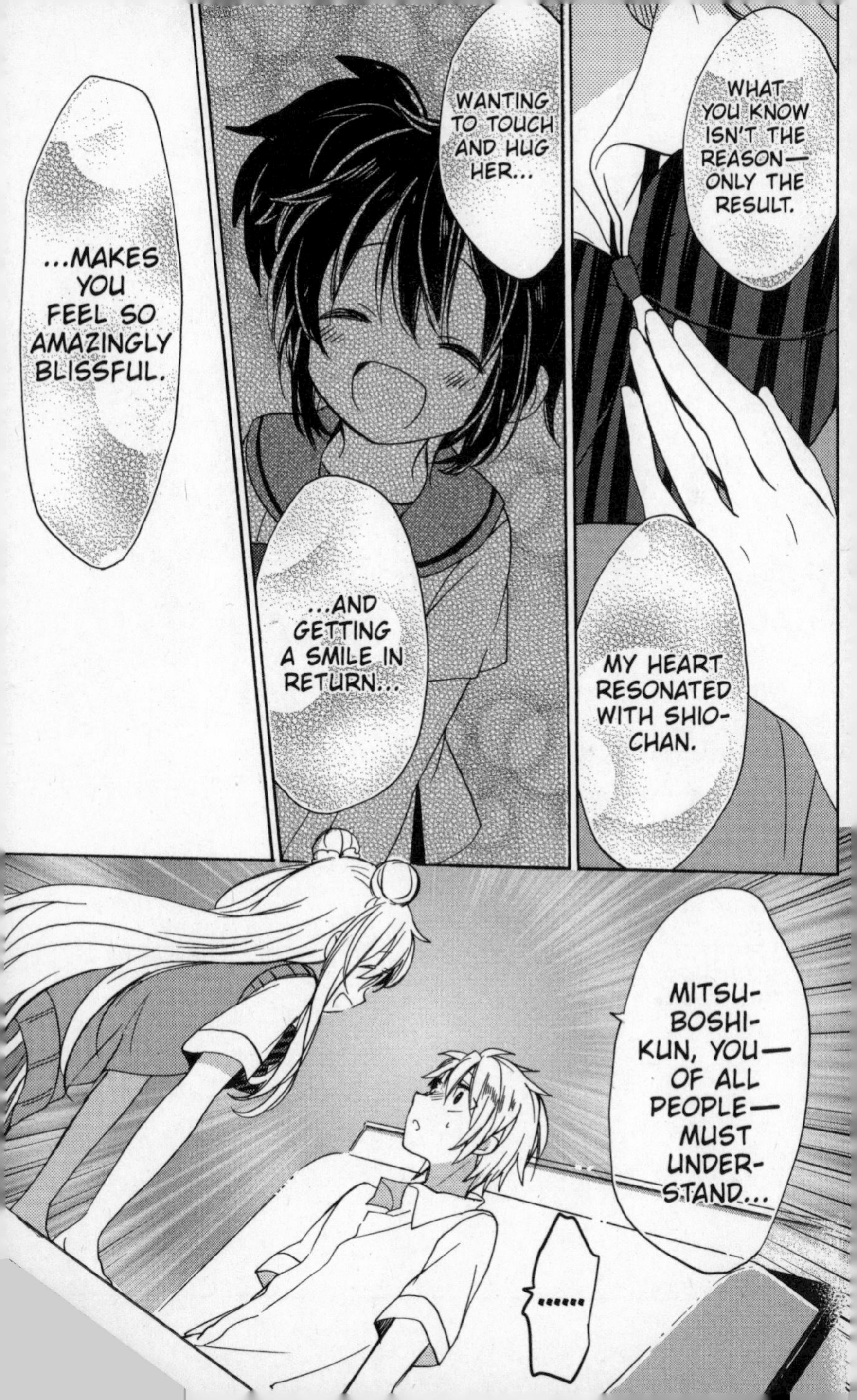
WHAT YOU KNOW ISN'T THE REASON—ONLY THE RESULT.
MY HEART RESONATED WITH SHIO-CHAN.
WANTING TO TOUCH AND HUG HER...
...AND GETTING A SMILE IN RETURN...
...MAKES YOU FEEL SO AMAZINGLY BLISSFUL.
MITSU-BOSHI-KUN, YOU—OF ALL PEOPLE—MUST UNDER-STAND...
......

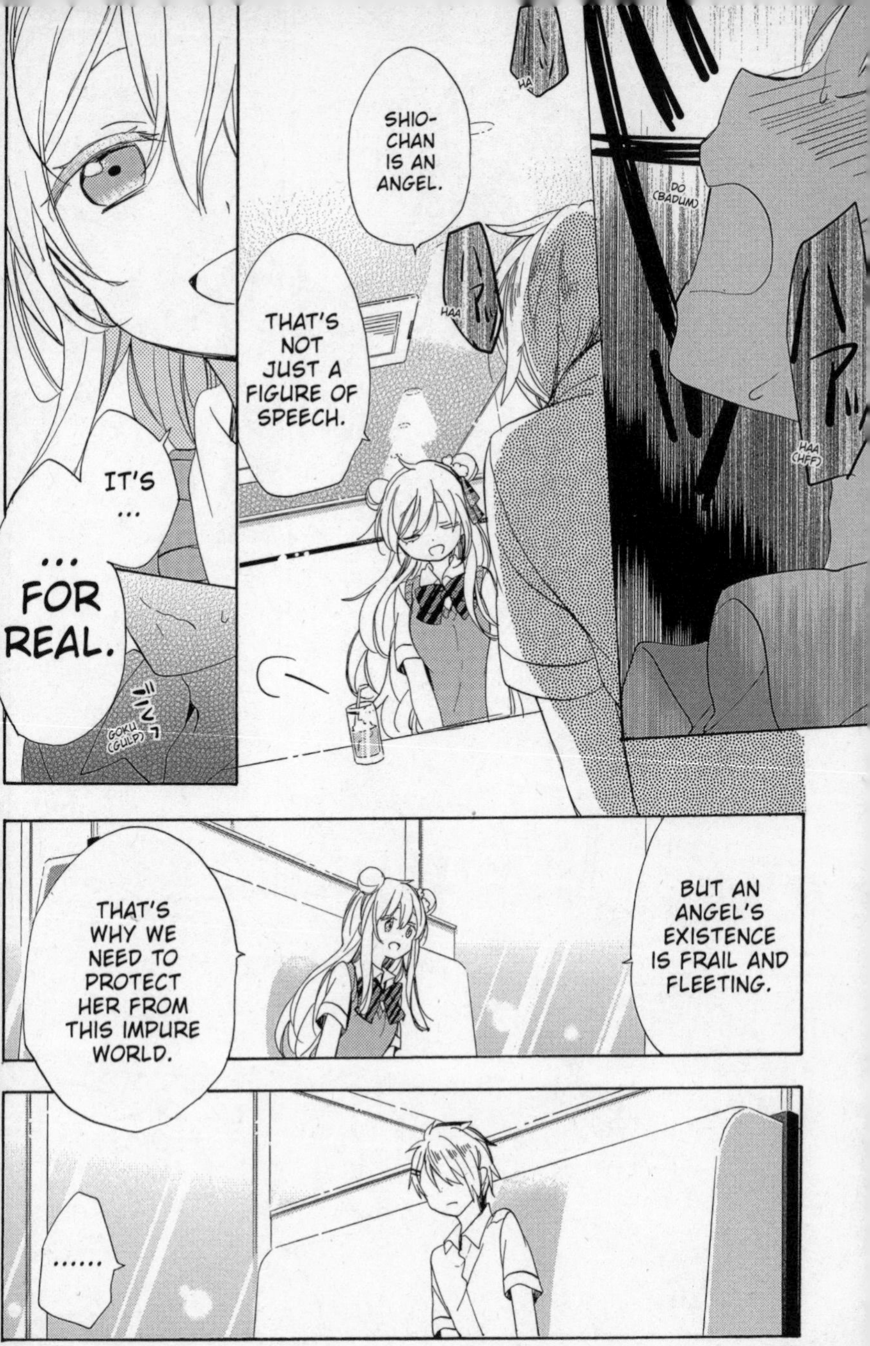
HA
DO (BADUM)
HAA (HFF)
SHIO-CHAN IS AN ANGEL.
HAA
THAT'S NOT JUST A FIGURE OF SPEECH.
IT'S ...
... FOR REAL.
GOKU (GULP)
BUT AN ANGEL'S EXISTENCE IS FRAIL AND FLEETING.
THAT'S WHY WE NEED TO PROTECT HER FROM THIS IMPURE WORLD.
......

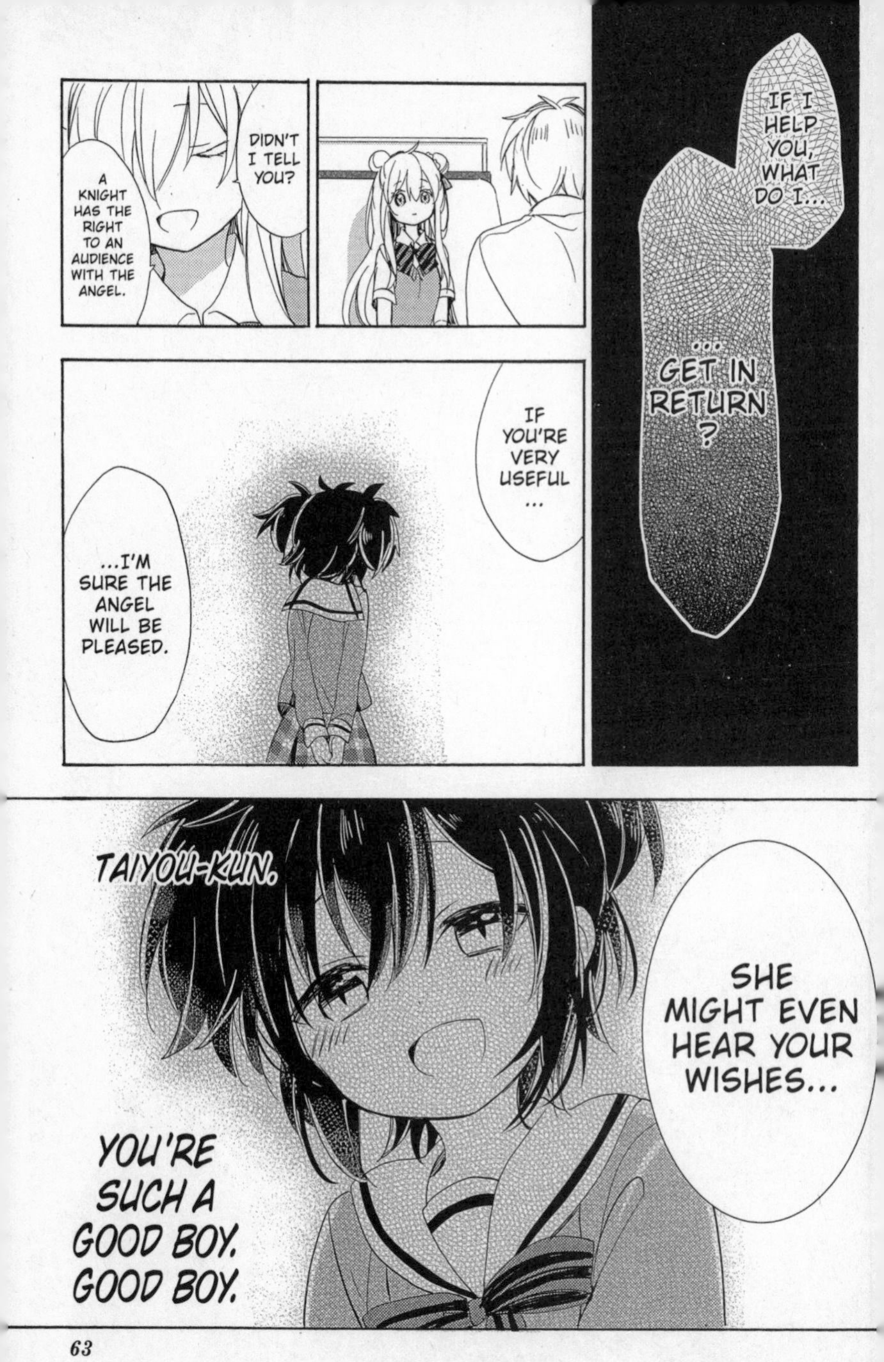
IF I HELP YOU, WHAT DO I...
...GET IN RETURN?
DIDN'T I TELL YOU?
A KNIGHT HAS THE RIGHT TO AN AUDIENCE WITH THE ANGEL.
IF YOU'RE VERY USEFUL...
...I'M SURE THE ANGEL WILL BE PLEASED.
SHE MIGHT EVEN HEAR YOUR WISHES...
TAIYOU-KUN.
YOU'RE SUCH A GOOD BOY. GOOD BOY.

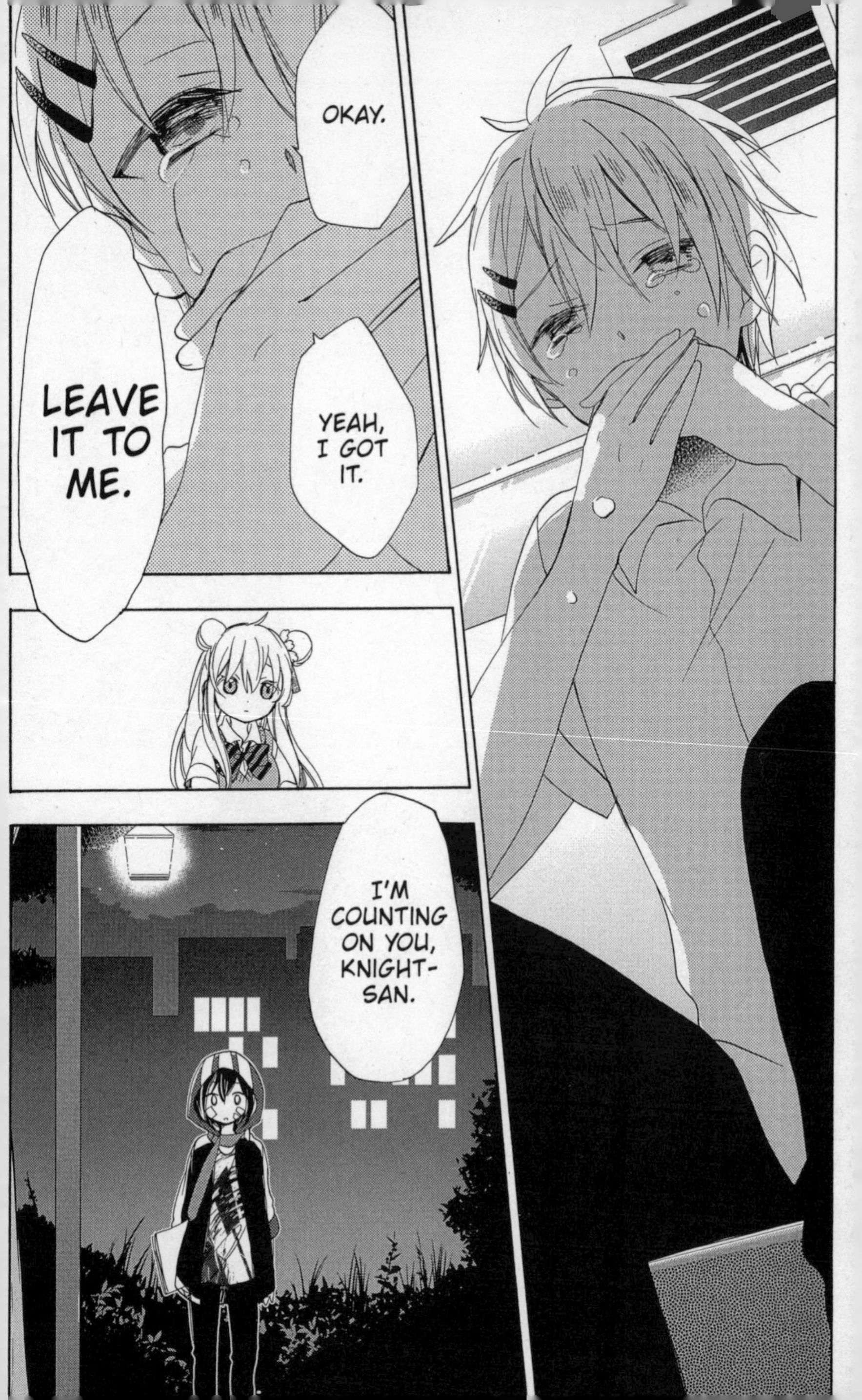
I'M COUNTING ON YOU, KNIGHT-SAN.
OKAY.
YEAH, I GOT IT.
LEAVE IT TO ME.

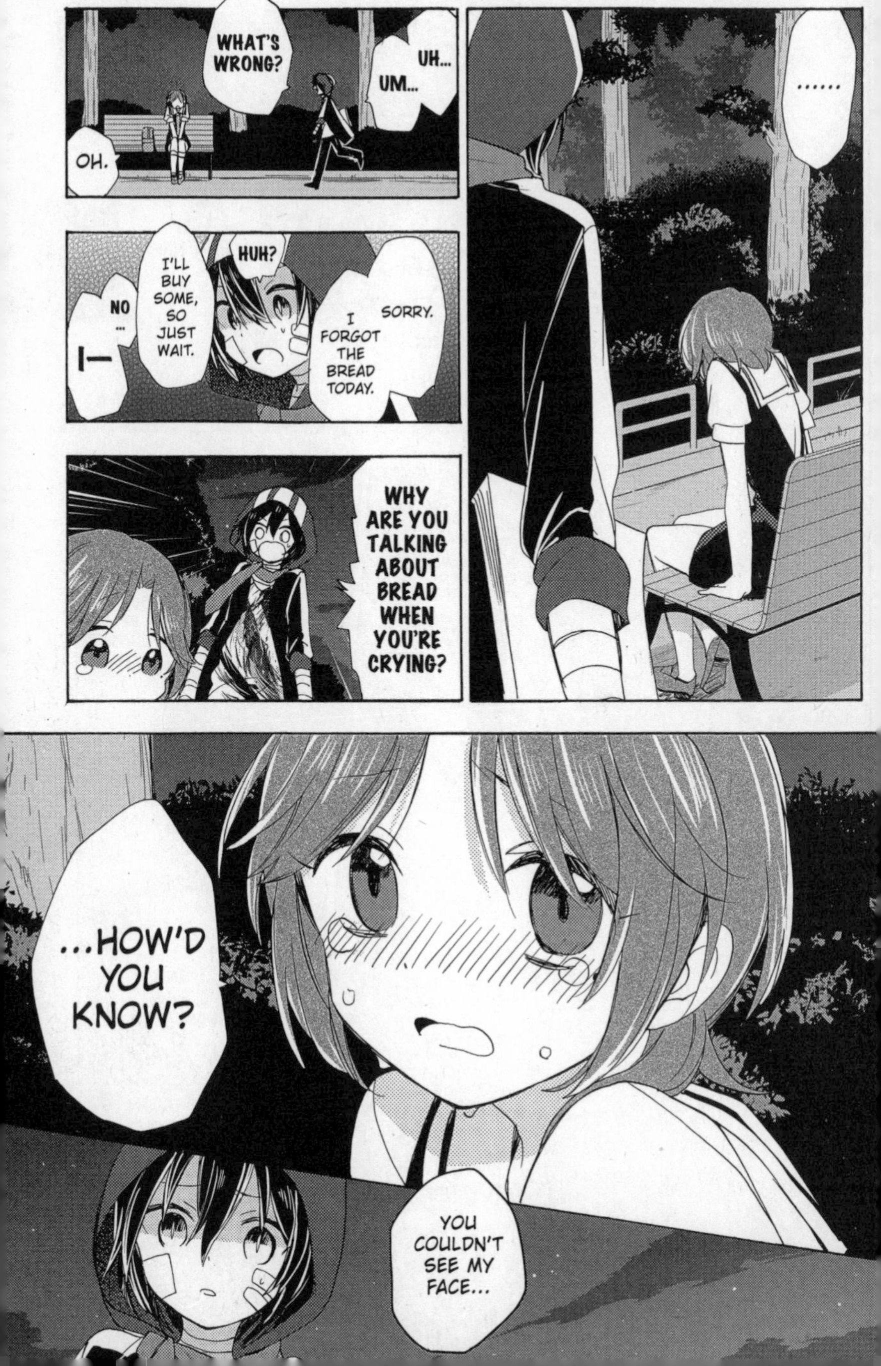
......
UH... UM...
WHAT'S WRONG?
OH.
SORRY. I FORGOT THE BREAD TODAY.
HUH?
I'LL BUY SOME, SO JUST WAIT.
NO ... I—
WHY ARE YOU TALKING ABOUT BREAD WHEN YOU'RE CRYING?
...HOW'D YOU KNOW?
YOU COULDN'T SEE MY FACE...

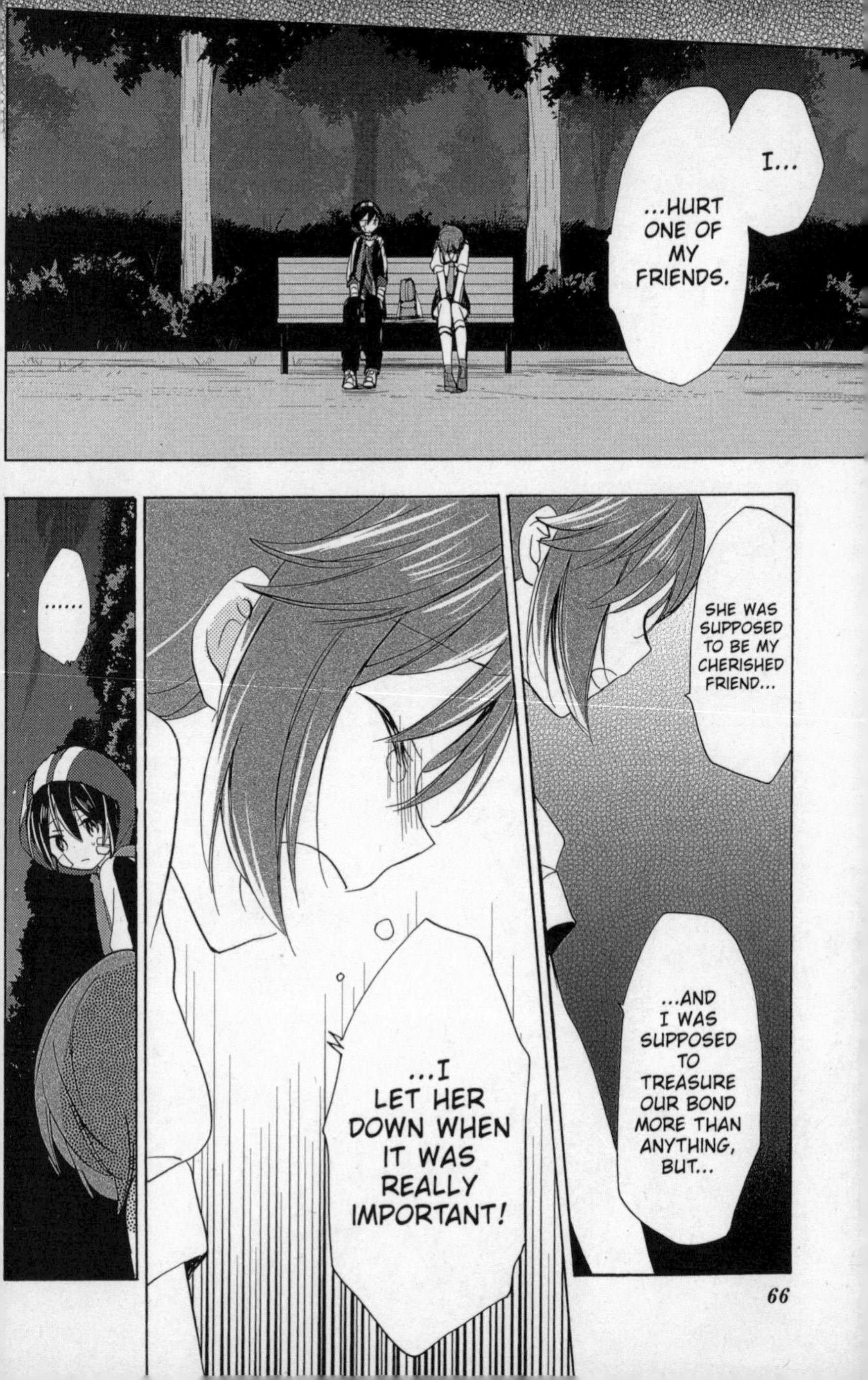
I...
...HURT ONE OF MY FRIENDS.
SHE WAS SUPPOSED TO BE MY CHERISHED FRIEND...
...AND I WAS SUPPOSED TO TREASURE OUR BOND MORE THAN ANYTHING, BUT...
...I LET HER DOWN WHEN IT WAS REALLY IMPORTANT!
......

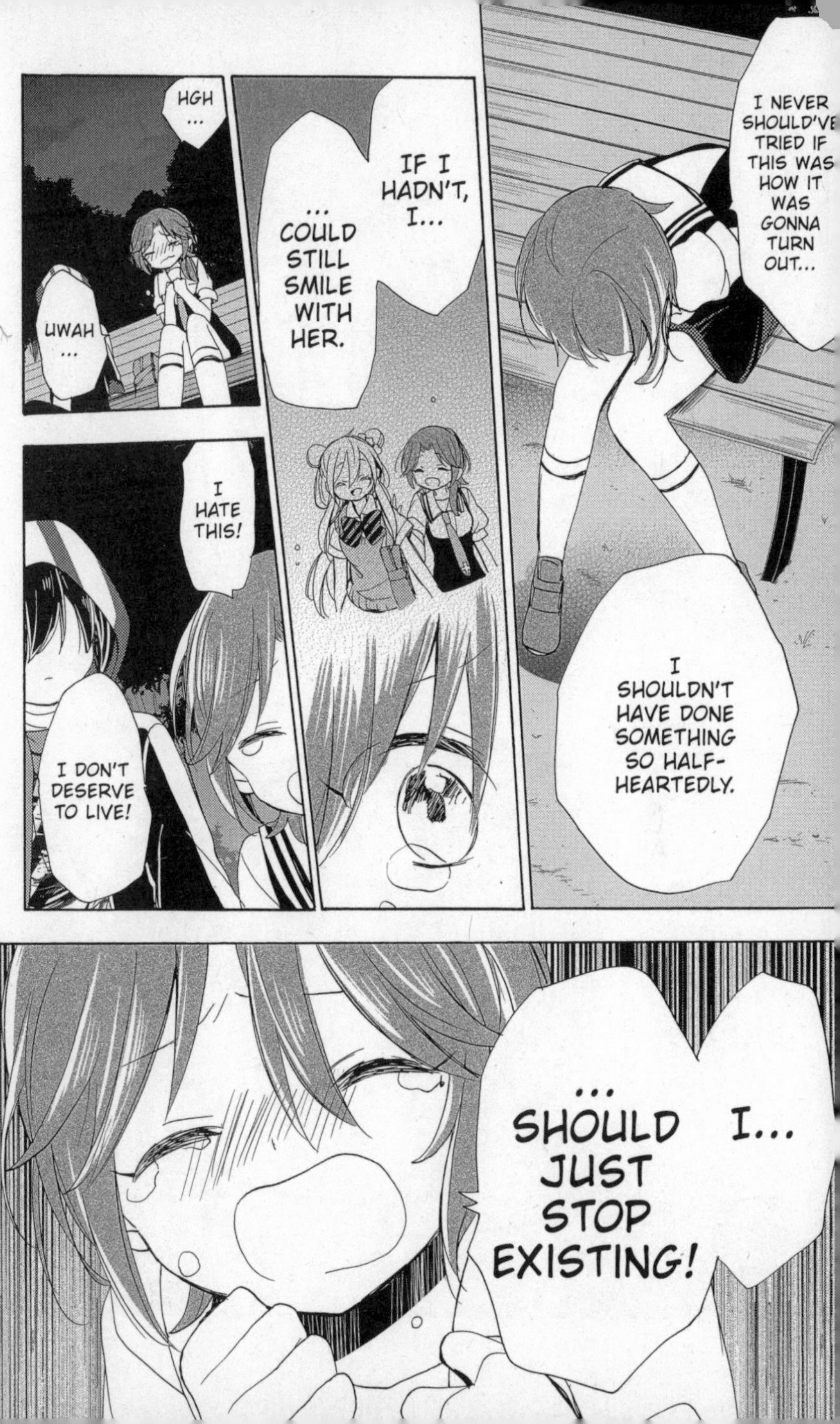
I NEVER SHOULD'VE TRIED IF THIS WAS HOW IT WAS GONNA TURN OUT...
I SHOULDN'T HAVE DONE SOMETHING SO HALF-HEARTEDLY.
IF I HADN'T, I...
...COULD STILL SMILE WITH HER.
HGH...
UWAH...
I HATE THIS!
I DON'T DESERVE TO LIVE!
I...
...SHOULD JUST STOP EXISTING!

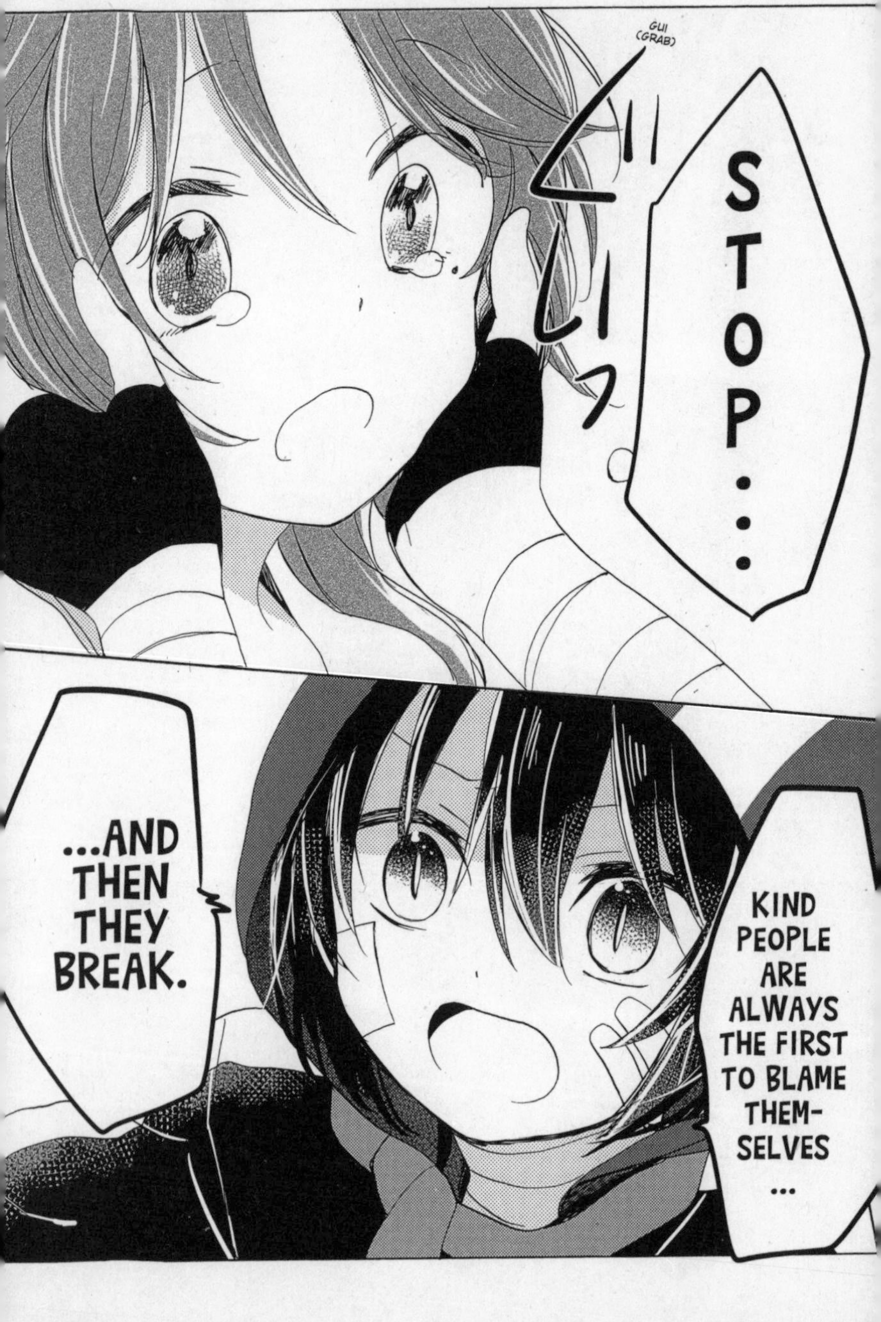
GUI (GRAB)
STOP...
KIND PEOPLE ARE ALWAYS THE FIRST TO BLAME THEM-SELVES ...
...AND THEN THEY BREAK.

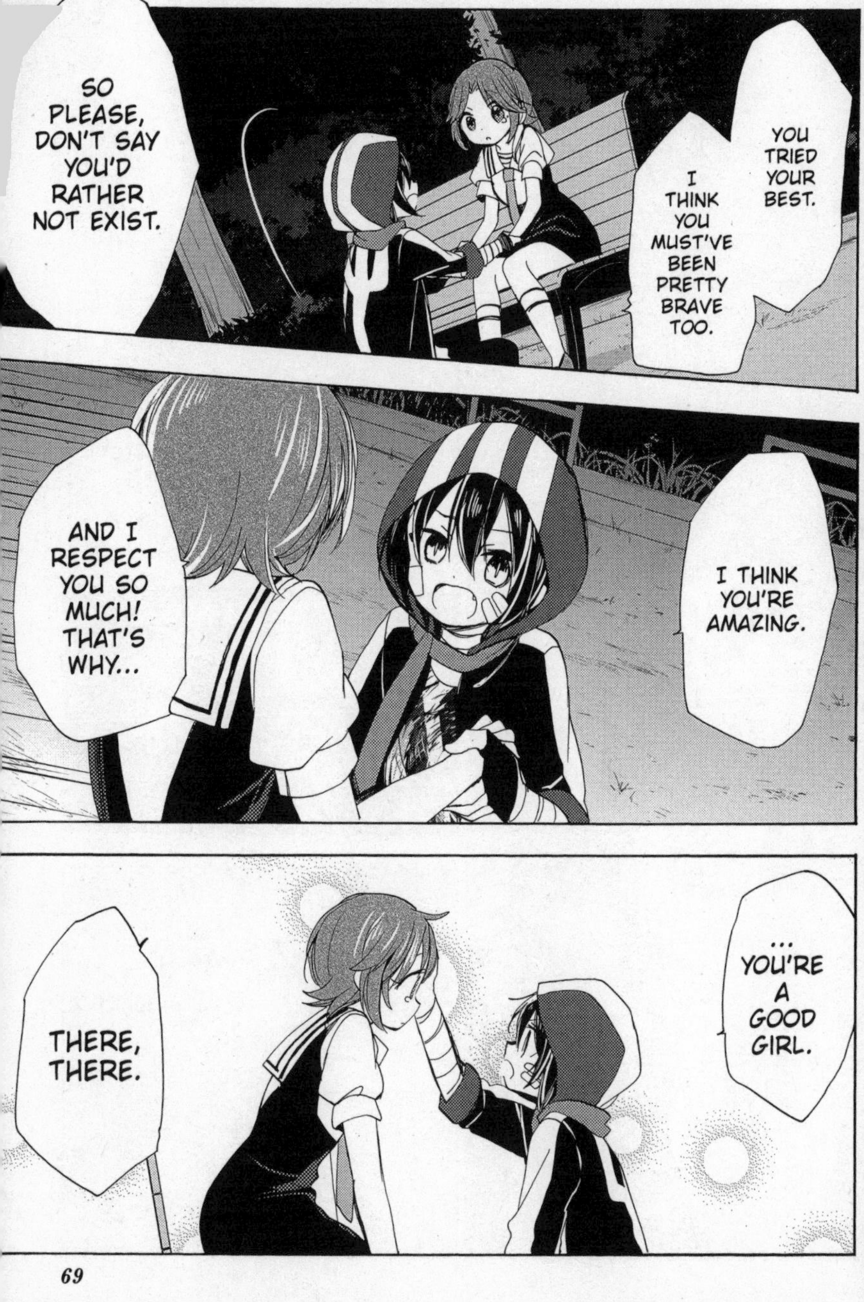
YOU TRIED YOUR BEST.
I THINK YOU MUST'VE BEEN PRETTY BRAVE TOO.
SO PLEASE, DON'T SAY YOU'D RATHER NOT EXIST.
I THINK YOU'RE AMAZING.
AND I RESPECT YOU SO MUCH! THAT'S WHY...
... YOU'RE A GOOD GIRL.
THERE, THERE.

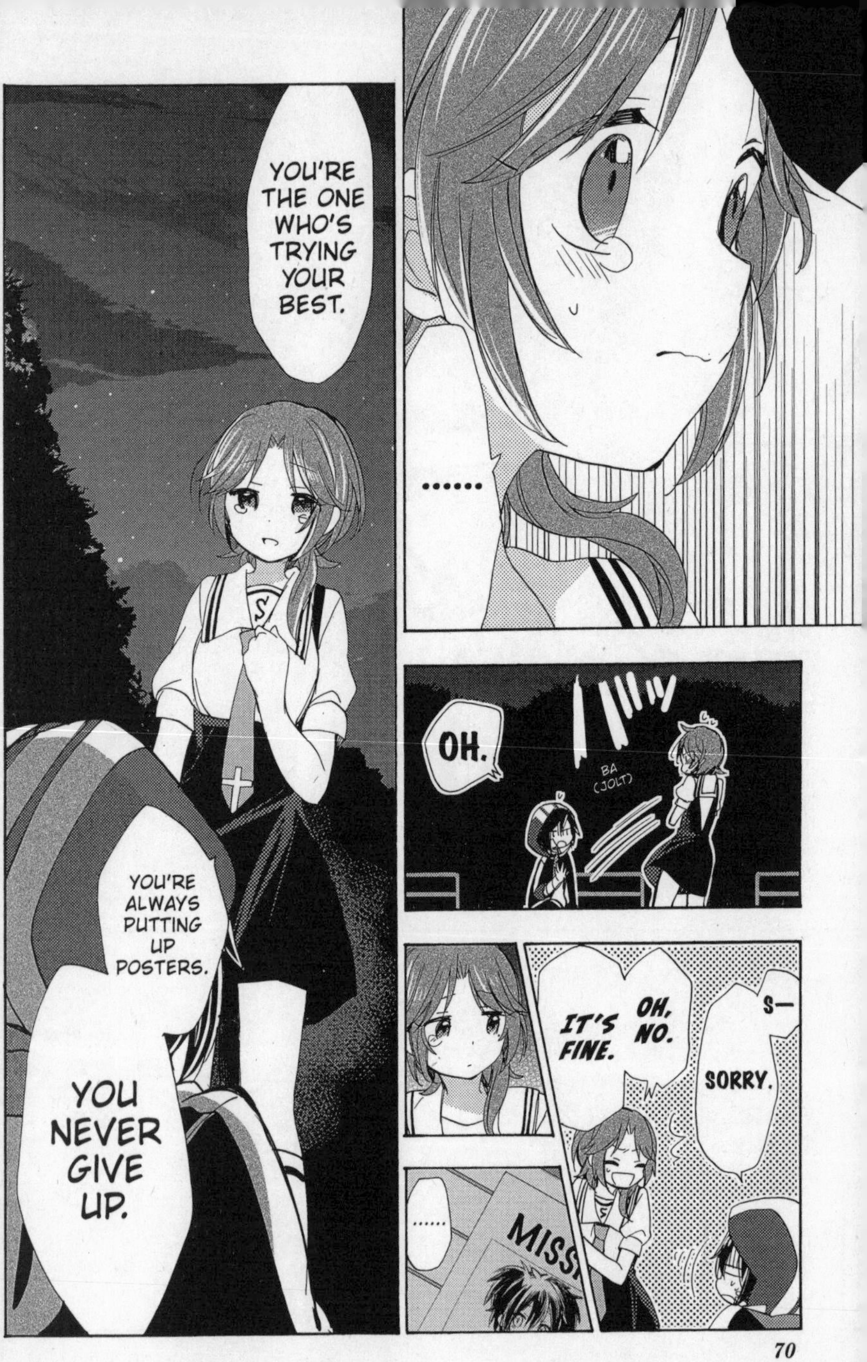
......
OH.
BA (JOLT)
S— SORRY.
OH, NO. IT'S FINE.
......
MISS
YOU'RE THE ONE WHO'S TRYING YOUR BEST.
YOU'RE ALWAYS PUTTING UP POSTERS.
YOU NEVER GIVE UP.

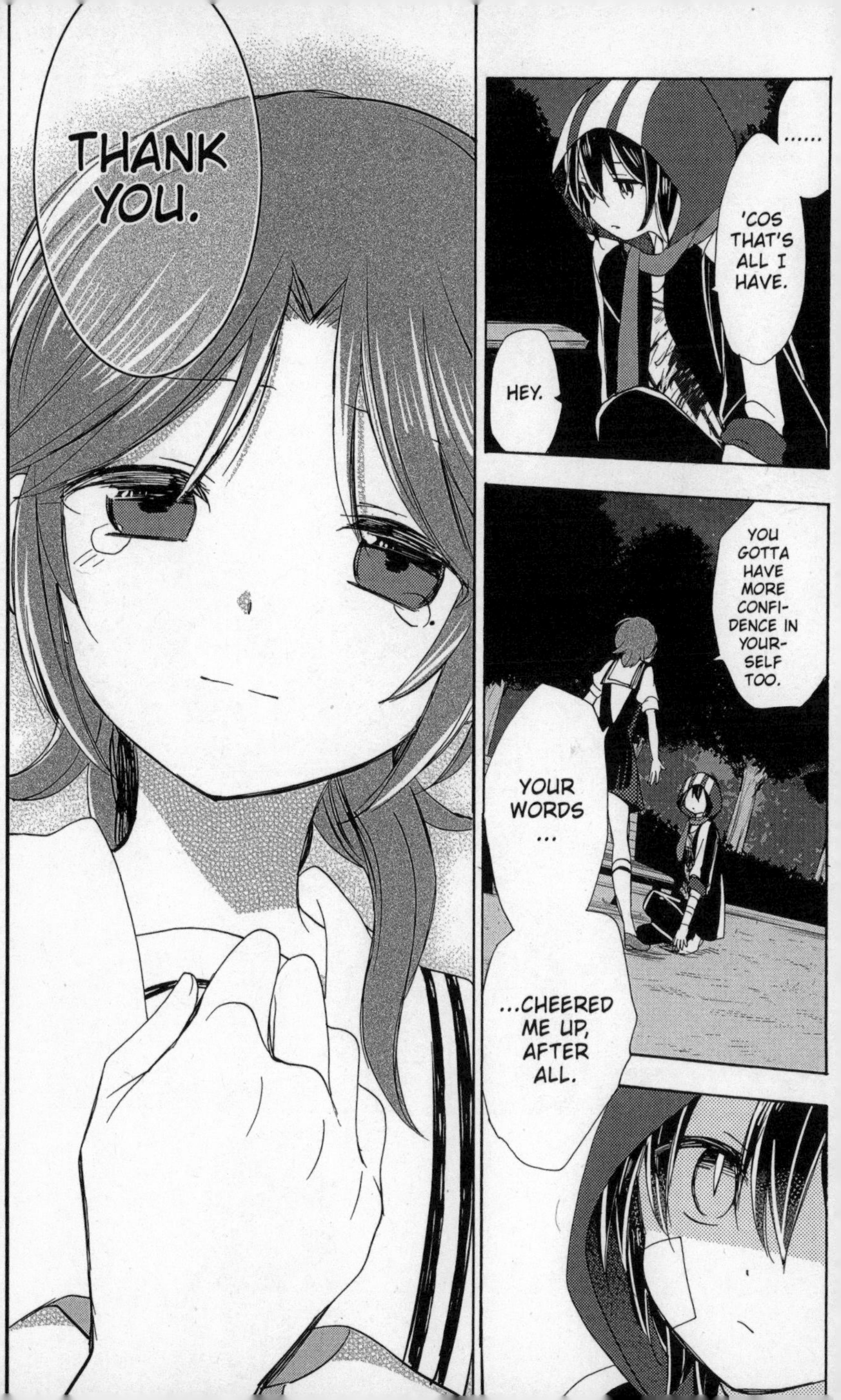
......
'COS THAT'S ALL I HAVE.
HEY.
YOU GOTTA HAVE MORE CONFI-DENCE IN YOUR-SELF TOO.
YOUR WORDS ...
...CHEERED ME UP, AFTER ALL.
THANK YOU.

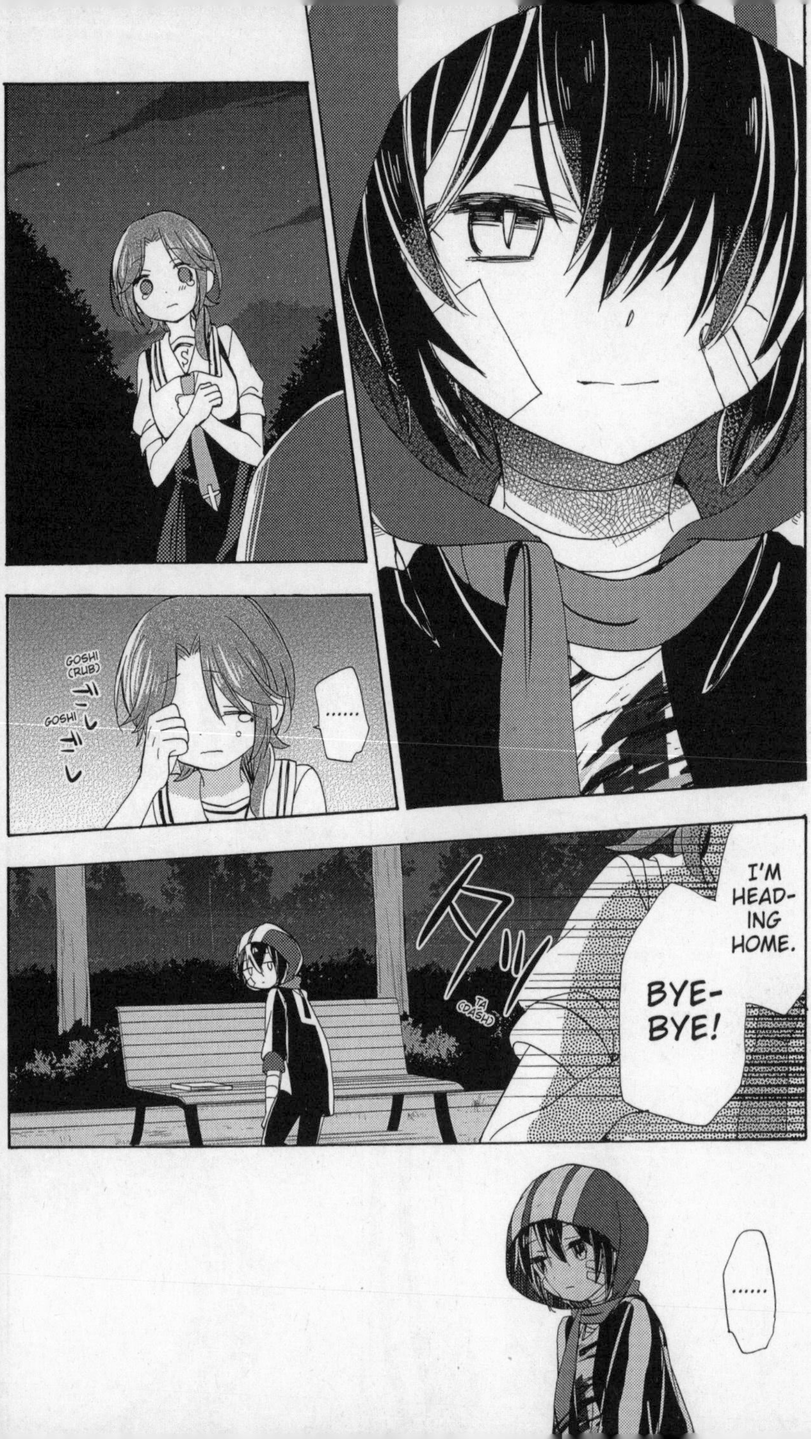
GOSHI (RUB) GOSHI
......
I'M HEADING HOME.
BYE-BYE!
TA (DASH)
......

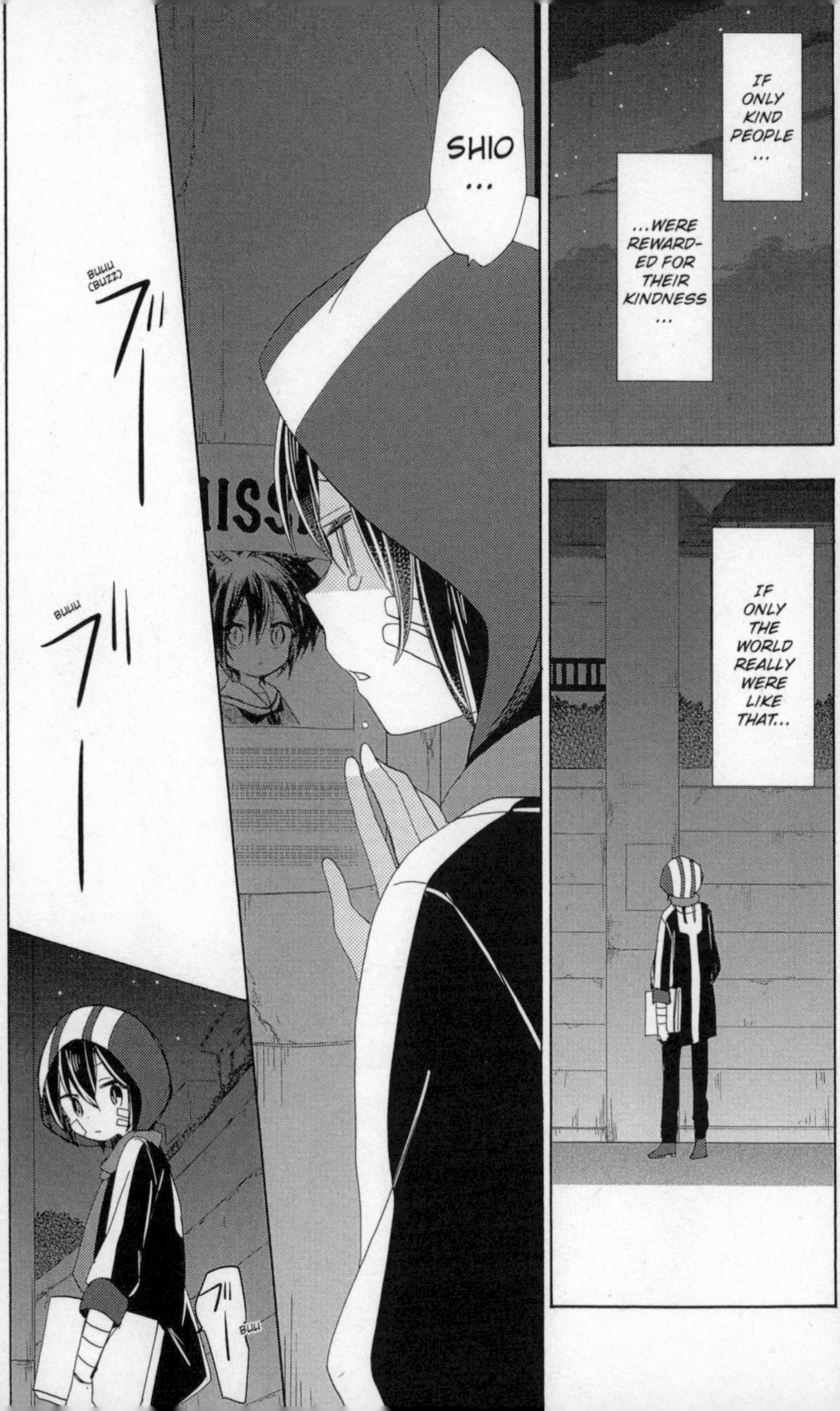
IF ONLY KIND PEOPLE...
...WERE REWARD-ED FOR THEIR KINDNESS...
IF ONLY THE WORLD REALLY WERE LIKE THAT...
SHIO...
BUUU (BUZZ)
BUUU
BUU

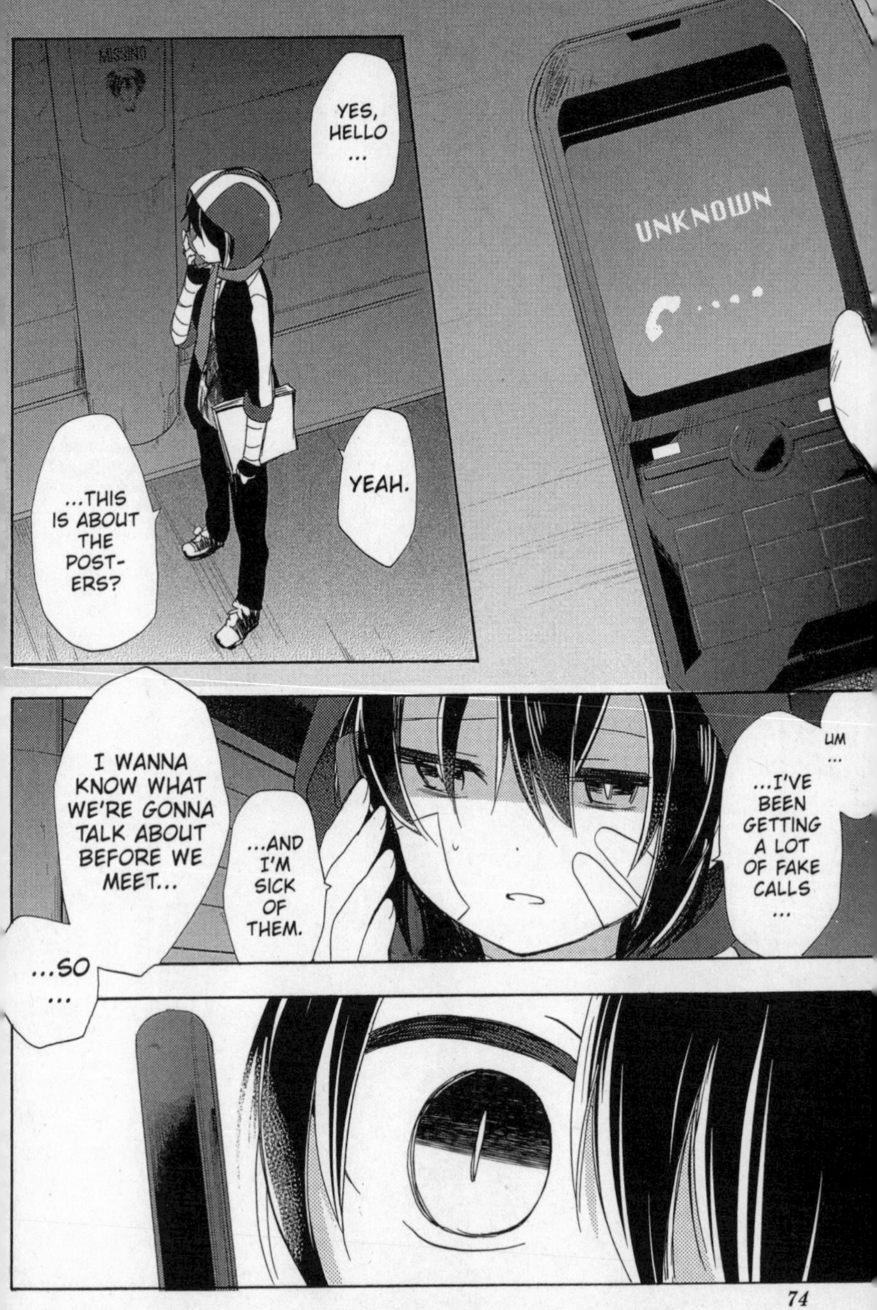
UNKNOWN
MISSING
YES, HELLO ...
YEAH.
...THIS IS ABOUT THE POSTERS?
UM ...
...I'VE BEEN GETTING A LOT OF FAKE CALLS ...
...AND I'M SICK OF THEM.
I WANNA KNOW WHAT WE'RE GONNA TALK ABOUT BEFORE WE MEET...
...SO ...

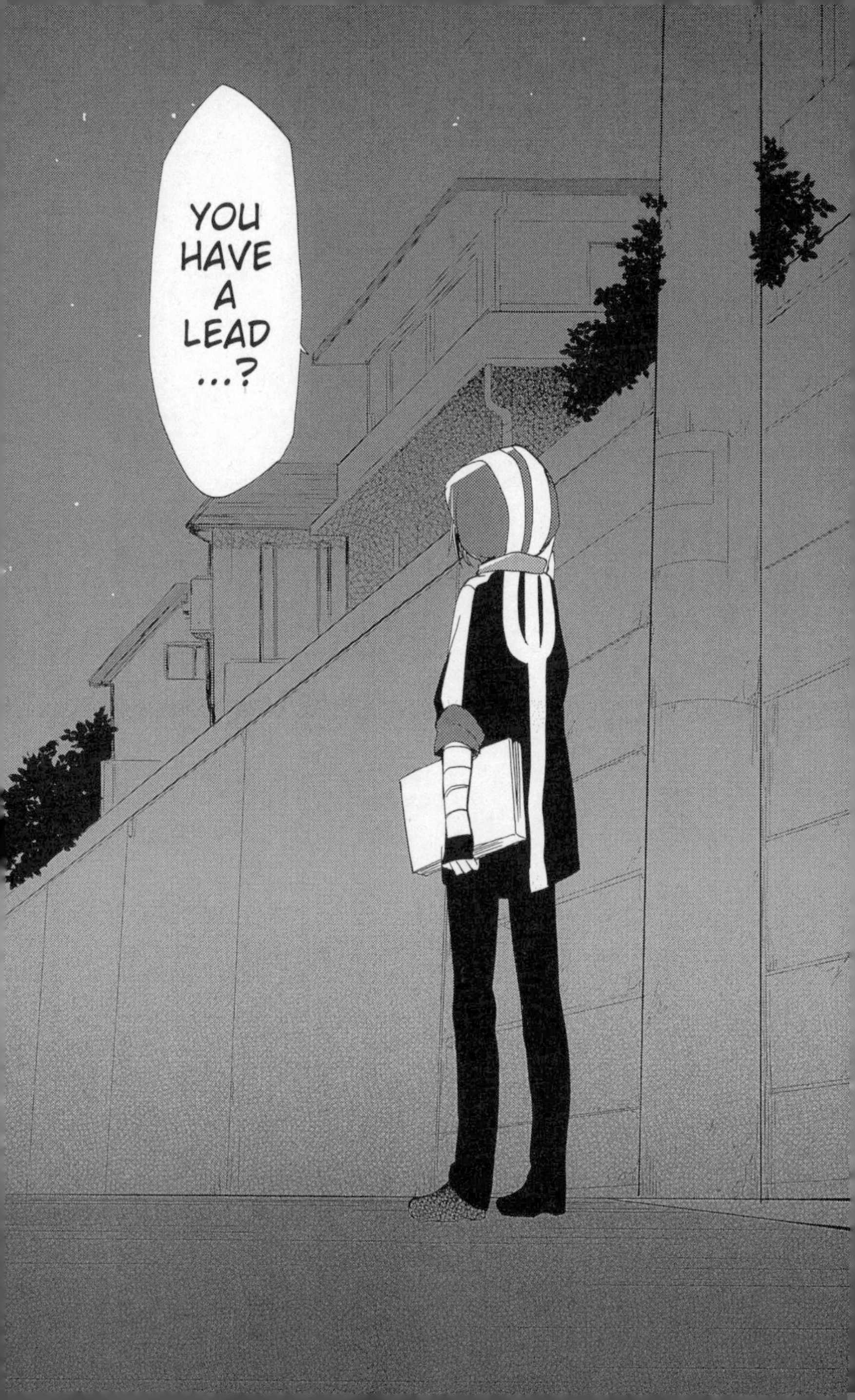
YOU HAVE A LEAD ...?

Happy
Sugar
Life

21ST LIFE: WAVERING THREAD

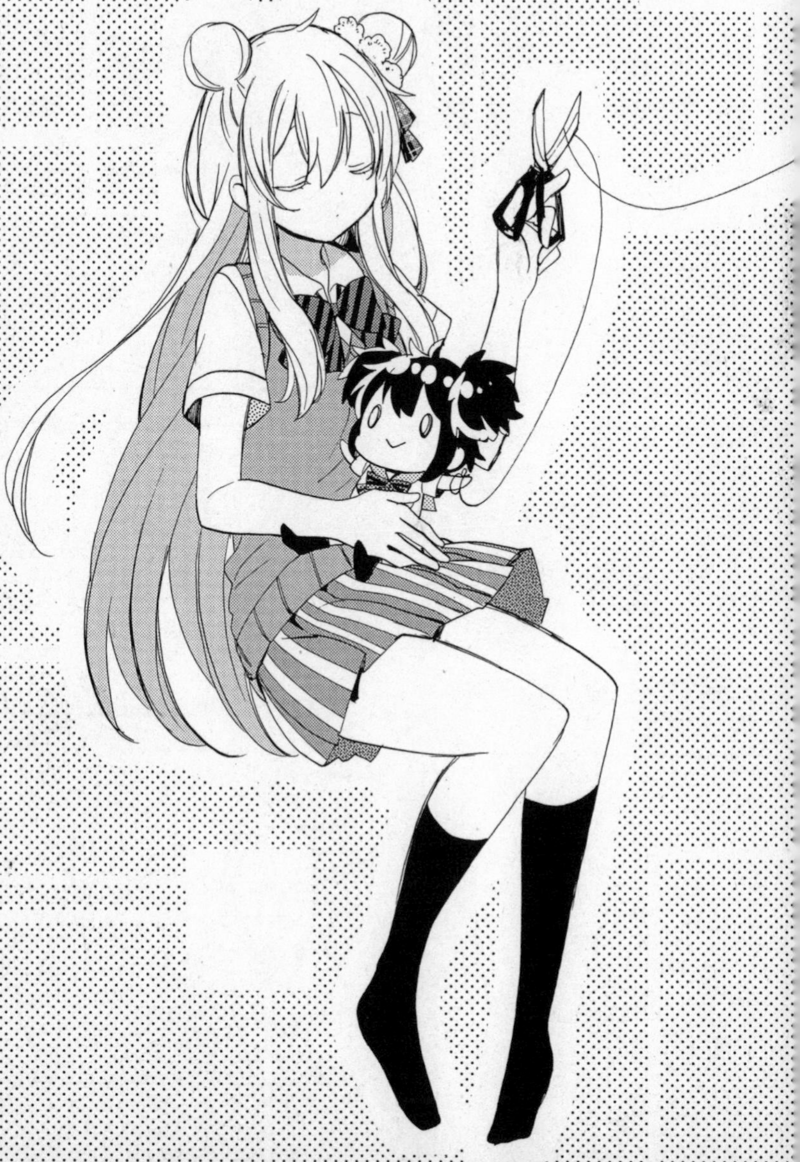

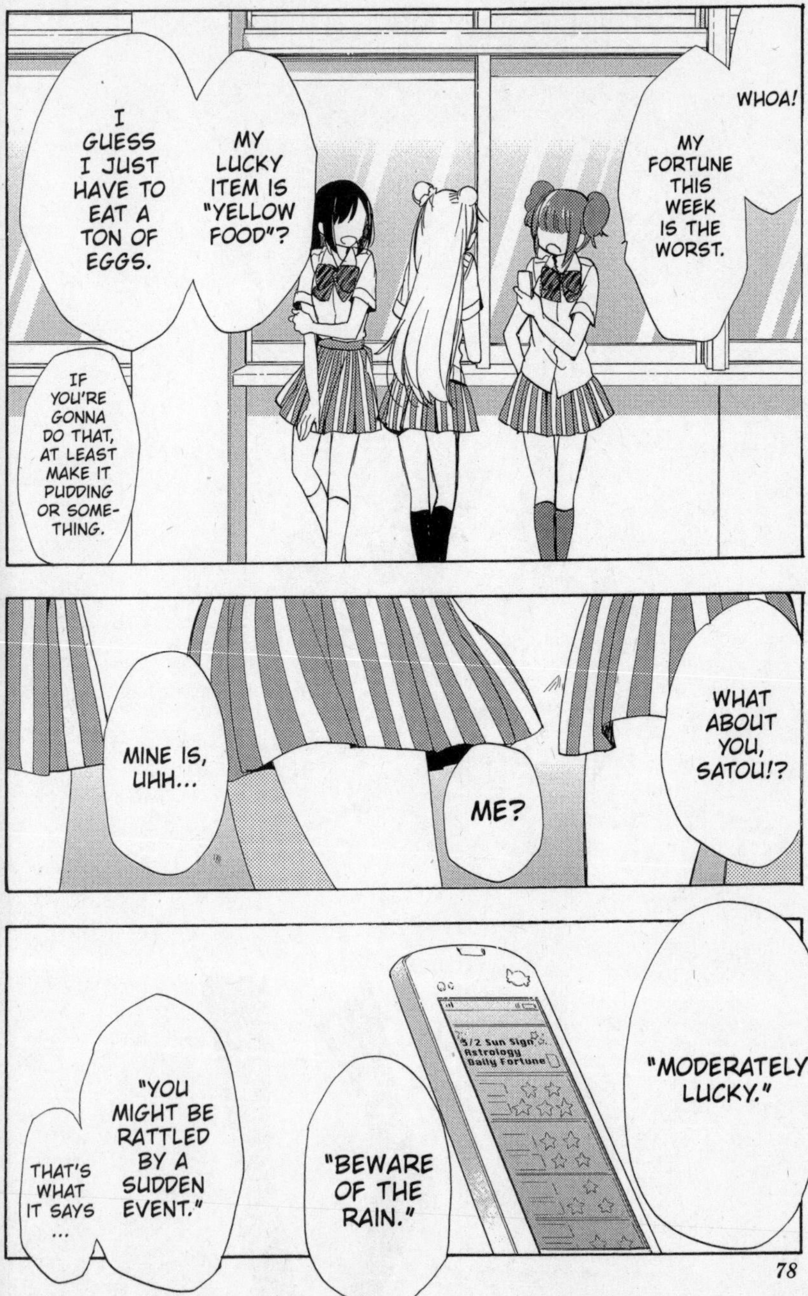
WHOA!
MY FORTUNE THIS WEEK IS THE WORST.
MY LUCKY ITEM IS "YELLOW FOOD"?
I GUESS I JUST HAVE TO EAT A TON OF EGGS.
IF YOU'RE GONNA DO THAT, AT LEAST MAKE IT PUDDING OR SOME-THING.
WHAT ABOUT YOU, SATOU!?
ME?
MINE IS, UHH...
"MODERATELY LUCKY."
3/2 Sun Sign Astrology Daily Fortune
"BEWARE OF THE RAIN."
"YOU MIGHT BE RATTLED BY A SUDDEN EVENT."
THAT'S WHAT IT SAYS ...

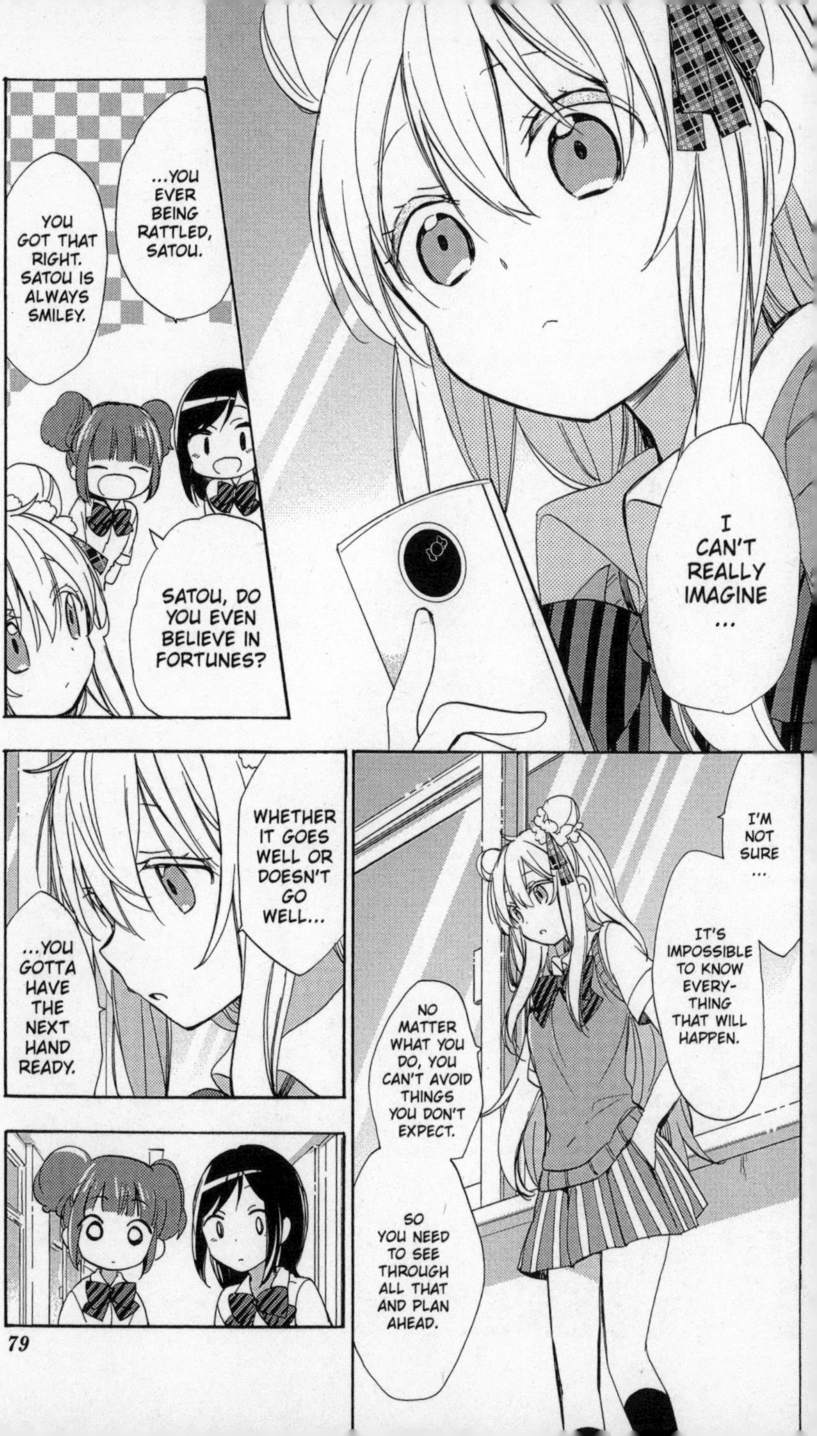
I CAN'T REALLY IMAGINE...
...YOU EVER BEING RATTLED, SATOU.
YOU GOT THAT RIGHT. SATOU IS ALWAYS SMILEY.
SATOU, DO YOU EVEN BELIEVE IN FORTUNES?
I'M NOT SURE...
IT'S IMPOSSIBLE TO KNOW EVERY-THING THAT WILL HAPPEN.
NO MATTER WHAT YOU DO, YOU CAN'T AVOID THINGS YOU DON'T EXPECT.
SO YOU NEED TO SEE THROUGH ALL THAT AND PLAN AHEAD.
WHETHER IT GOES WELL OR DOESN'T GO WELL...
...YOU GOTTA HAVE THE NEXT HAND READY.

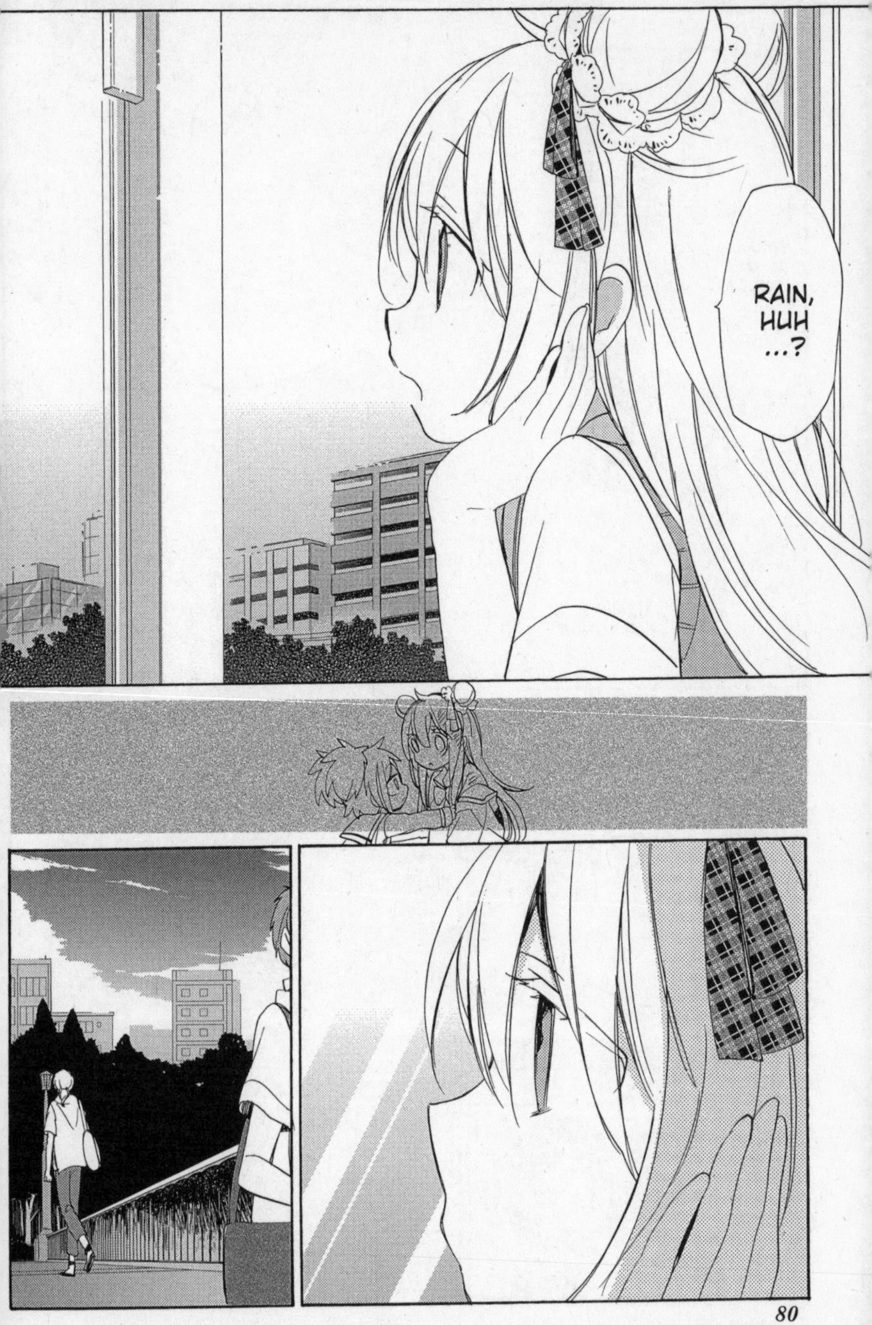
RAIN, HUH ...?

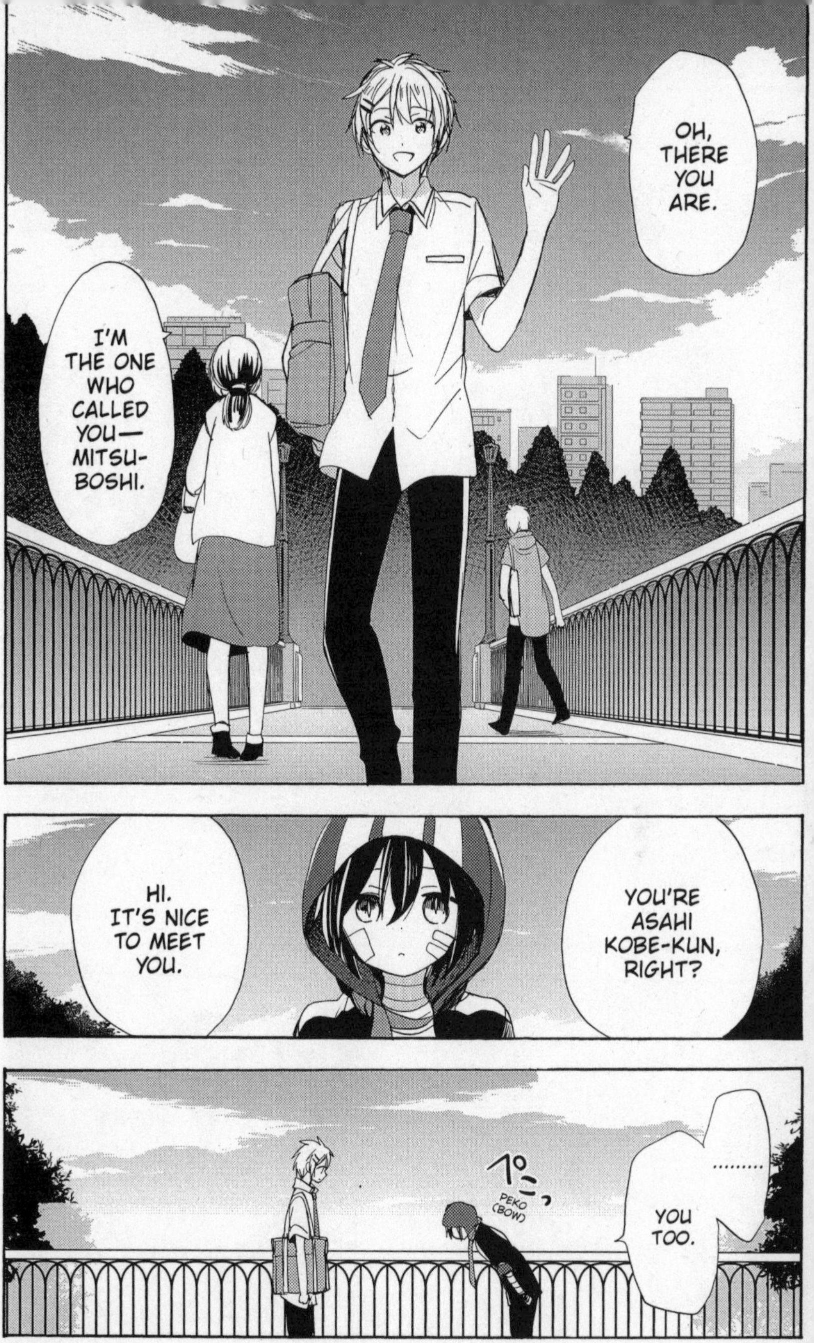
OH, THERE YOU ARE.
I'M THE ONE WHO CALLED YOU— MITSU-BOSHI.
YOU'RE ASAHI KOBE-KUN, RIGHT?
HI. IT'S NICE TO MEET YOU.
.... YOU TOO.
ペこっ
PEKO (BOW)

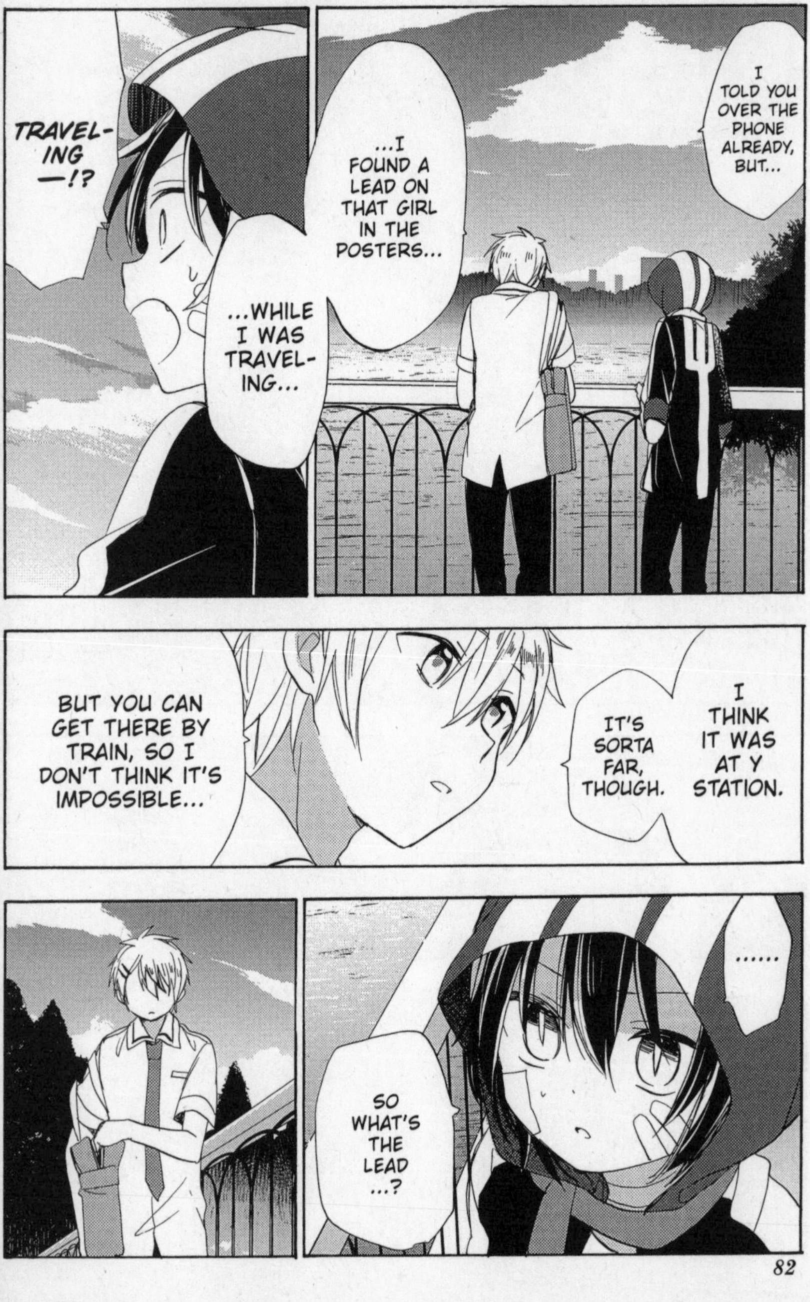
I TOLD YOU OVER THE PHONE ALREADY, BUT...
...I FOUND A LEAD ON THAT GIRL IN THE POSTERS...
...WHILE I WAS TRAVELING...
TRAVELING—!?
I THINK IT WAS AT Y STATION.
IT'S SORTA FAR, THOUGH.
BUT YOU CAN GET THERE BY TRAIN, SO I DON'T THINK IT'S IMPOSSIBLE...
......
SO WHAT'S THE LEAD...?

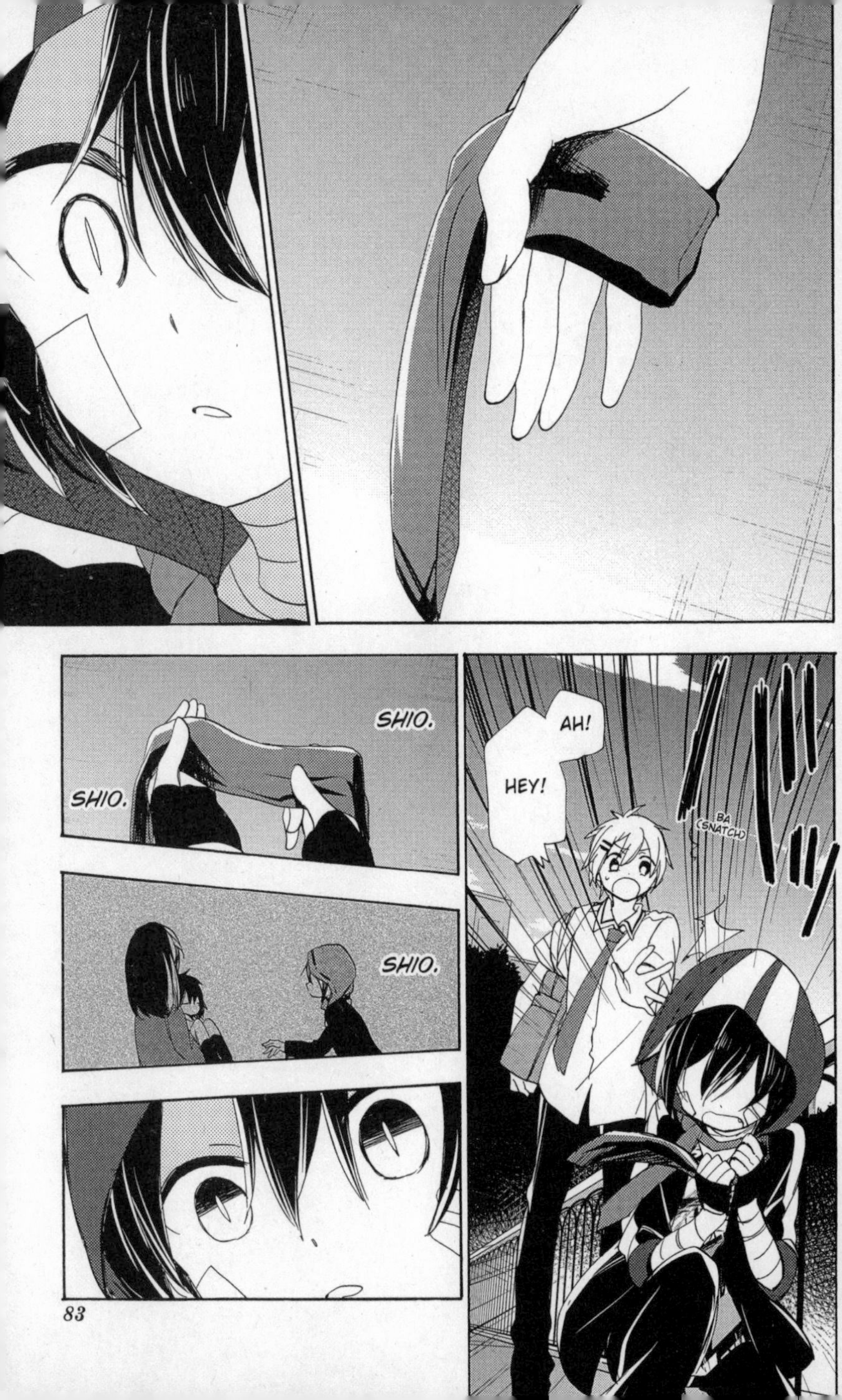
AH!
HEY!
BA (SNATCH)
SHIO.
SHIO.
SHIO.

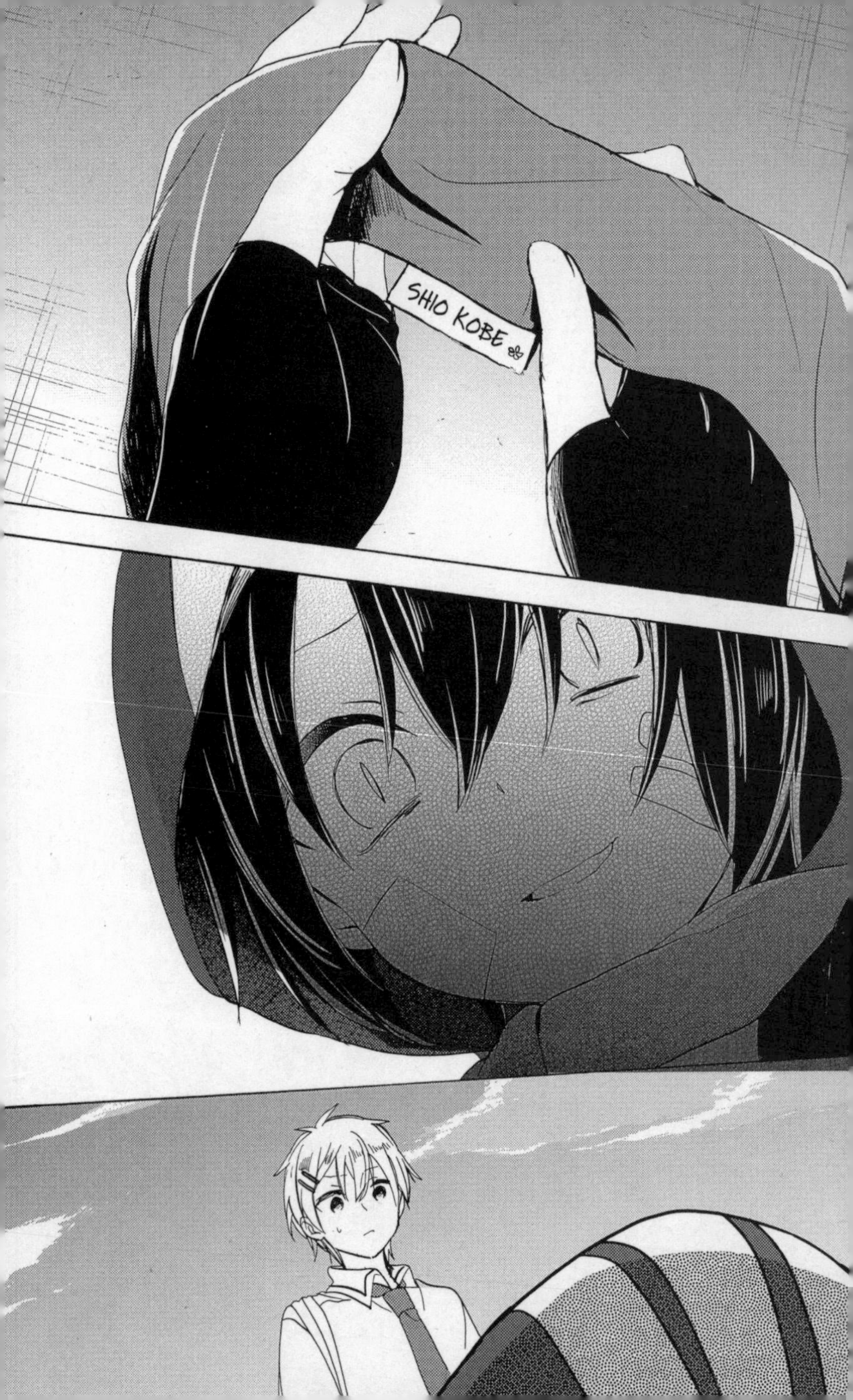
SHIO KOBE

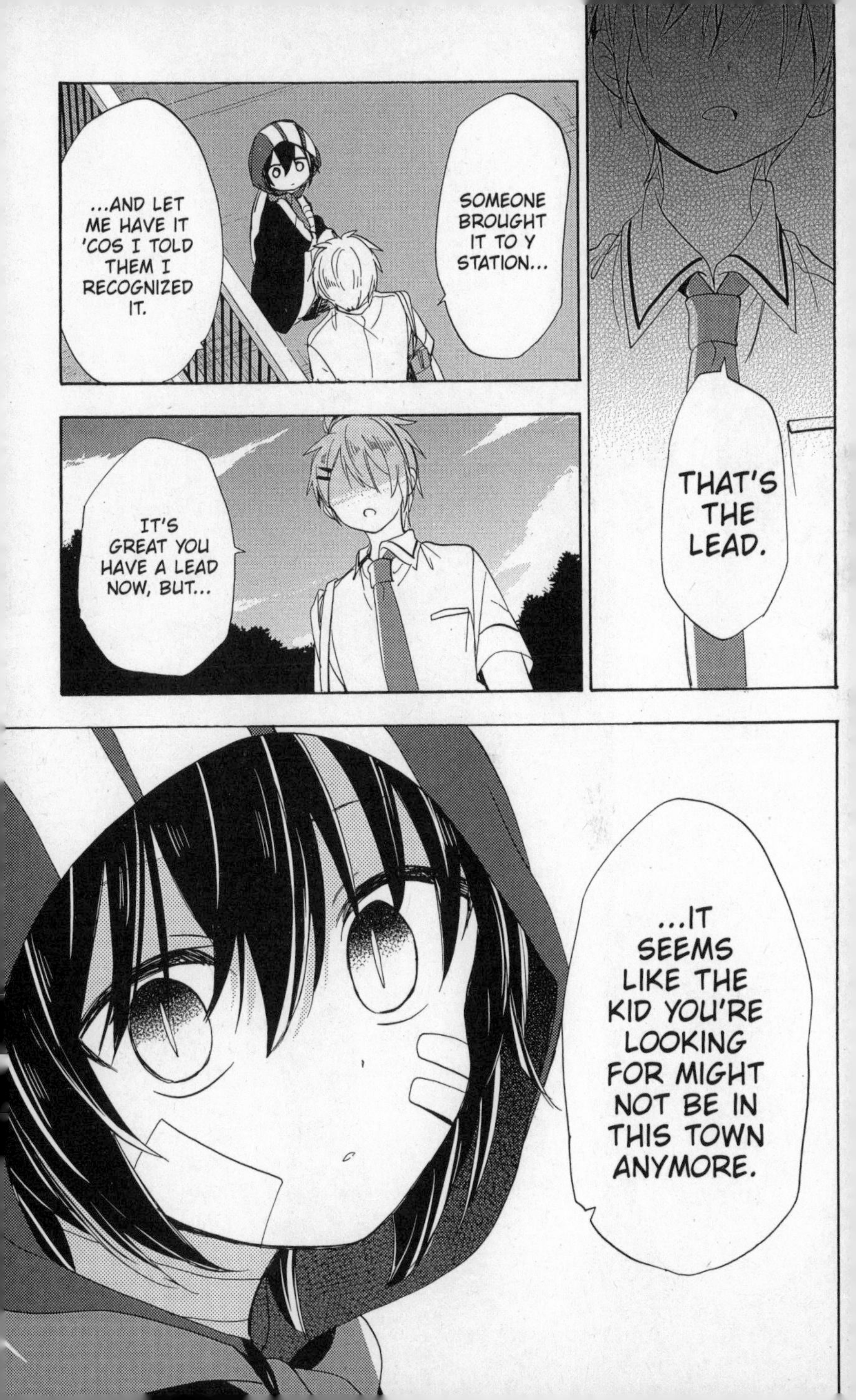
THAT'S THE LEAD.
SOMEONE BROUGHT IT TO Y STATION...
...AND LET ME HAVE IT 'COS I TOLD THEM I RECOGNIZED IT.
IT'S GREAT YOU HAVE A LEAD NOW, BUT...
...IT SEEMS LIKE THE KID YOU'RE LOOKING FOR MIGHT NOT BE IN THIS TOWN ANYMORE.

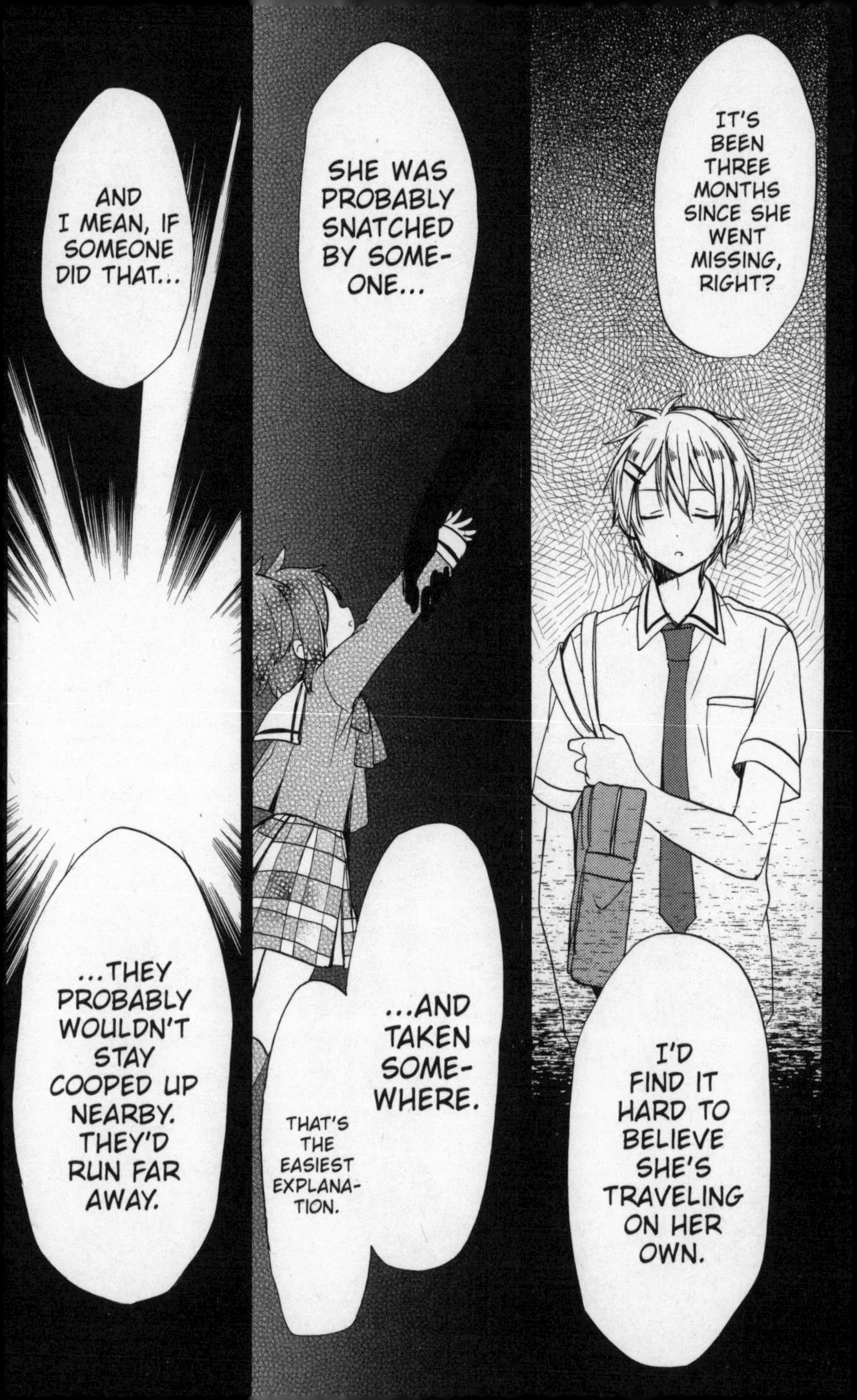
IT'S BEEN THREE MONTHS SINCE SHE WENT MISSING, RIGHT?
I'D FIND IT HARD TO BELIEVE SHE'S TRAVELING ON HER OWN.
SHE WAS PROBABLY SNATCHED BY SOMEONE...
...AND TAKEN SOMEWHERE.
THAT'S THE EASIEST EXPLANATION.
AND I MEAN, IF SOMEONE DID THAT...
...THEY PROBABLY WOULDN'T STAY COOPED UP NEARBY. THEY'D RUN FAR AWAY.

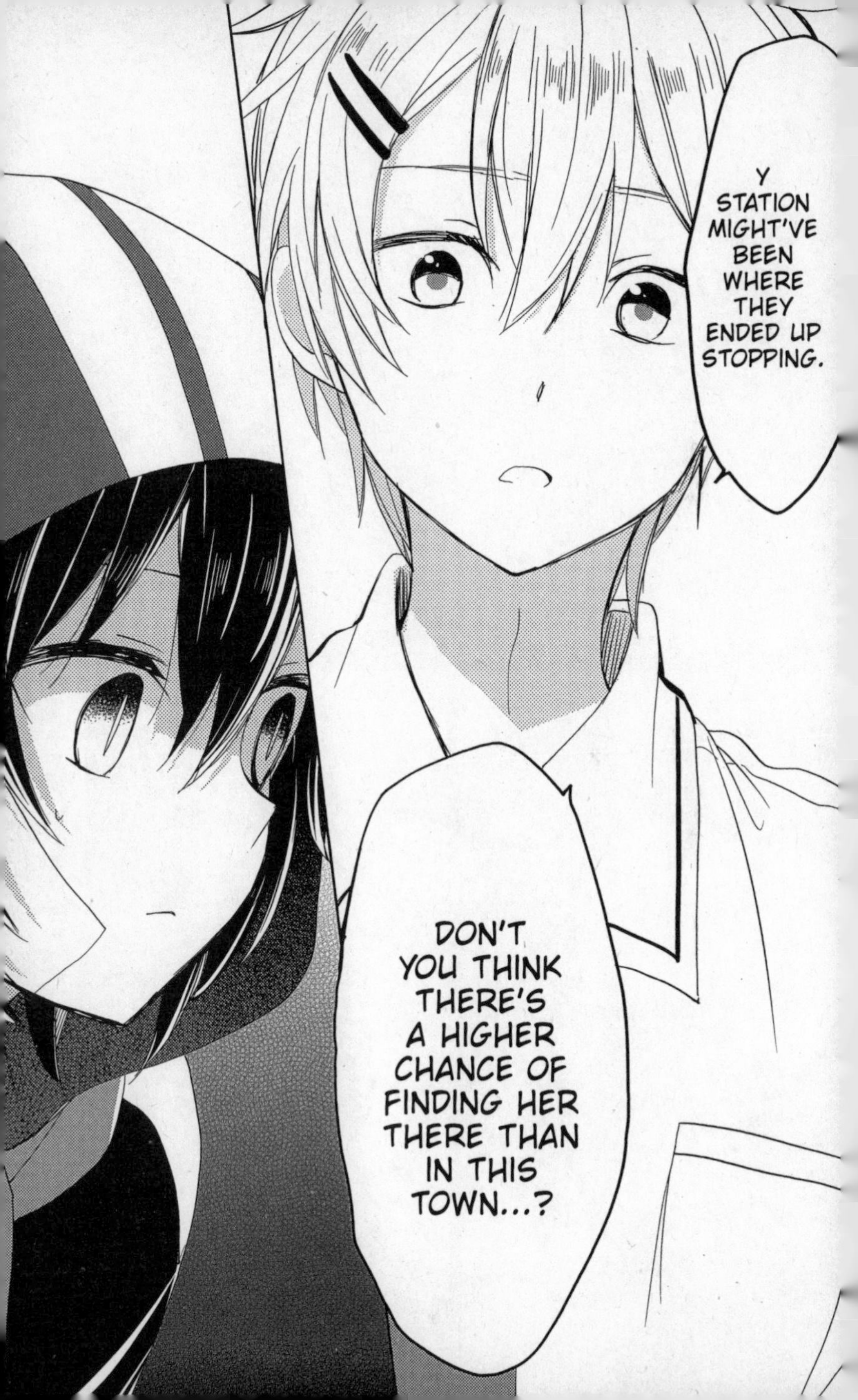
Y STATION MIGHT'VE BEEN WHERE THEY ENDED UP STOPPING.
DON'T YOU THINK THERE'S A HIGHER CHANCE OF FINDING HER THERE THAN IN THIS TOWN...?

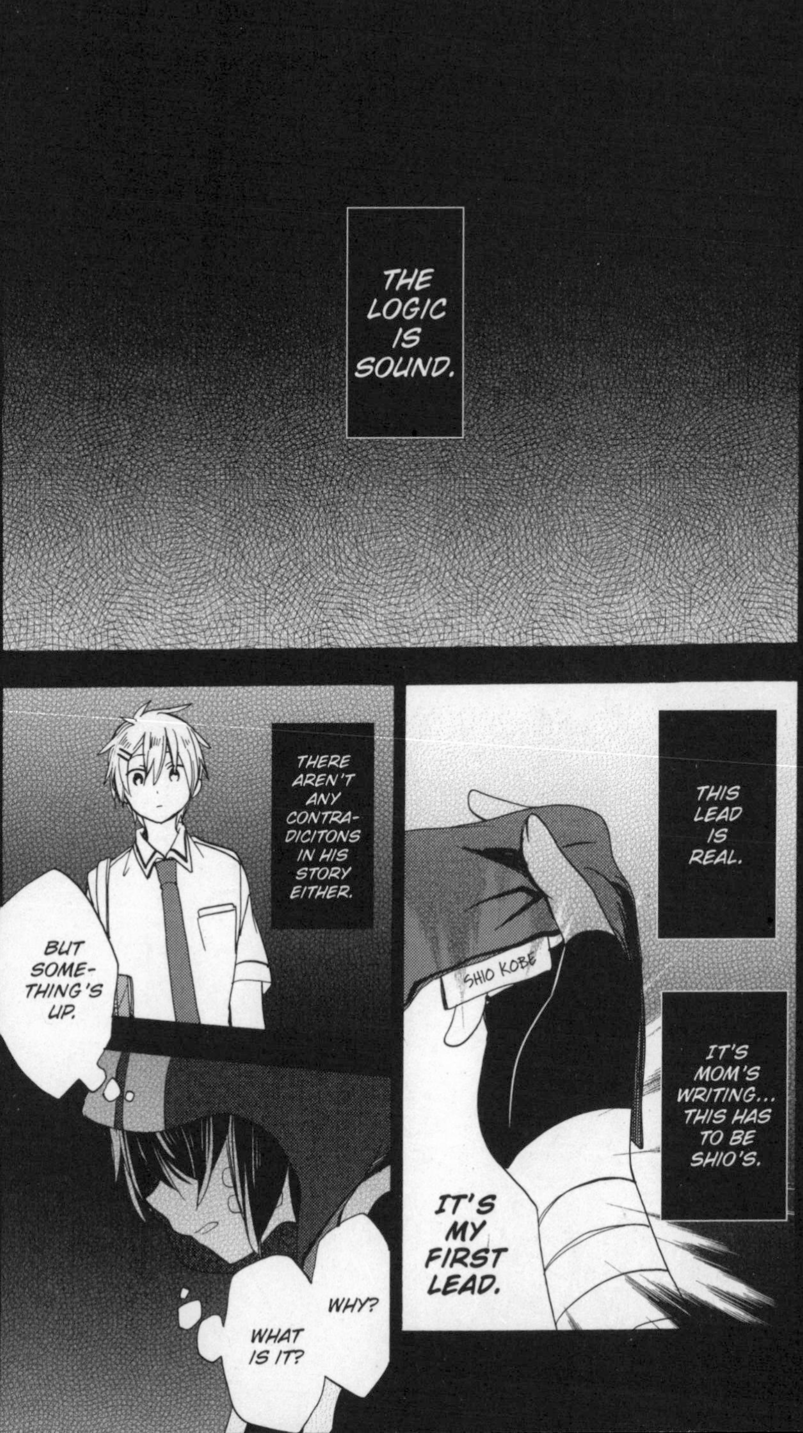
THE LOGIC IS SOUND.
THIS LEAD IS REAL.
SHIO KOBE
IT'S MOM'S WRITING... THIS HAS TO BE SHIO'S.
IT'S MY FIRST LEAD.
THERE AREN'T ANY CONTRA-DICITONS IN HIS STORY EITHER.
BUT SOME-THING'S UP.
WHY?
WHAT IS IT?

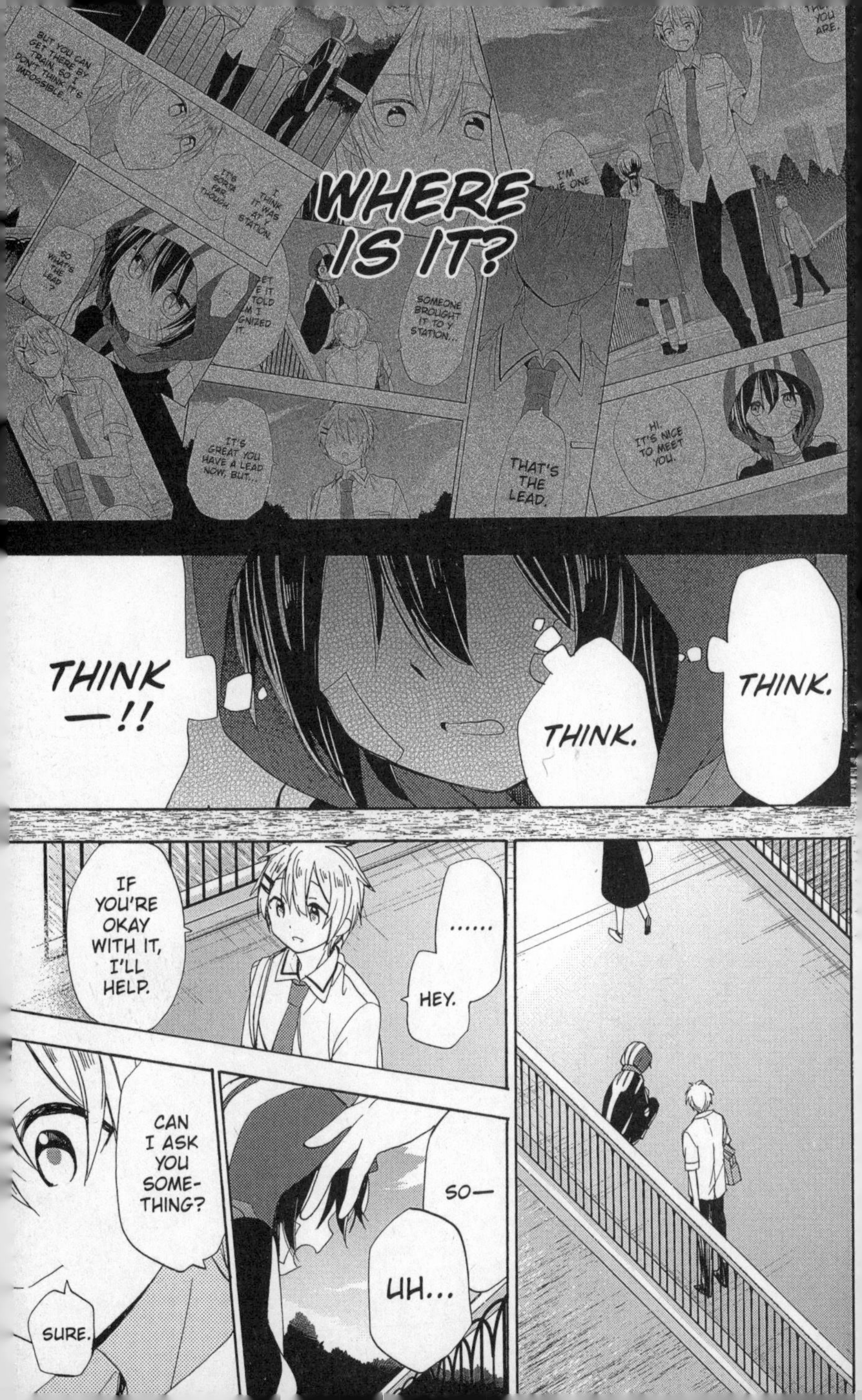

HI. IT'S NICE TO MEET YOU.
THAT'S THE LEAD.
SOMEONE BROUGHT IT TO Y STATION...
WHERE IS IT?
IT'S GREAT YOU HAVE A LEAD NOW, BUT...
I THINK IT WAS AT Y STATION.
IT'S SORTA FAR, THOUGH.
SO WHAT'S THE LEAD?
BUT YOU CAN GET THERE BY TRAIN, SO I DON'T THINK IT'S IMPOSSIBLE...
THINK.
THINK.
THINK—!!
......
HEY.
IF YOU'RE OKAY WITH IT, I'LL HELP.
SO—
UH...
CAN I ASK YOU SOMETHING?
SURE.

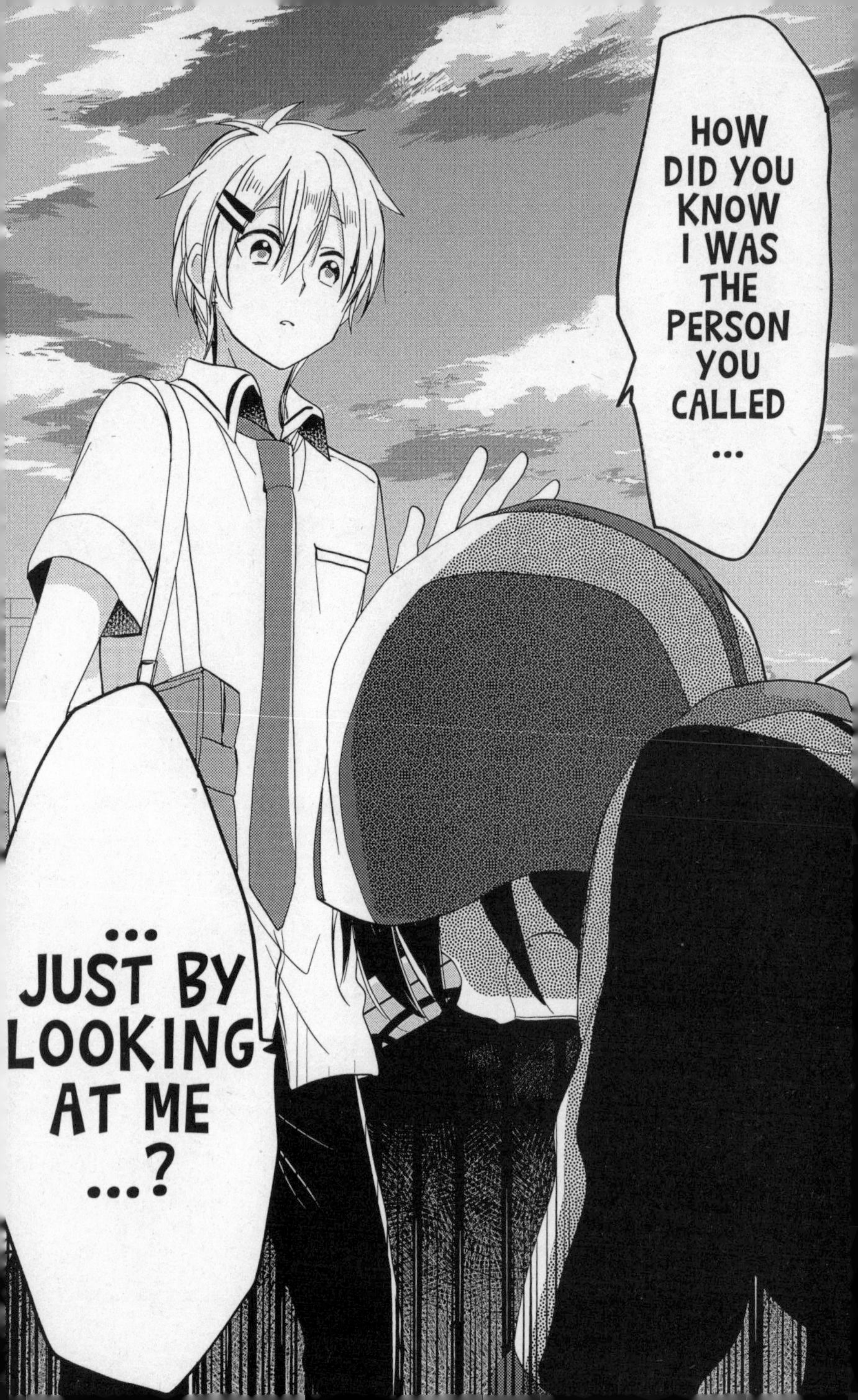
HOW DID YOU KNOW I WAS THE PERSON YOU CALLED ...
... JUST BY LOOKING AT ME ...?

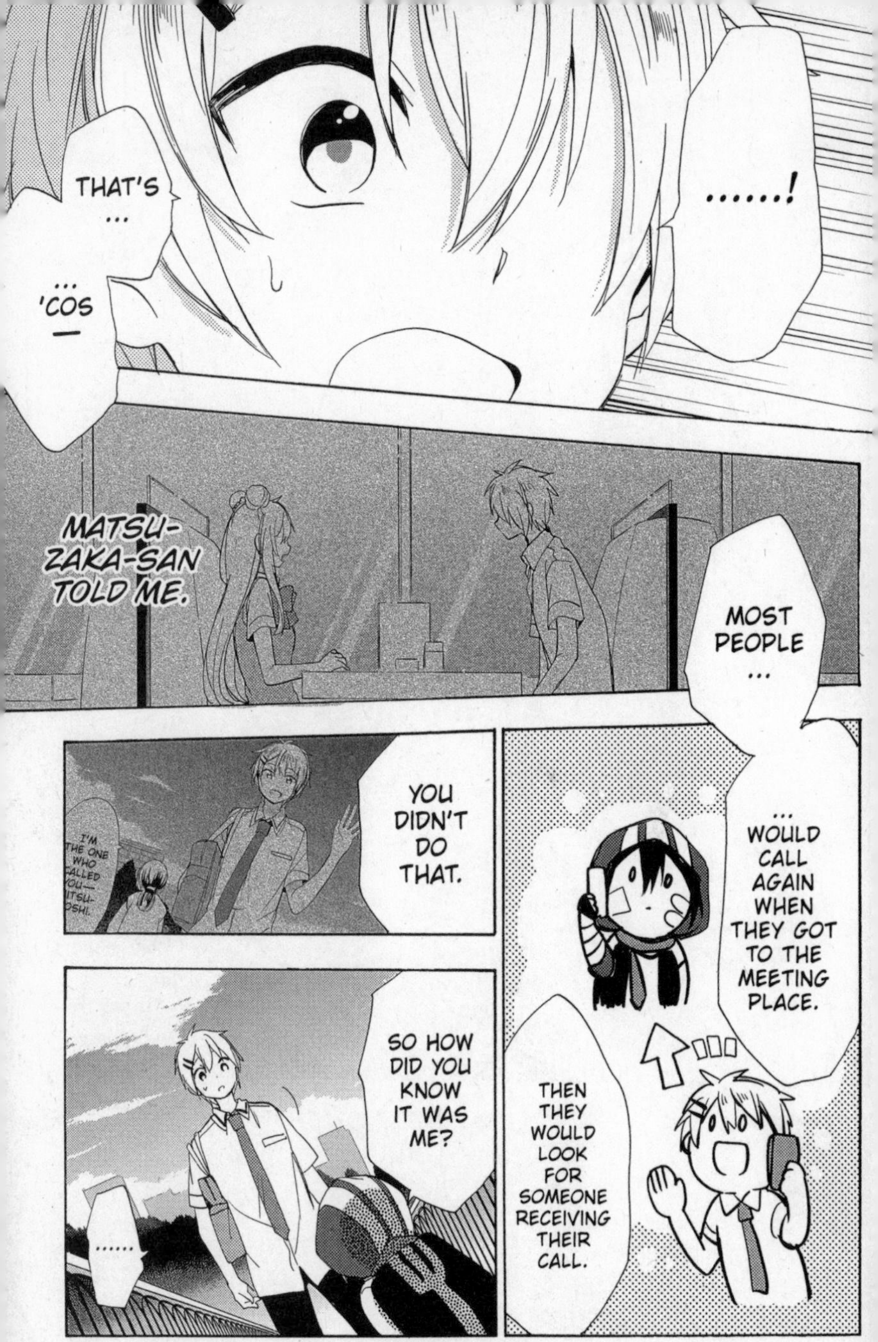
......!
THAT'S ...
... 'COS —
MATSU-ZAKA-SAN TOLD ME.
MOST PEOPLE ...
... WOULD CALL AGAIN WHEN THEY GOT TO THE MEETING PLACE.
THEN THEY WOULD LOOK FOR SOMEONE RECEIVING THEIR CALL.
YOU DIDN'T DO THAT.
I'M THE ONE WHO CALLED YOU— ITSU-OSHI.
SO HOW DID YOU KNOW IT WAS ME?
......

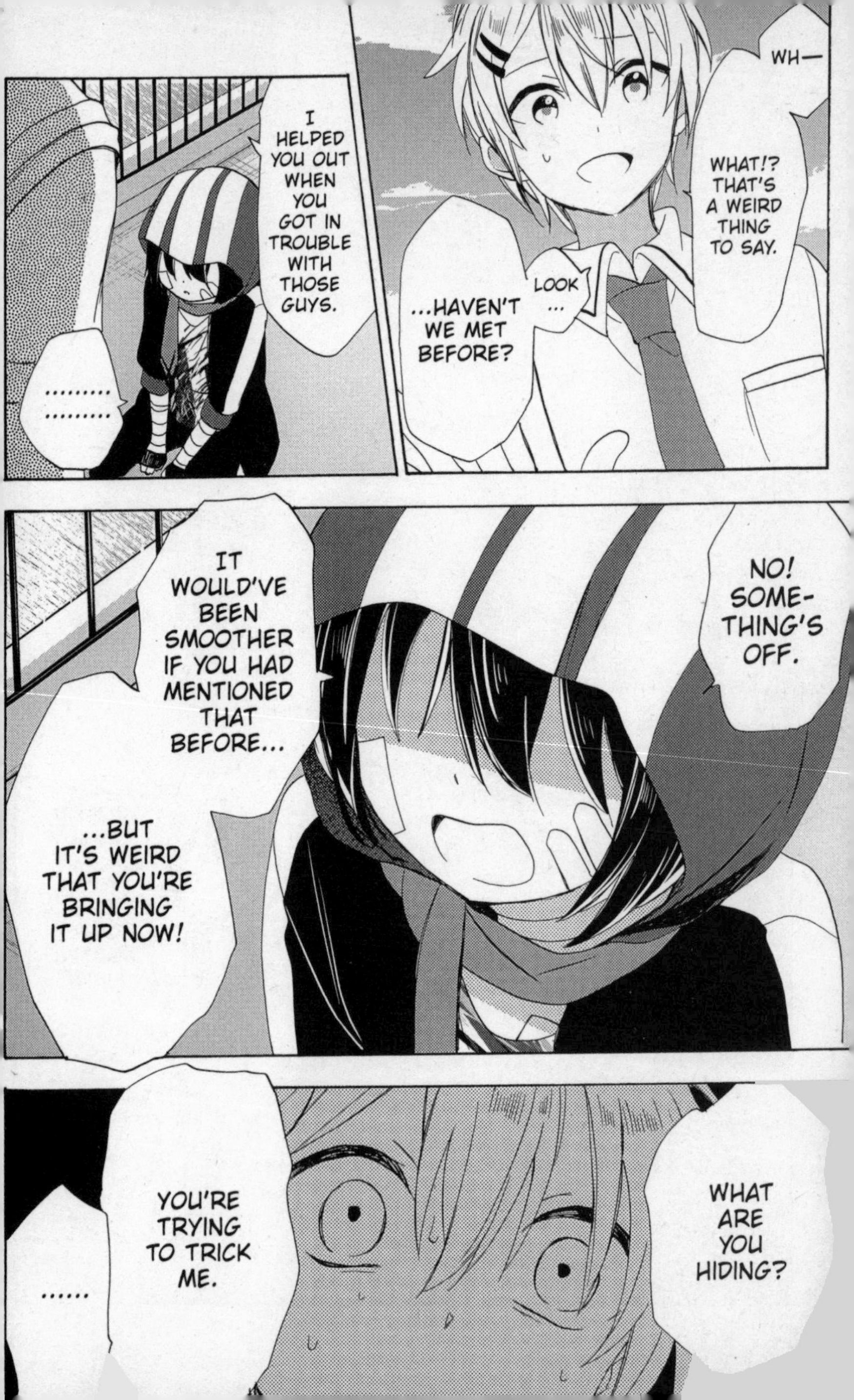
WH—
WHAT!? THAT'S A WEIRD THING TO SAY.
LOOK ...
...HAVEN'T WE MET BEFORE?
I HELPED YOU OUT WHEN YOU GOT IN TROUBLE WITH THOSE GUYS.
....
NO! SOME-THING'S OFF.
IT WOULD'VE BEEN SMOOTHER IF YOU HAD MENTIONED THAT BEFORE...
...BUT IT'S WEIRD THAT YOU'RE BRINGING IT UP NOW!
WHAT ARE YOU HIDING?
YOU'RE TRYING TO TRICK ME.
......

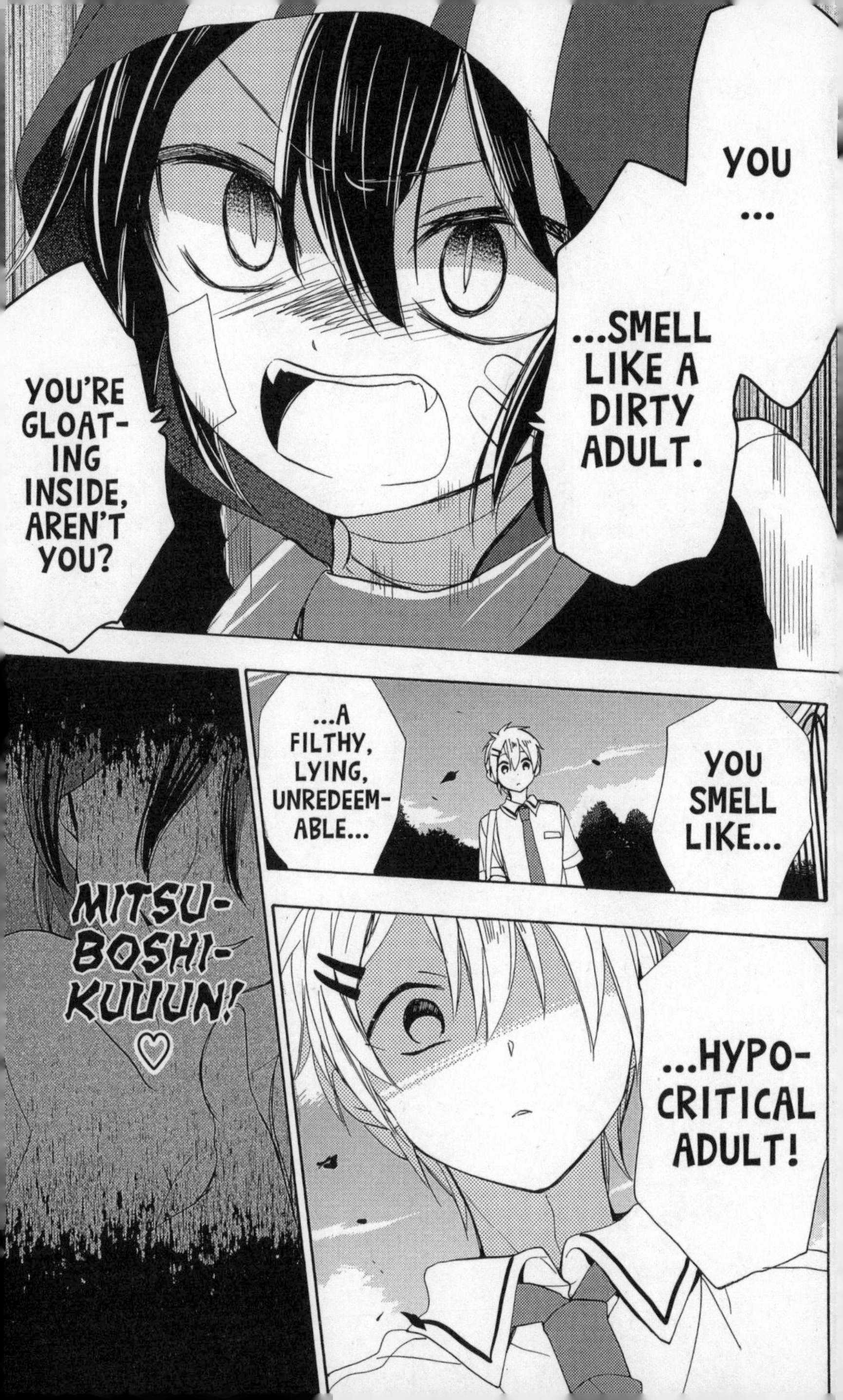
YOU ...
...SMELL LIKE A DIRTY ADULT.
YOU'RE GLOAT-ING INSIDE, AREN'T YOU?
YOU SMELL LIKE...
...A FILTHY, LYING, UNREDEEM-ABLE...
...HYPO-CRITICAL ADULT!
MITSU-BOSHI-KUUUN! ♡

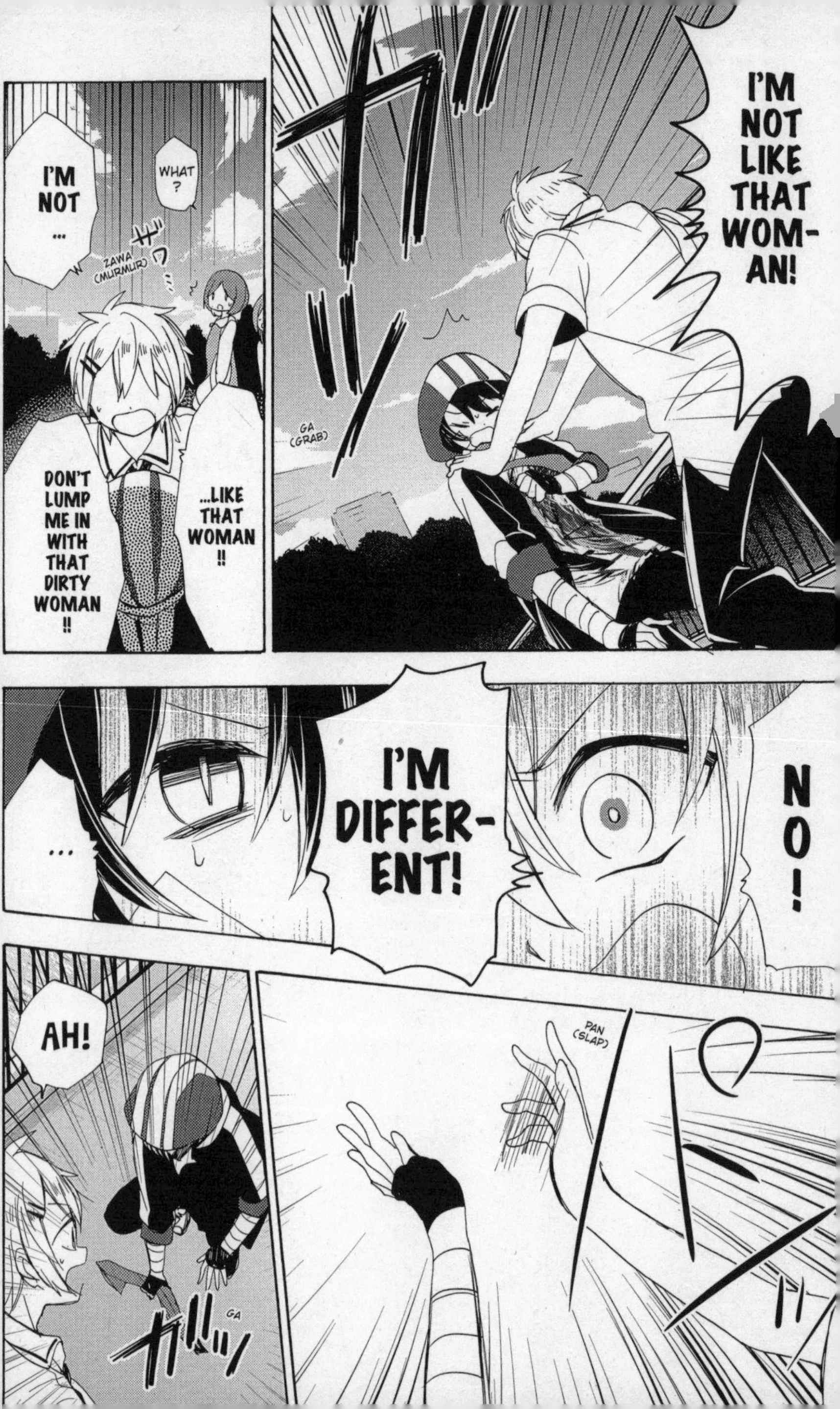
I'M NOT LIKE THAT WOM-AN!
GA (GRAB)
WHAT?
I'M NOT ...
ZAWA (MURMUR)
...LIKE THAT WOMAN!!
DON'T LUMP ME IN WITH THAT DIRTY WOMAN!!
NO!
I'M DIFFER-ENT!
...
PAN (SLAP)
AH!
GA

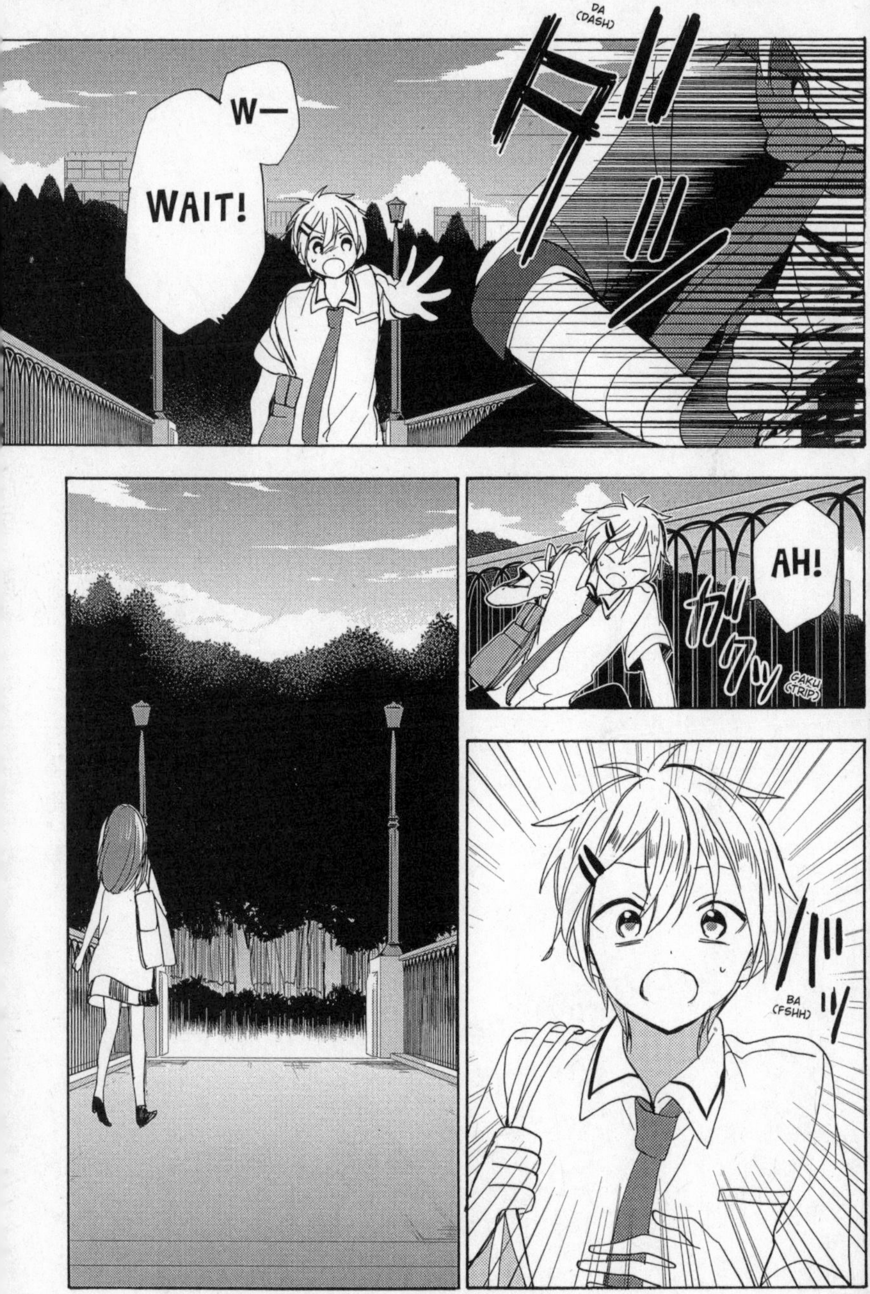
DA
(DASH)
W—
WAIT!
AH!
GAKU
(TRIP)
BA
(FSHH)

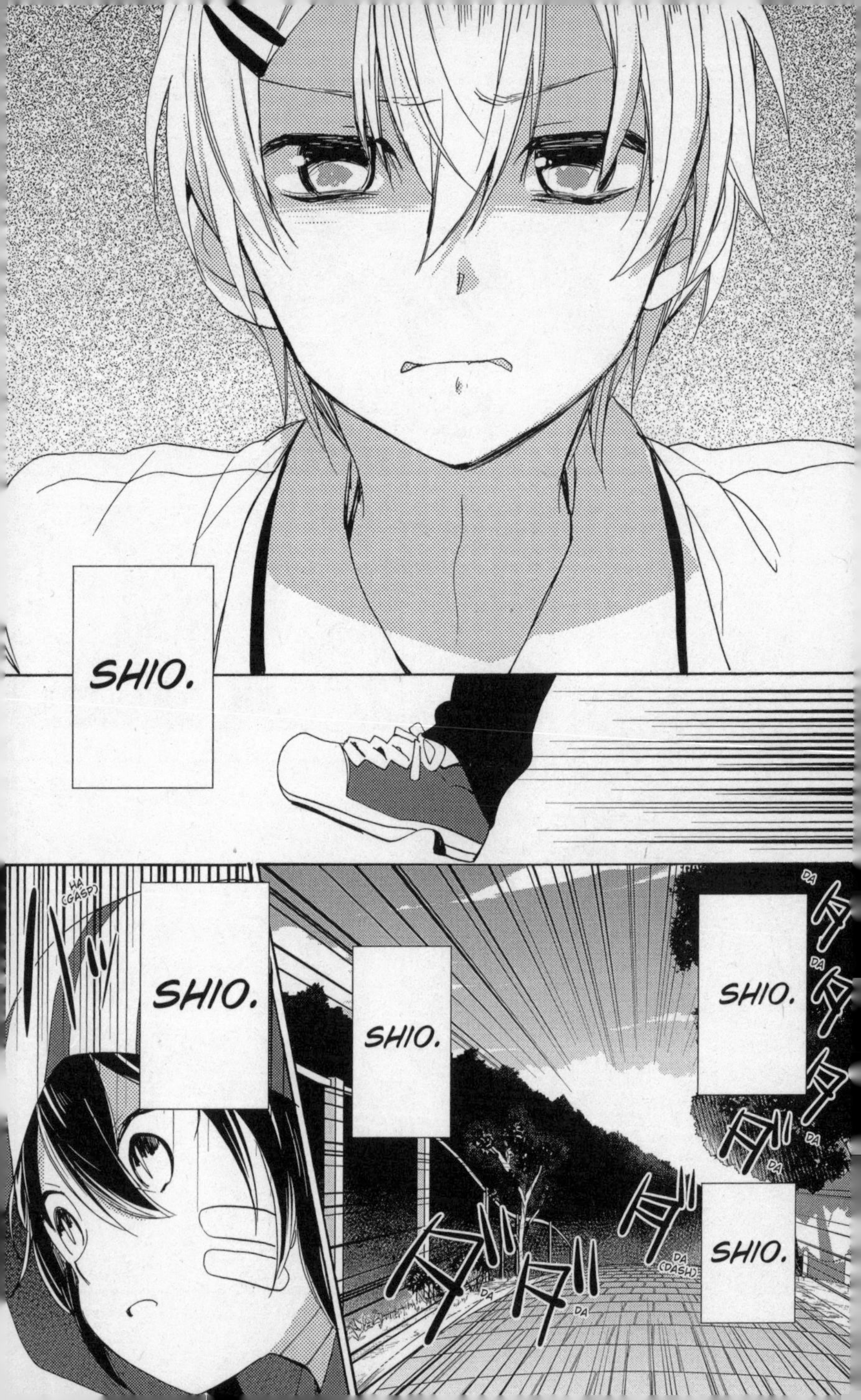

SHIO.
DA
DA
SHIO.
DA
DA
SHIO.
DA (DASH)
DA
DA
SHIO.
SHIO.
HA (GASP)

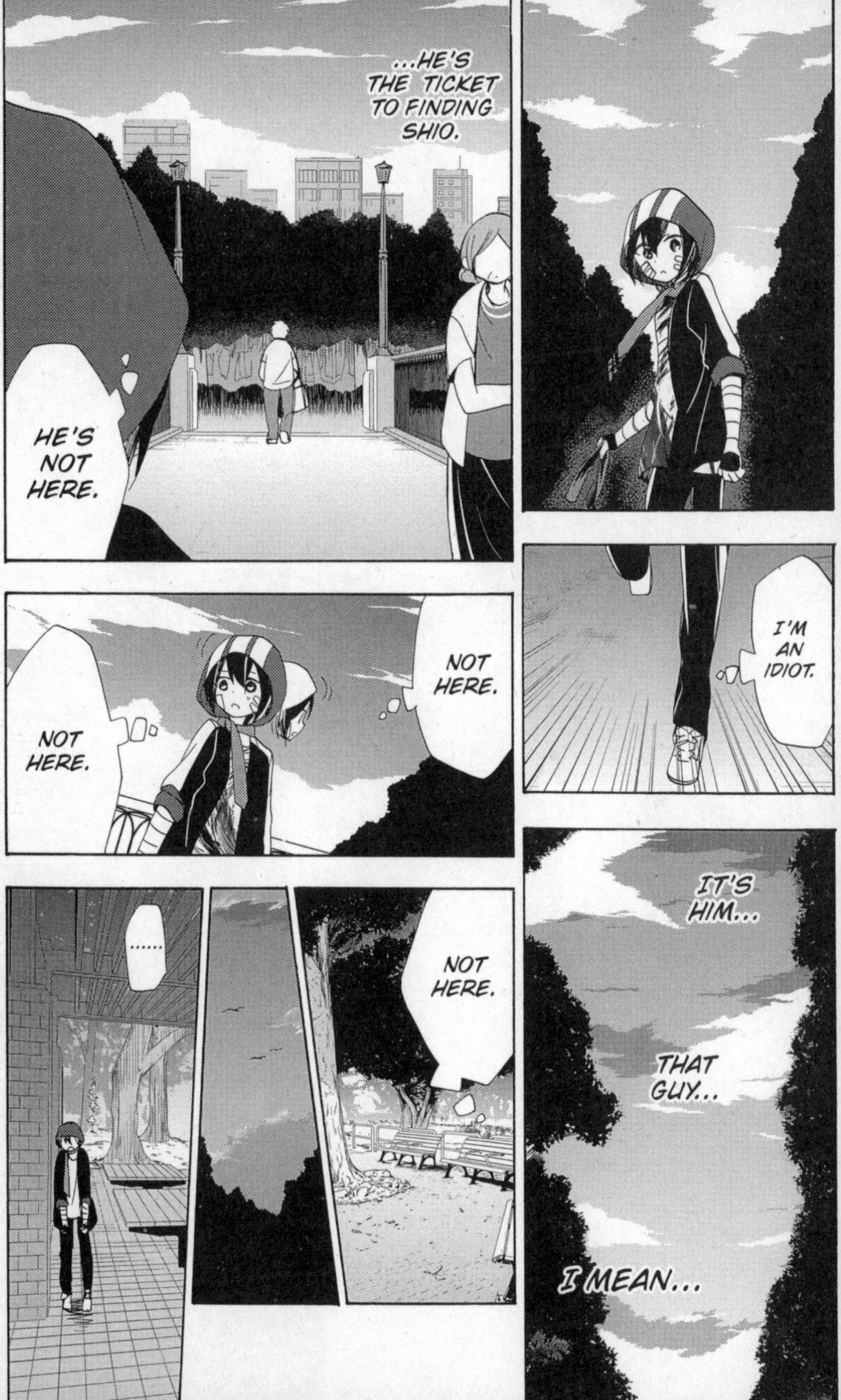
...HE'S THE TICKET TO FINDING SHIO.
HE'S NOT HERE.
I'M AN IDIOT.
NOT HERE.
NOT HERE.
IT'S HIM...
THAT GUY...
I MEAN...
NOT HERE.
......

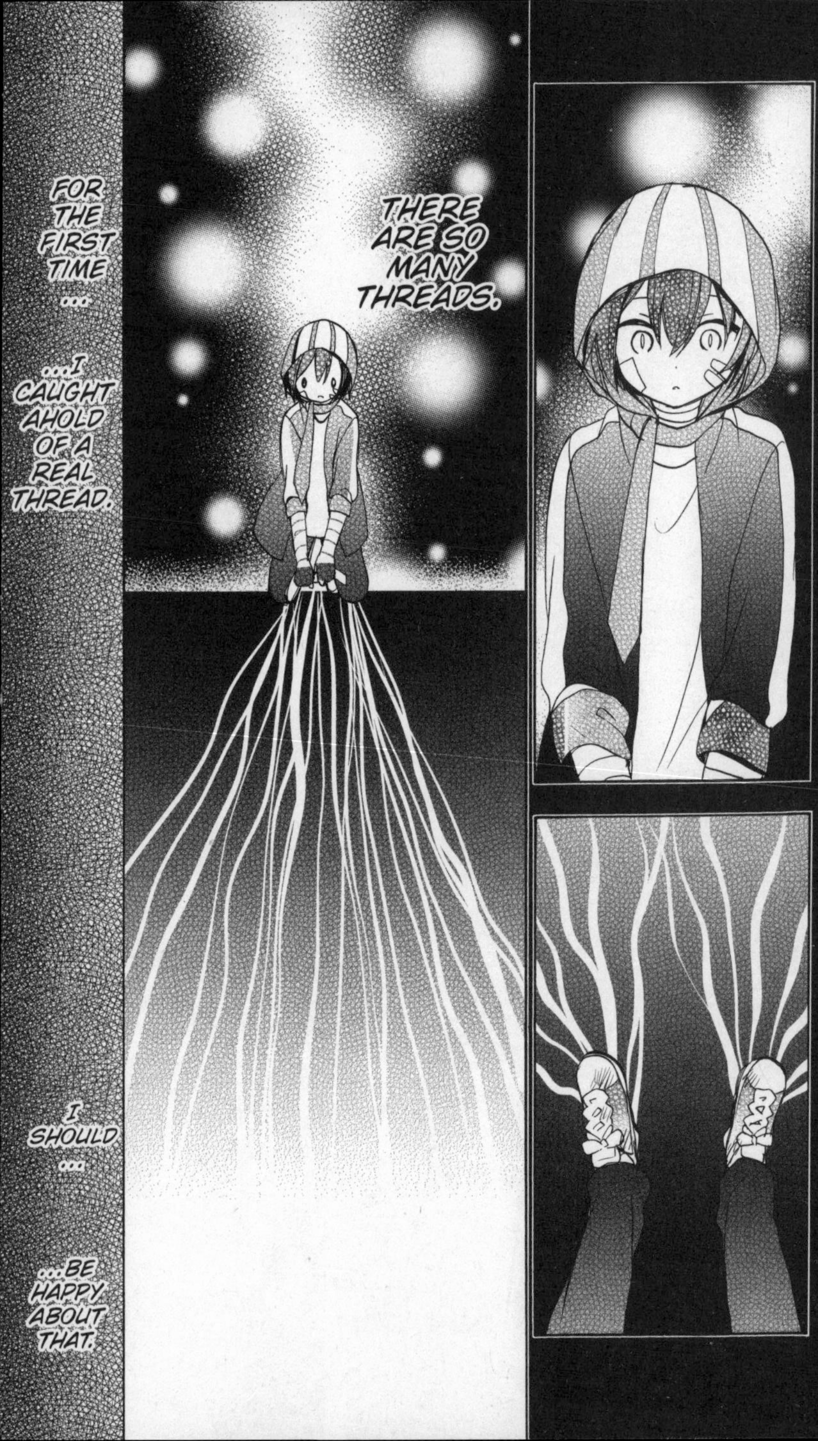
THERE ARE SO MANY THREADS.
FOR THE FIRST TIME...
...I CAUGHT AHOLD OF A REAL THREAD.
I SHOULD...
...BE HAPPY ABOUT THAT.

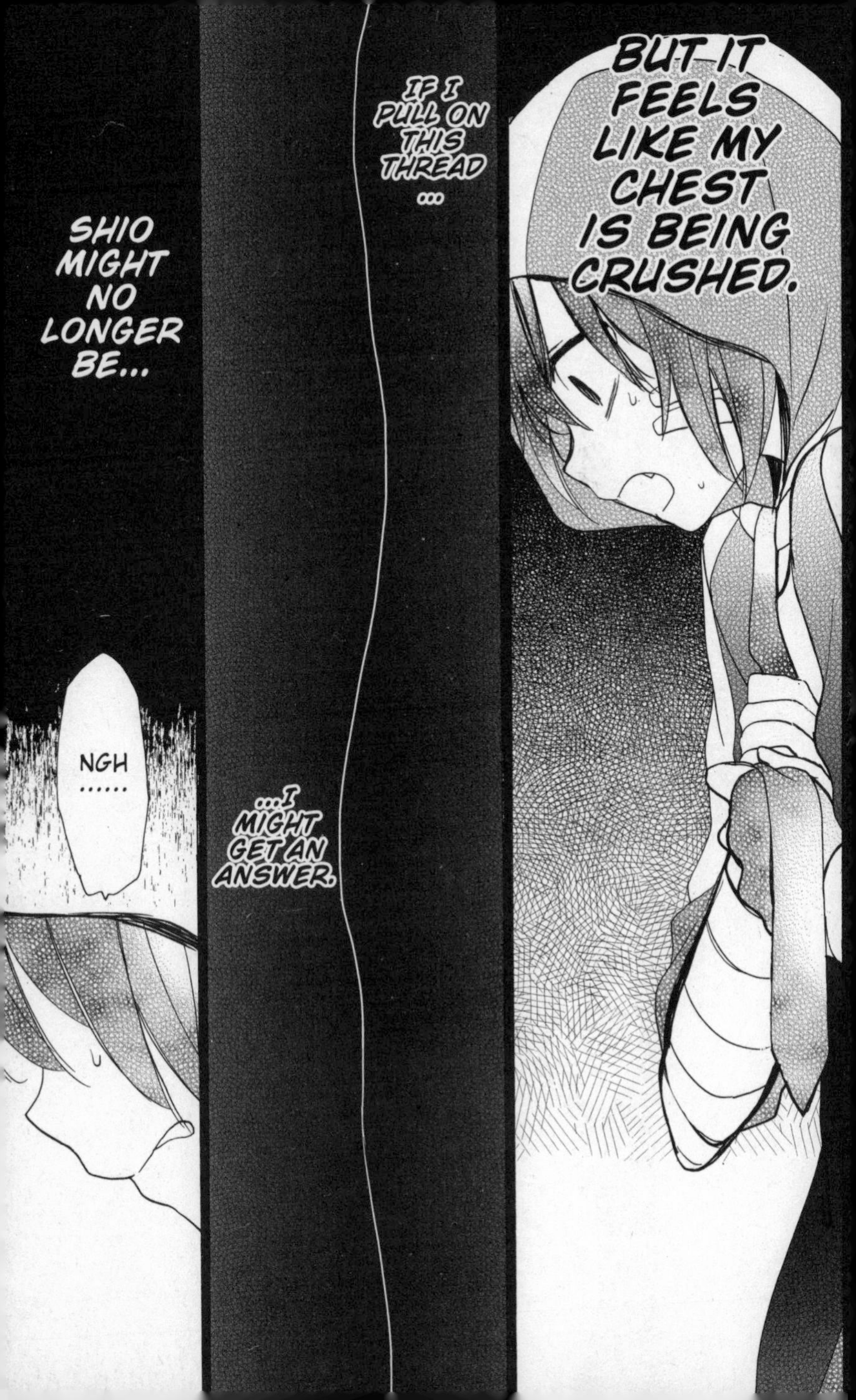
BUT IT FEELS LIKE MY CHEST IS BEING CRUSHED.
IF I PULL ON THIS THREAD ...
...I MIGHT GET AN ANSWER.
SHIO MIGHT NO LONGER BE...
NGH ......

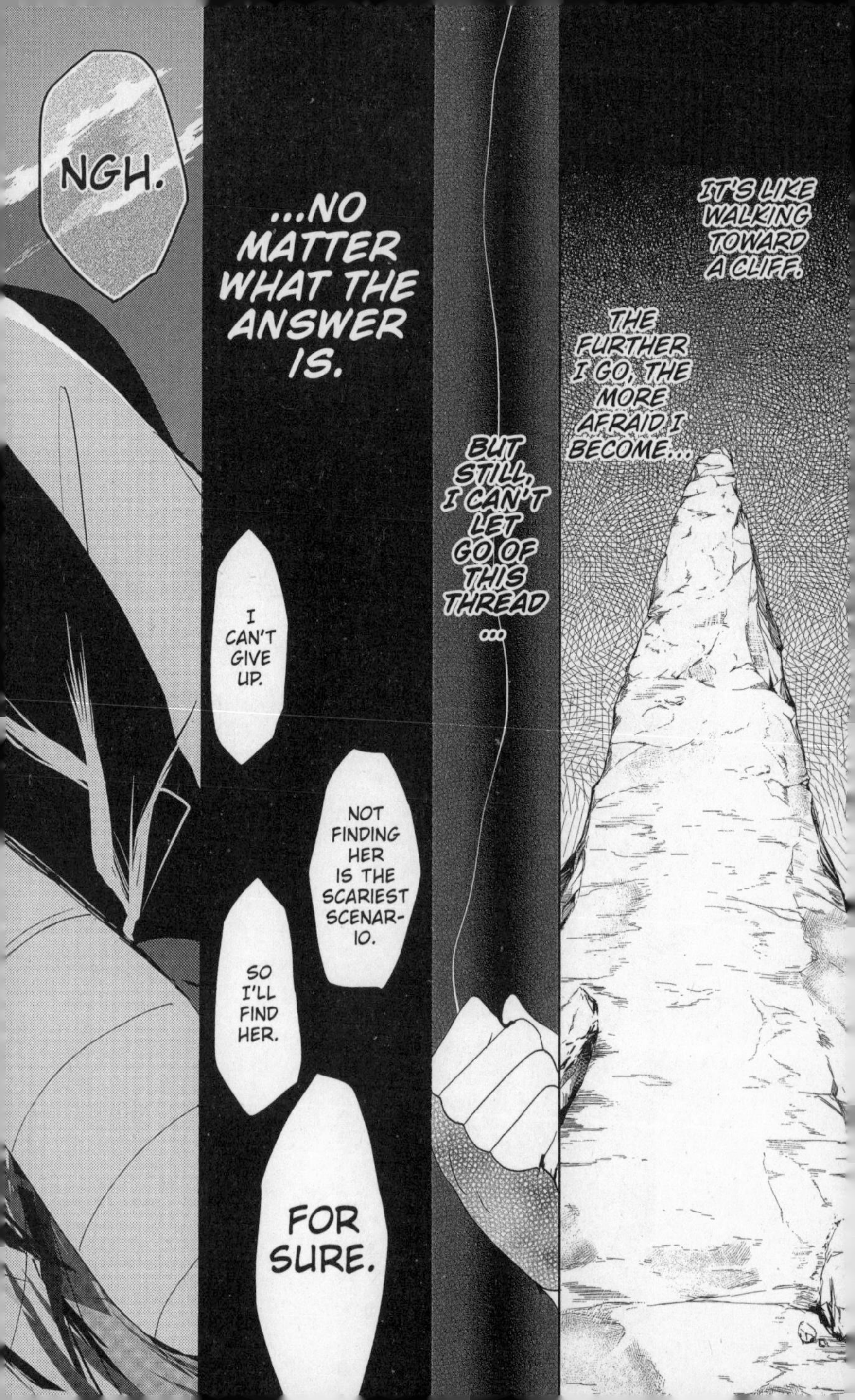
IT'S LIKE WALKING TOWARD A CLIFF.
THE FURTHER I GO, THE MORE AFRAID I BECOME...
BUT STILL, I CAN'T LET GO OF THIS THREAD...
...NO MATTER WHAT THE ANSWER IS.
I CAN'T GIVE UP.
NOT FINDING HER IS THE SCARIEST SCENARIO.
SO I'LL FIND HER.
FOR SURE.
NGH.

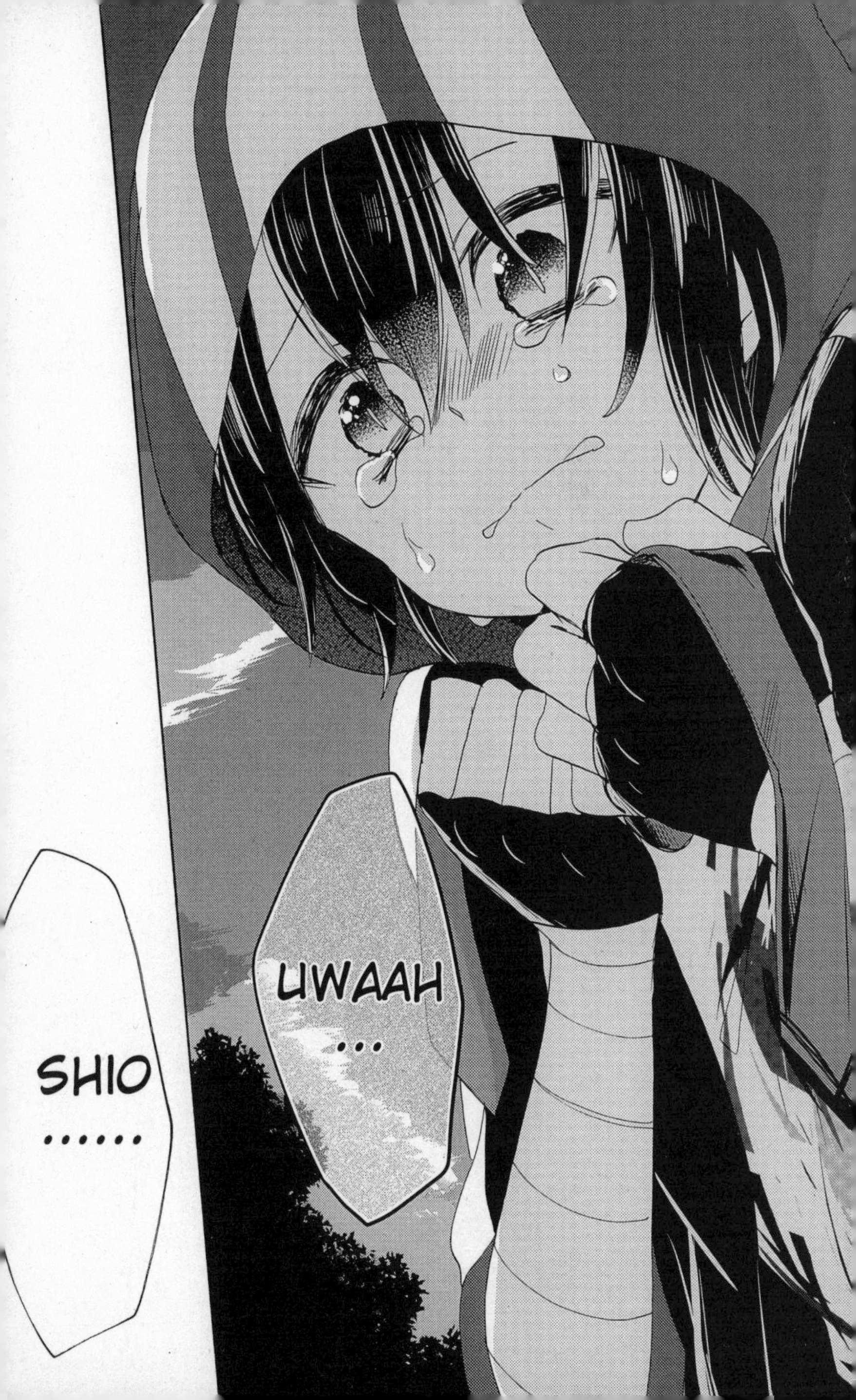
UWAAH ...
SHIO ......

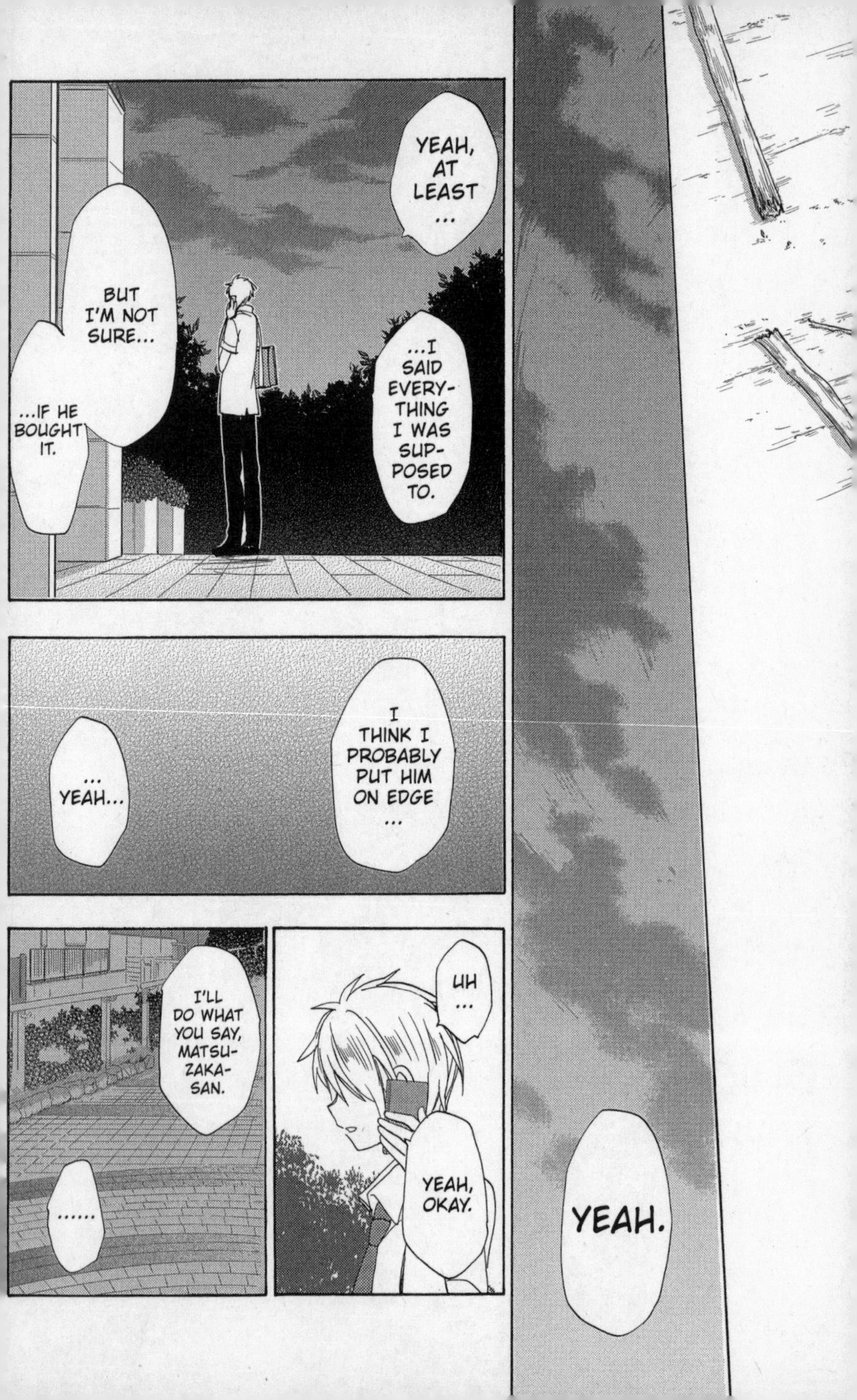
YEAH.
YEAH, AT LEAST ...
...I SAID EVERYTHING I WAS SUPPOSED TO.
BUT I'M NOT SURE...
...IF HE BOUGHT IT.
I THINK I PROBABLY PUT HIM ON EDGE ...
... YEAH...
UH ...
YEAH, OKAY.
I'LL DO WHAT YOU SAY, MATSUZAKA-SAN.
......

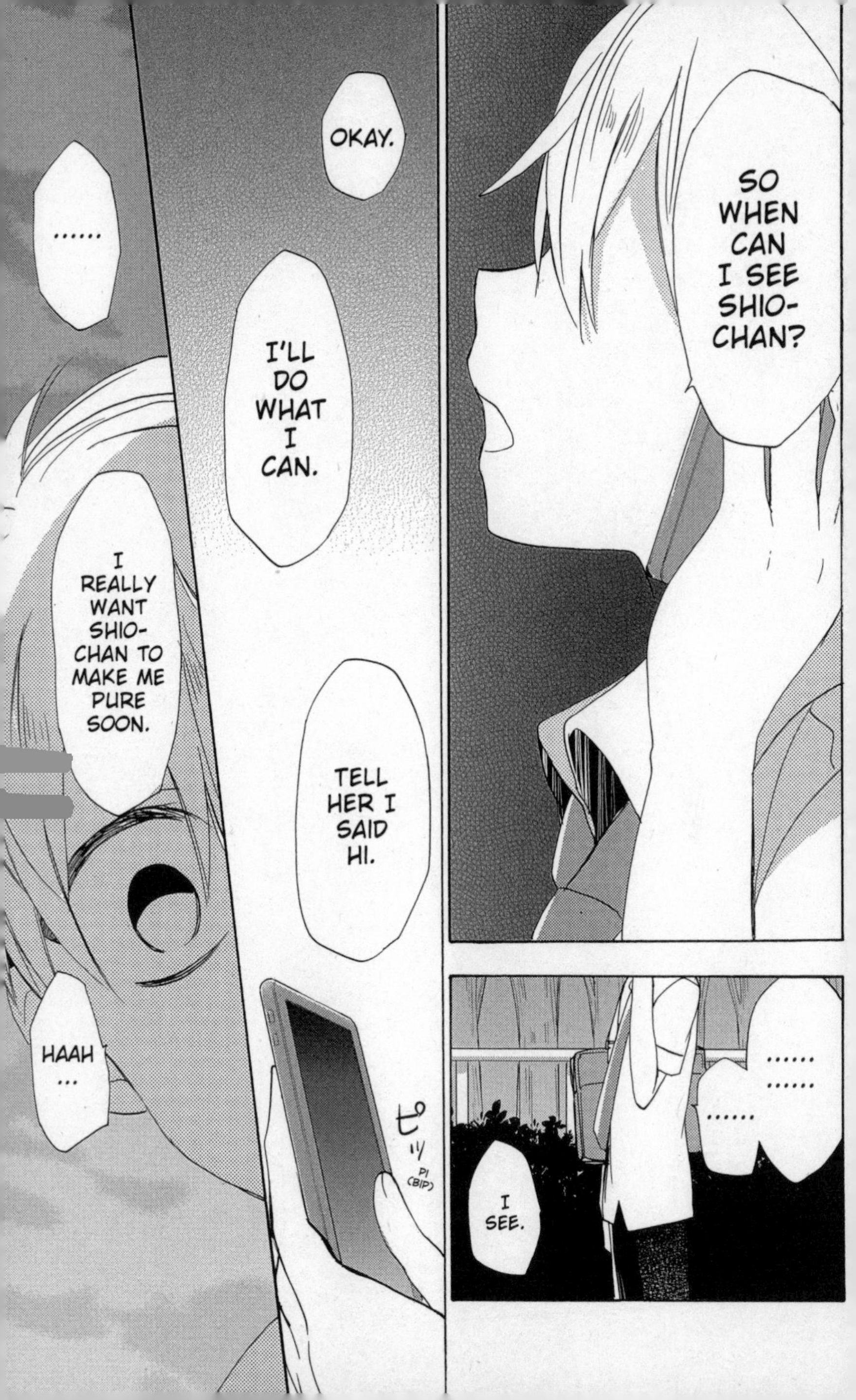
SO WHEN CAN I SEE SHIO-CHAN?
......
......
......
I SEE.
OKAY.
I'LL DO WHAT I CAN.
TELL HER I SAID HI.
ピッ
PI (BIP)
......
I REALLY WANT SHIO-CHAN TO MAKE ME PURE SOON.
HAAH...

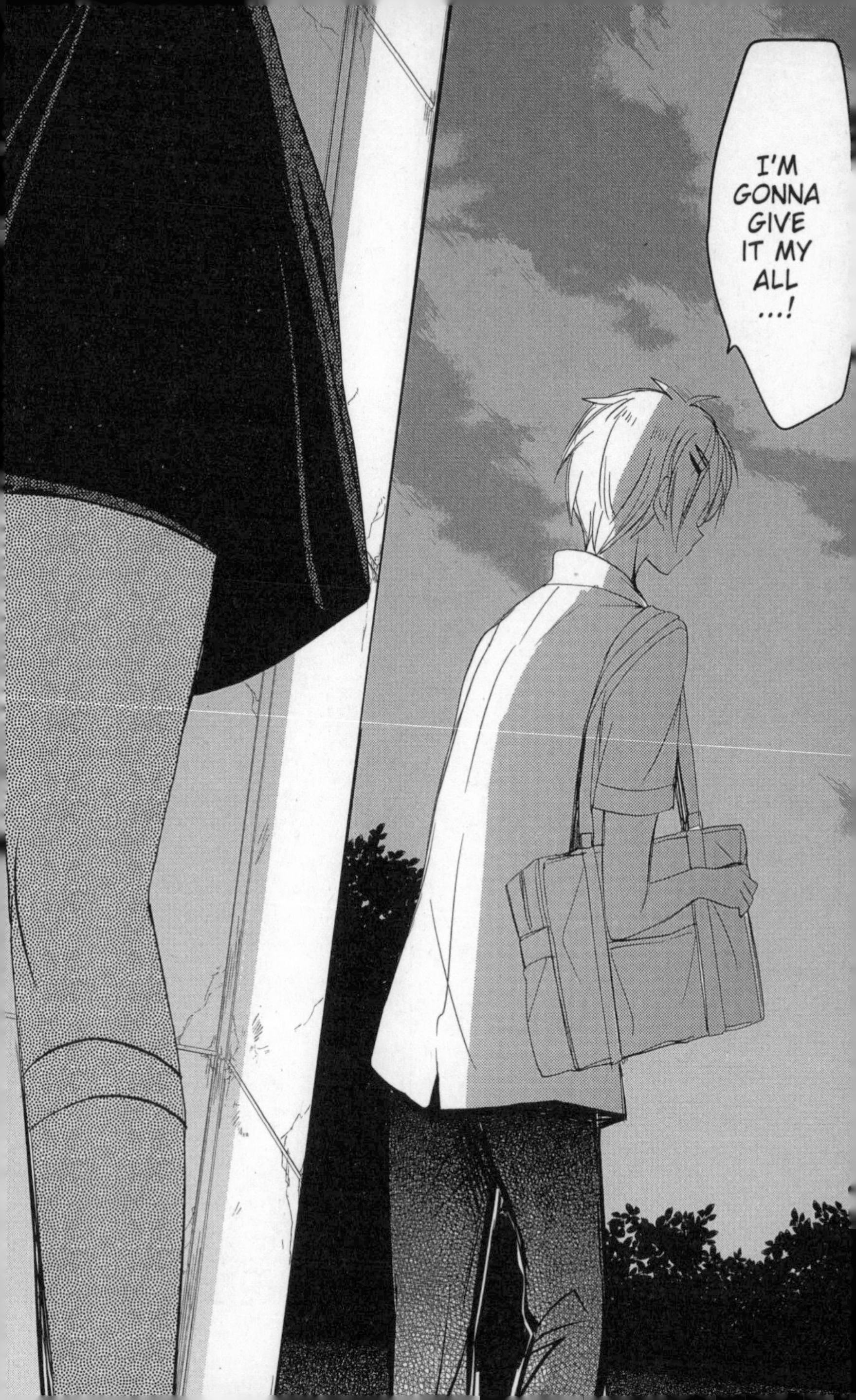
I'M GONNA GIVE IT MY ALL ...!

22ND LIFE

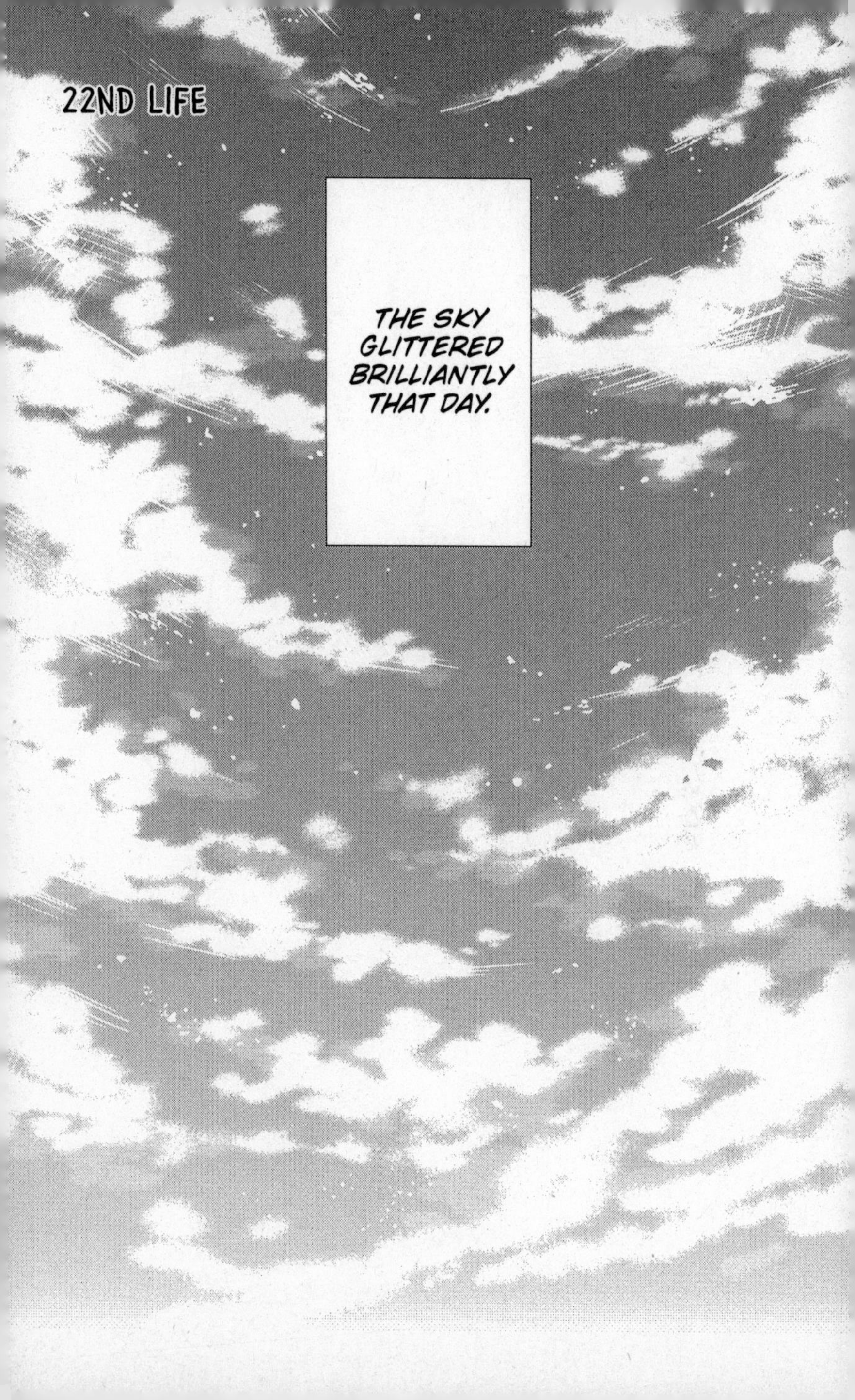
THE SKY GLITTERED BRILLIANTLY THAT DAY.

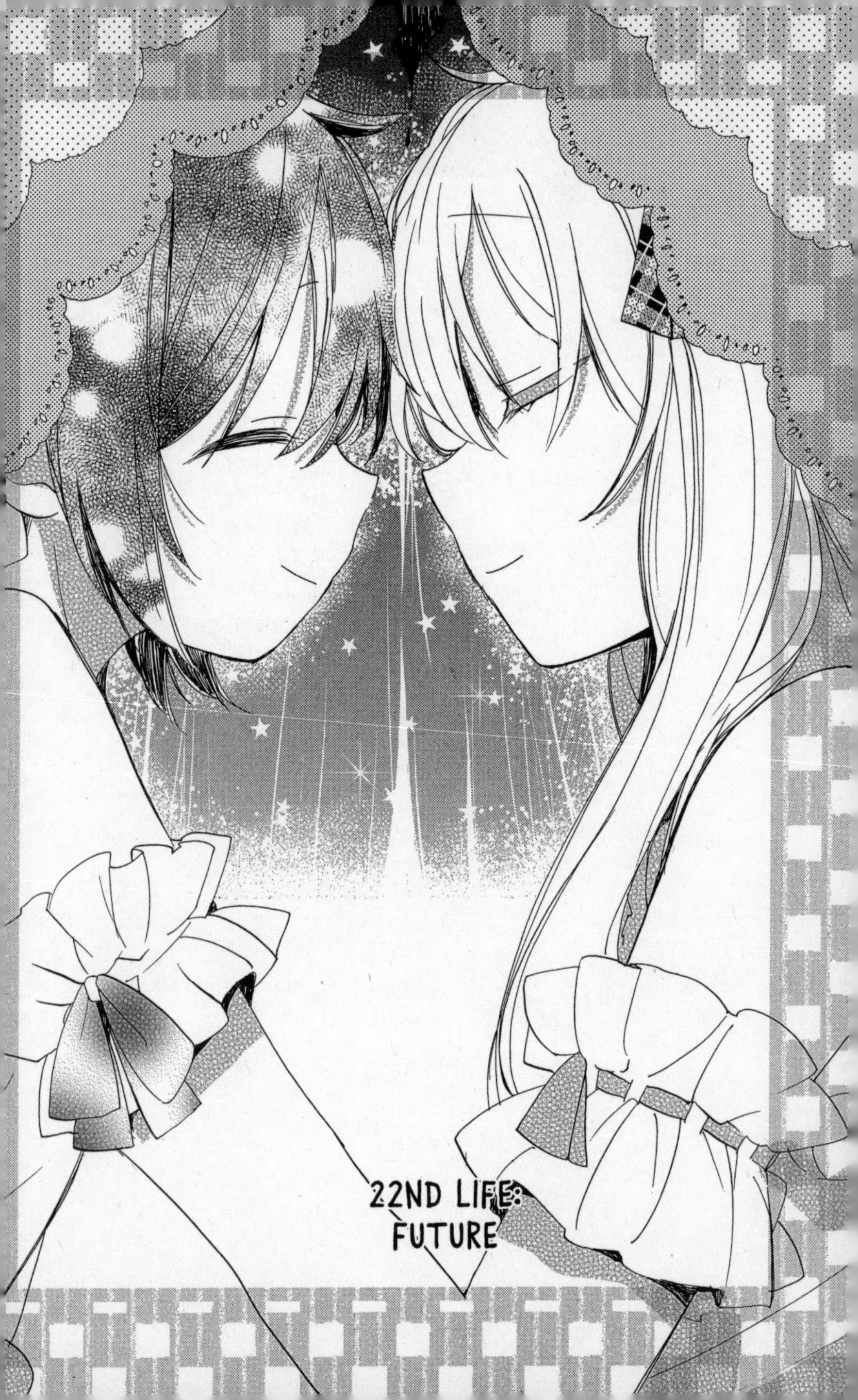
22ND LIFE:
FUTURE

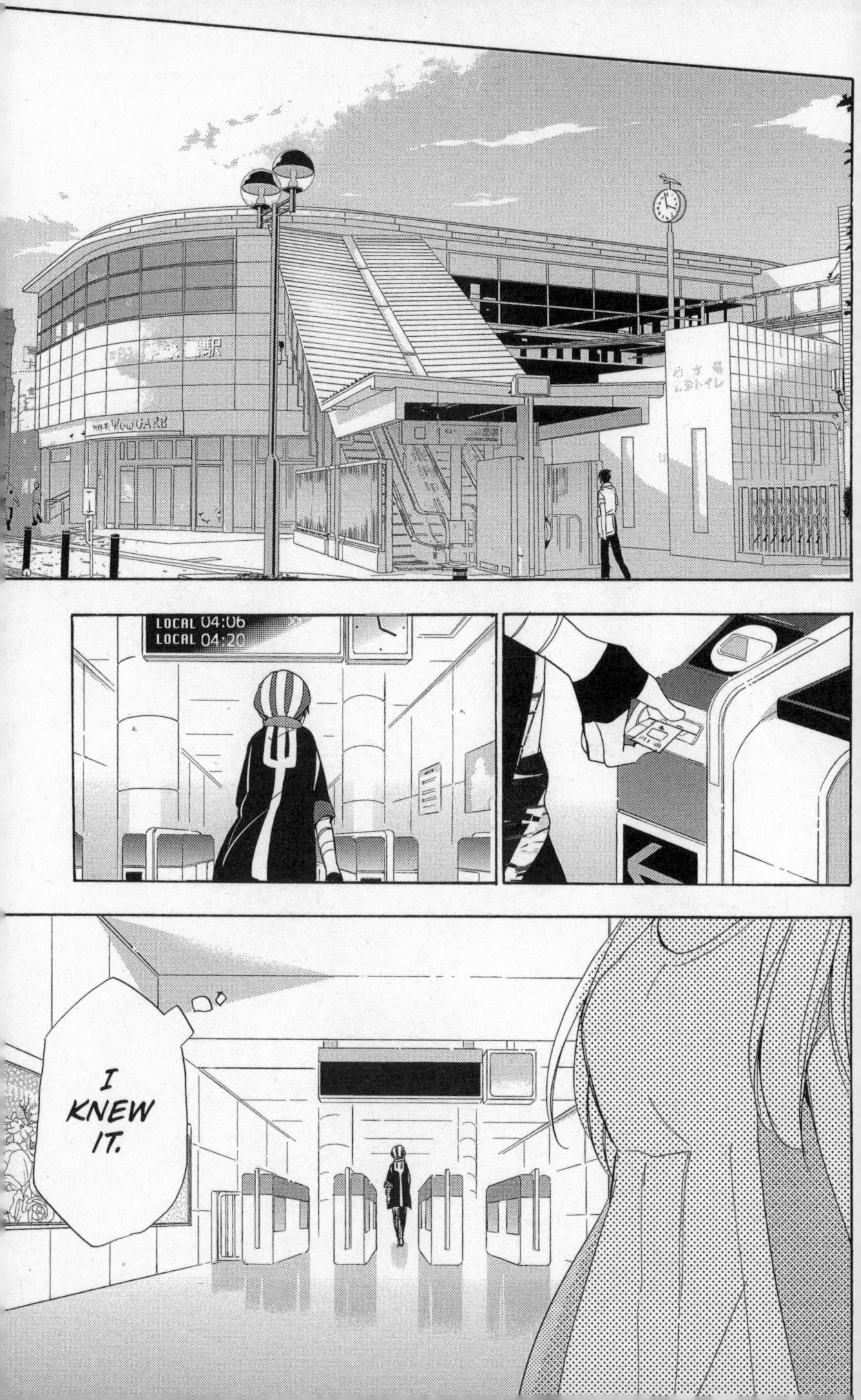
LOCAL 04:06
LOCAL 04:20
I KNEW IT.

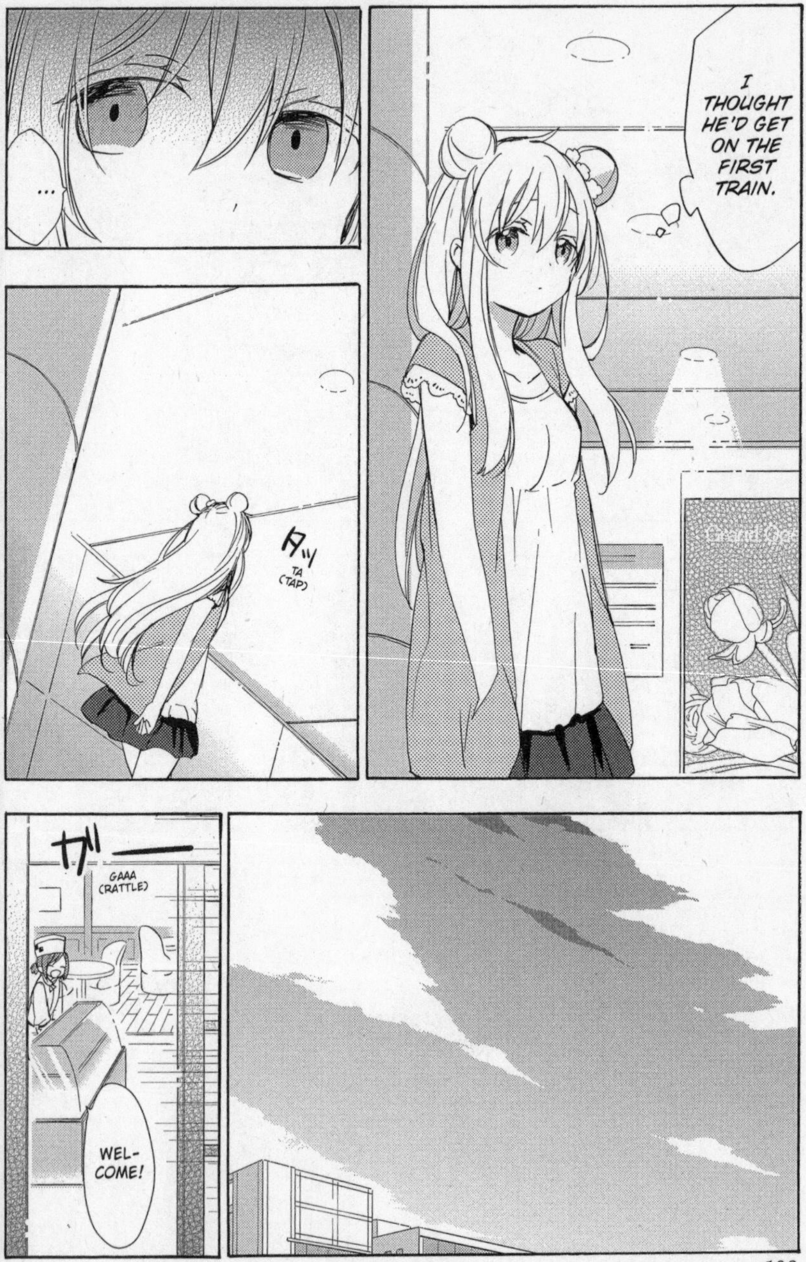

I THOUGHT HE'D GET ON THE FIRST TRAIN.
...
タッ
TA (TAP)
ガー
GAAA (RATTLE)
WEL-COME!

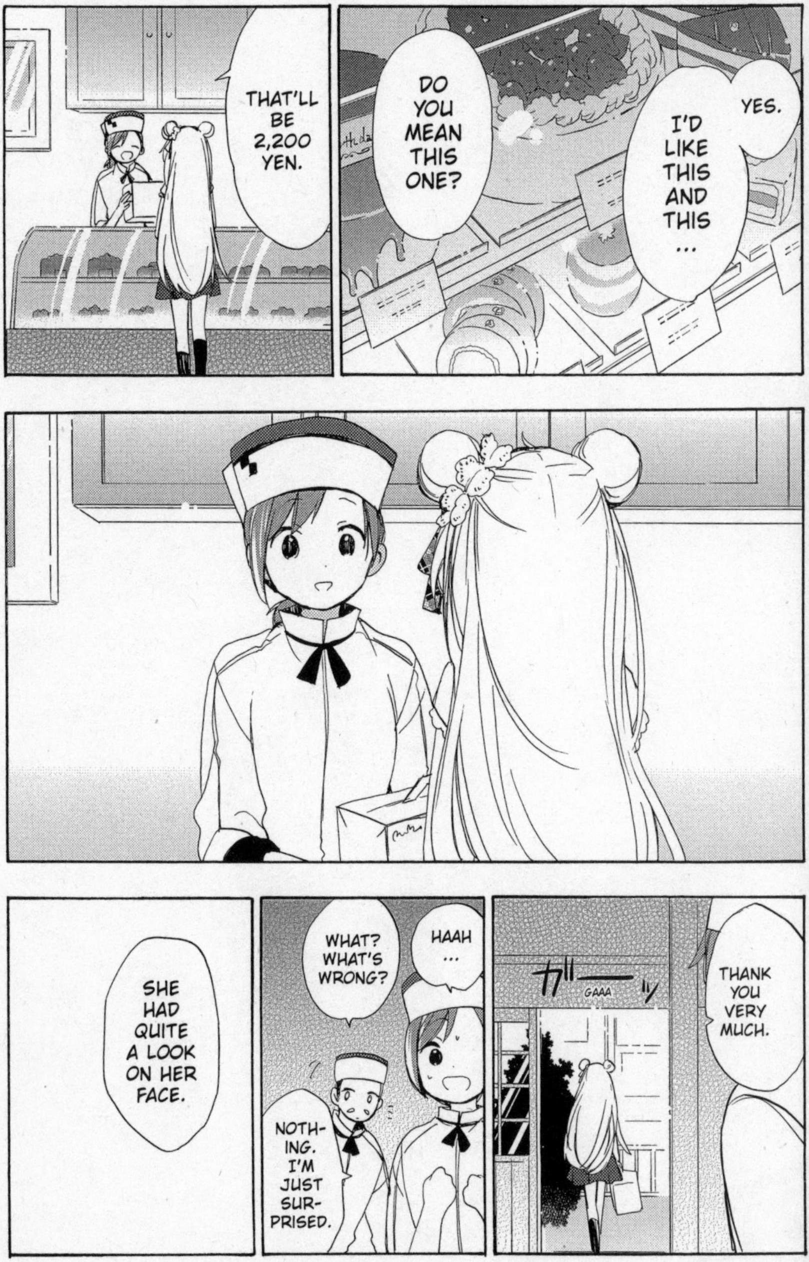
YES.
I'D LIKE THIS AND THIS...
DO YOU MEAN THIS ONE?
THAT'LL BE 2,200 YEN.
THANK YOU VERY MUCH.
GAAA
HAAH...
WHAT? WHAT'S WRONG?
NOTH-ING. I'M JUST SUR-PRISED.
SHE HAD QUITE A LOOK ON HER FACE.

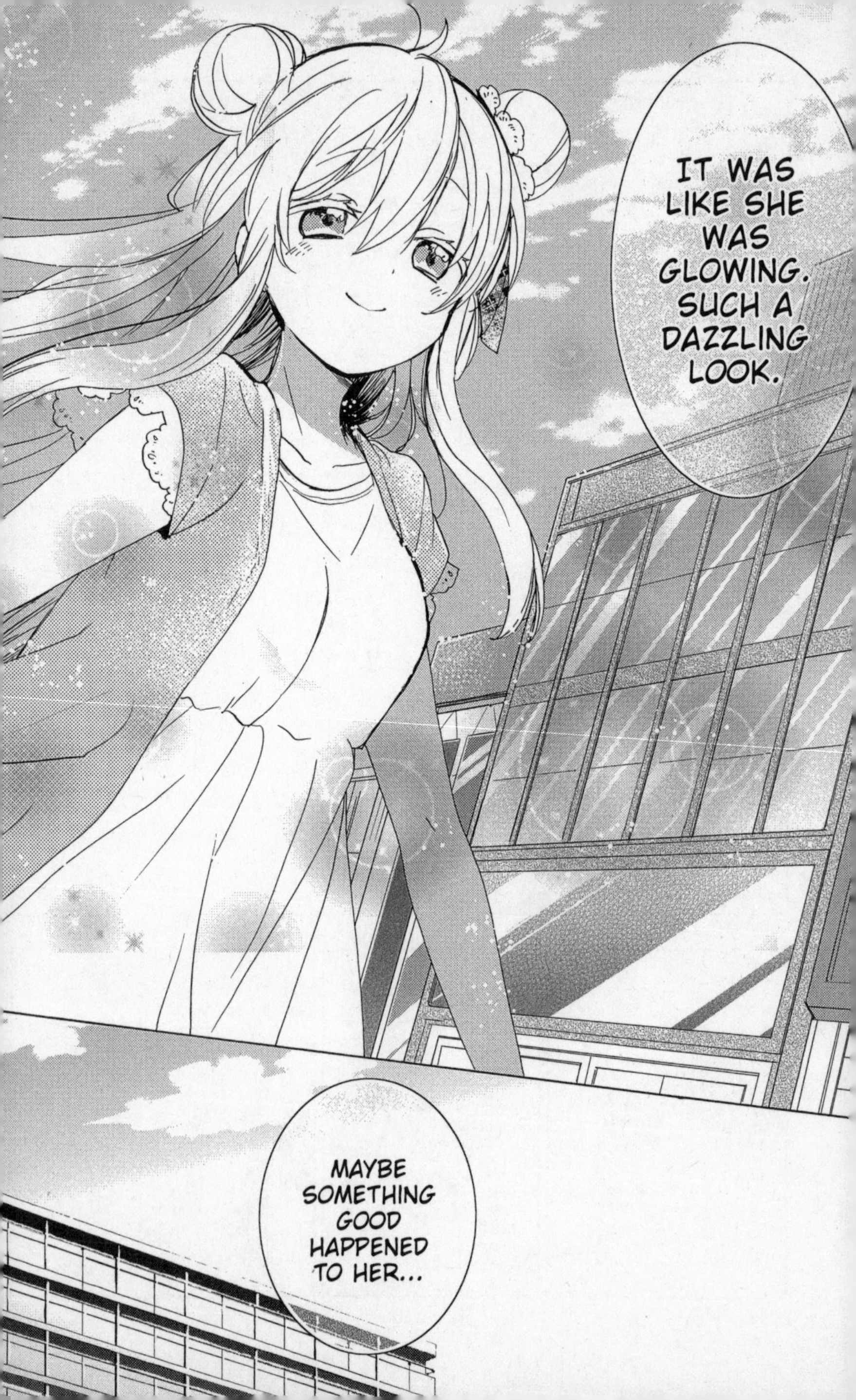
IT WAS LIKE SHE WAS GLOWING. SUCH A DAZZLING LOOK.
MAYBE SOMETHING GOOD HAPPENED TO HER...

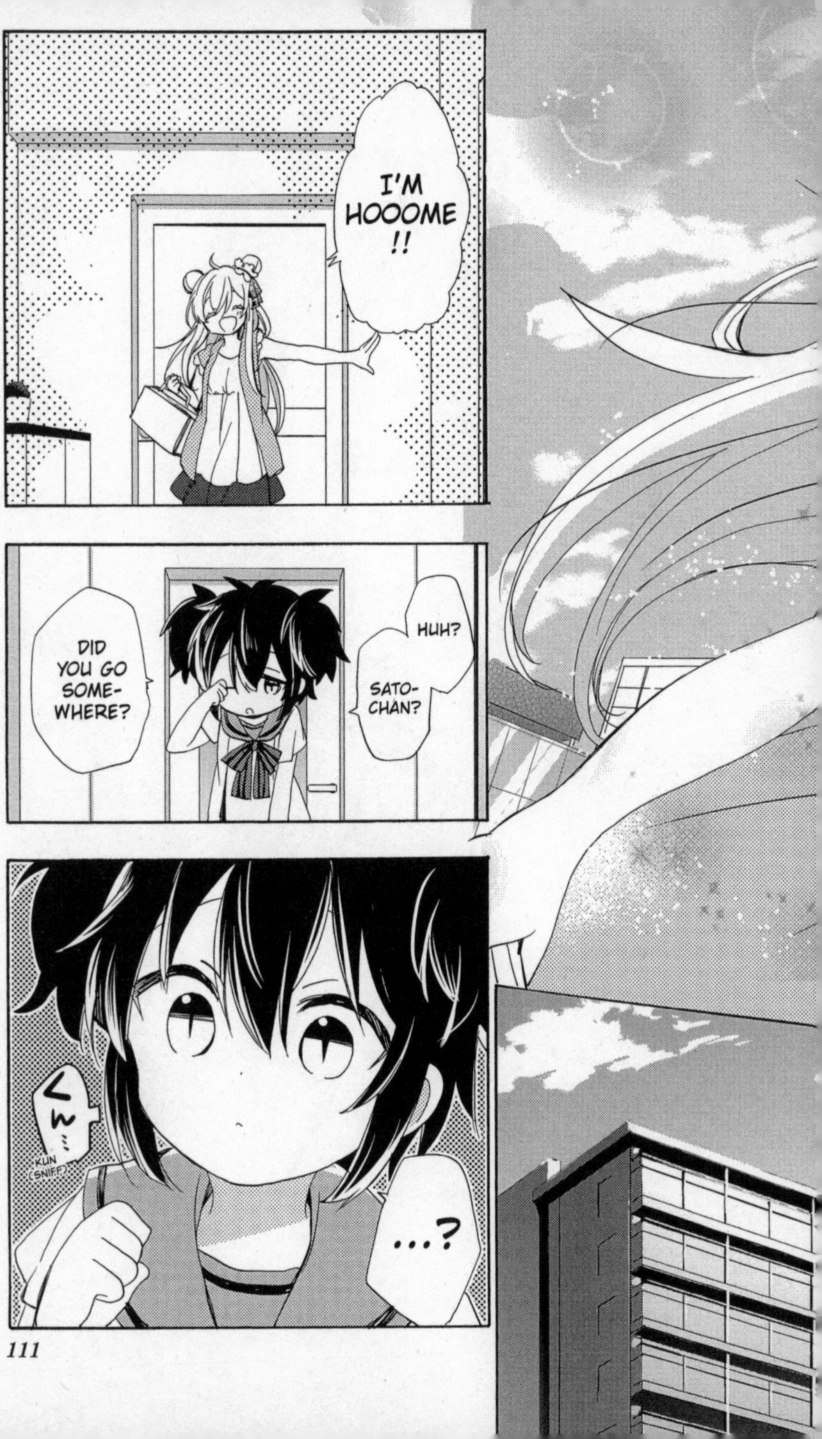
I'M HOOOME!!
HUH?
SATO-CHAN?
DID YOU GO SOME-WHERE?
くん…
KUN (SNIFF)
...?

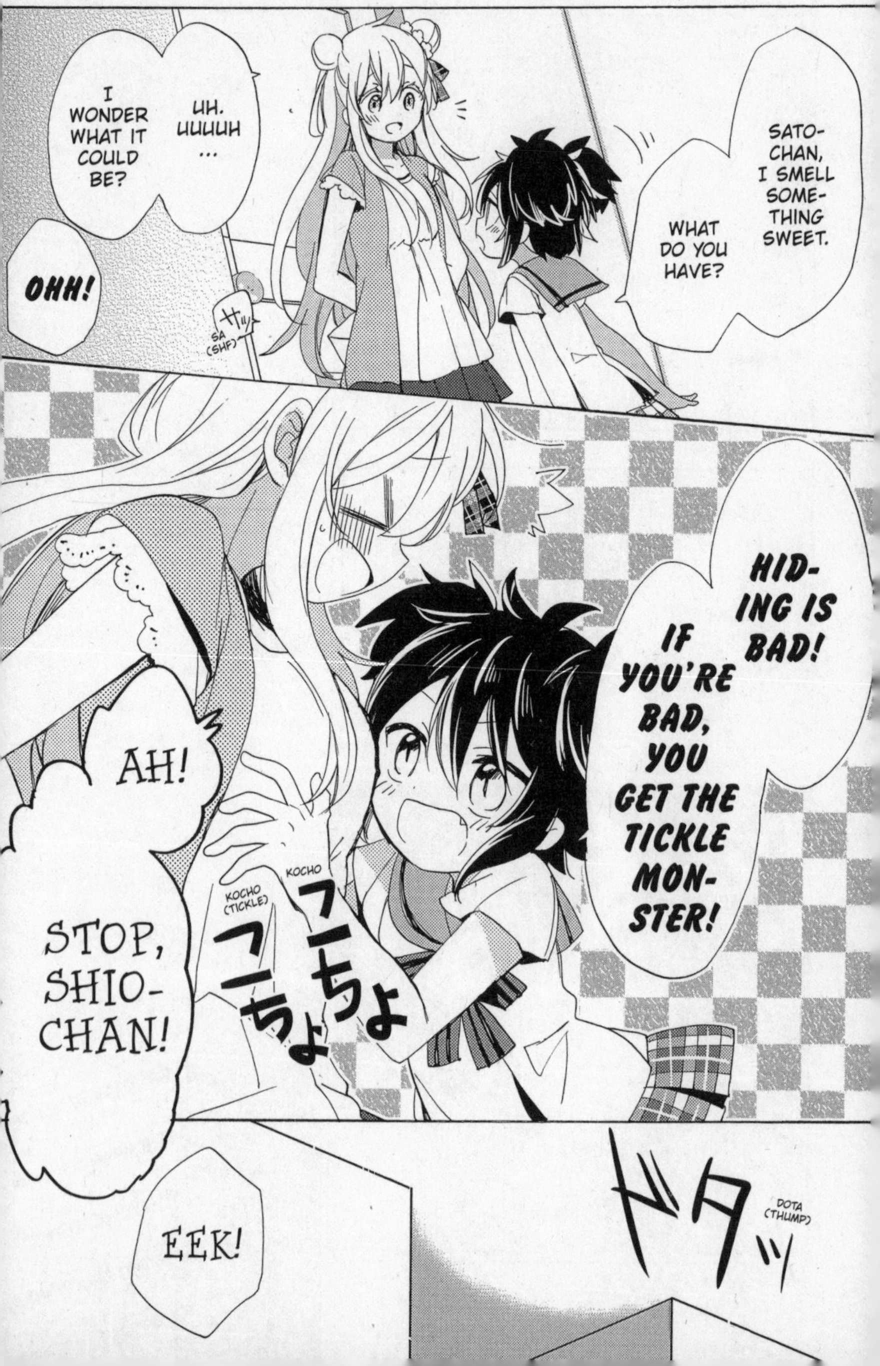
SATO-CHAN, I SMELL SOME-THING SWEET.
WHAT DO YOU HAVE?
UH. UUUUH ...
I WONDER WHAT IT COULD BE?
サッ
SA (SHF)
OHH!
HID-ING IS BAD!
IF YOU'RE BAD, YOU GET THE TICKLE MON-STER!
こちょ
KOCHO
こちょ
KOCHO (TICKLE)
AH!
STOP, SHIO-CHAN!
ドタッ
DOTA (THUMP)
EEK!

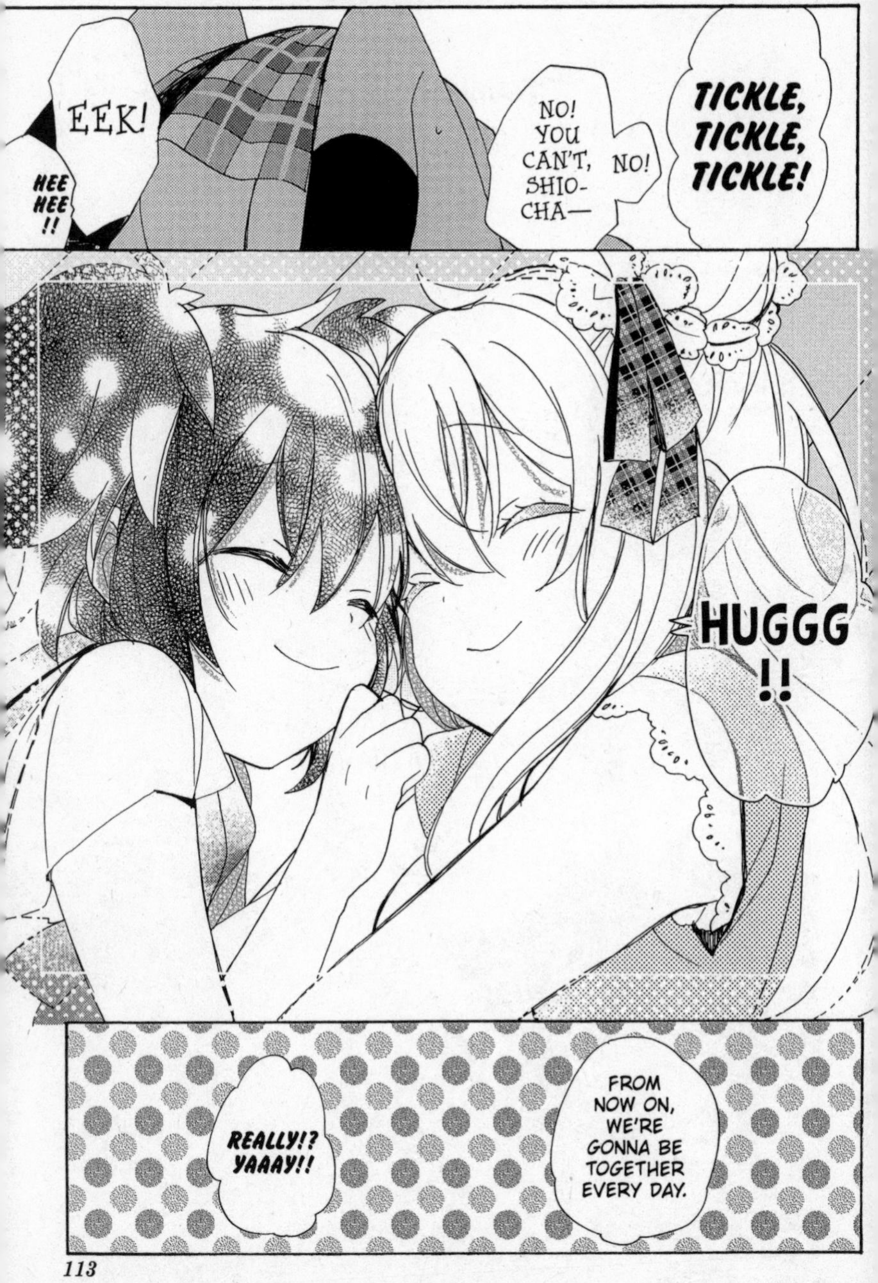
TICKLE, TICKLE, TICKLE!
NO! YOU CAN'T, SHIO-CHA—
NO!
EEK!
HEE HEE!!
HUGGG!!
FROM NOW ON, WE'RE GONNA BE TOGETHER EVERY DAY.
REALLY!? YAAAY!!

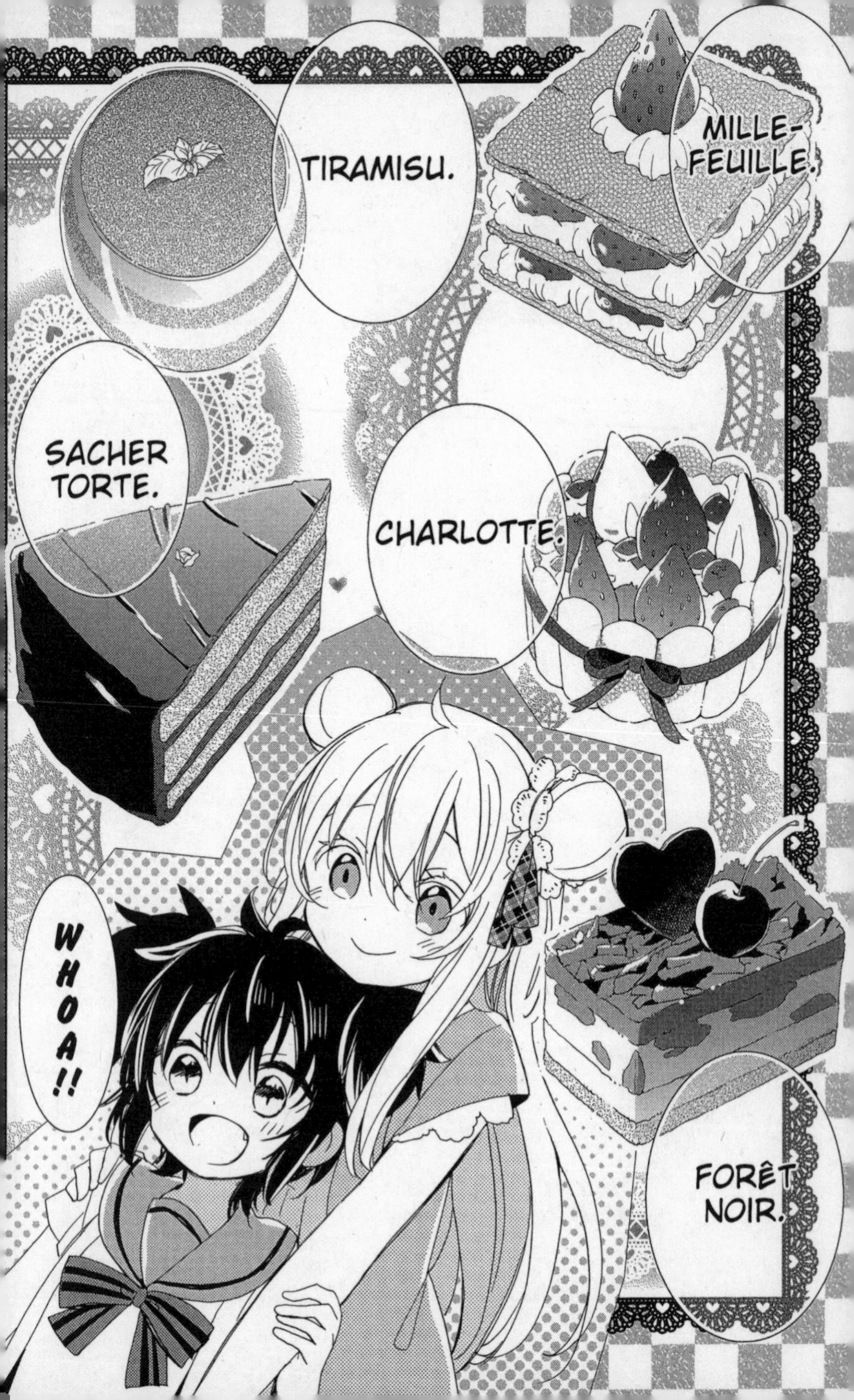
MILLE-FEUILLE.
TIRAMISU.
CHARLOTTE.
SACHER TORTE.
FORÊT NOIR.
WHOA!!

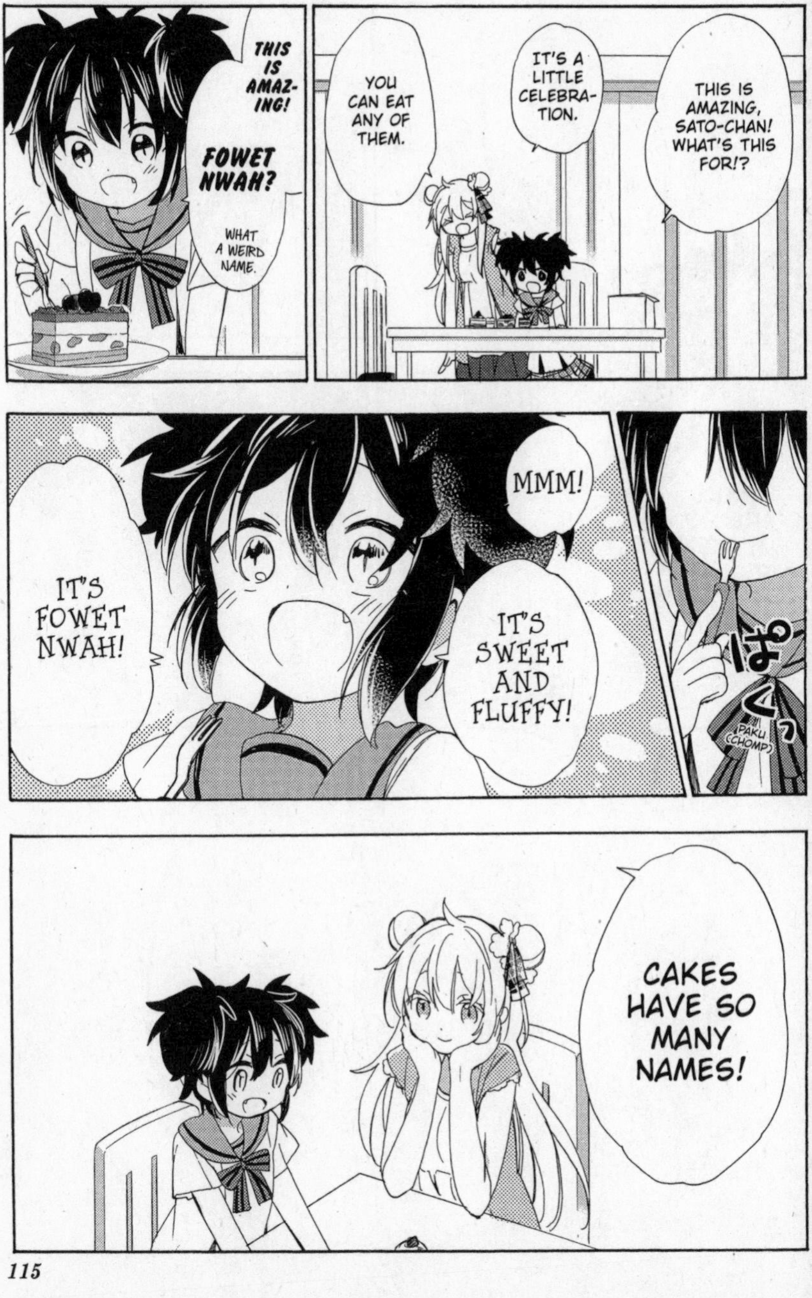
THIS IS AMAZING, SATO-CHAN! WHAT'S THIS FOR!?
IT'S A LITTLE CELEBRATION.
YOU CAN EAT ANY OF THEM.
THIS IS AMAZING!
FOWET NWAH?
WHAT A WEIRD NAME.
ぱくっ
PAKU (CHOMP)
MMM!
IT'S SWEET AND FLUFFY!
IT'S FOWET NWAH!
CAKES HAVE SO MANY NAMES!

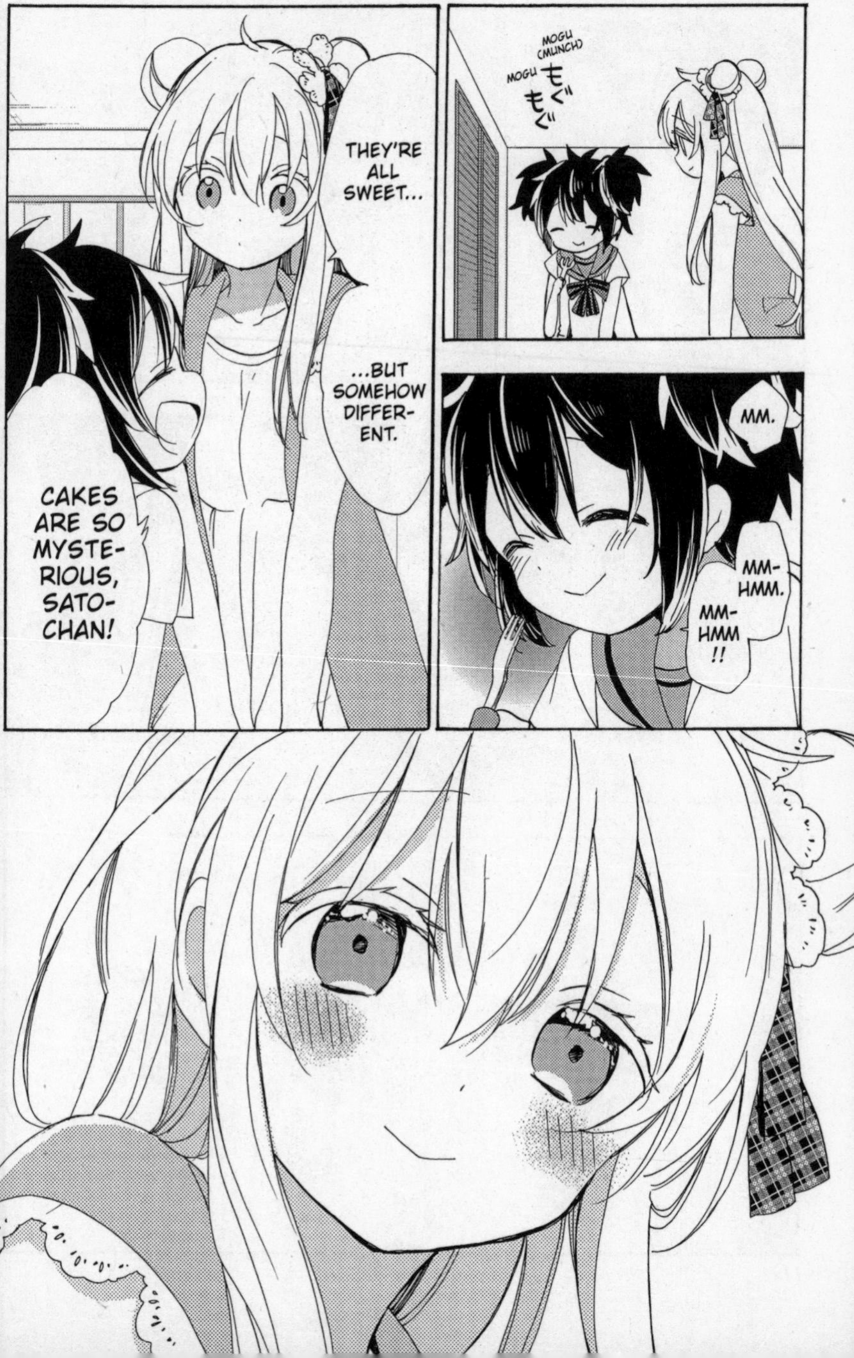

MOGU (MUNCH)
もぐ
MOGU
もぐ
MM.
MM-HMM.
MM-HMM!!
THEY'RE ALL SWEET...
...BUT SOMEHOW DIFFER-ENT.
CAKES ARE SO MYSTE-RIOUS, SATO-CHAN!

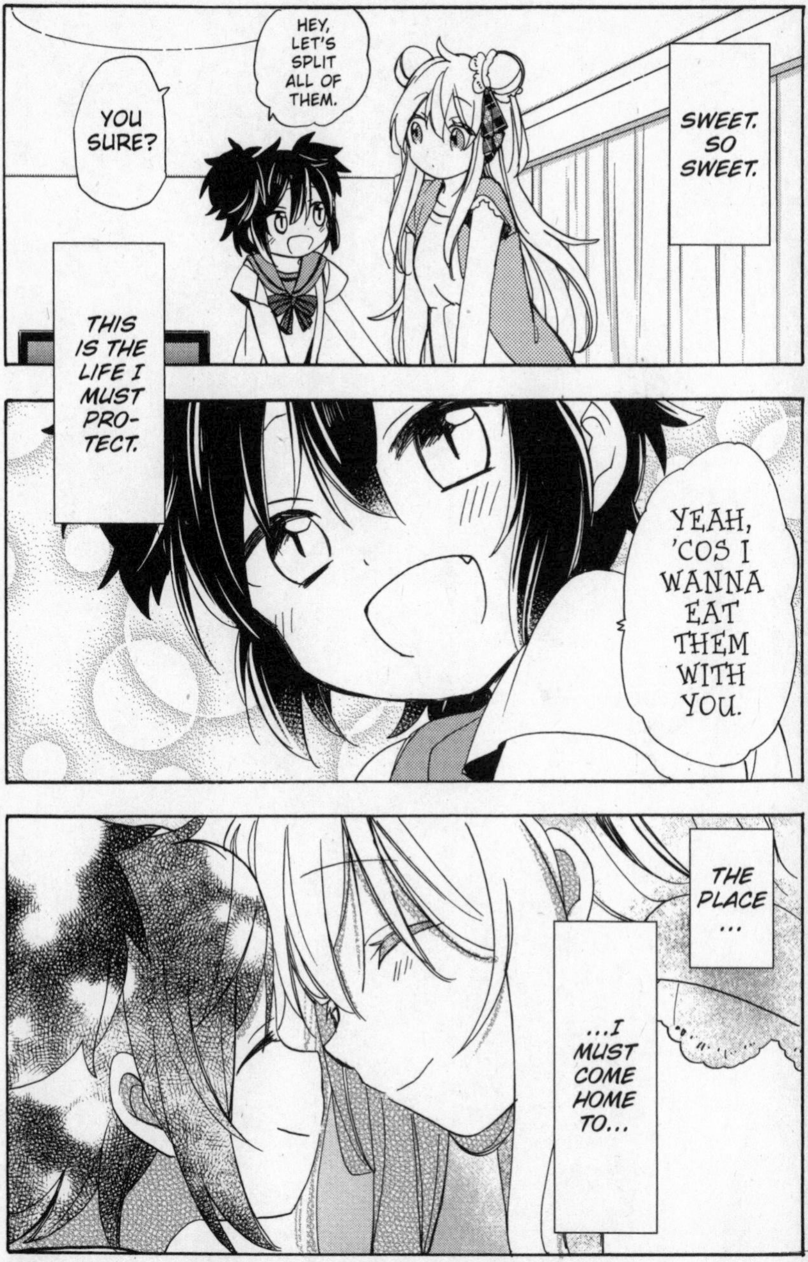
SWEET. SO SWEET.
HEY, LET'S SPLIT ALL OF THEM.
YOU SURE?
THIS IS THE LIFE I MUST PRO-TECT.
YEAH, 'COS I WANNA EAT THEM WITH YOU.
THE PLACE...
...I MUST COME HOME TO...

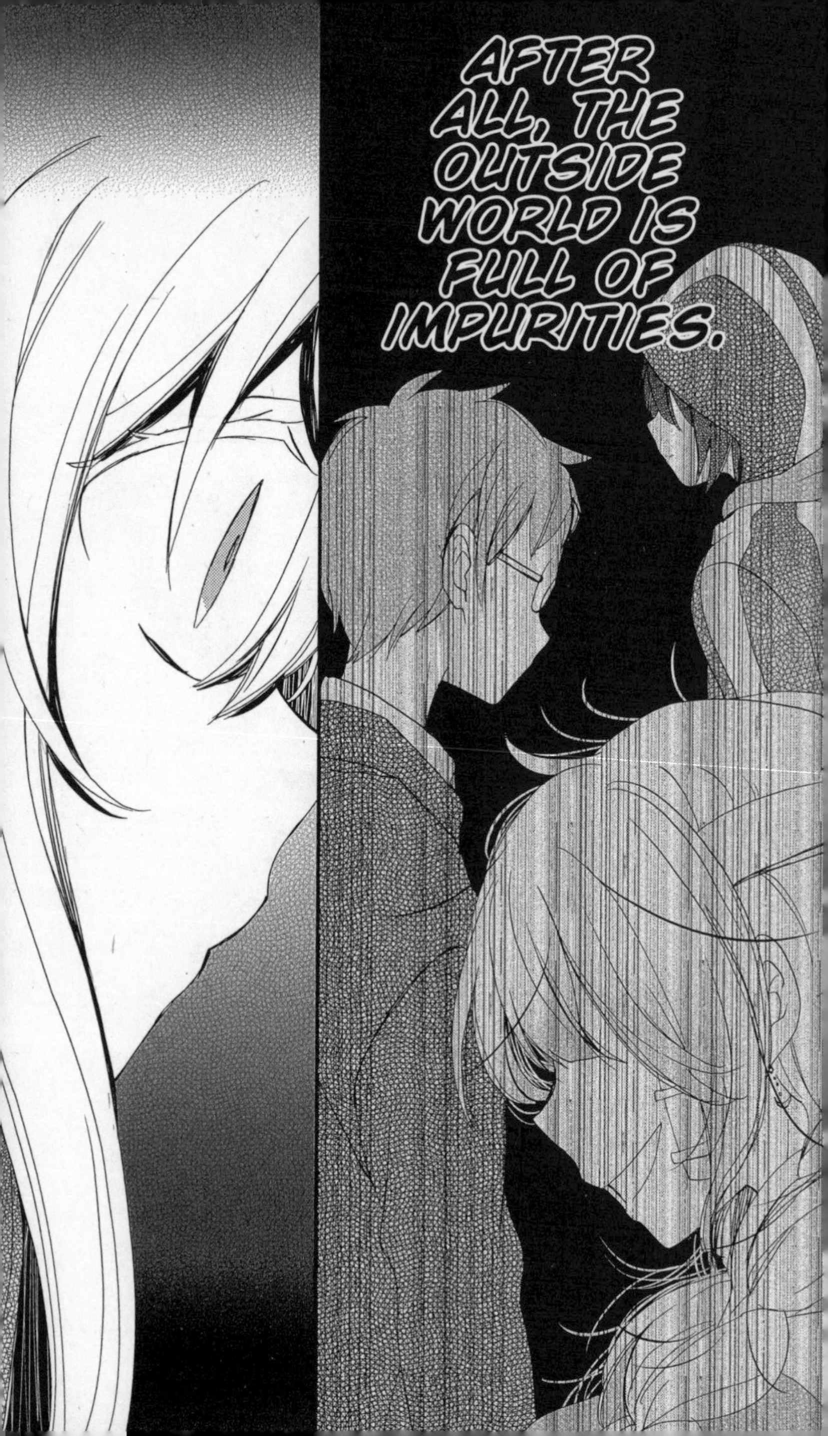
AFTER ALL, THE OUTSIDE WORLD IS FULL OF IMPURITIES.

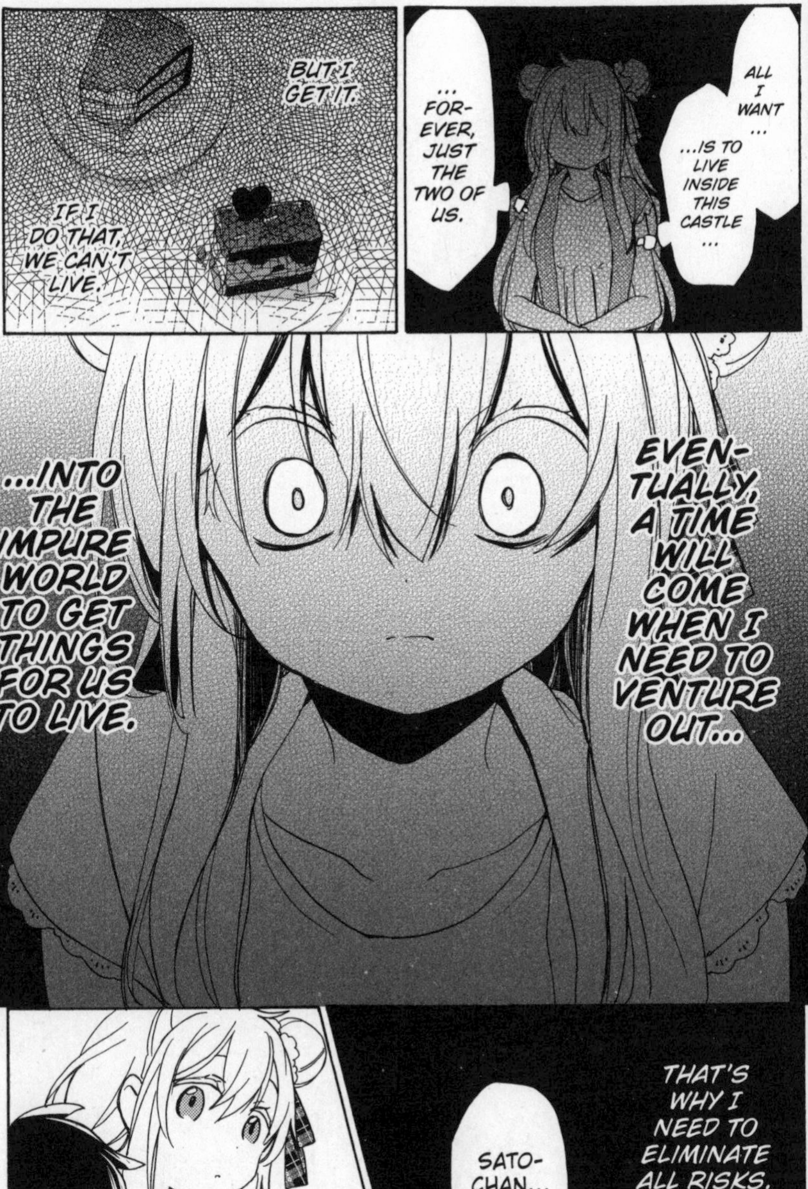
ALL I WANT ...
...IS TO LIVE INSIDE THIS CASTLE ...
... FOREVER, JUST THE TWO OF US.
BUT I GET IT.
IF I DO THAT, WE CAN'T LIVE.
EVENTUALLY, A TIME WILL COME WHEN I NEED TO VENTURE OUT...
...INTO THE IMPURE WORLD TO GET THINGS FOR US TO LIVE.
THAT'S WHY I NEED TO ELIMINATE ALL RISKS.
SATO-CHAN...

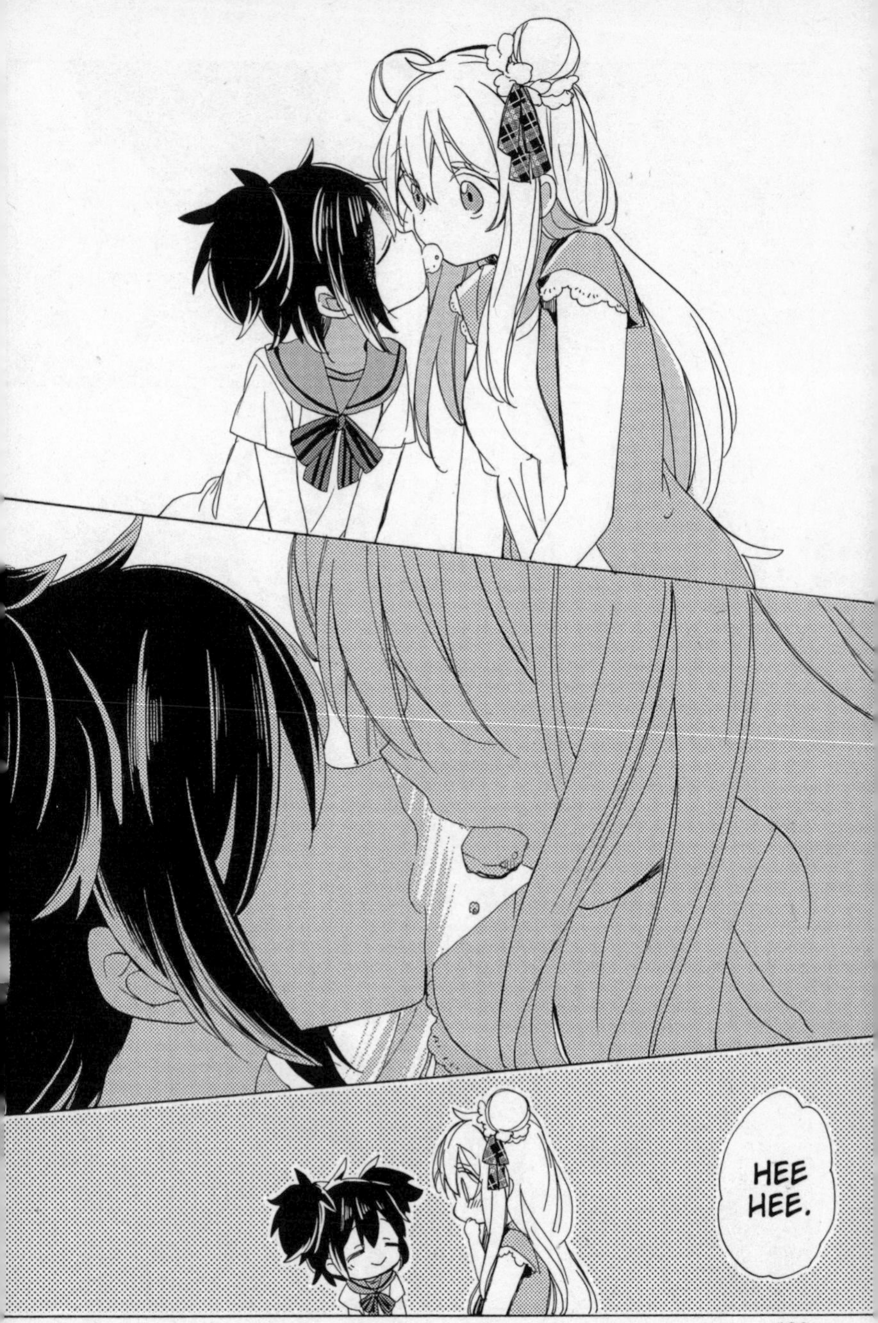
HEE HEE.

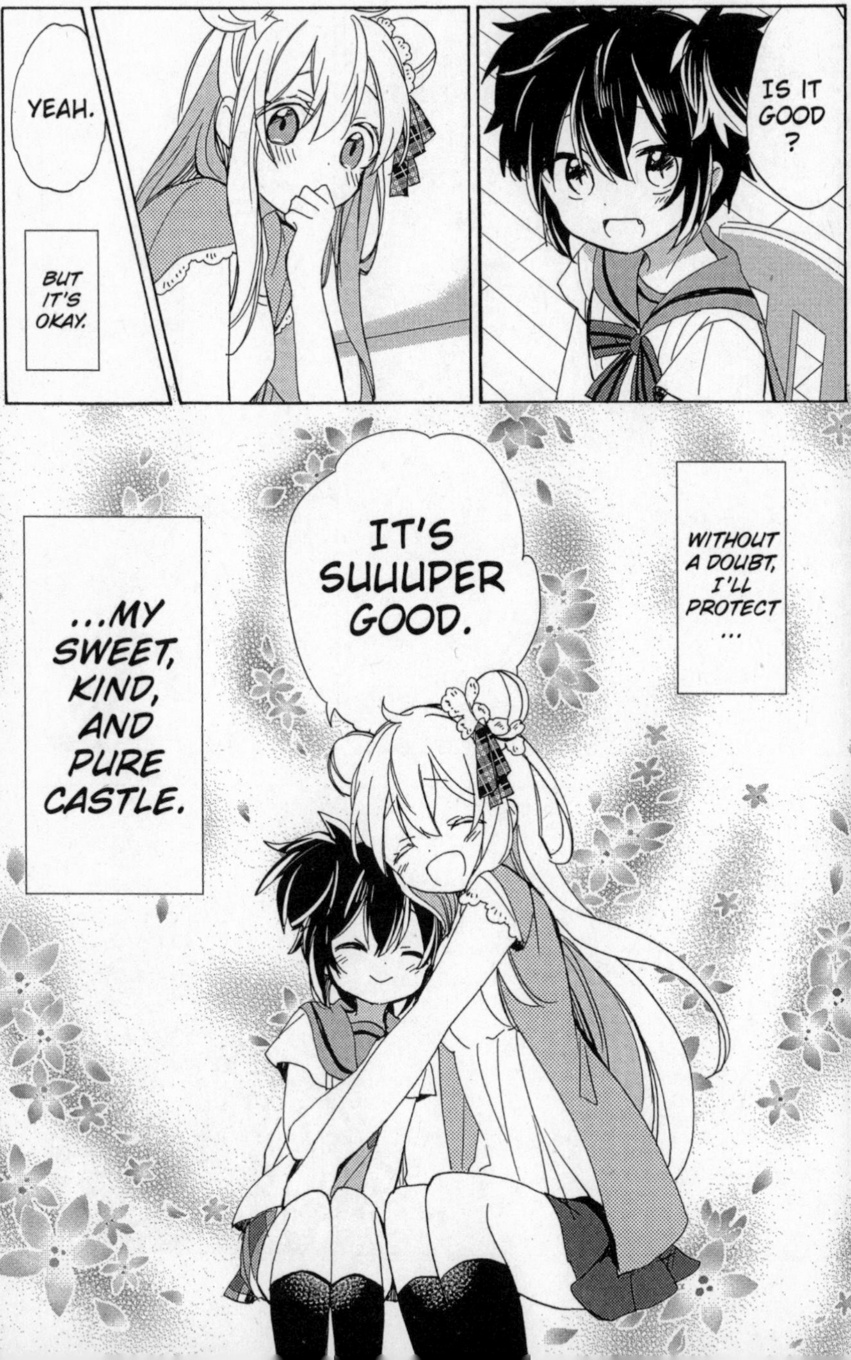
IS IT GOOD?
YEAH.
BUT IT'S OKAY.
WITHOUT A DOUBT, I'LL PROTECT...
IT'S SUUUPER GOOD.
...MY SWEET, KIND, AND PURE CASTLE.

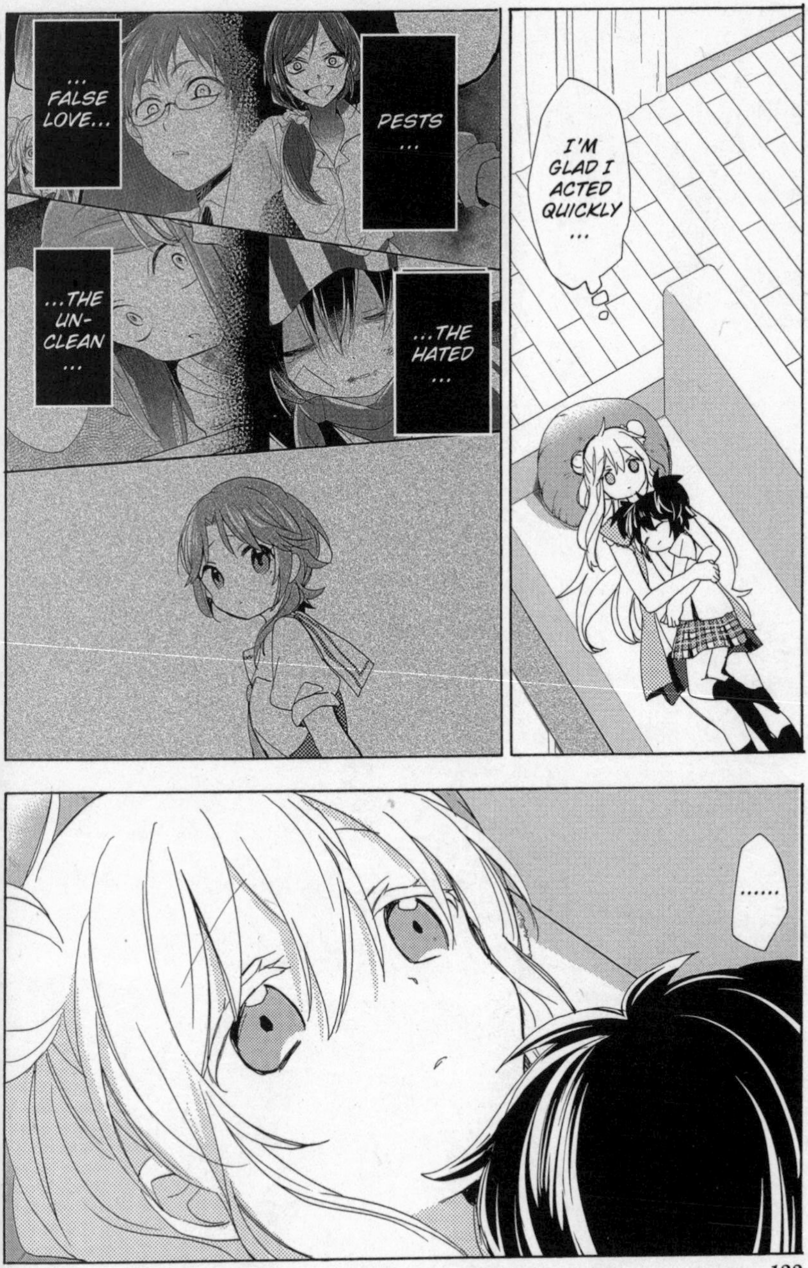
I'M GLAD I ACTED QUICKLY ...
PESTS ...
... FALSE LOVE...
...THE HATED ...
...THE UN-CLEAN ...
......

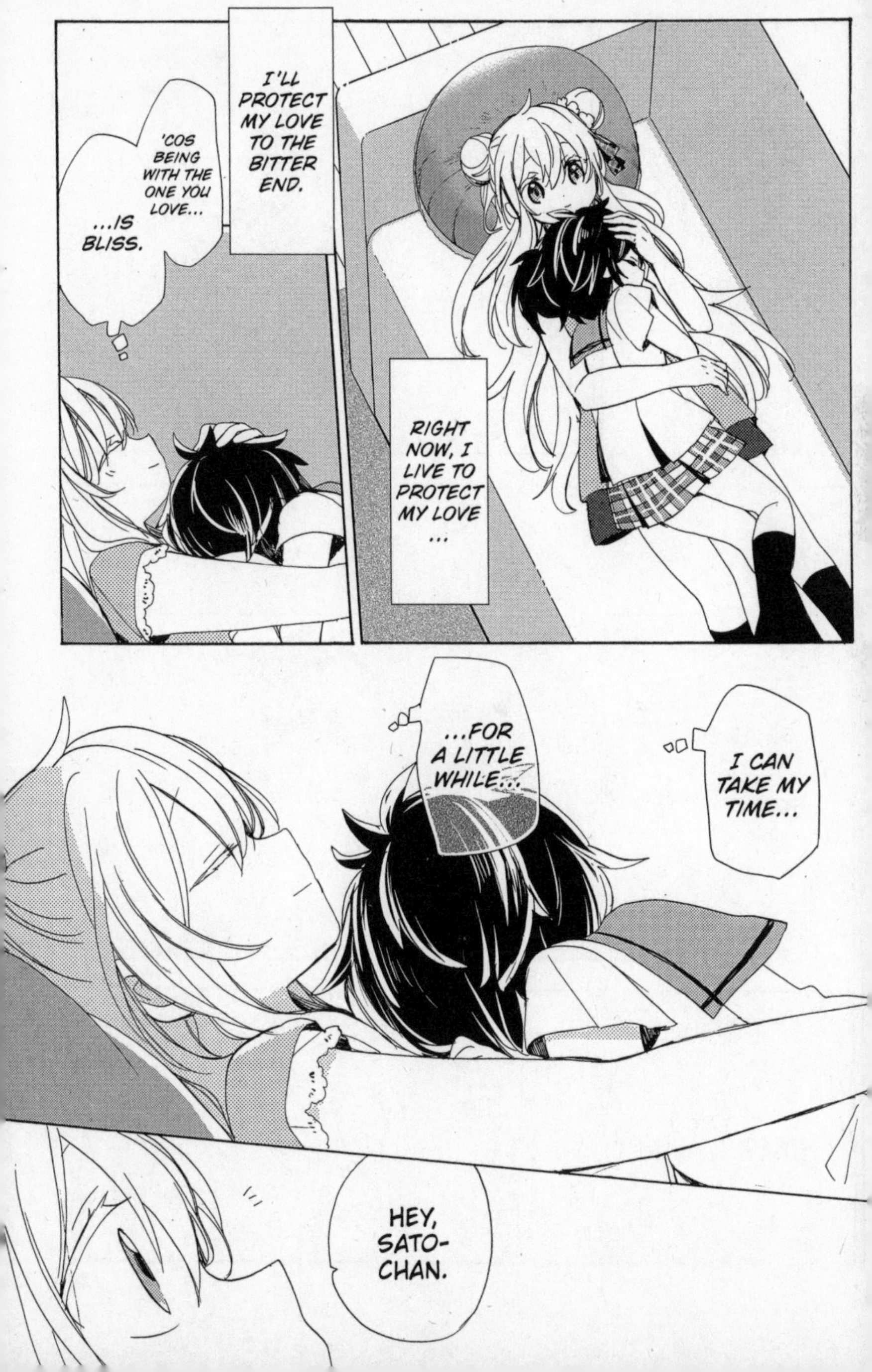
RIGHT NOW, I LIVE TO PROTECT MY LOVE ...
I'LL PROTECT MY LOVE TO THE BITTER END.
'COS BEING WITH THE ONE YOU LOVE...
...IS BLISS.
I CAN TAKE MY TIME...
...FOR A LITTLE WHILE...
HEY, SATO-CHAN.

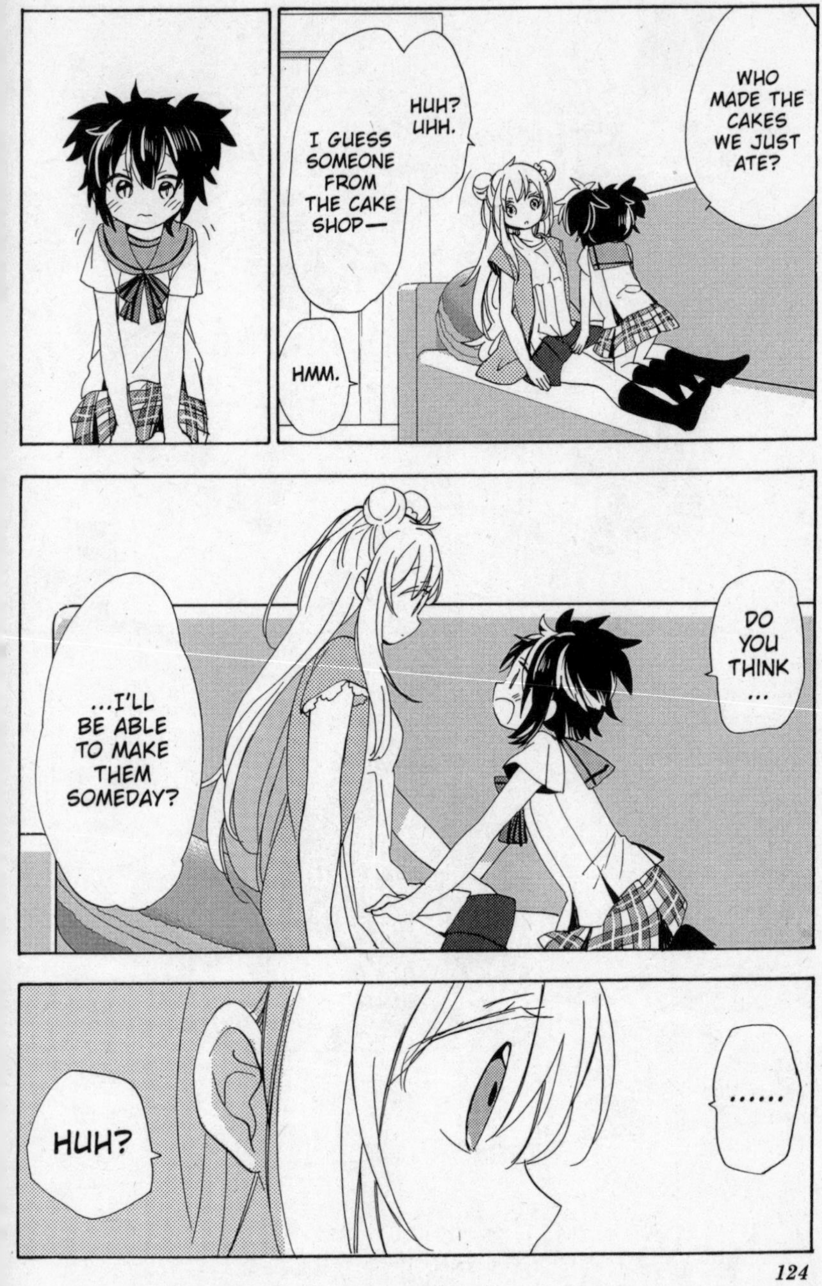
WHO MADE THE CAKES WE JUST ATE?
HUH? UHH.
I GUESS SOMEONE FROM THE CAKE SHOP—
HMM.
DO YOU THINK...
...I'LL BE ABLE TO MAKE THEM SOMEDAY?
......
HUH?

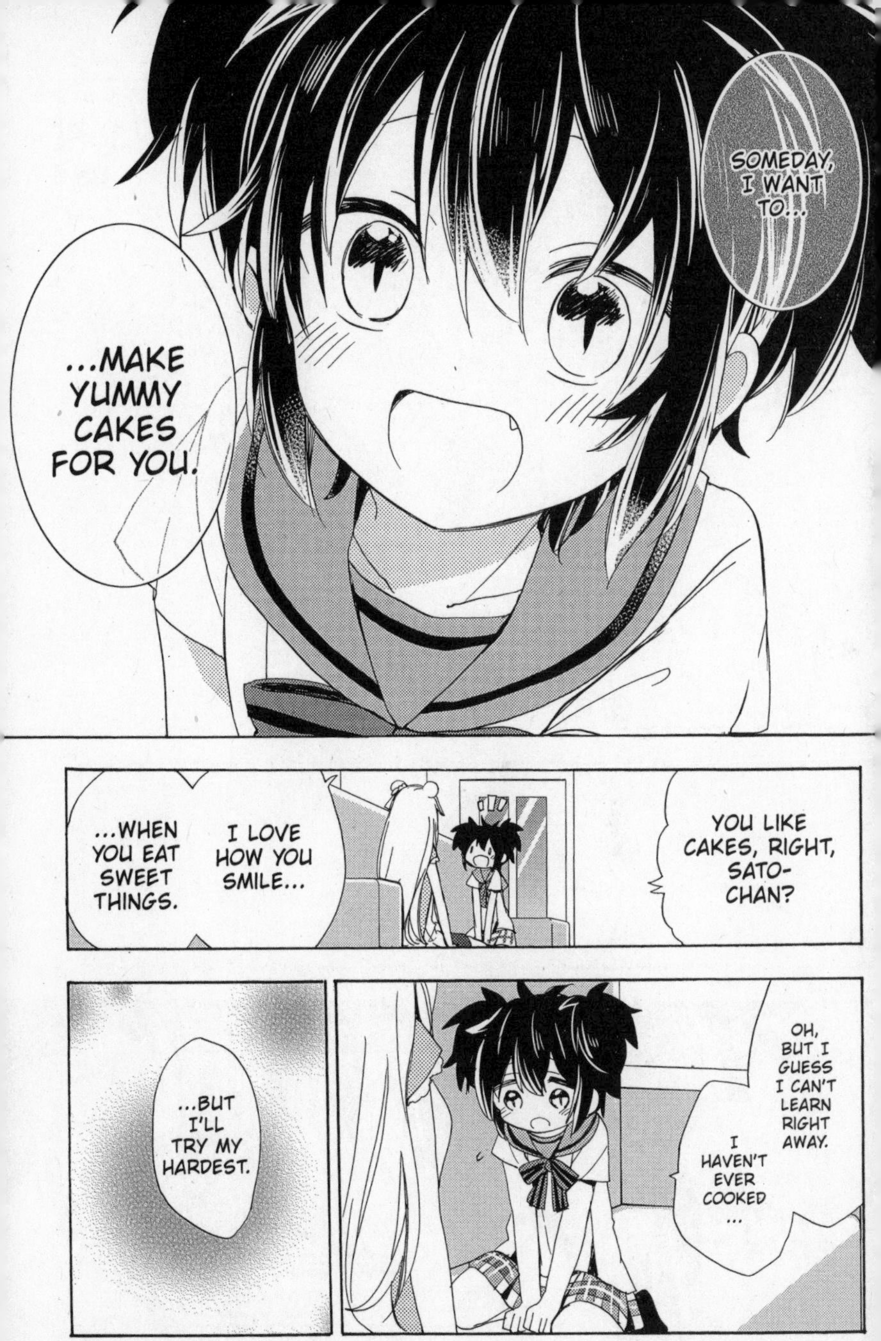
SOMEDAY, I WANT TO...
...MAKE YUMMY CAKES FOR YOU.
YOU LIKE CAKES, RIGHT, SATO-CHAN?
I LOVE HOW YOU SMILE...
...WHEN YOU EAT SWEET THINGS.
OH, BUT I GUESS I CAN'T LEARN RIGHT AWAY.
I HAVEN'T EVER COOKED...
...BUT I'LL TRY MY HARDEST.

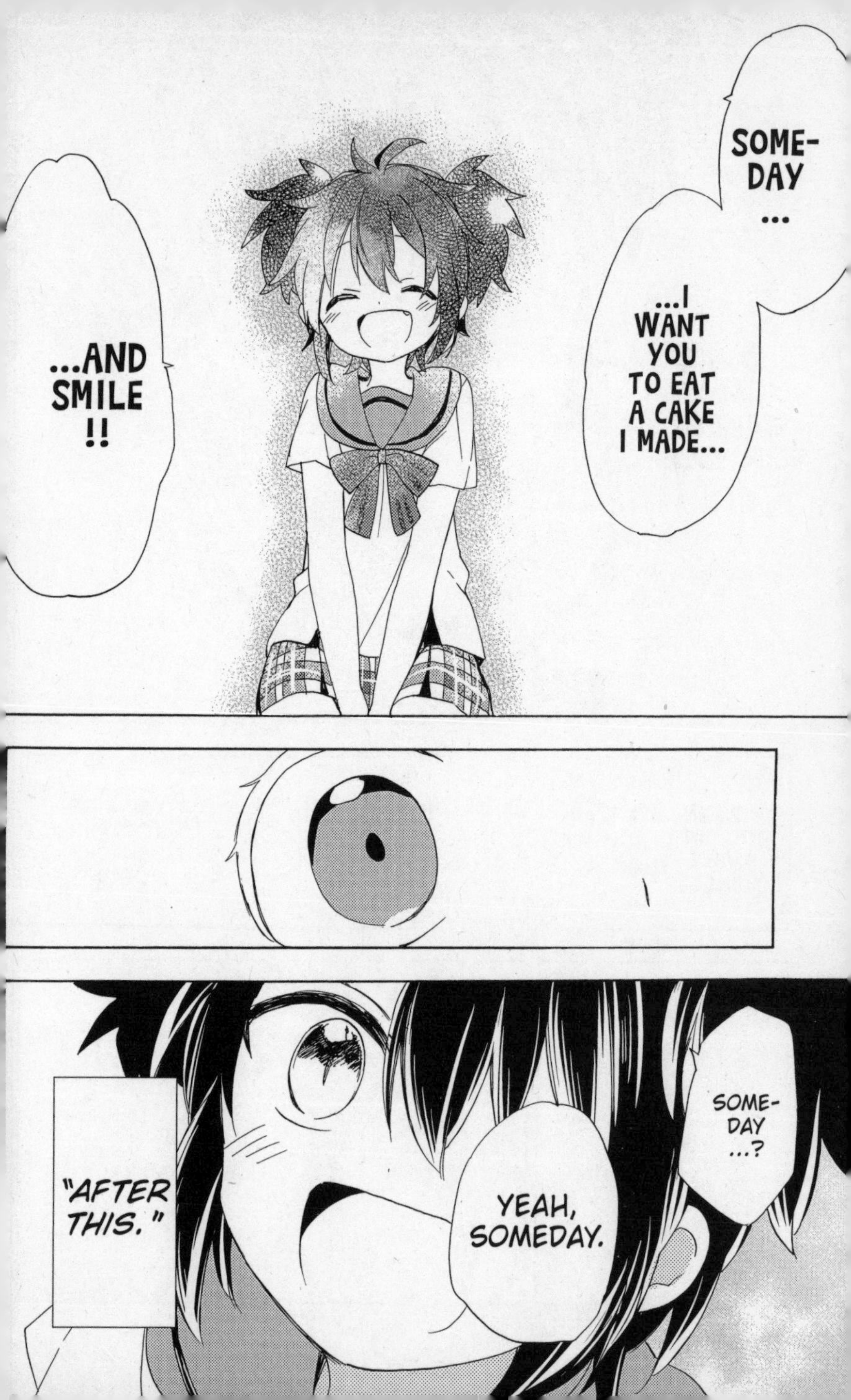
SOME-DAY...
...I WANT YOU TO EAT A CAKE I MADE...
...AND SMILE!!
SOME-DAY...?
YEAH, SOMEDAY.
"AFTER THIS."

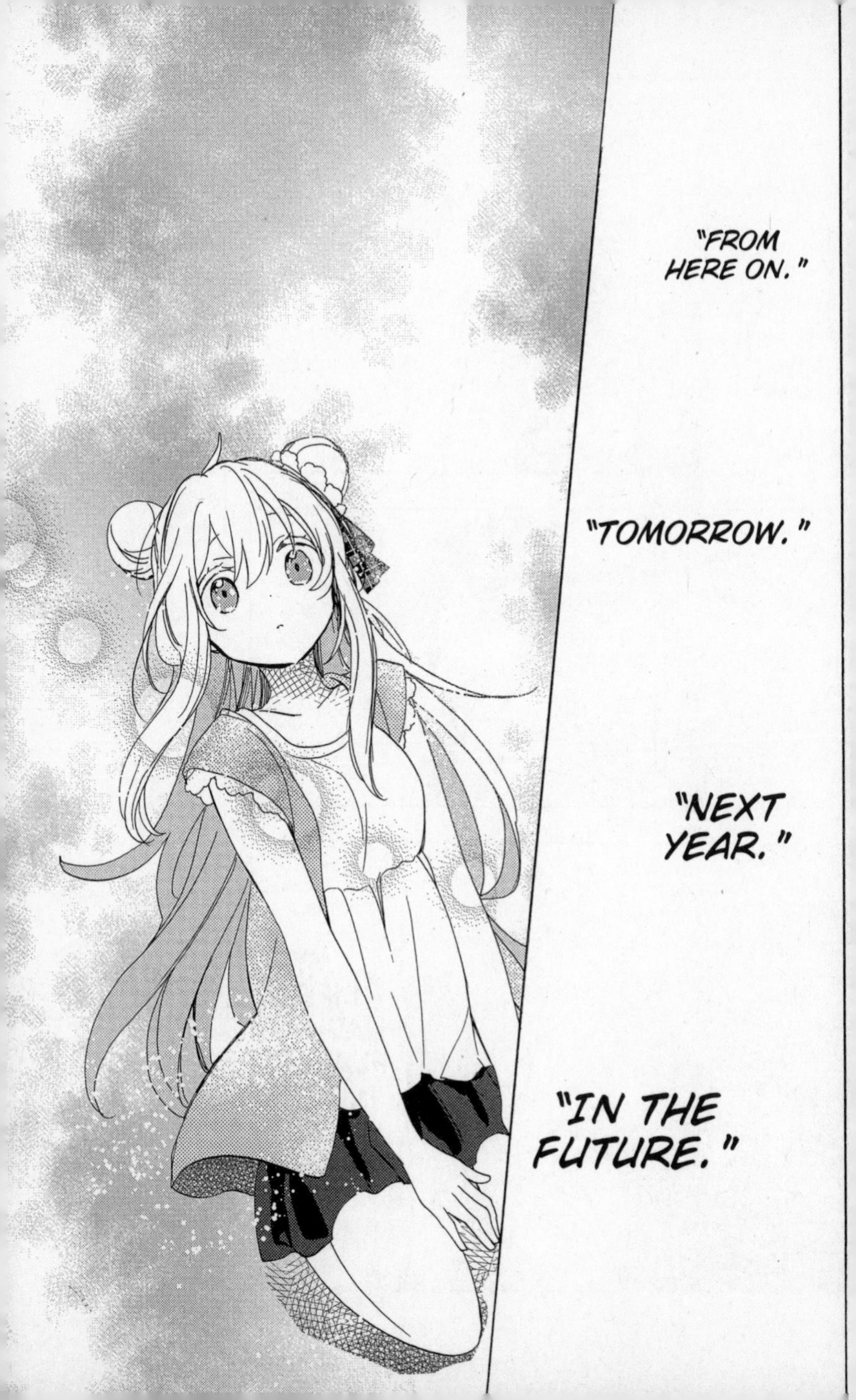
"FROM HERE ON."
"TOMORROW."
"NEXT YEAR."
"IN THE FUTURE."

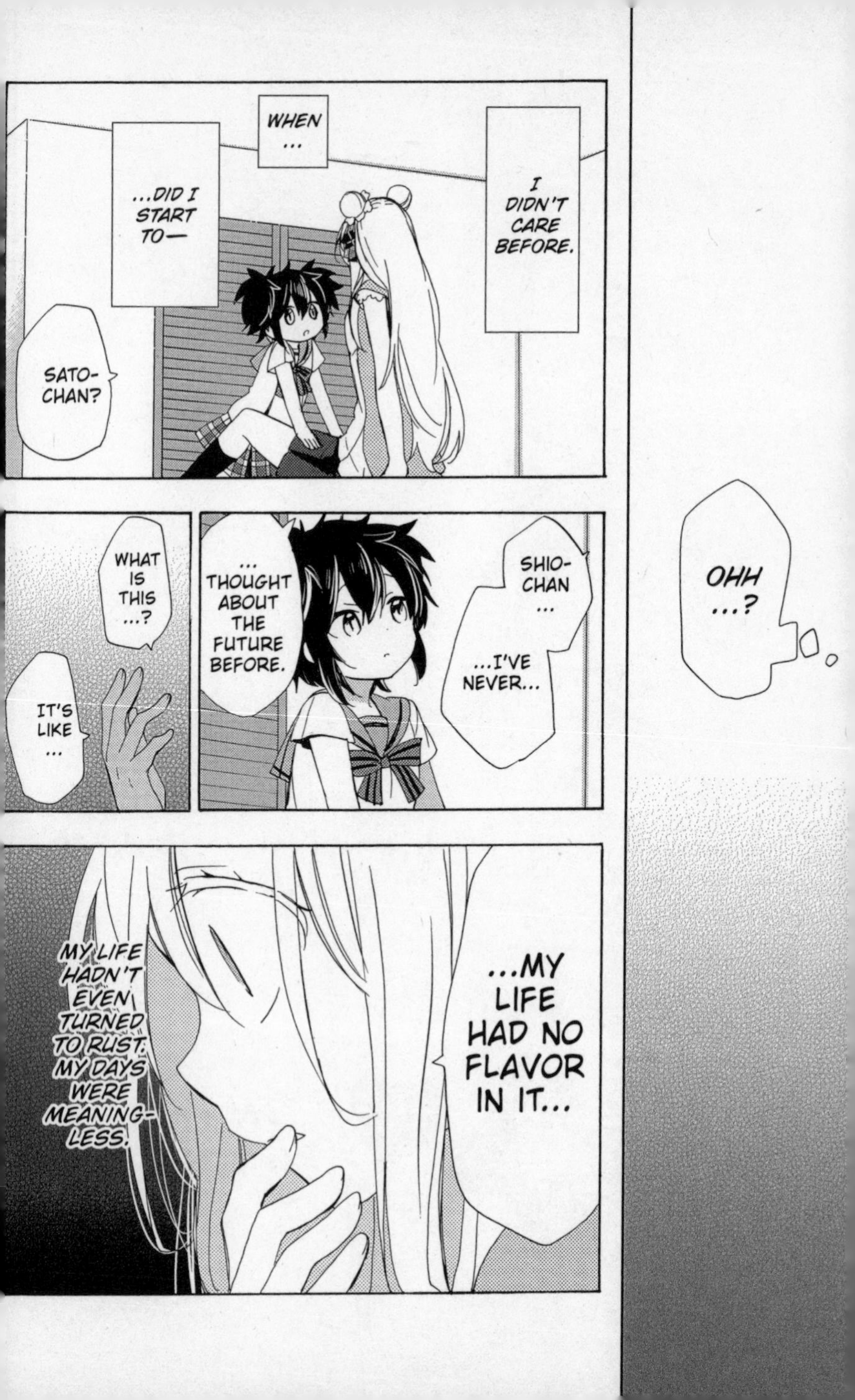
OHH ...?
I DIDN'T CARE BEFORE.
WHEN ...
...DID I START TO—
SATO-CHAN?
SHIO-CHAN ...
...I'VE NEVER...
... THOUGHT ABOUT THE FUTURE BEFORE.
WHAT IS THIS ...?
IT'S LIKE ...
...MY LIFE HAD NO FLAVOR IN IT...
MY LIFE HADN'T EVEN TURNED TO RUST. MY DAYS WERE MEANING-LESS.

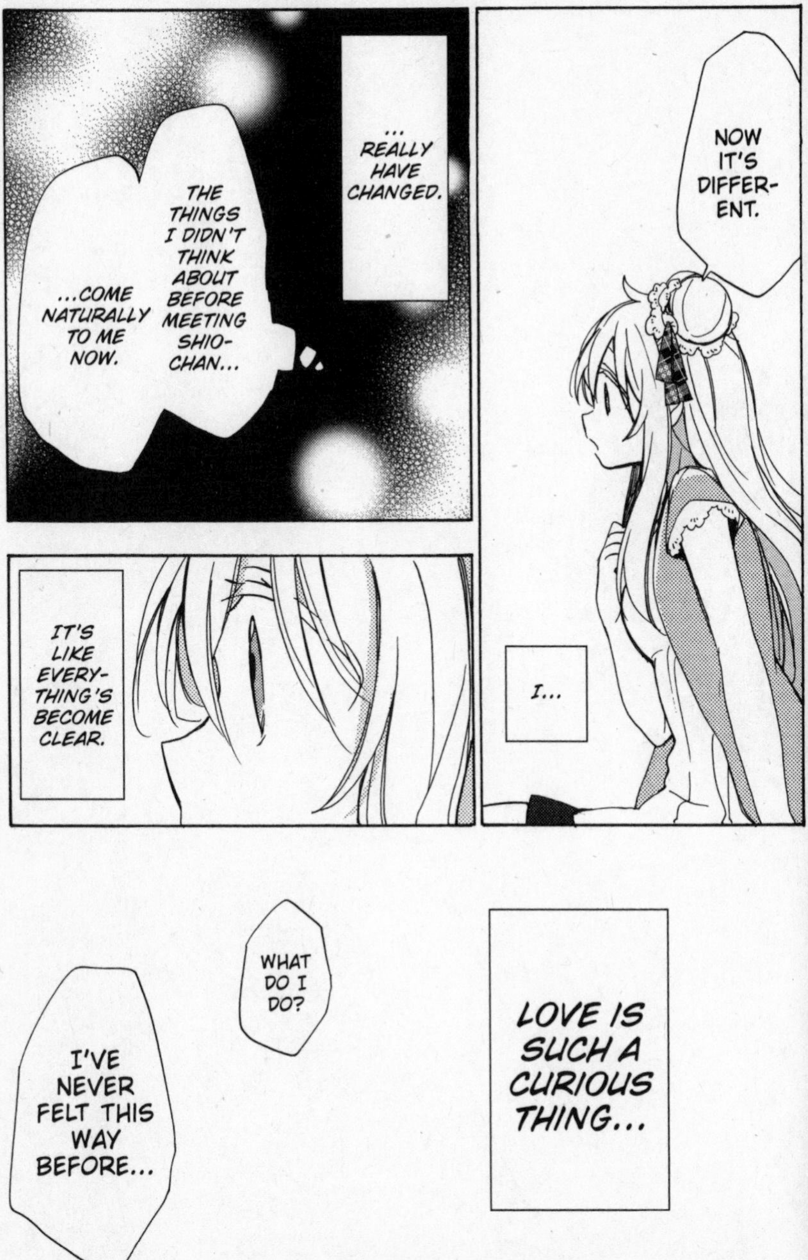
NOW IT'S DIFFER-ENT.
I...
...REALLY HAVE CHANGED.
THE THINGS I DIDN'T THINK ABOUT BEFORE MEETING SHIO-CHAN...
...COME NATURALLY TO ME NOW.
IT'S LIKE EVERY-THING'S BECOME CLEAR.
LOVE IS SUCH A CURIOUS THING...
WHAT DO I DO?
I'VE NEVER FELT THIS WAY BEFORE...

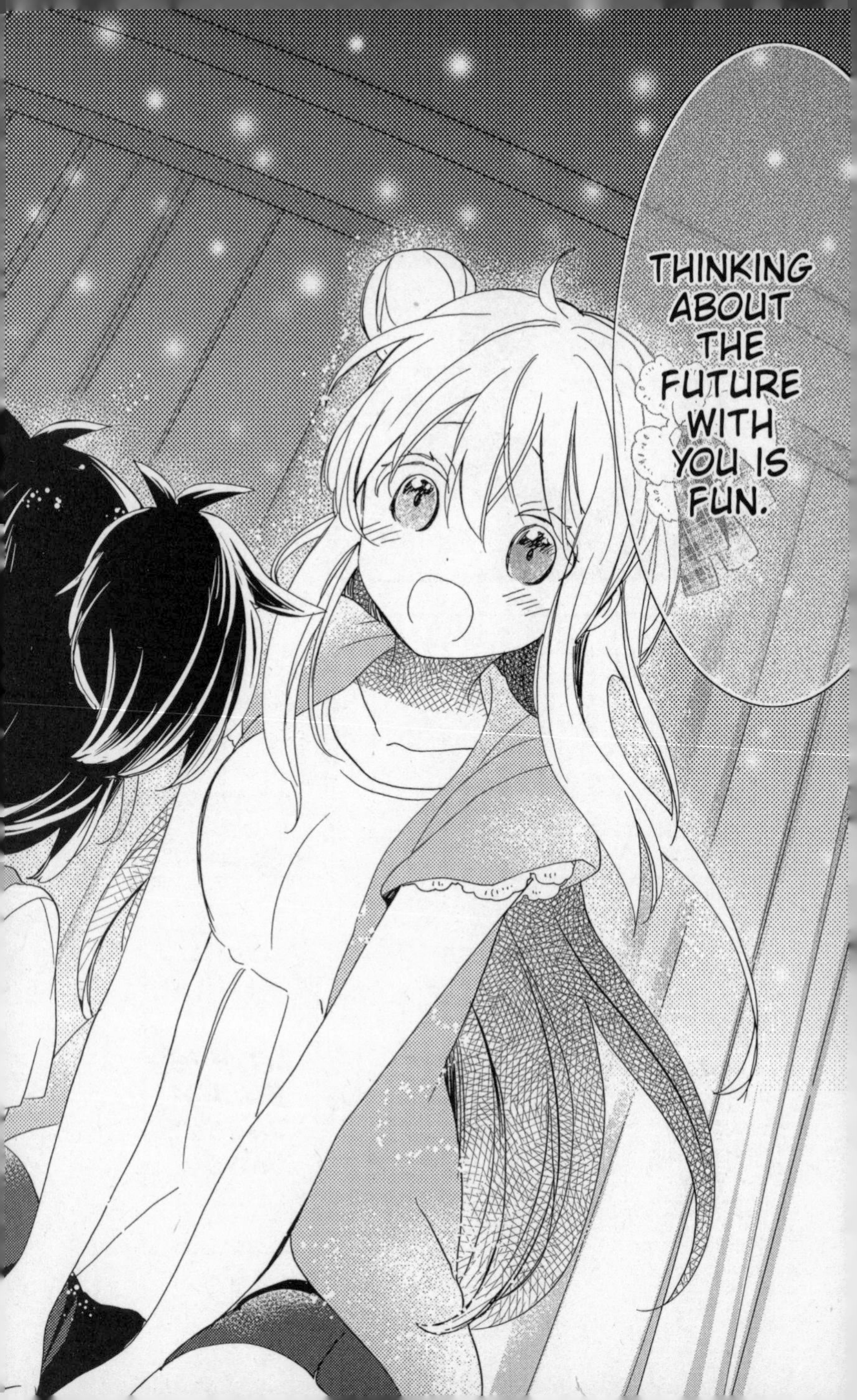
THINKING ABOUT THE FUTURE WITH YOU IS FUN.

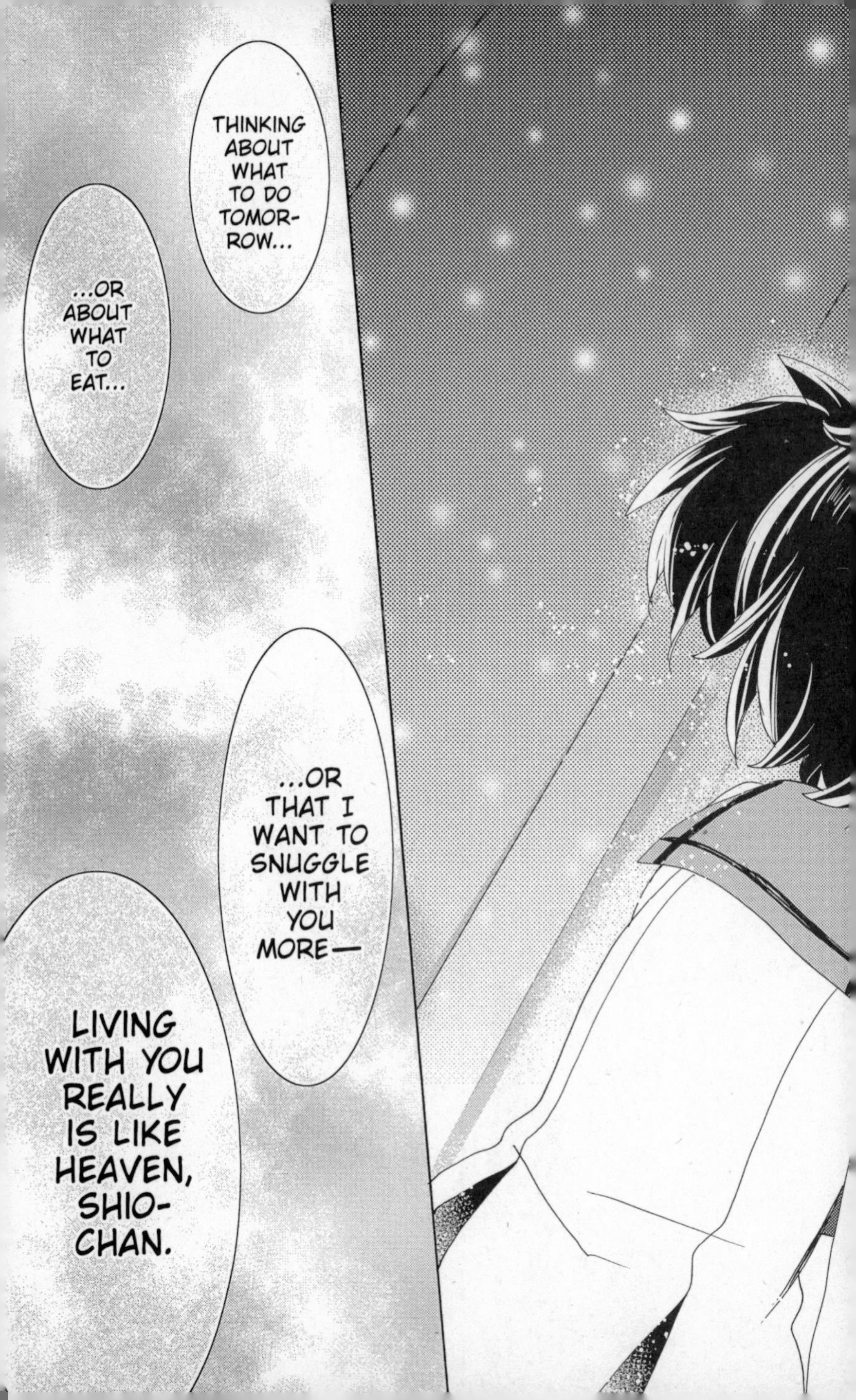
THINKING ABOUT WHAT TO DO TOMORROW...
...OR ABOUT WHAT TO EAT...
...OR THAT I WANT TO SNUGGLE WITH YOU MORE—
LIVING WITH YOU REALLY IS LIKE HEAVEN, SHIO-CHAN.

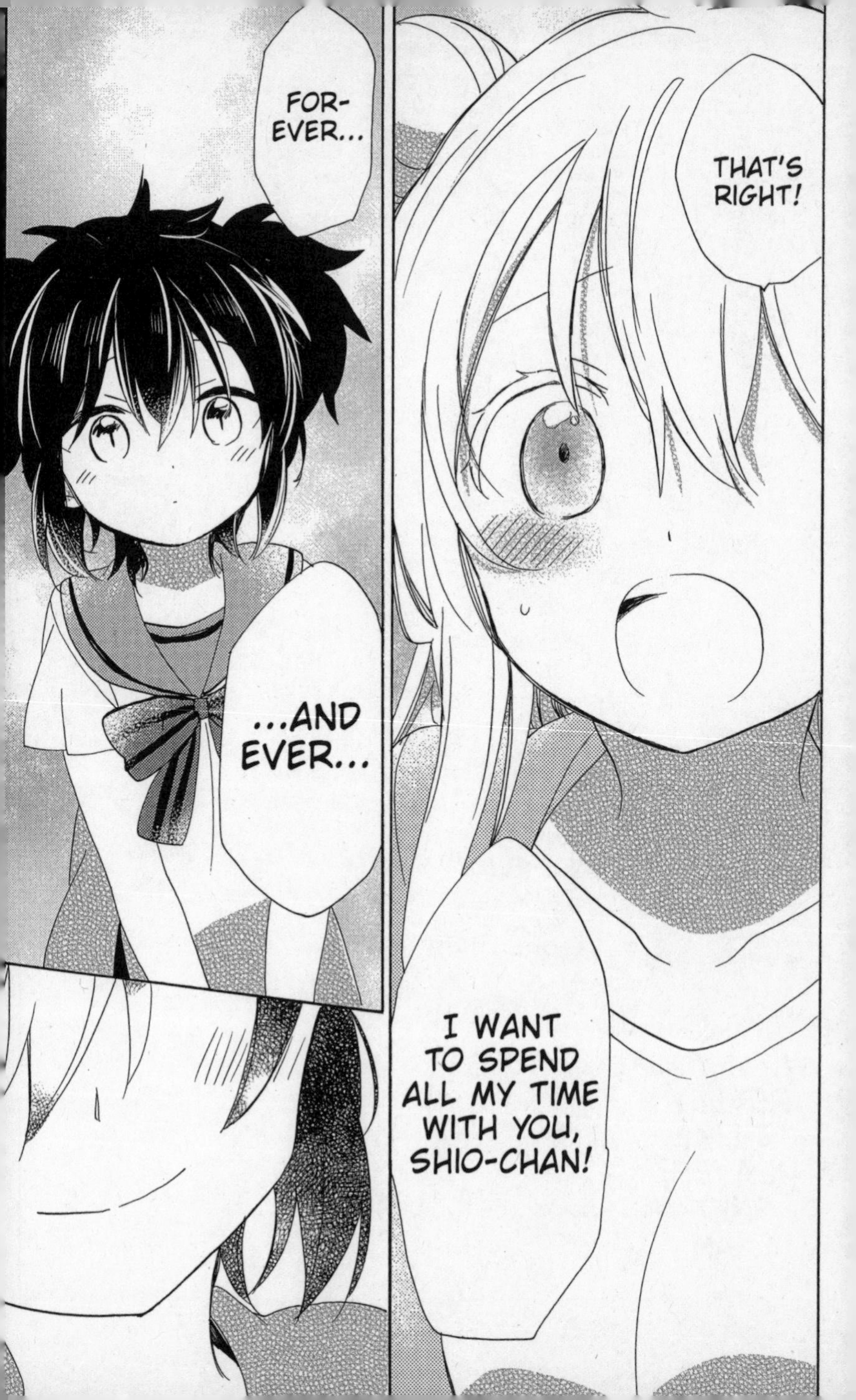
THAT'S RIGHT!
I WANT TO SPEND ALL MY TIME WITH YOU, SHIO-CHAN!
FOR-EVER...
...AND EVER...

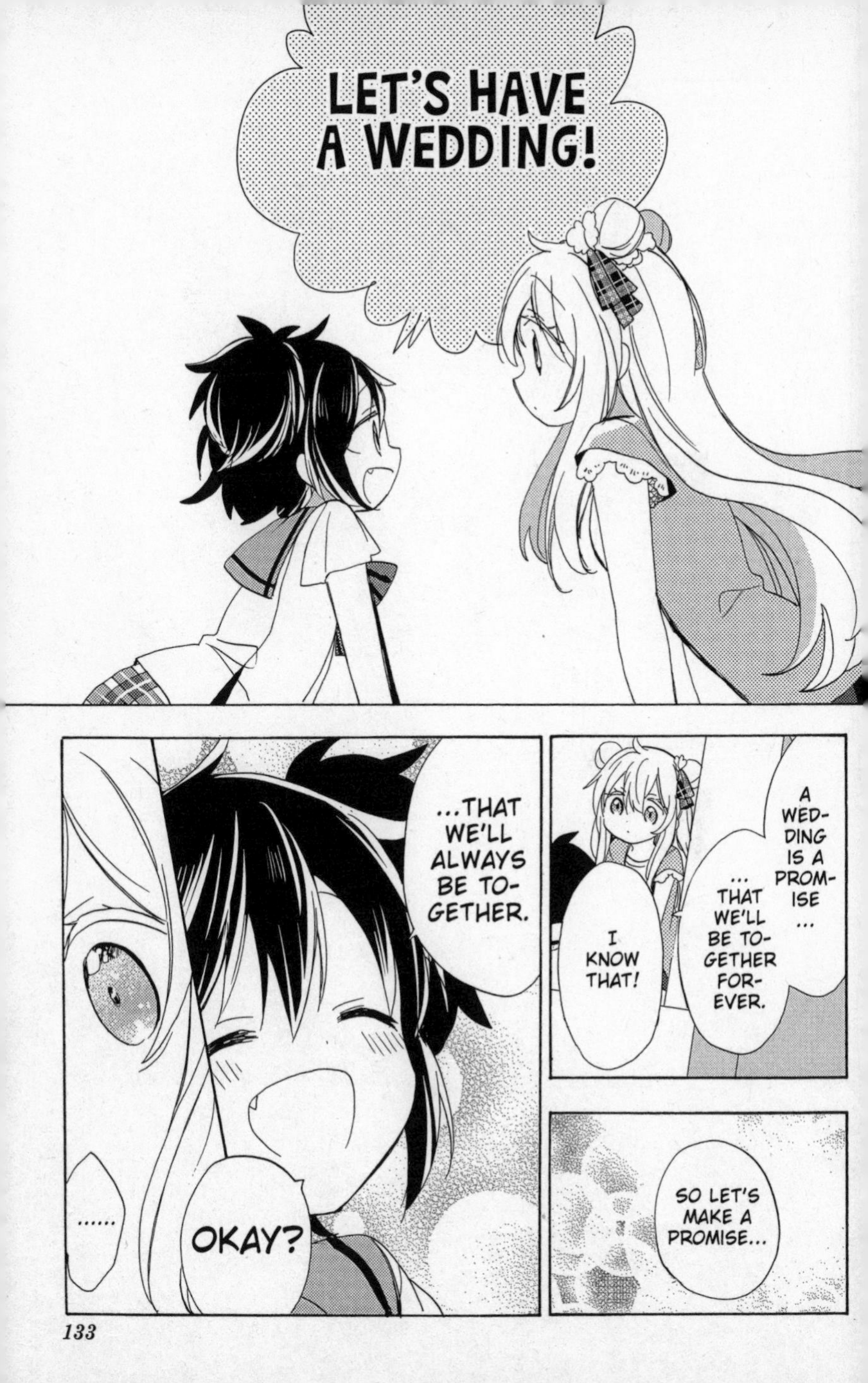
LET'S HAVE A WEDDING!
A WEDDING IS A PROMISE...
...THAT WE'LL BE TOGETHER FOREVER.
I KNOW THAT!
SO LET'S MAKE A PROMISE...
...THAT WE'LL ALWAYS BE TOGETHER.
OKAY?
......

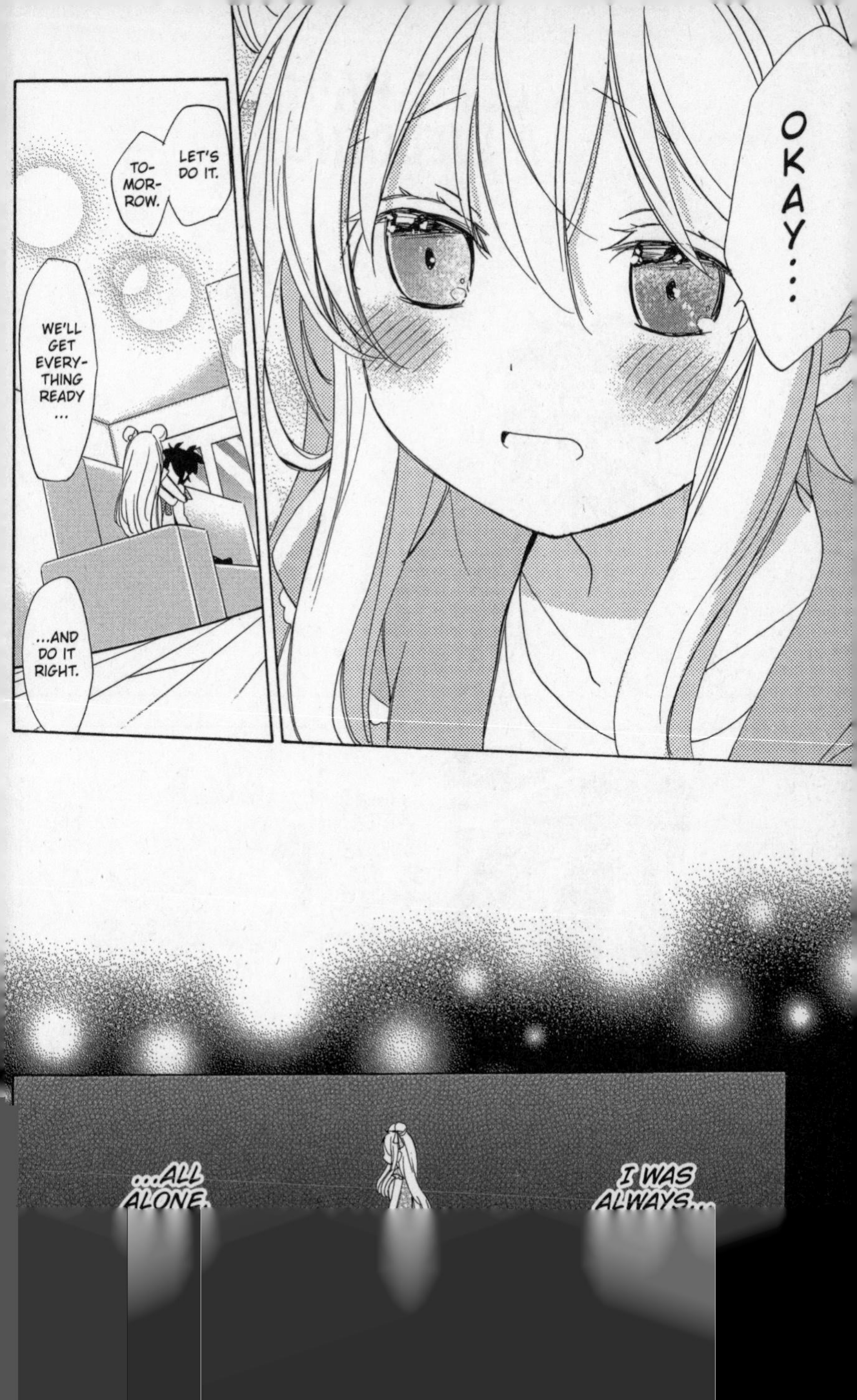
OKAY...
TO-MOR-ROW. LET'S DO IT.
WE'LL GET EVERY-THING READY ...
...AND DO IT RIGHT.
I WAS ALWAYS...
...ALL ALONE.

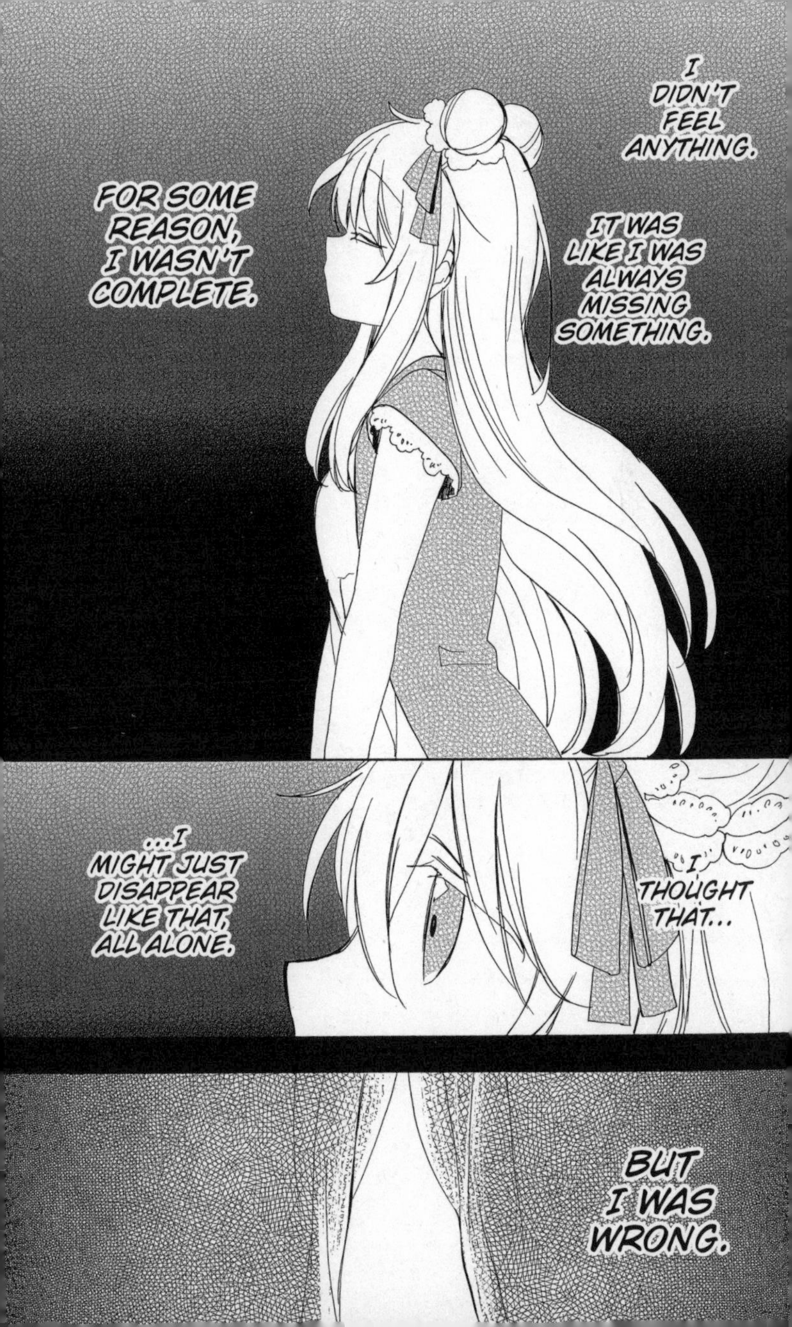
I DIDN'T FEEL ANYTHING.
IT WAS LIKE I WAS ALWAYS MISSING SOMETHING.
FOR SOME REASON, I WASN'T COMPLETE.
I THOUGHT THAT...
...I MIGHT JUST DISAPPEAR LIKE THAT, ALL ALONE.
BUT I WAS WRONG.

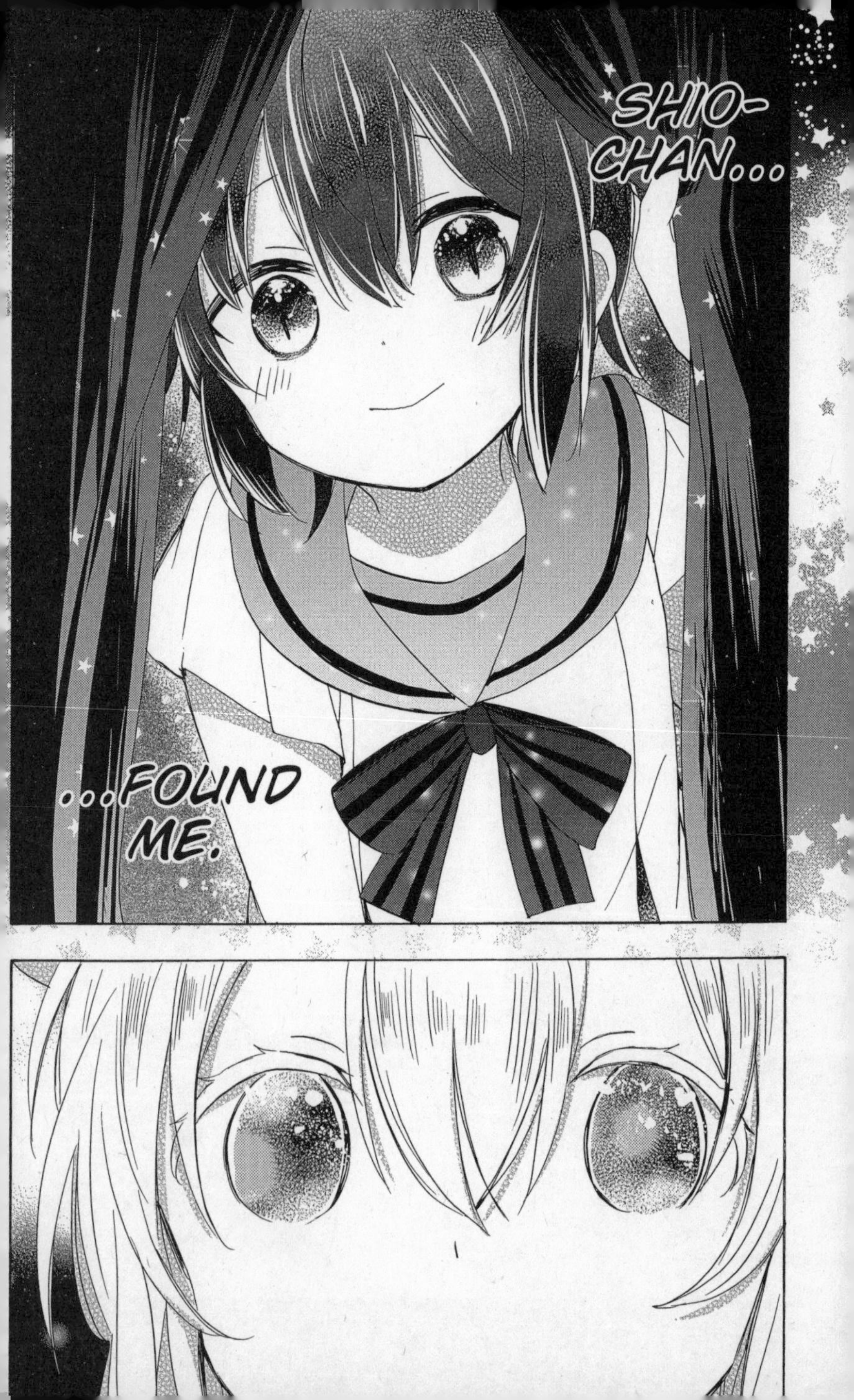
SHIO-CHAN...
...FOUND ME.

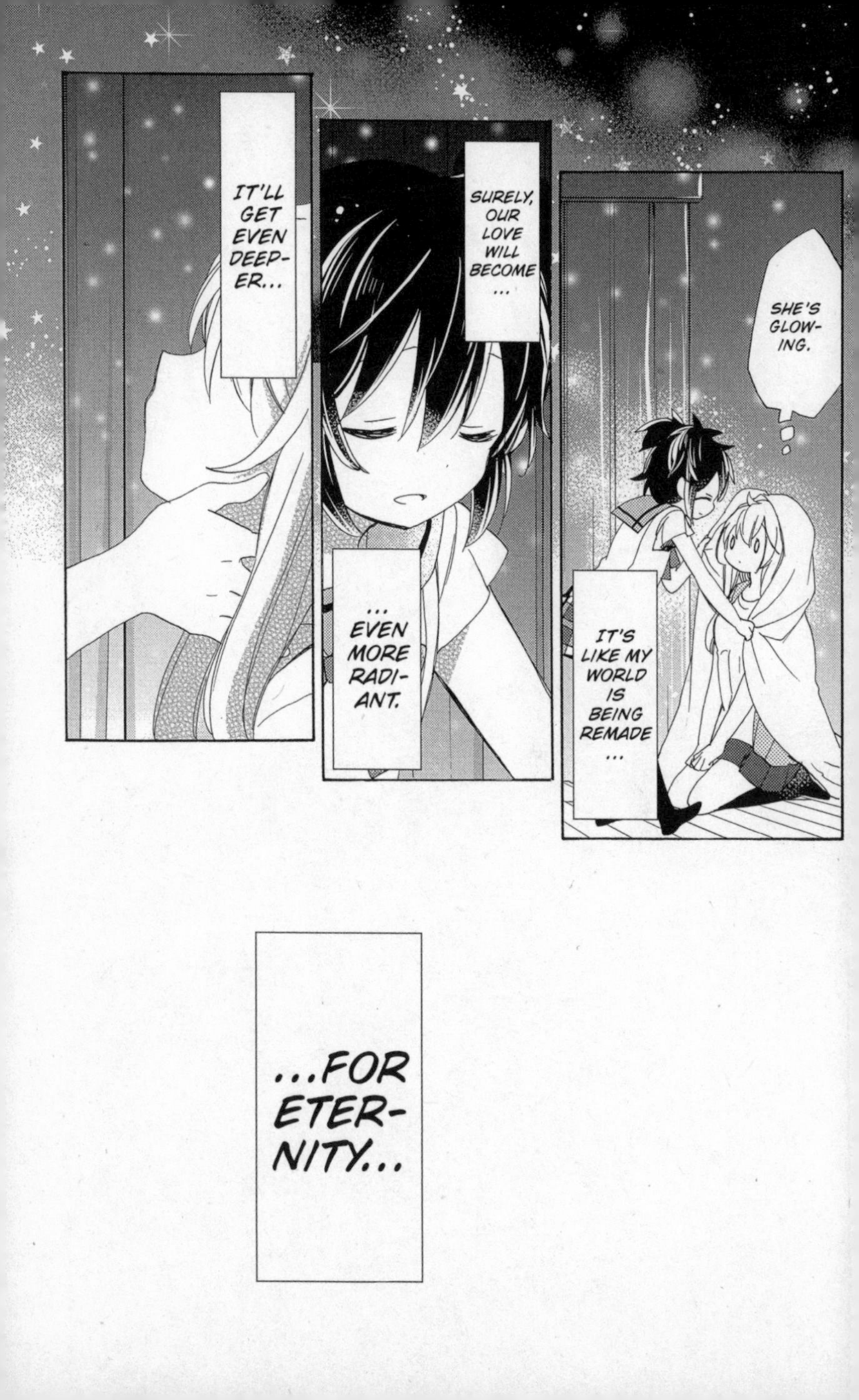
SHE'S GLOWING.
IT'S LIKE MY WORLD IS BEING REMADE...
SURELY, OUR LOVE WILL BECOME...
...EVEN MORE RADIANT.
IT'LL GET EVEN DEEPER...
...FOR ETERNITY...

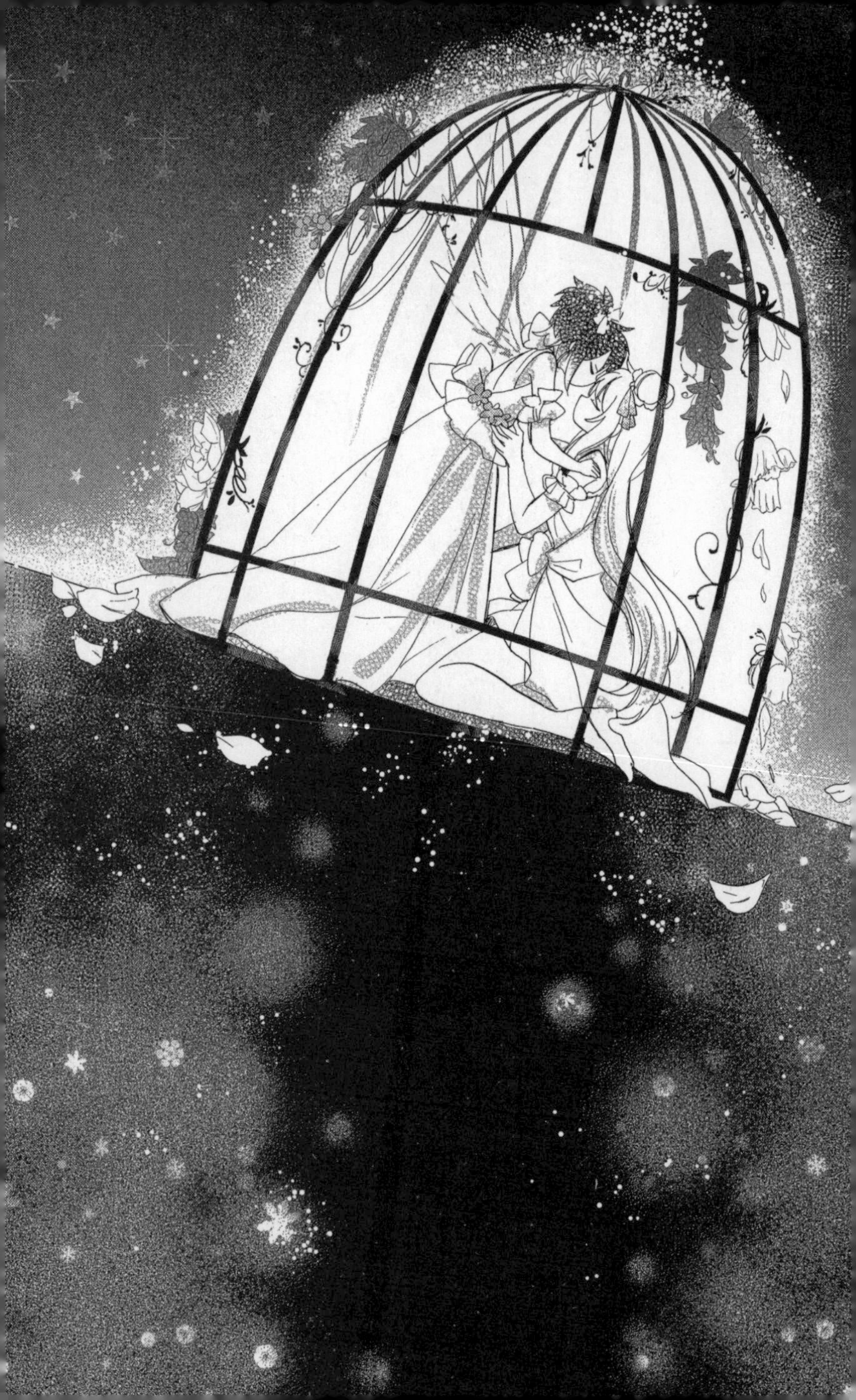

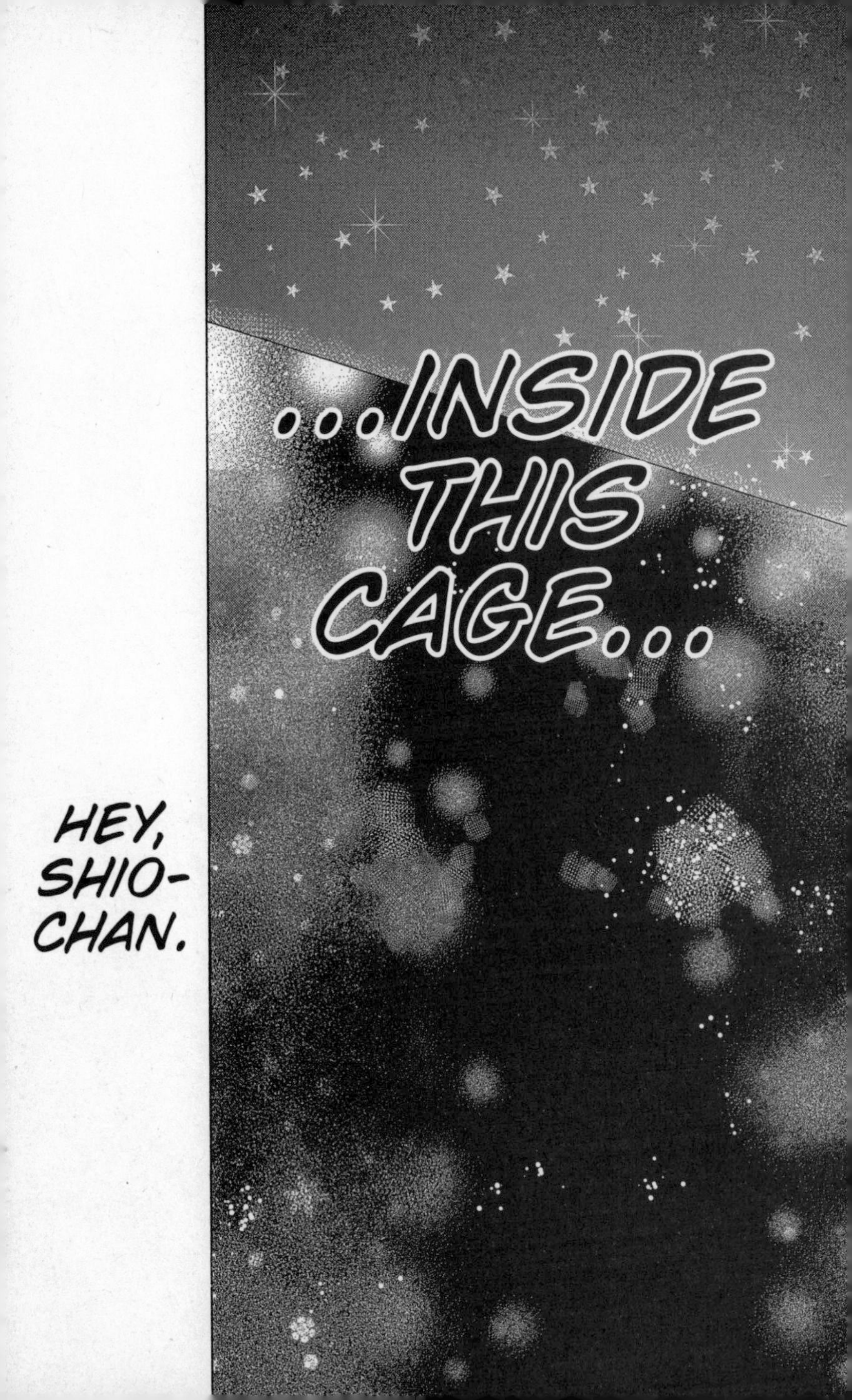
...INSIDE THIS CAGE...
HEY, SHIO-CHAN.

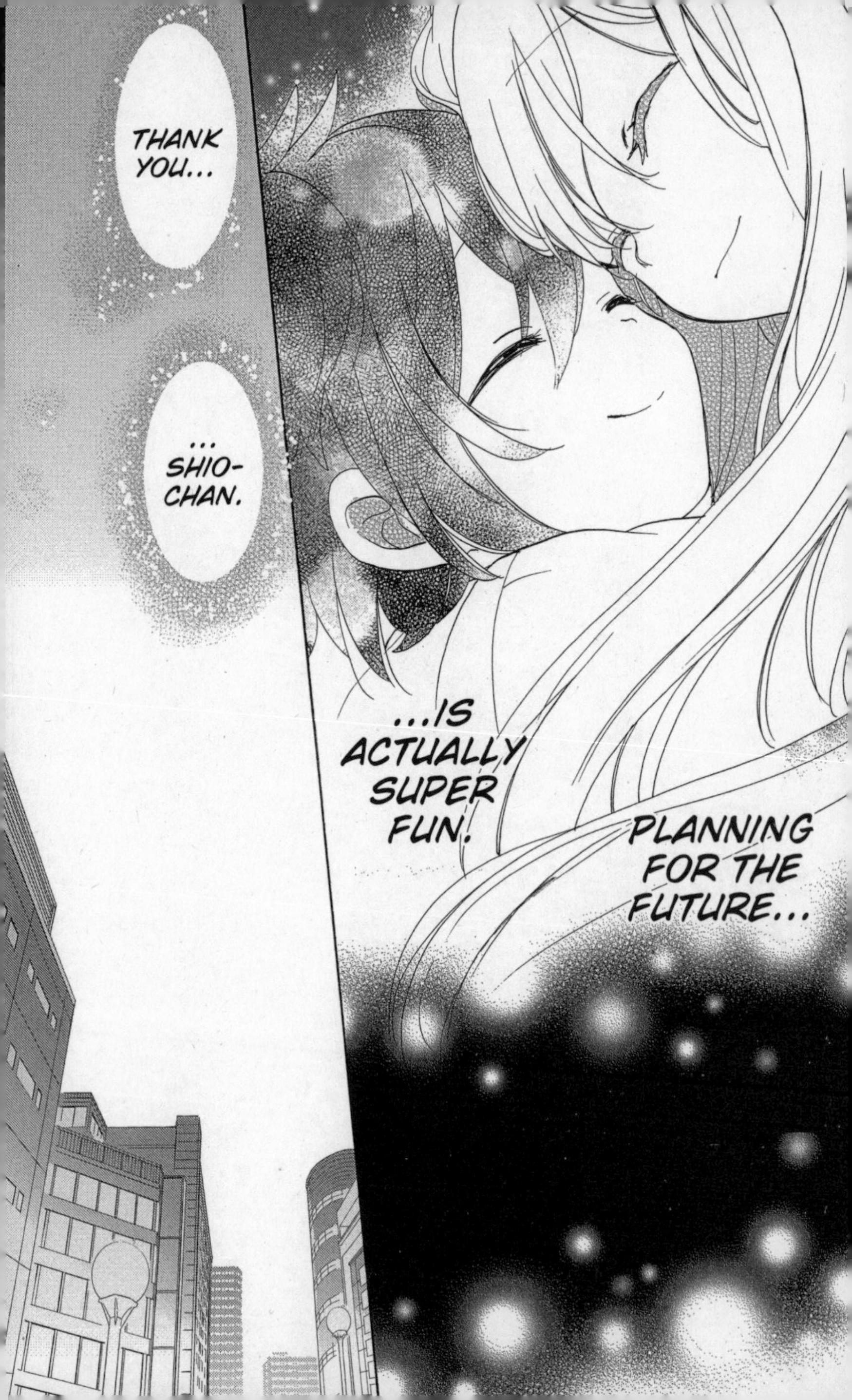
THANK YOU...
...SHIO-CHAN.
PLANNING FOR THE FUTURE...
...IS ACTUALLY SUPER FUN.

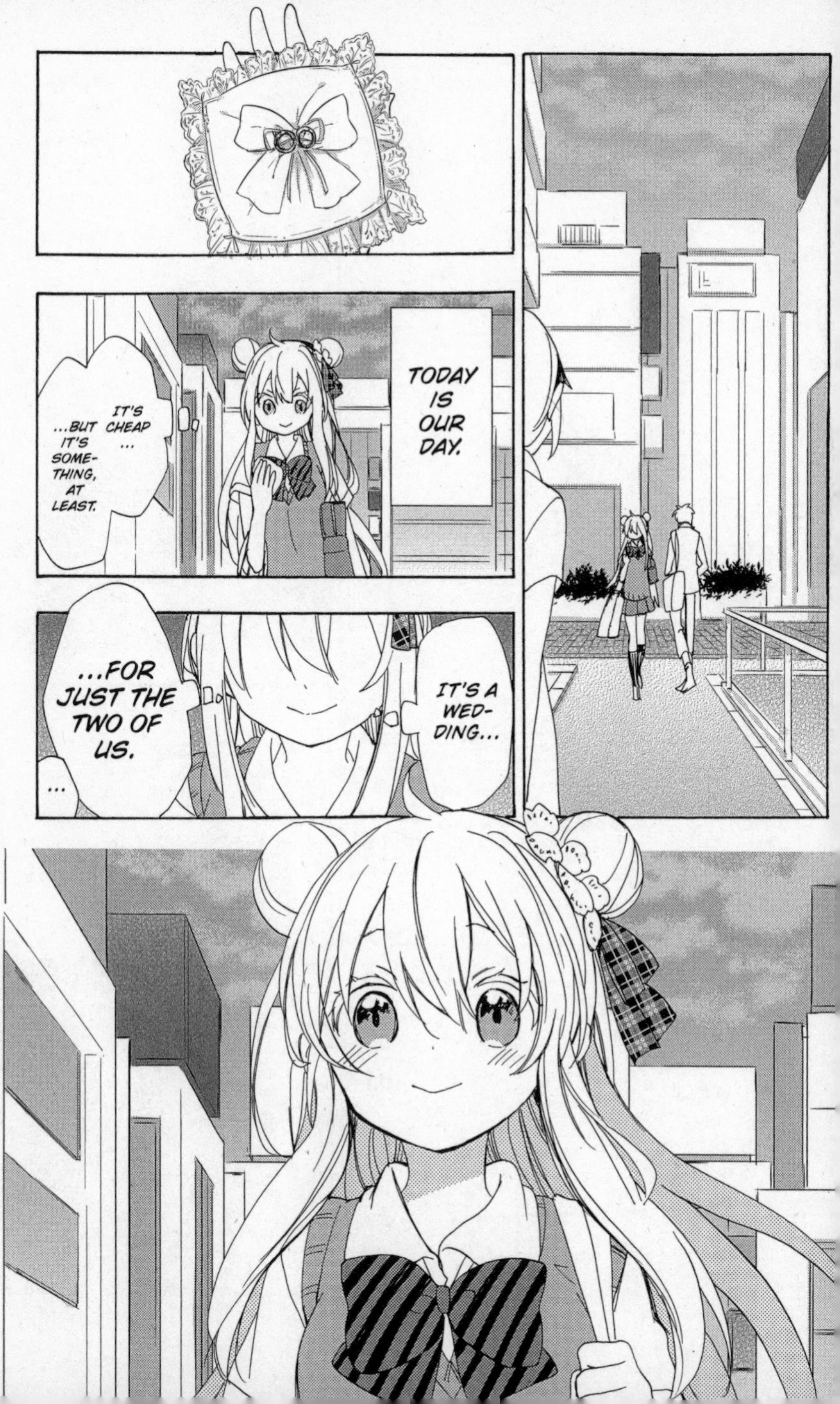
TODAY IS OUR DAY.
IT'S CHEAP...
...BUT IT'S SOMETHING, AT LEAST.
IT'S A WEDDING...
...FOR JUST THE TWO OF US.
...

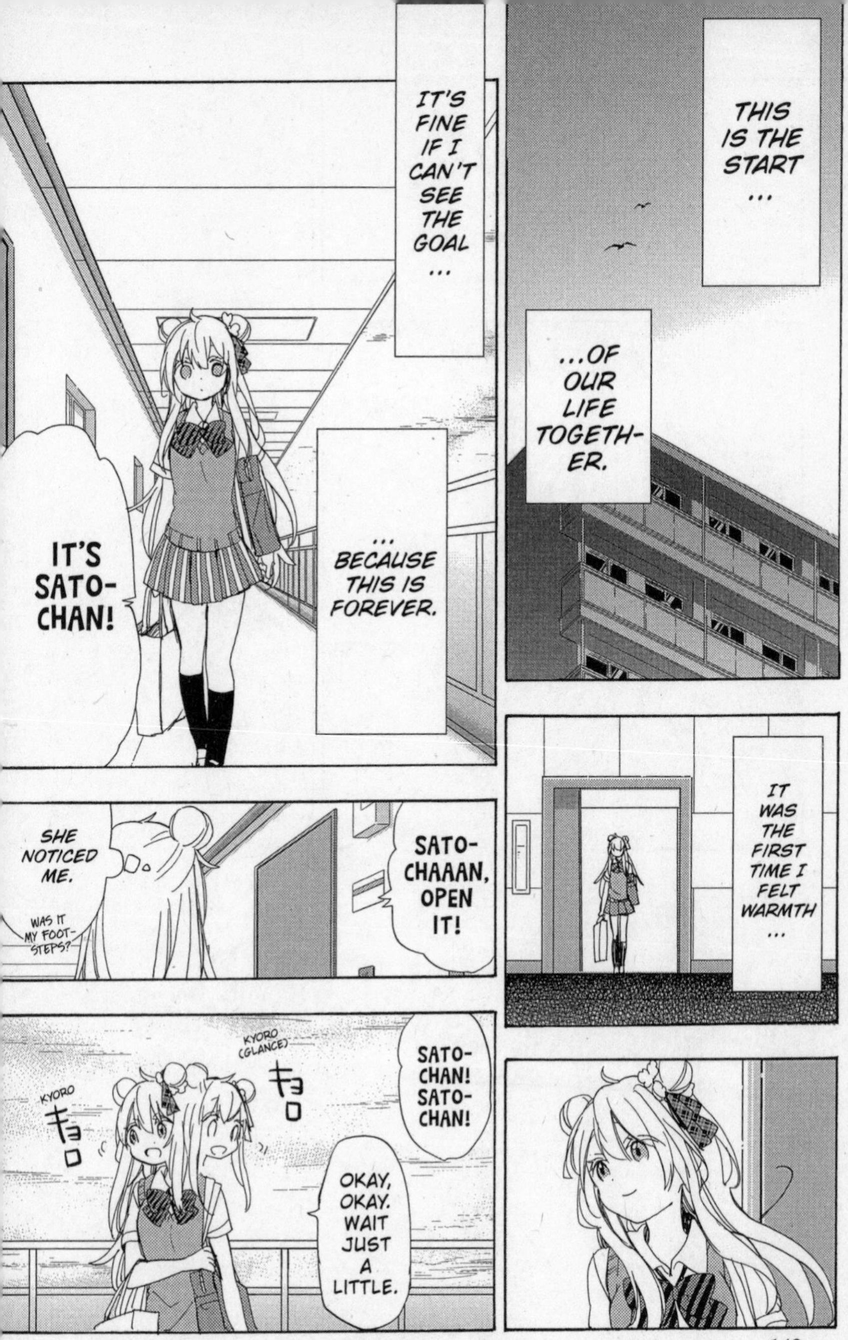
THIS IS THE START...
...OF OUR LIFE TOGETHER.
IT'S FINE IF I CAN'T SEE THE GOAL...
...BECAUSE THIS IS FOREVER.
IT'S SATO-CHAN!
IT WAS THE FIRST TIME I FELT WARMTH...
SATO-CHAAAN, OPEN IT!
SHE NOTICED ME.
WAS IT MY FOOTSTEPS?
SATO-CHAN! SATO-CHAN!
OKAY, OKAY. WAIT JUST A LITTLE.
KYORO (GLANCE)
キョロ
KYORO
キョロ

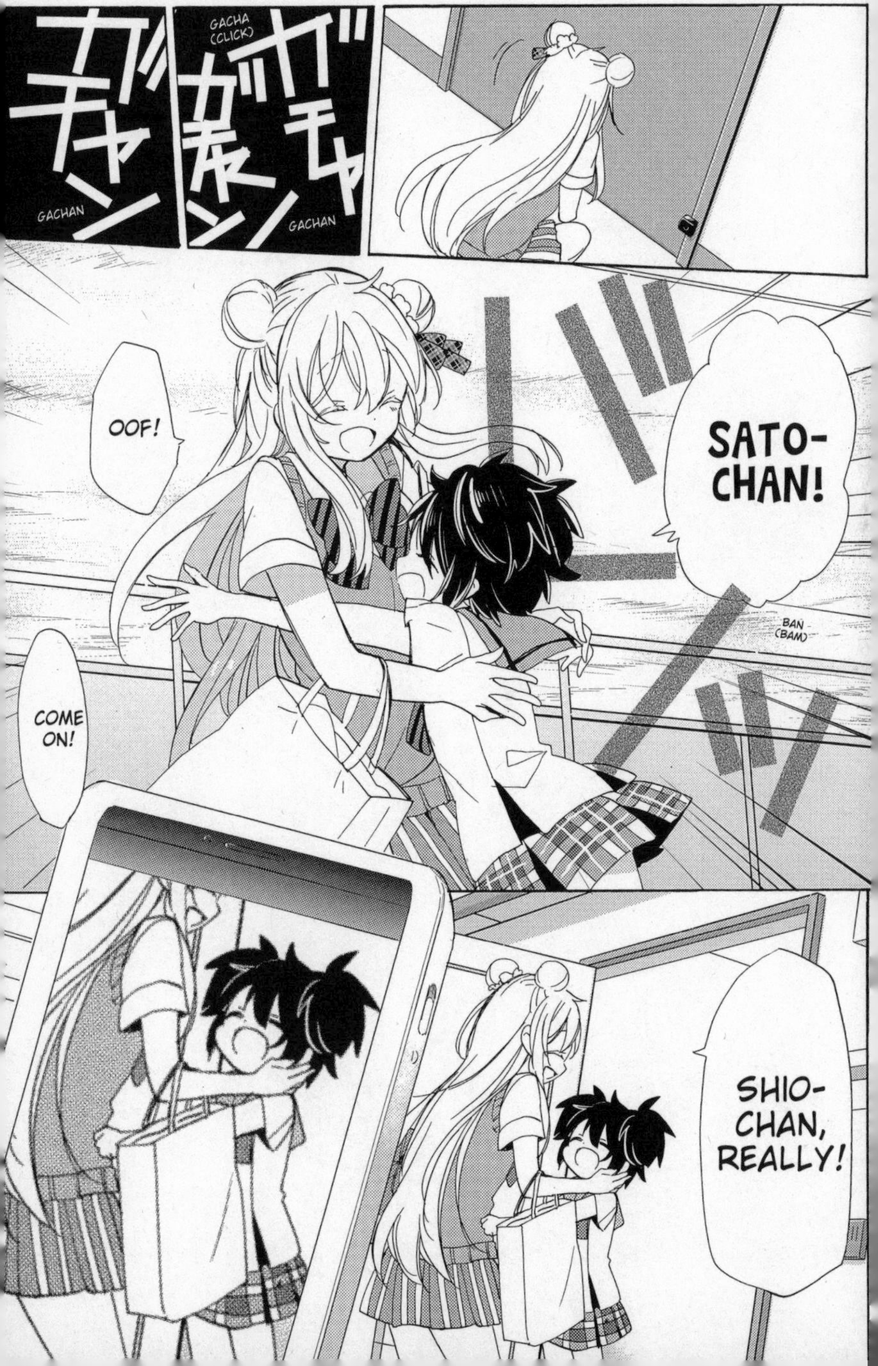
GACHA (CLICK)
GACHAN
GACHAN
SATO-CHAN!
BAN (BAM)
OOF!
COME ON!
SHIO-CHAN, REALLY!

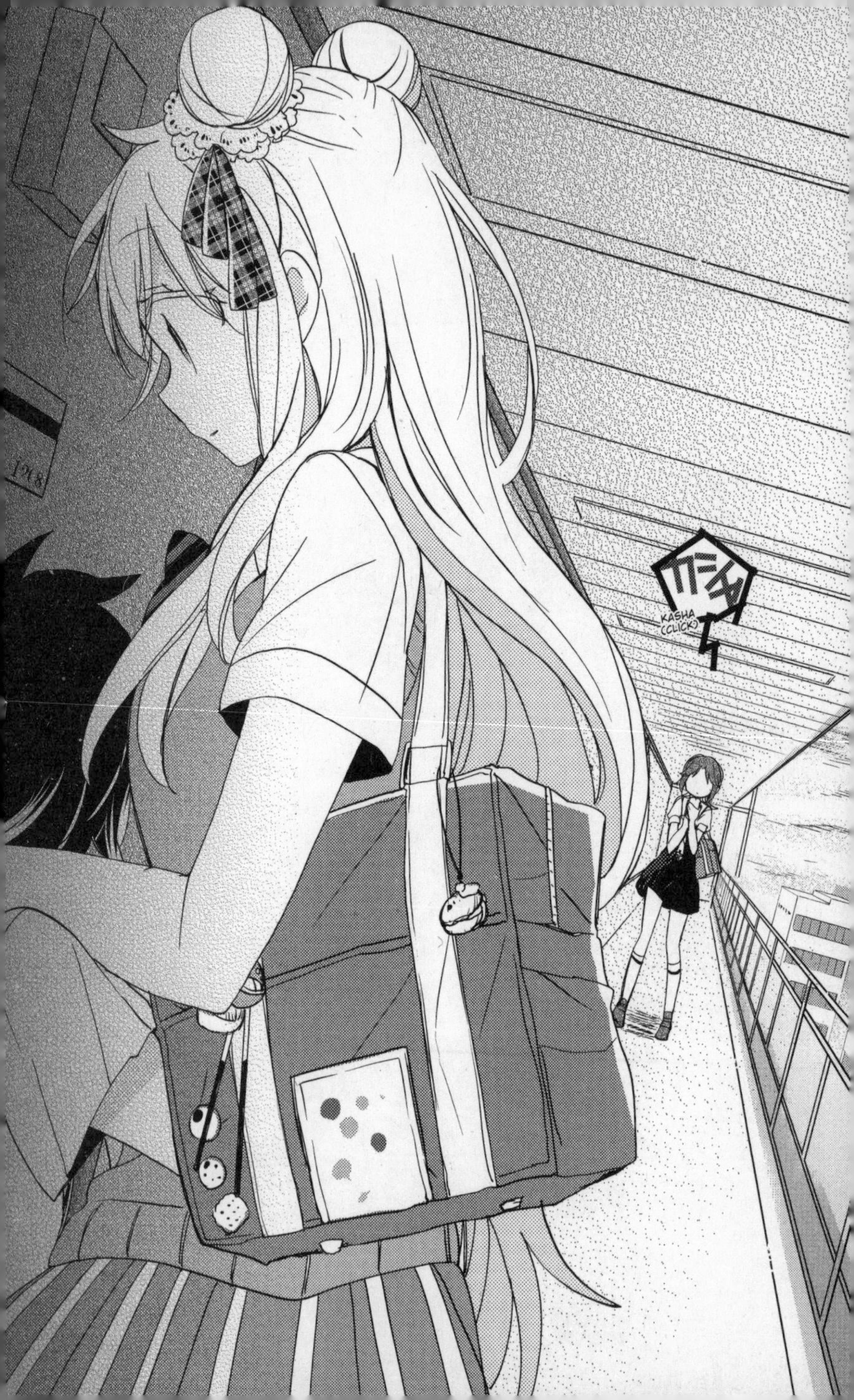
KASHA
(CLICK)

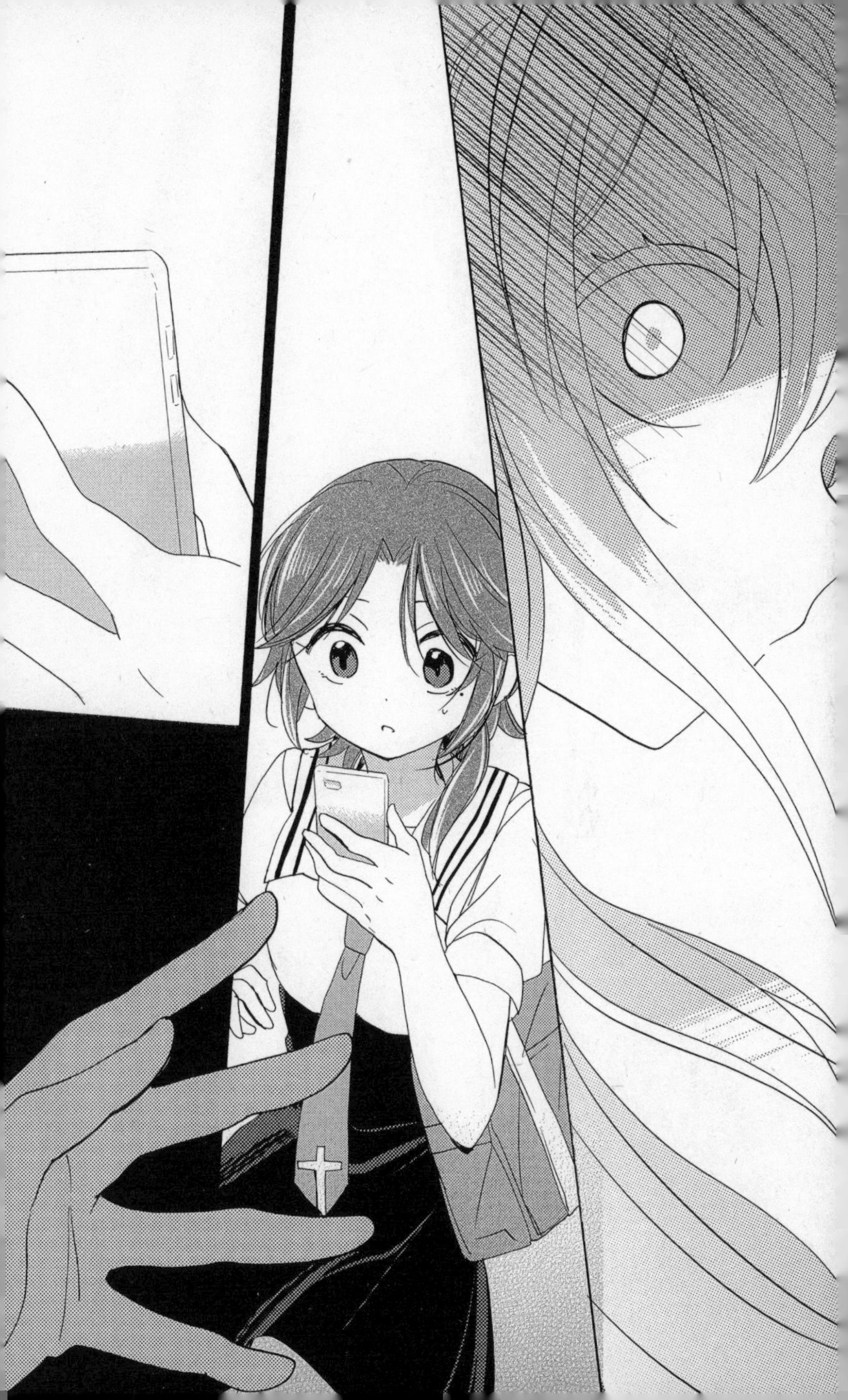

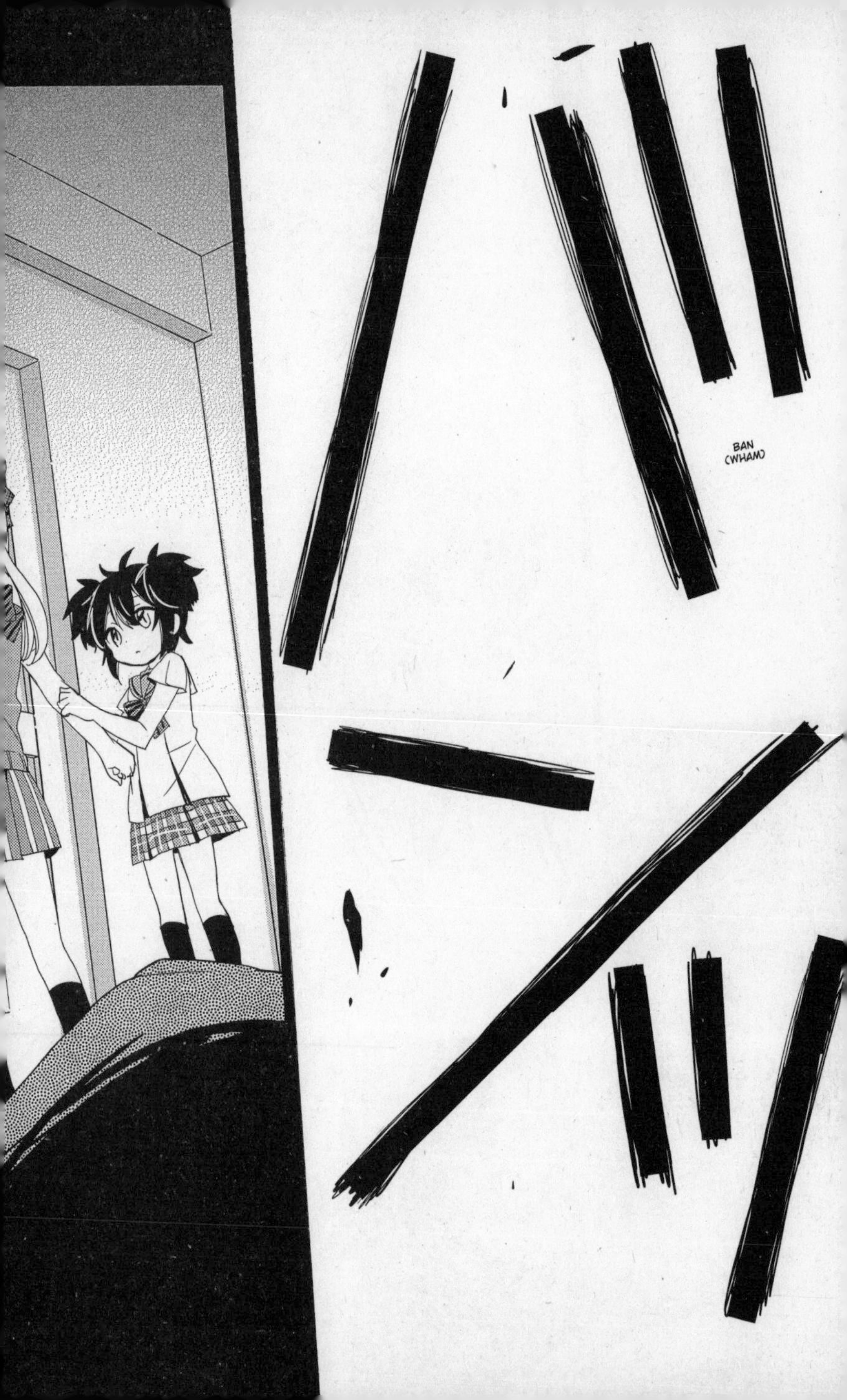
BAN
(WHAM)

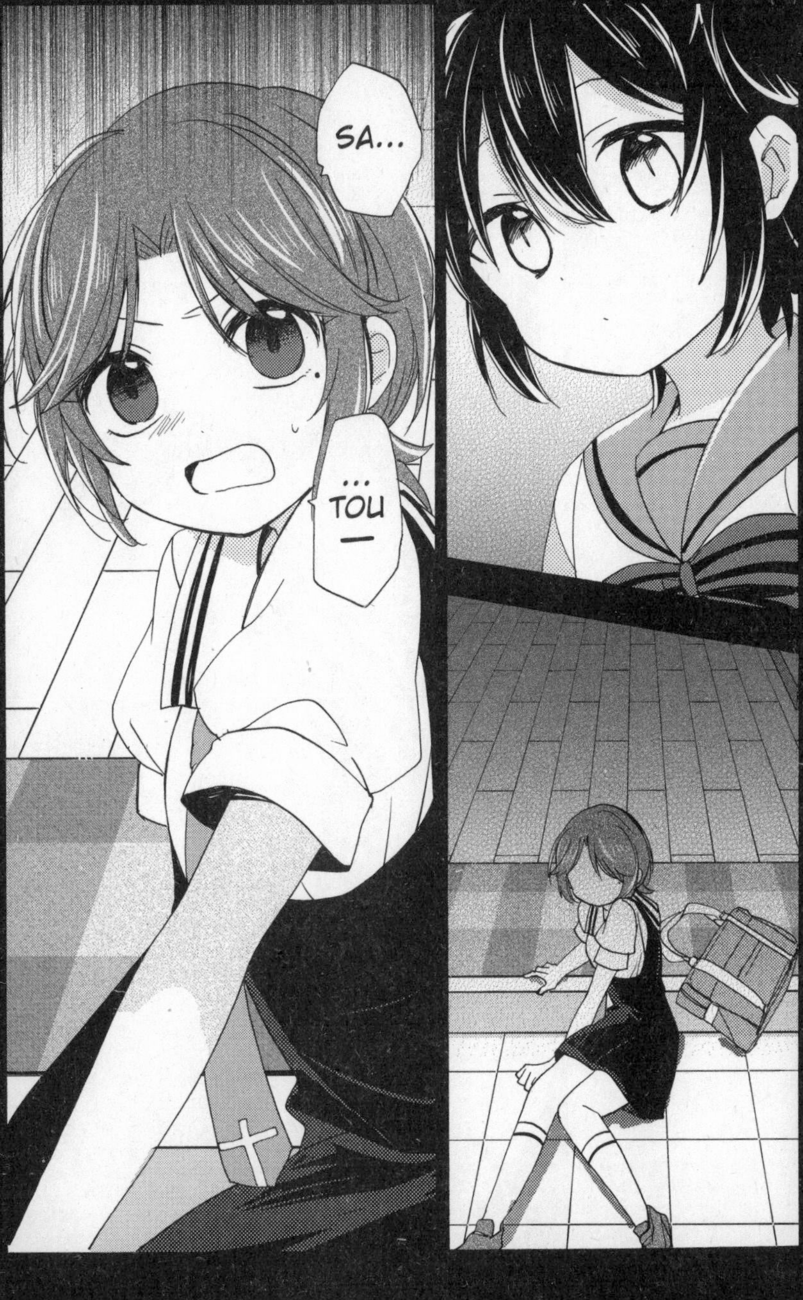
SA...
...TOU—

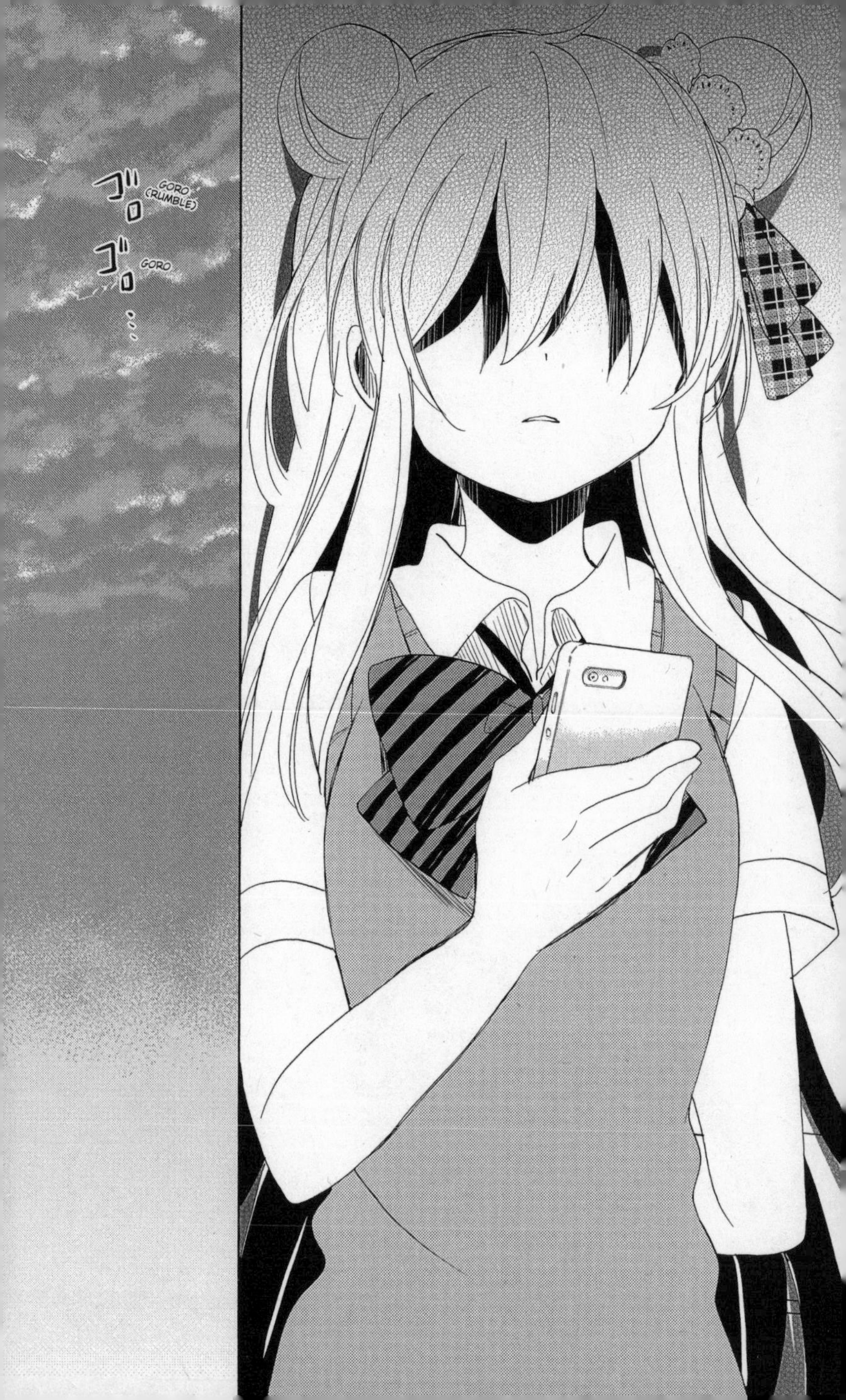
ゴロ GORO (RUMBLE)
ゴロ… GORO

Happy
Sugar
Life

Happy
Sugar
Life

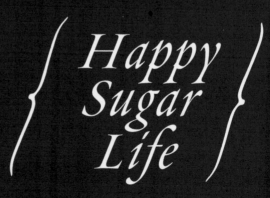

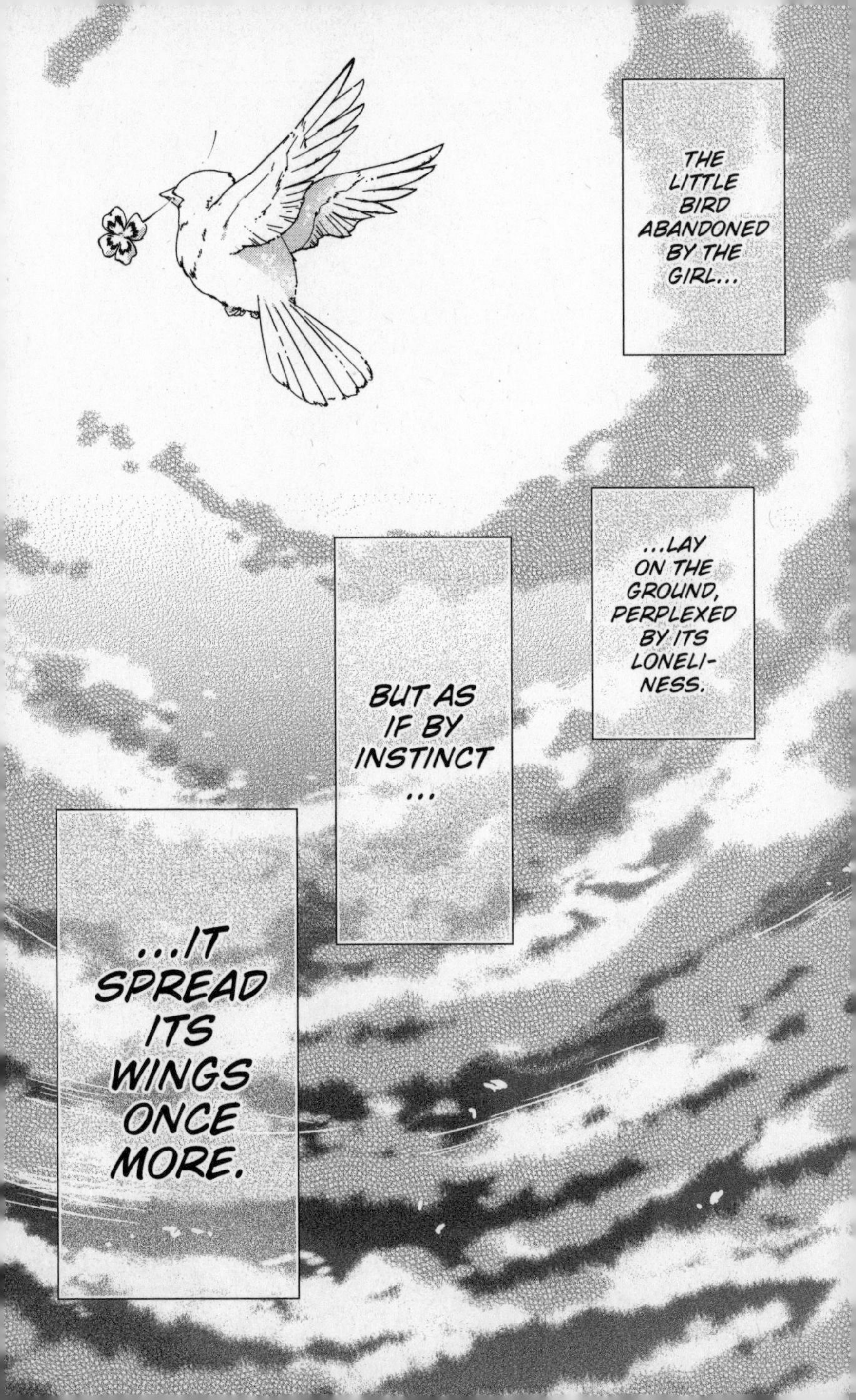
THE LITTLE BIRD ABANDONED BY THE GIRL...
...LAY ON THE GROUND, PERPLEXED BY ITS LONELI-NESS.
BUT AS IF BY INSTINCT ...
...IT SPREAD ITS WINGS ONCE MORE.

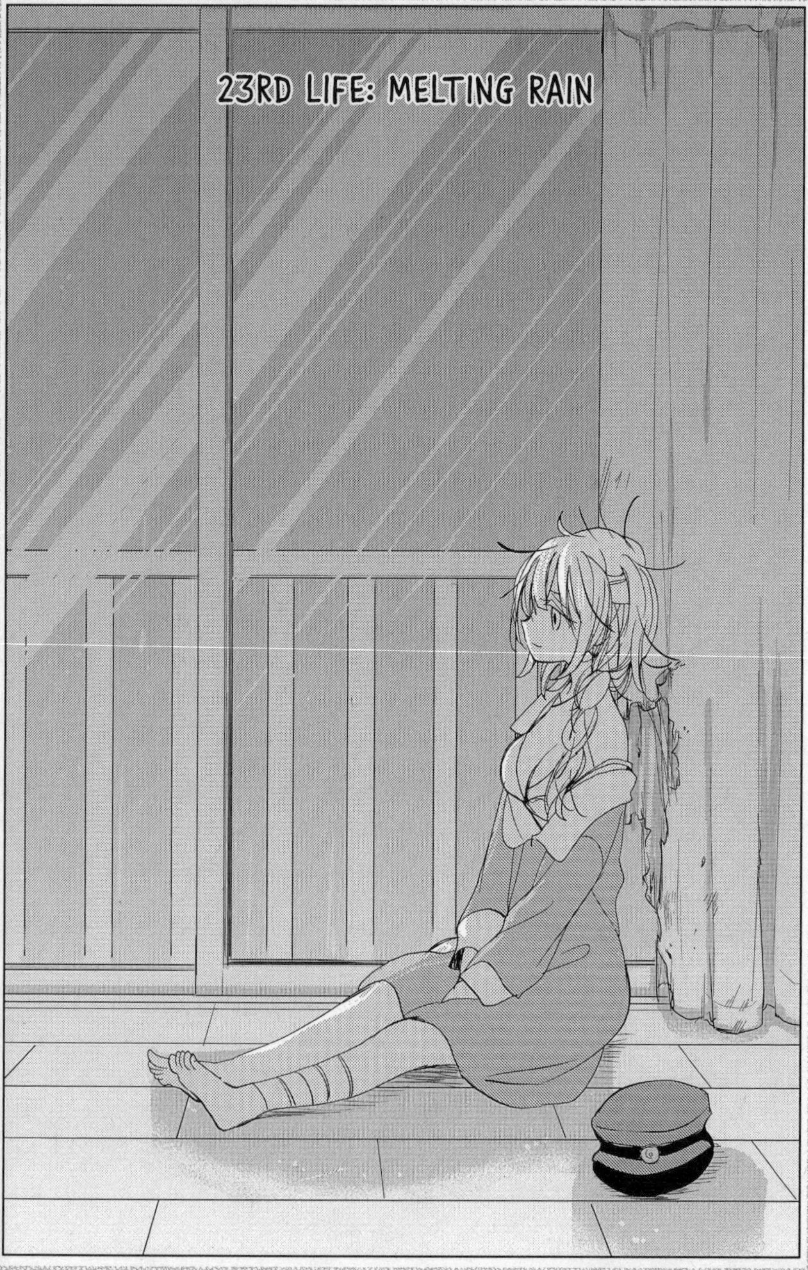
23RD LIFE: MELTING RAIN

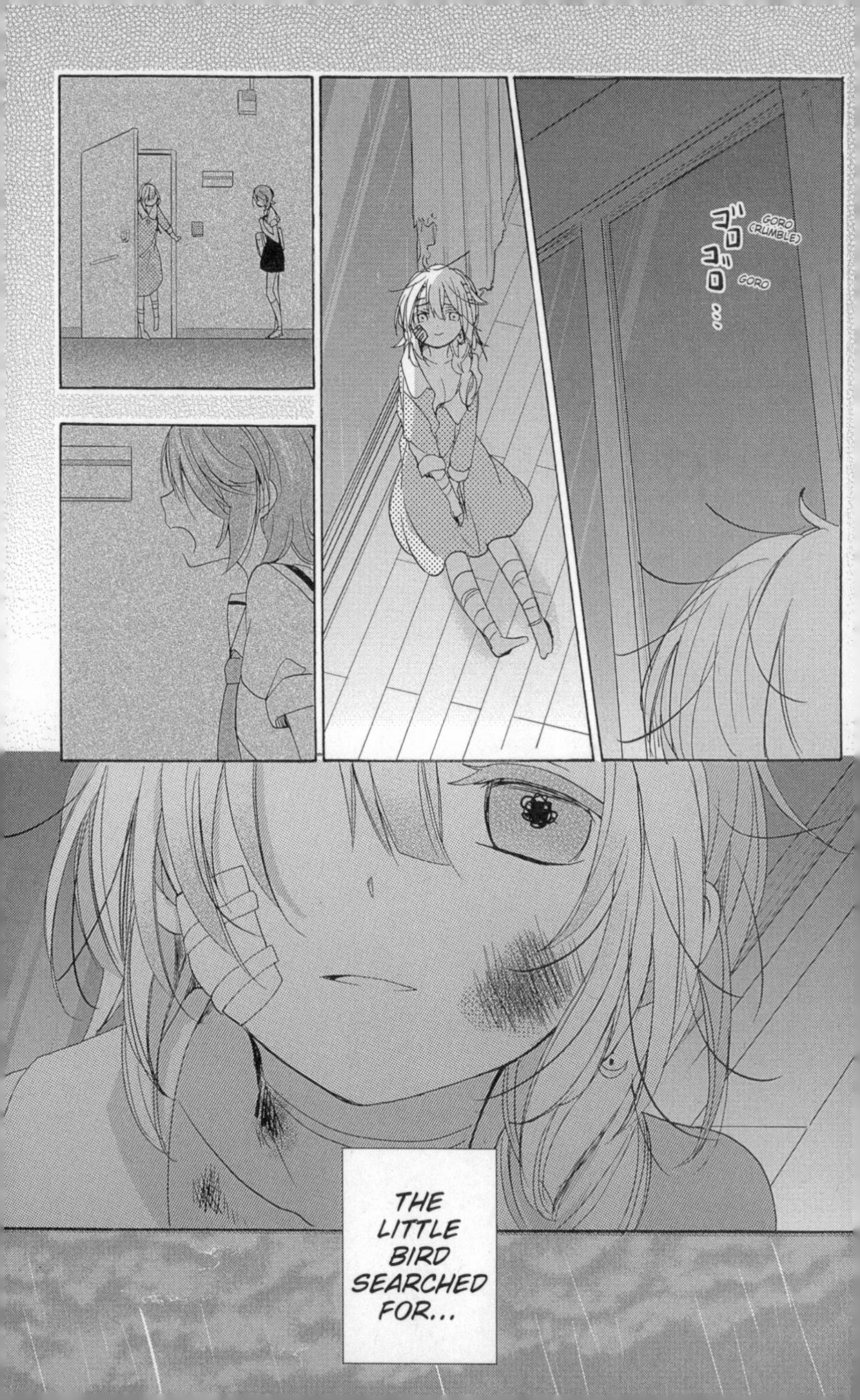
ゴロゴロ…
GORO (RUMBLE)
GORO
THE LITTLE BIRD SEARCHED FOR...

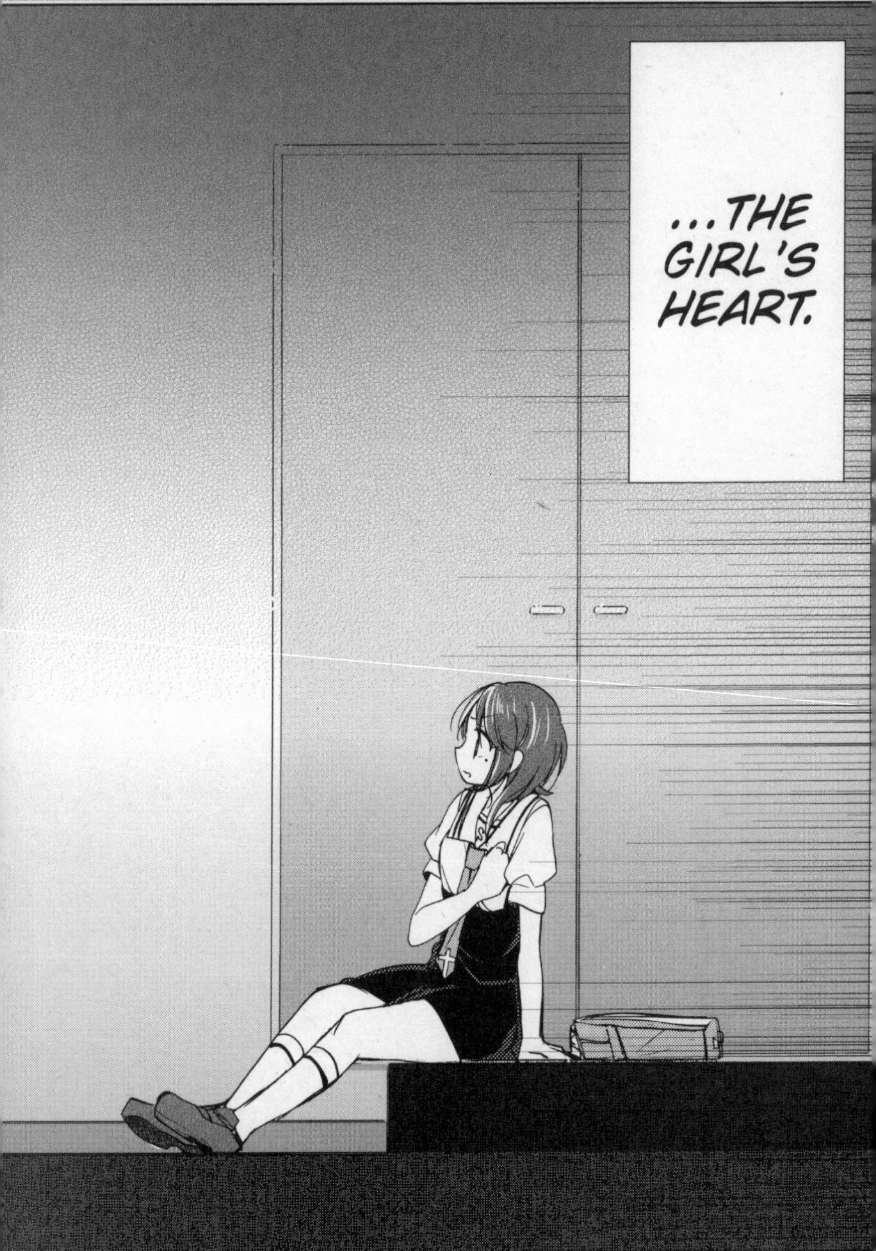
...THE GIRL'S HEART.

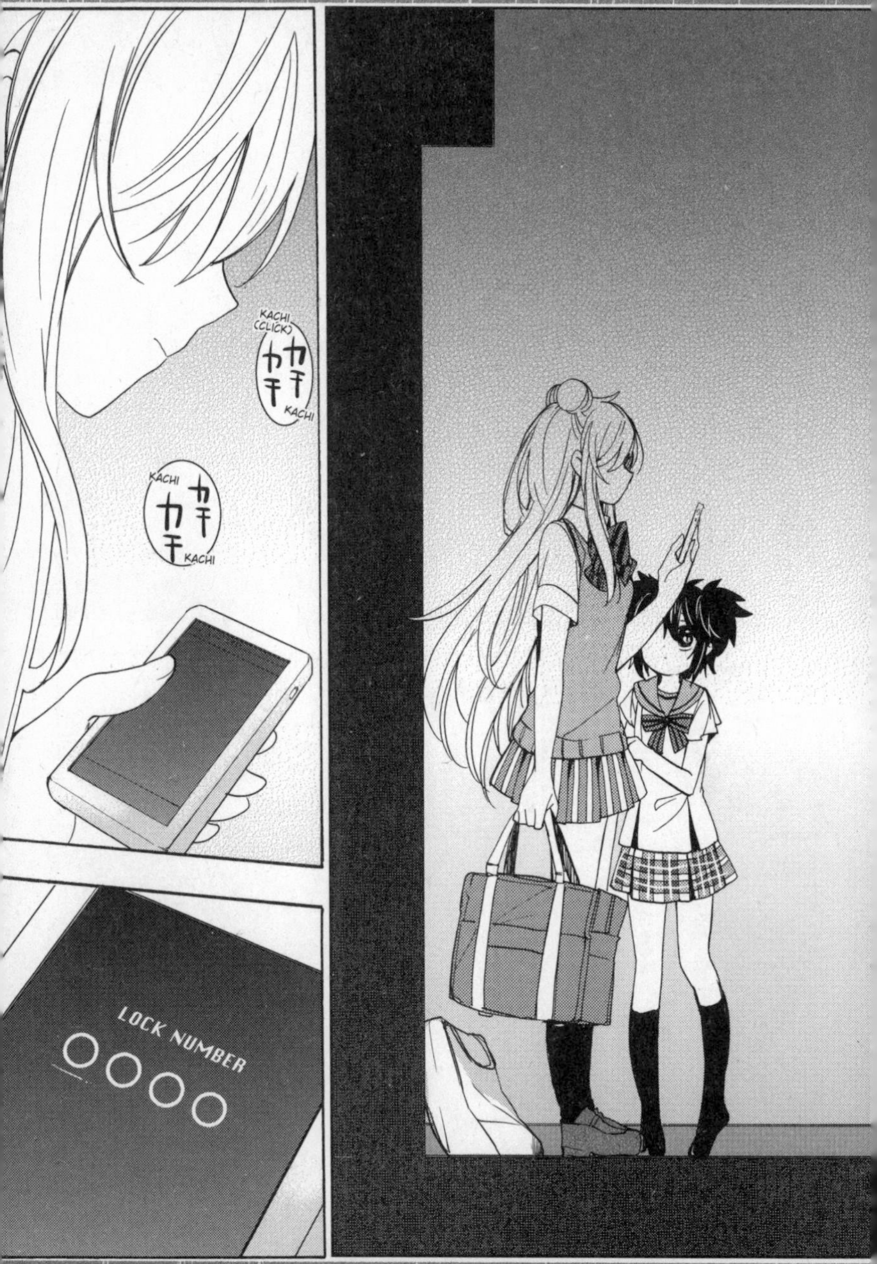
KACHI (CLICK)
カチカチ
KACHI
KACHI
カチカチ
KACHI
LOCK NUMBER

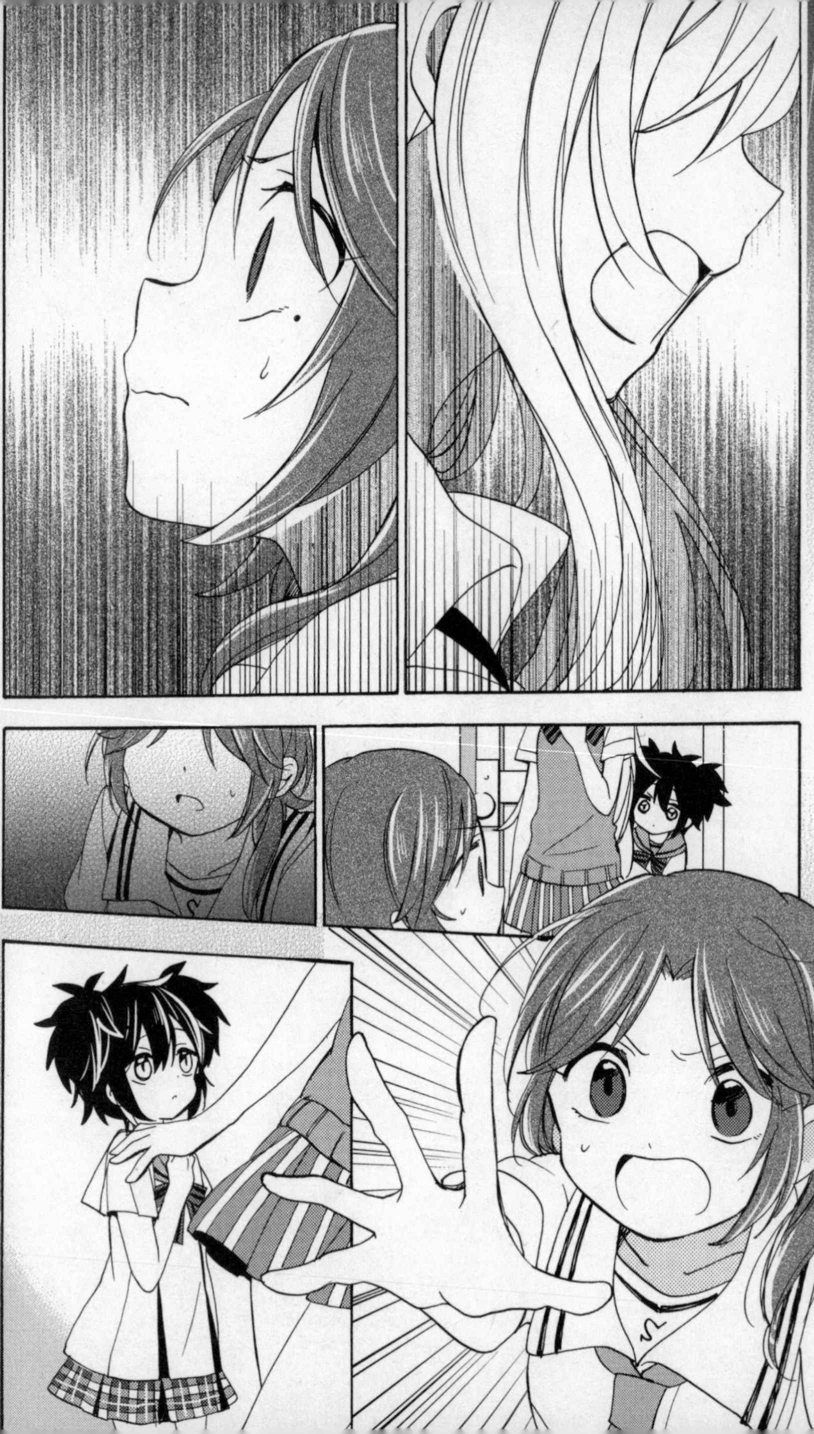

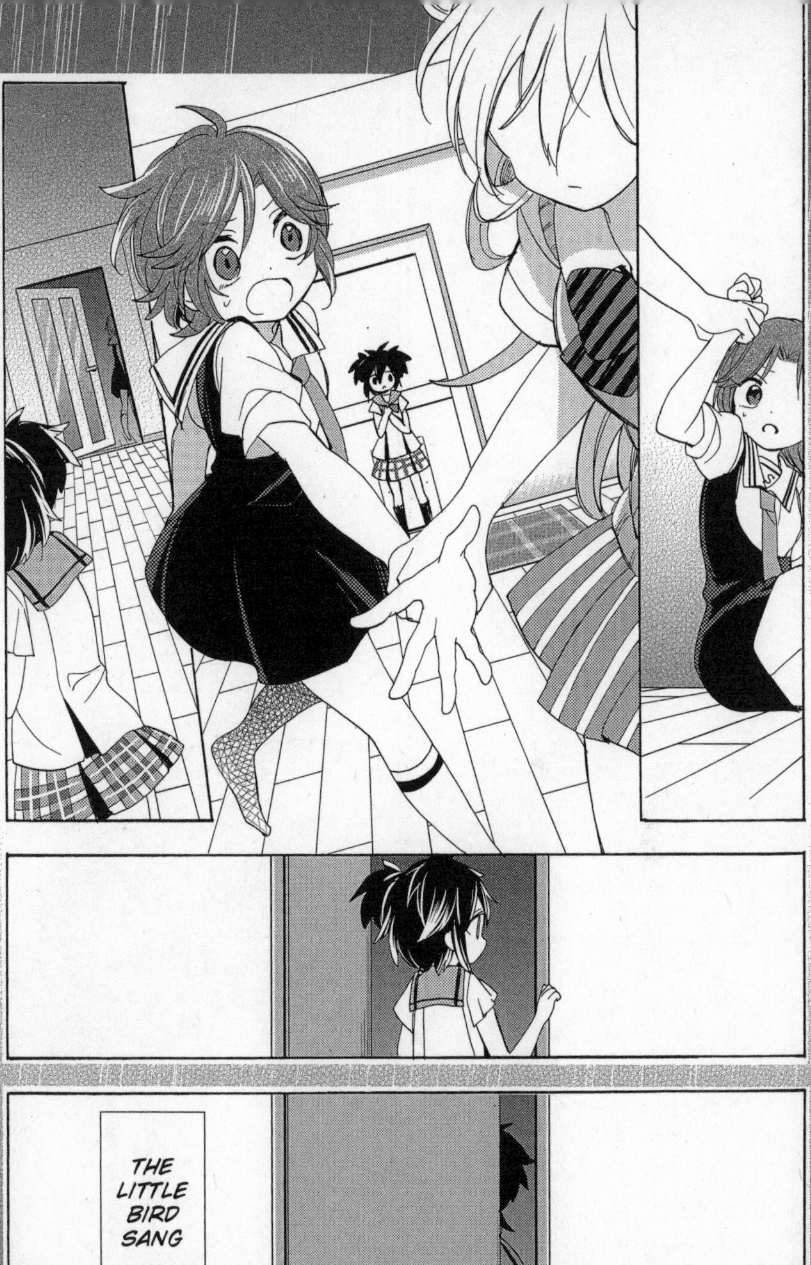
THE LITTLE BIRD SANG ...

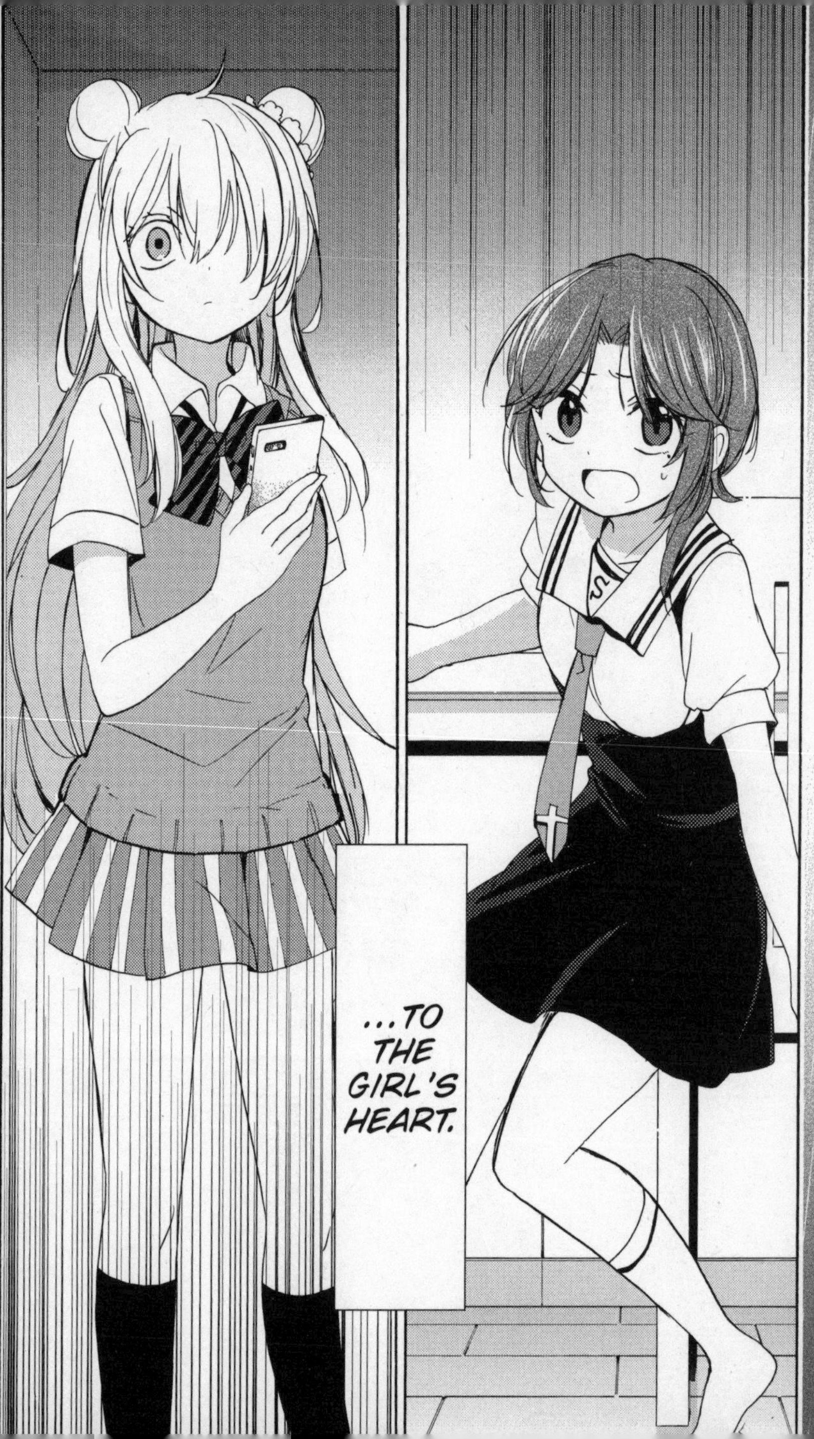
...TO THE GIRL'S HEART.

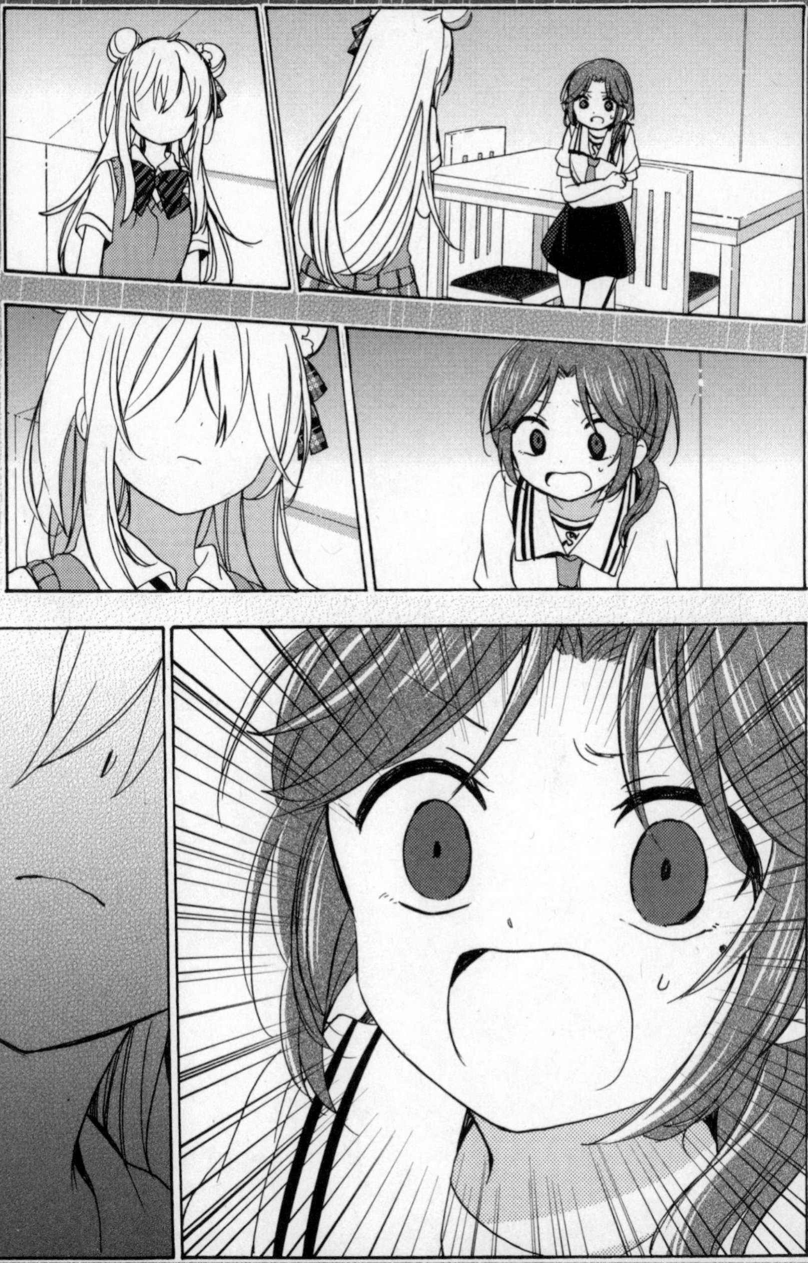

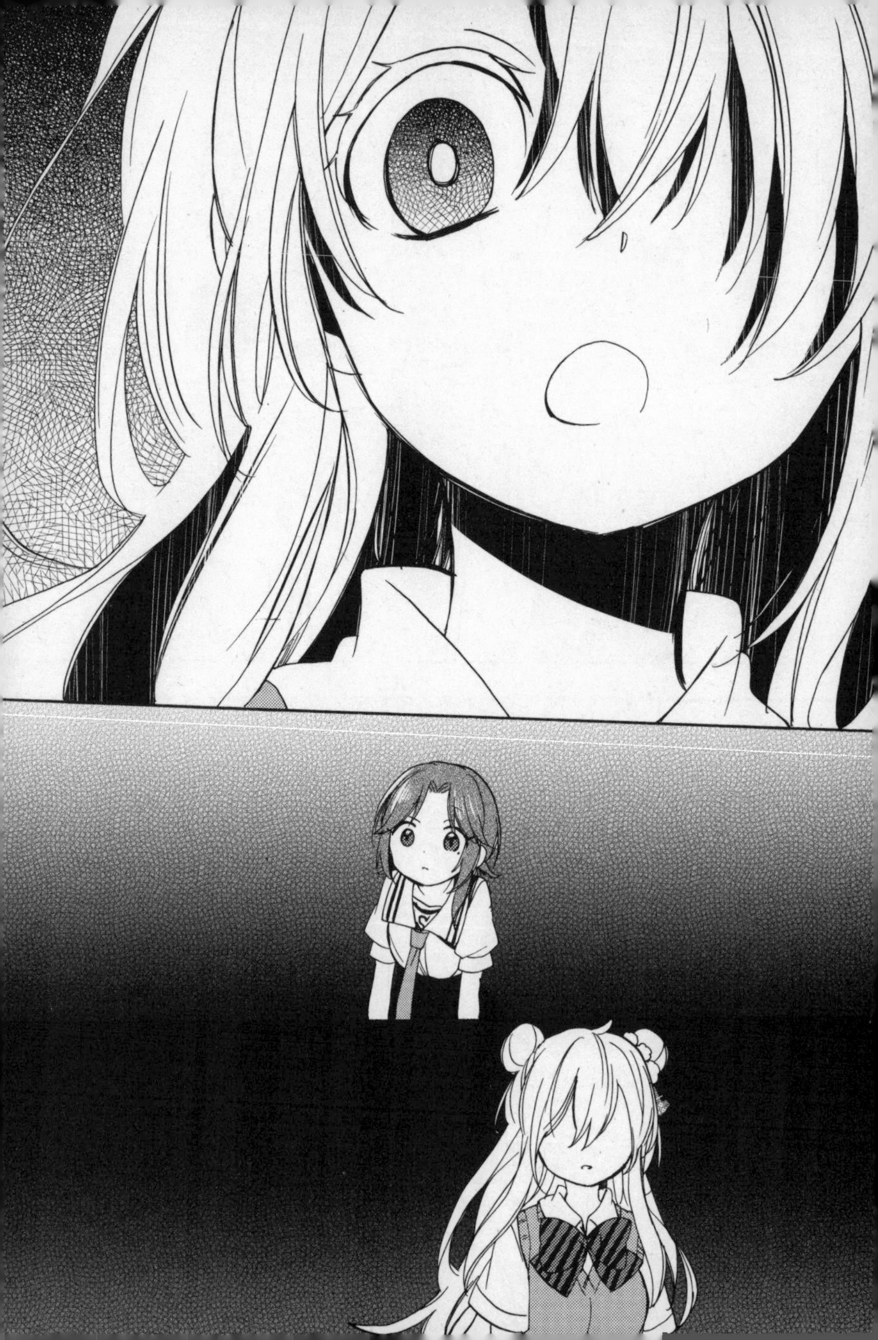

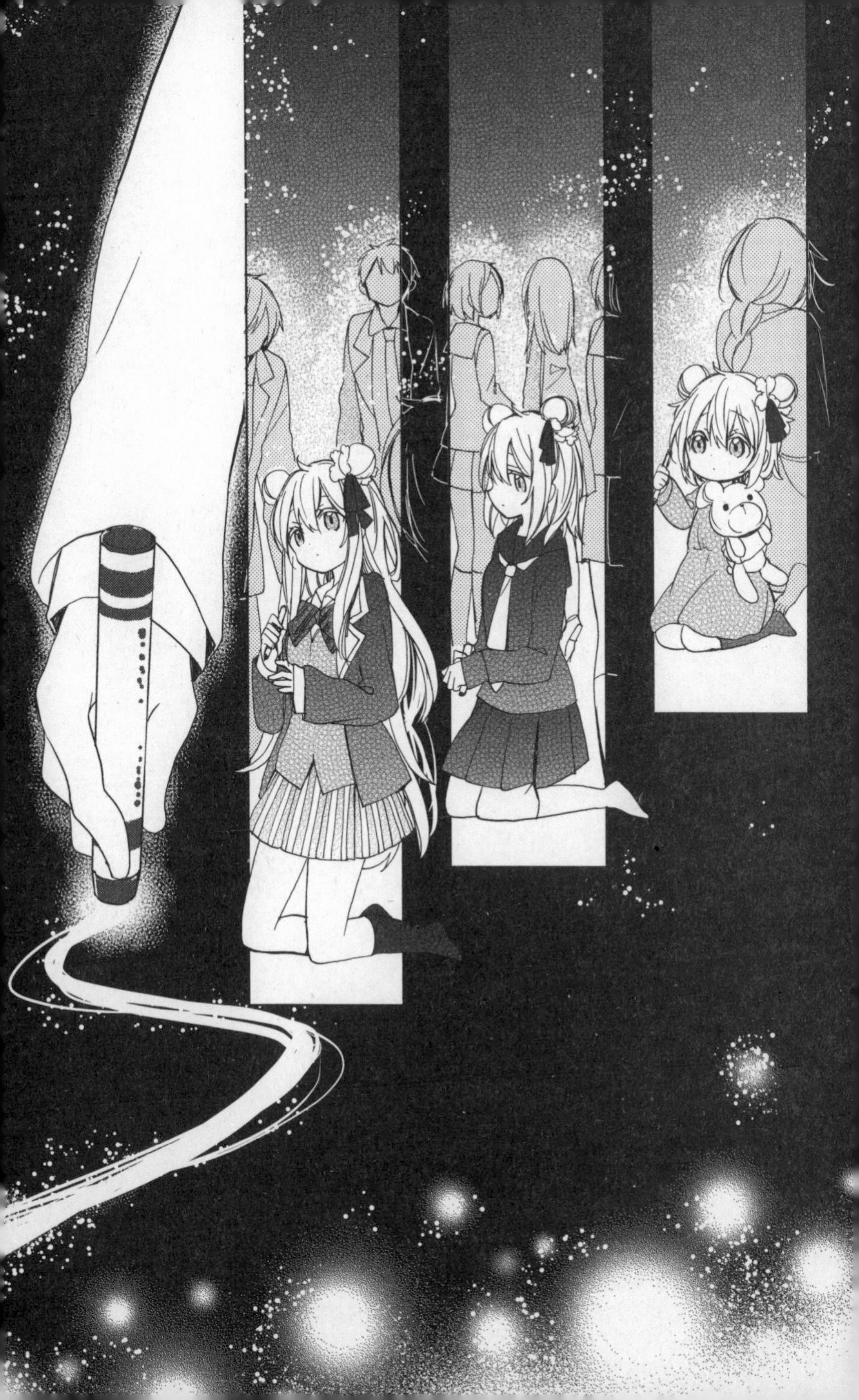

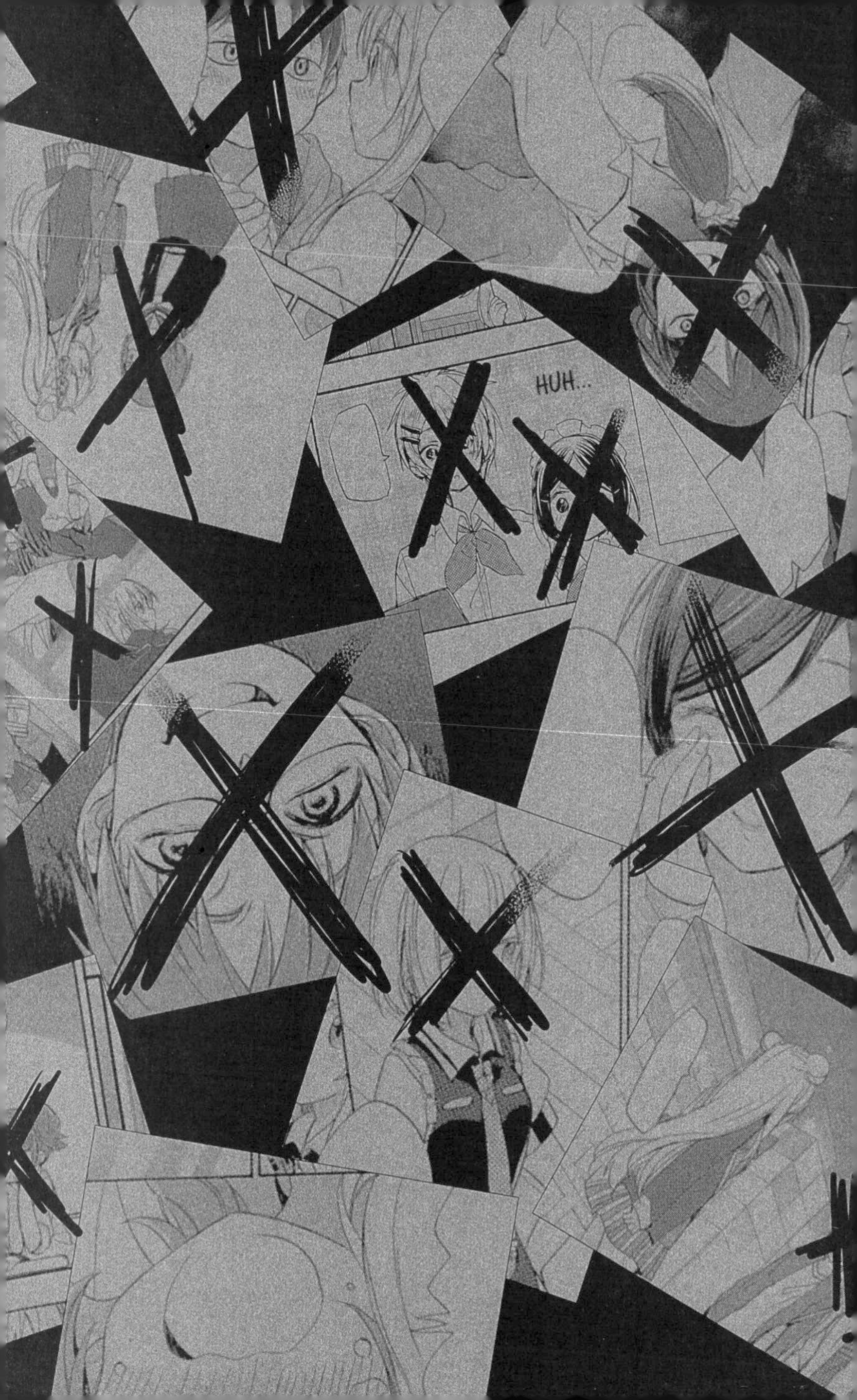
HUH...

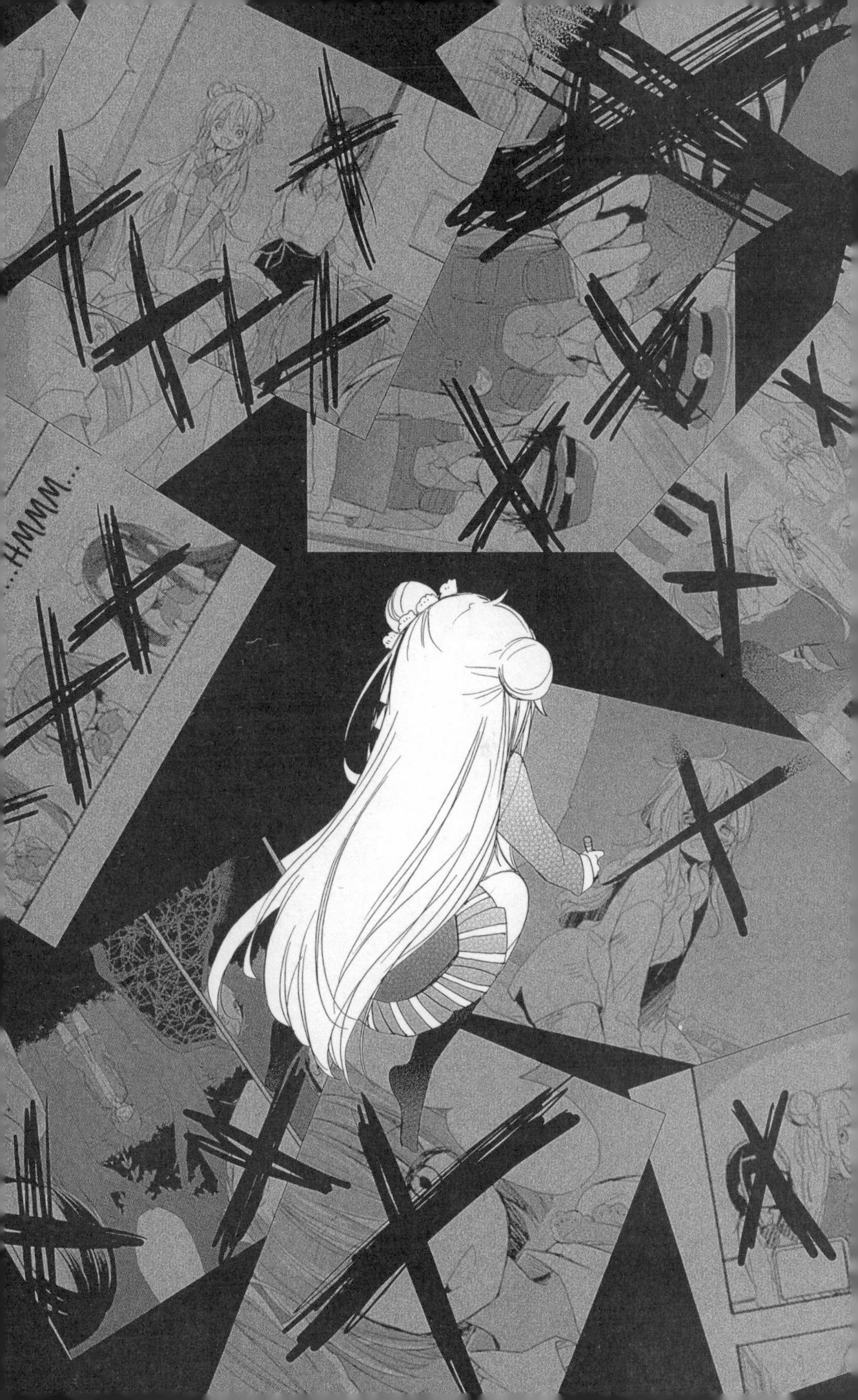
...HMMM....

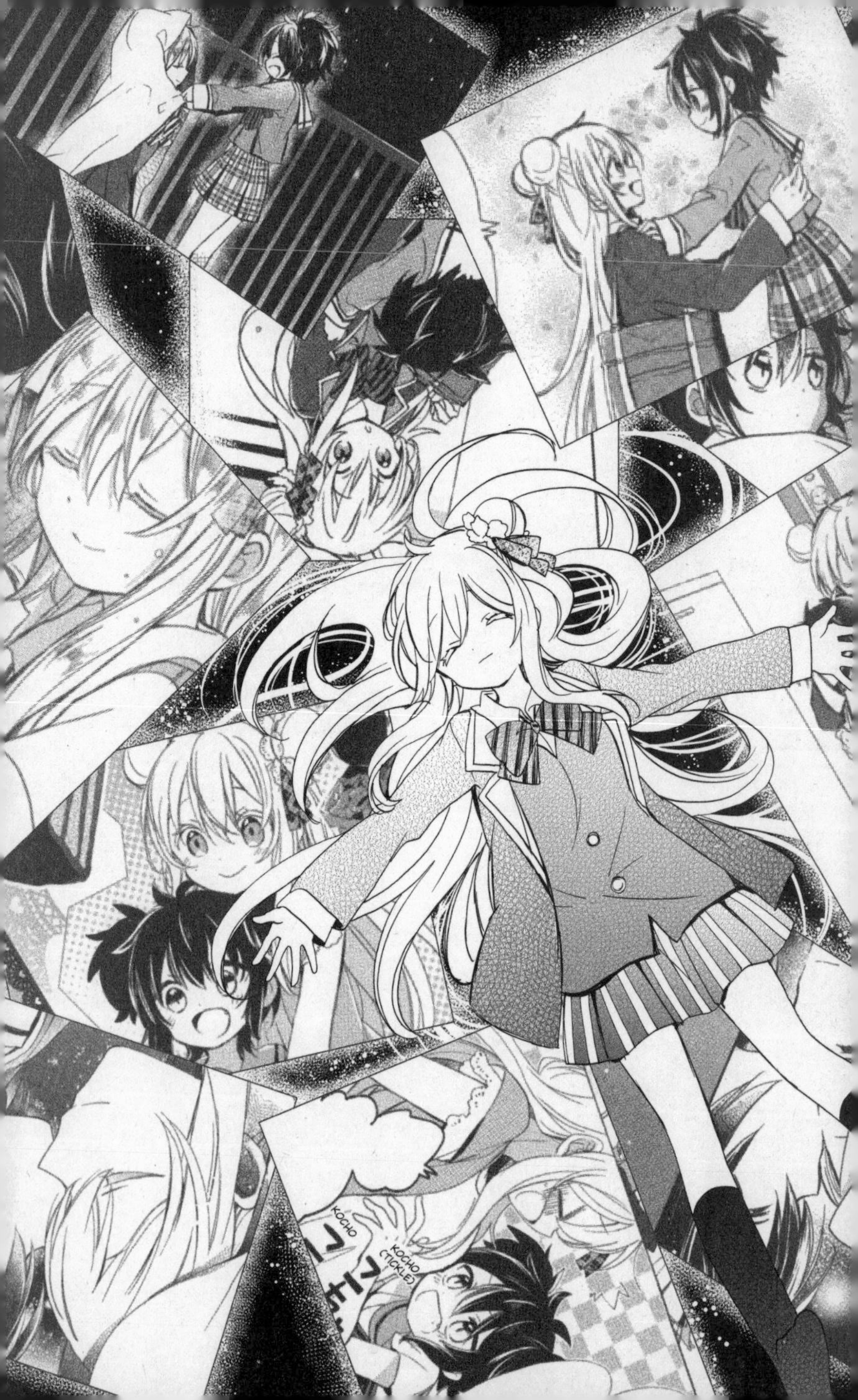
KOCHO (TICKLE)
KOCHO

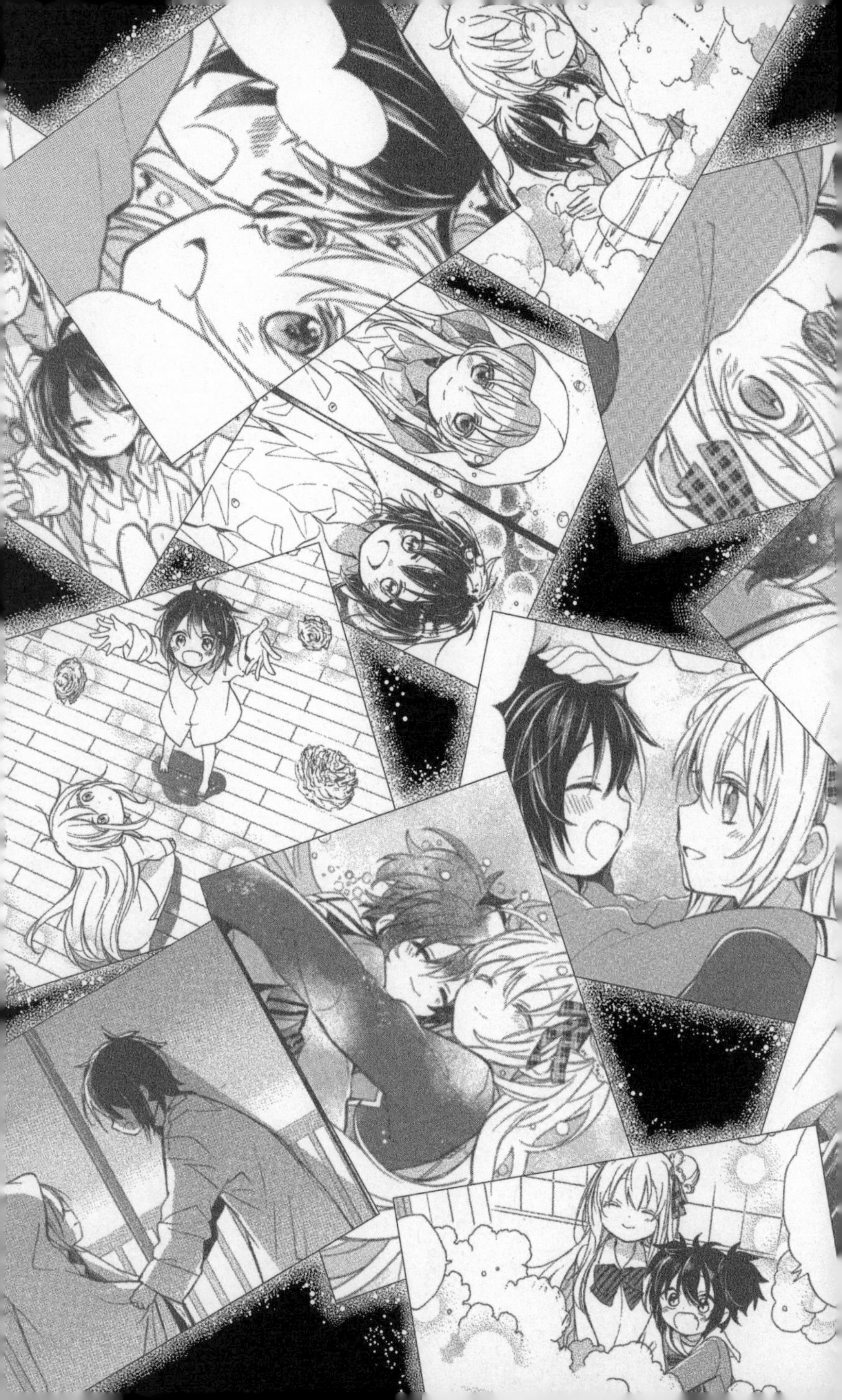

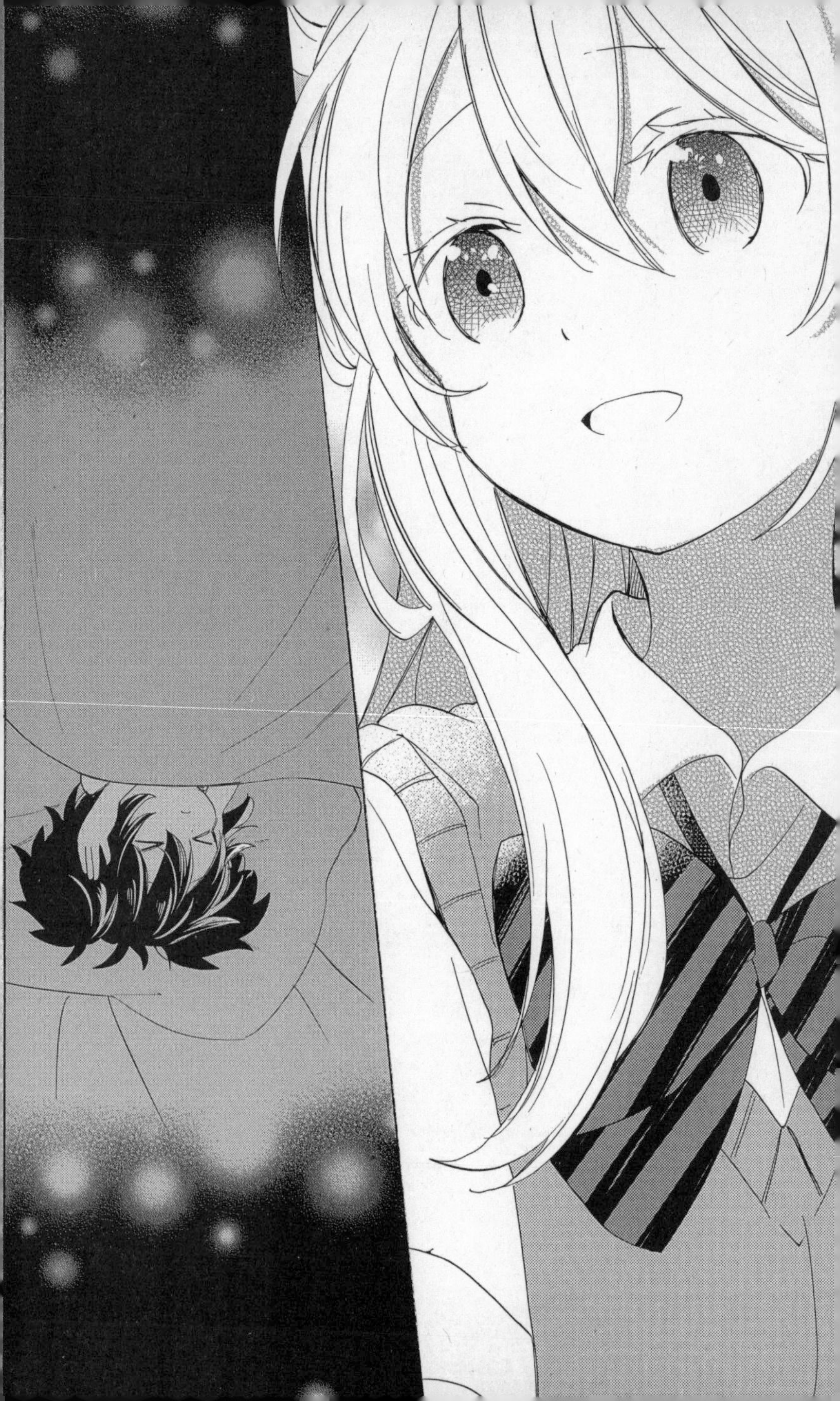

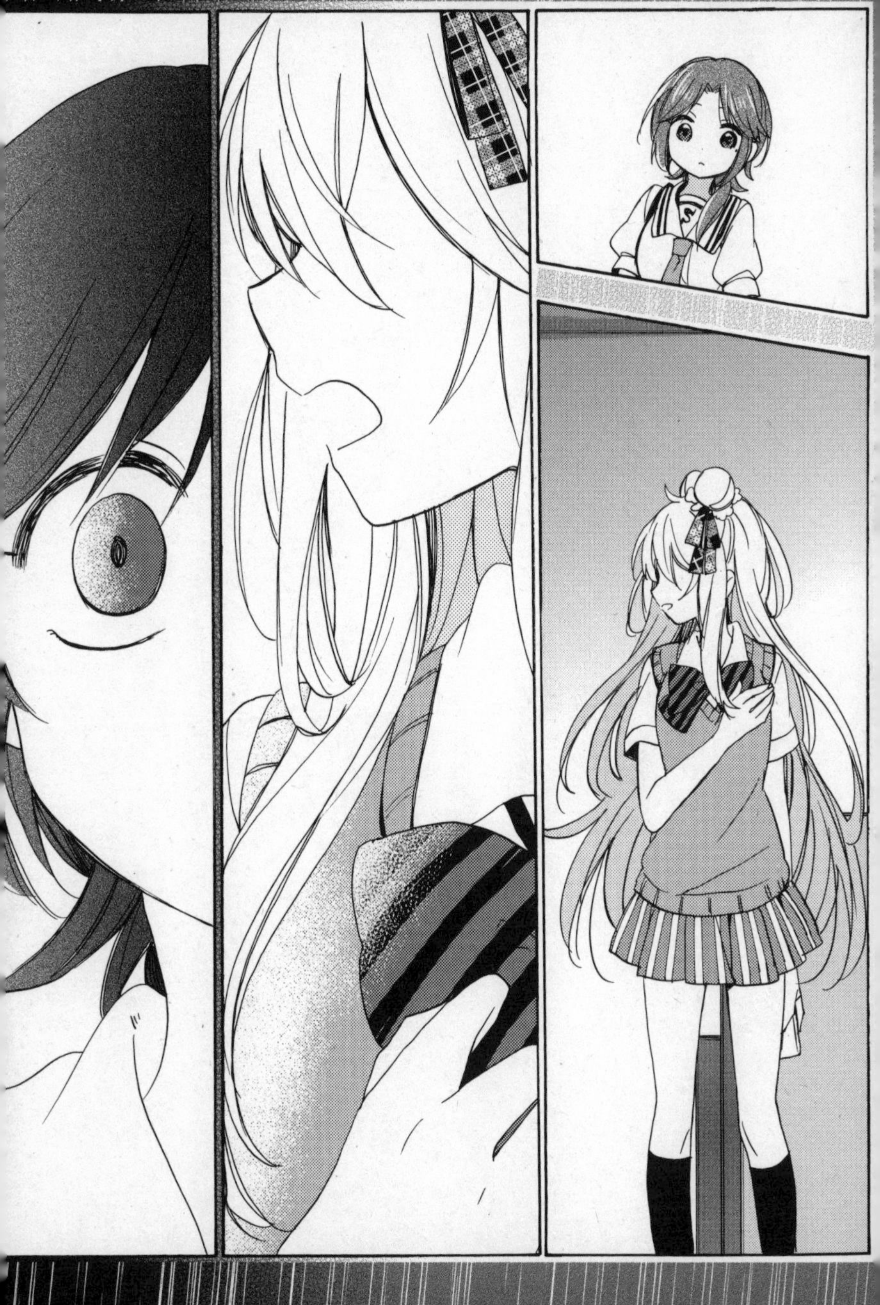

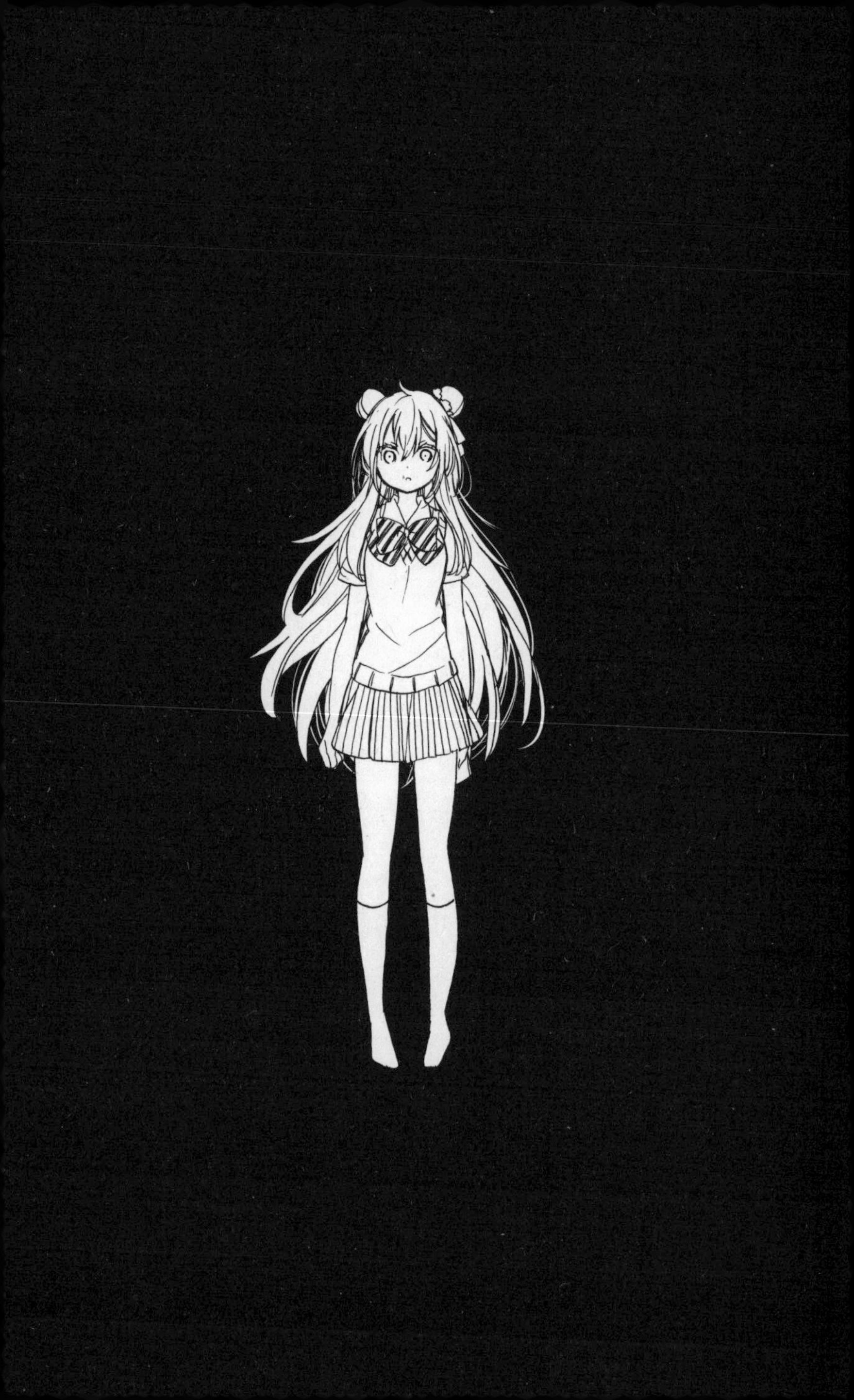

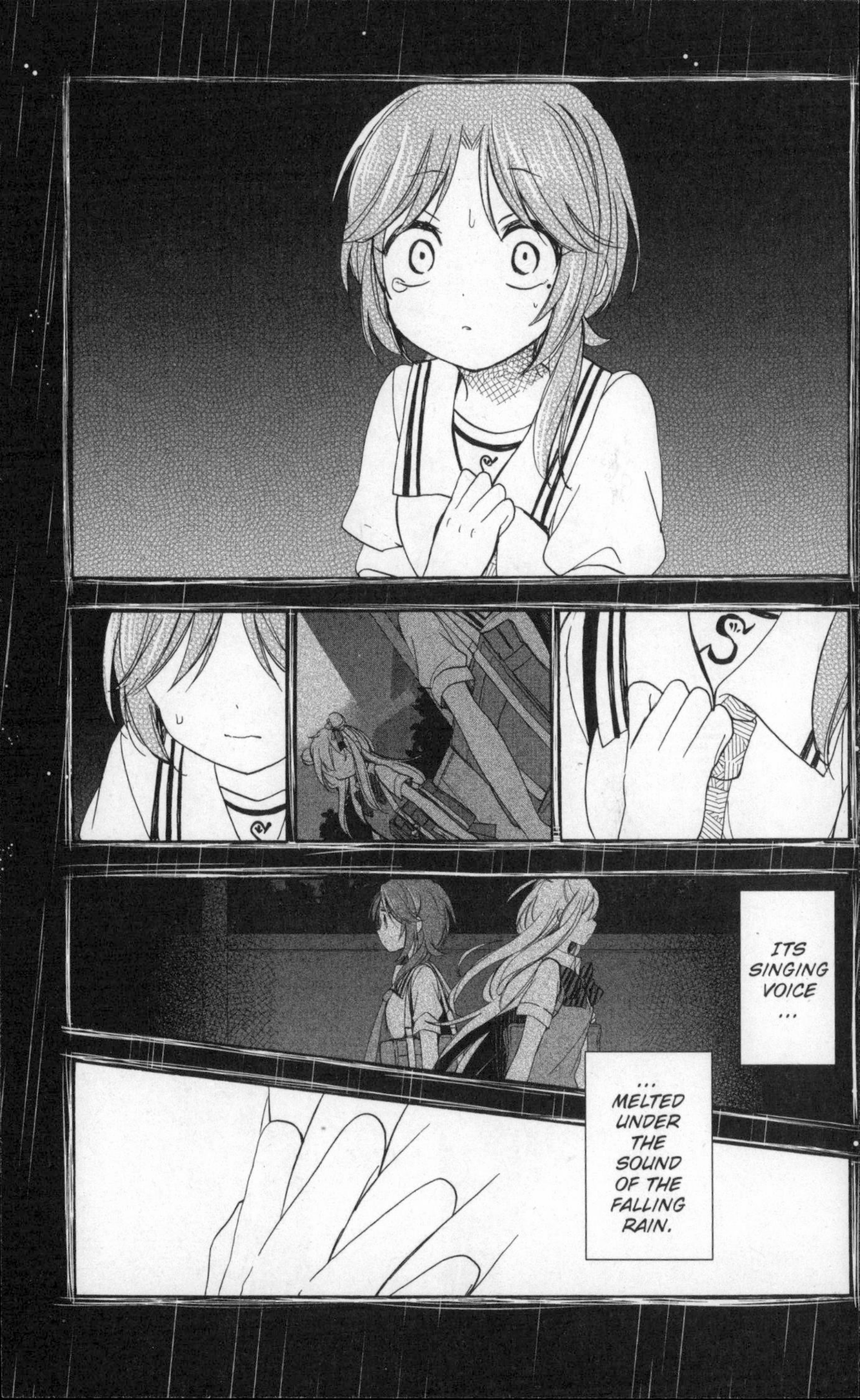
ITS SINGING VOICE ...
... MELTED UNDER THE SOUND OF THE FALLING RAIN.

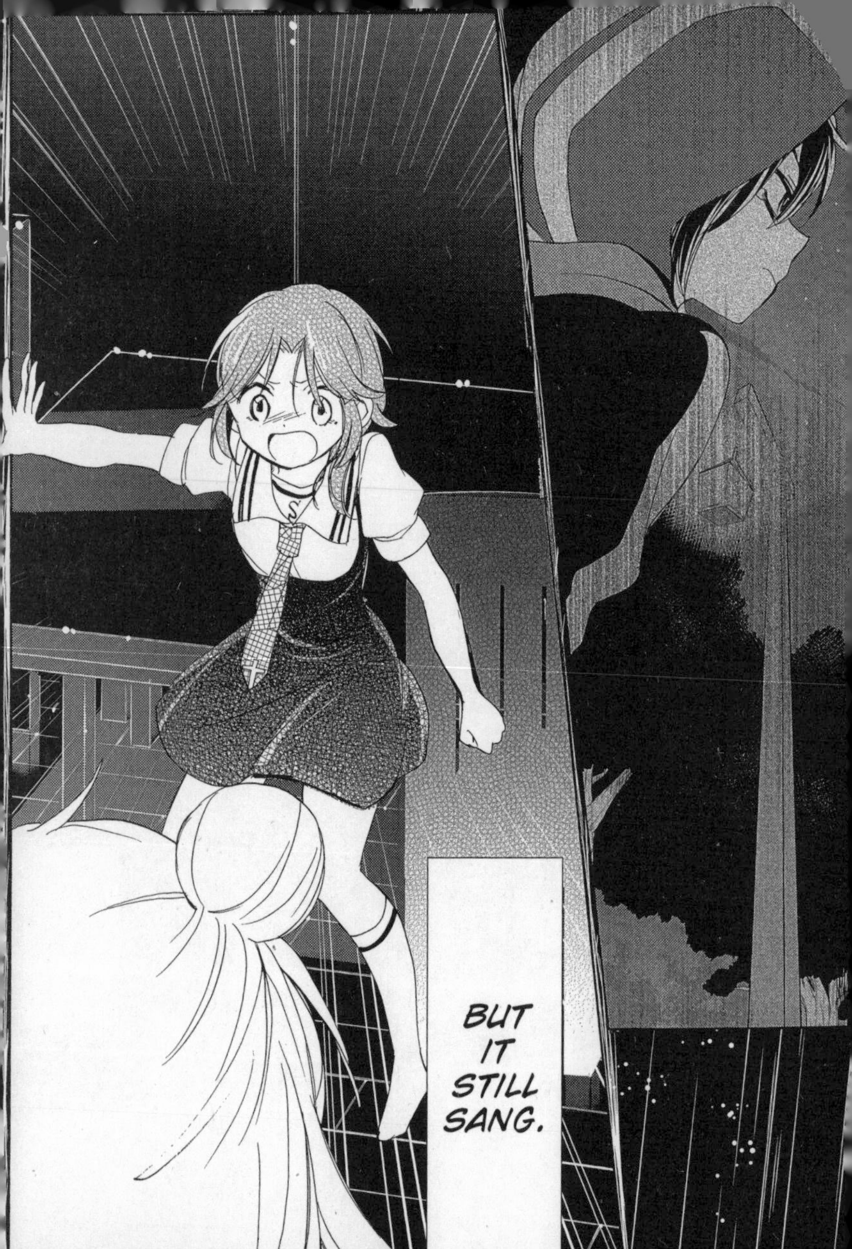
BUT IT STILL SANG.

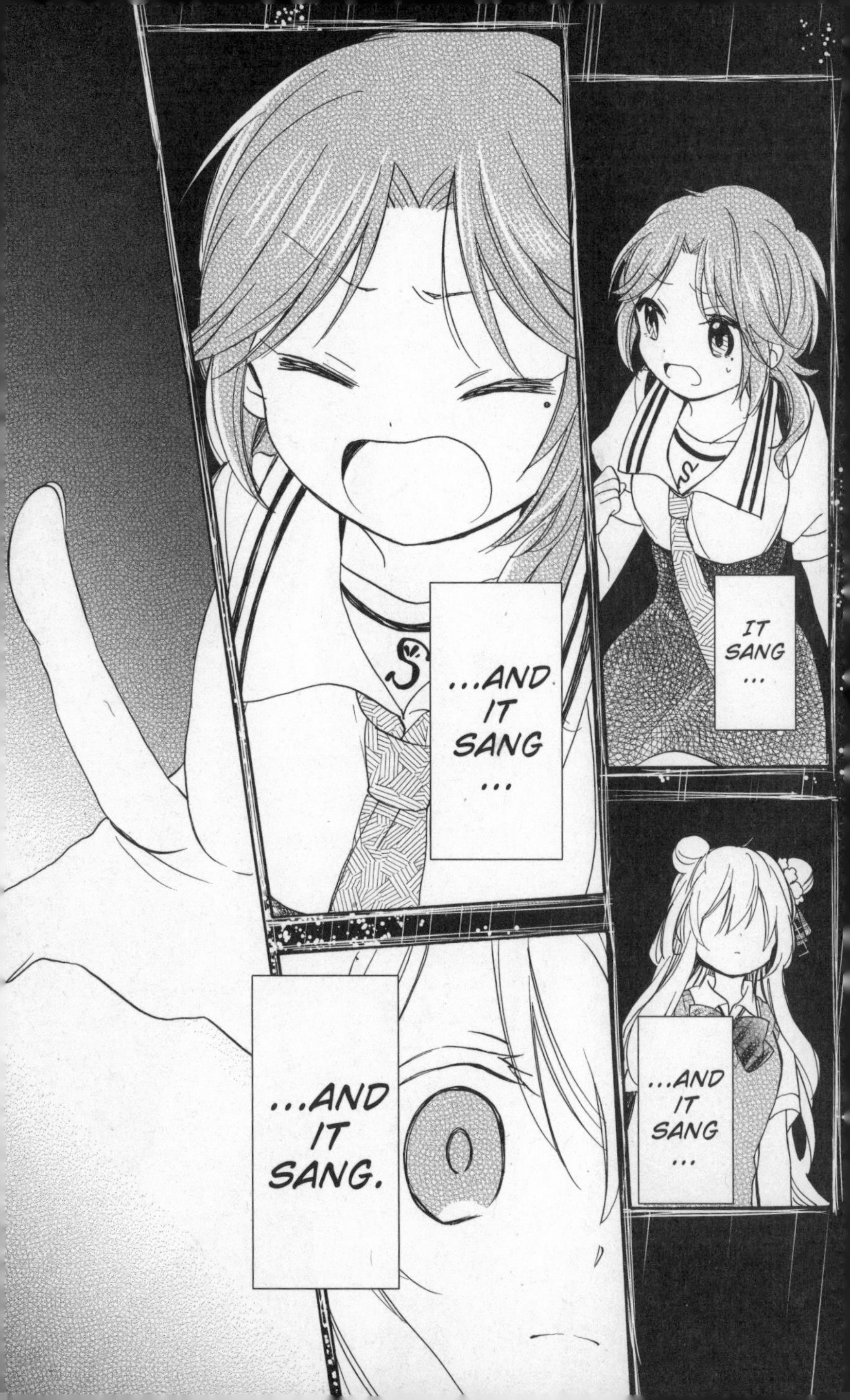
IT SANG ...
...AND IT SANG ...
...AND IT SANG ...
...AND IT SANG.

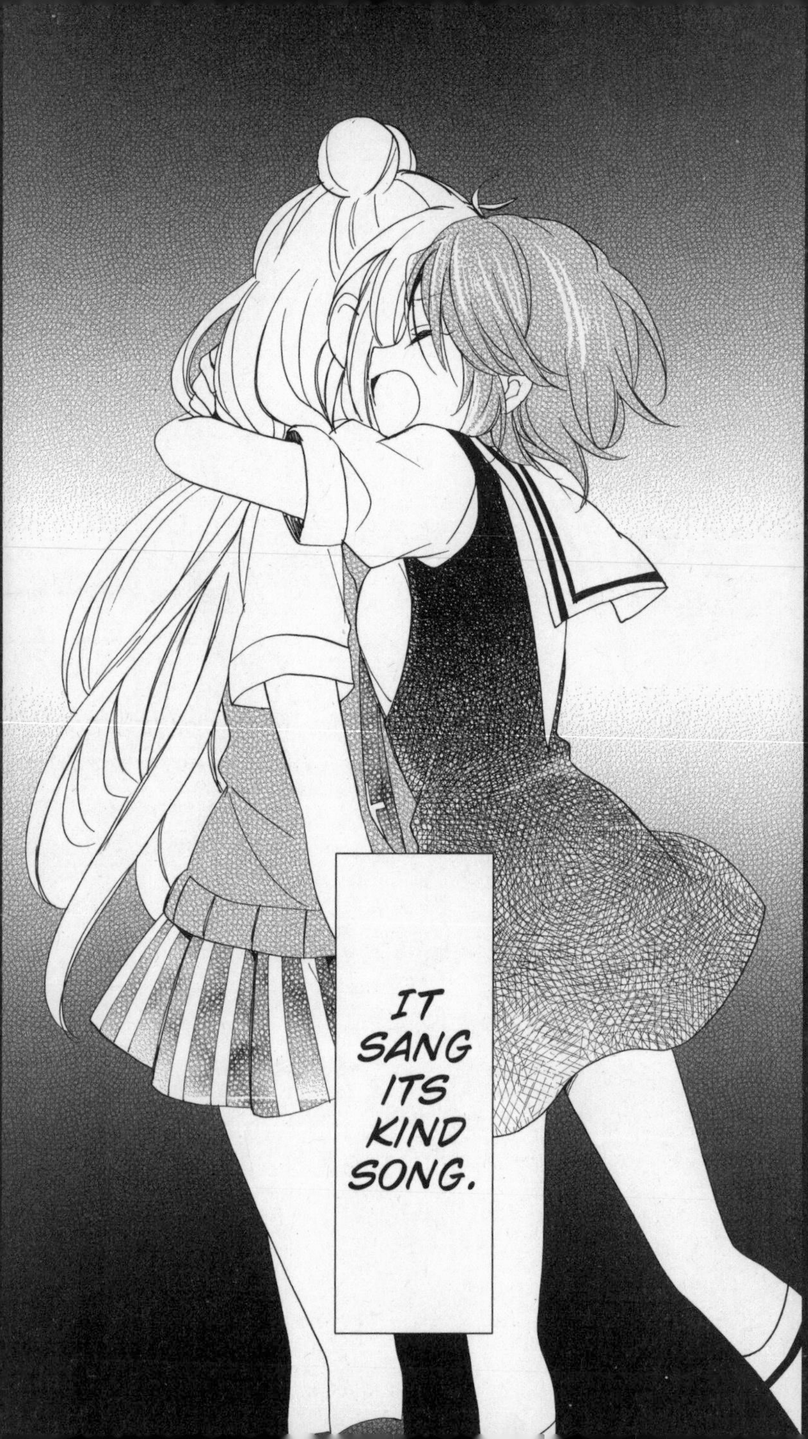
IT SANG ITS KIND SONG.

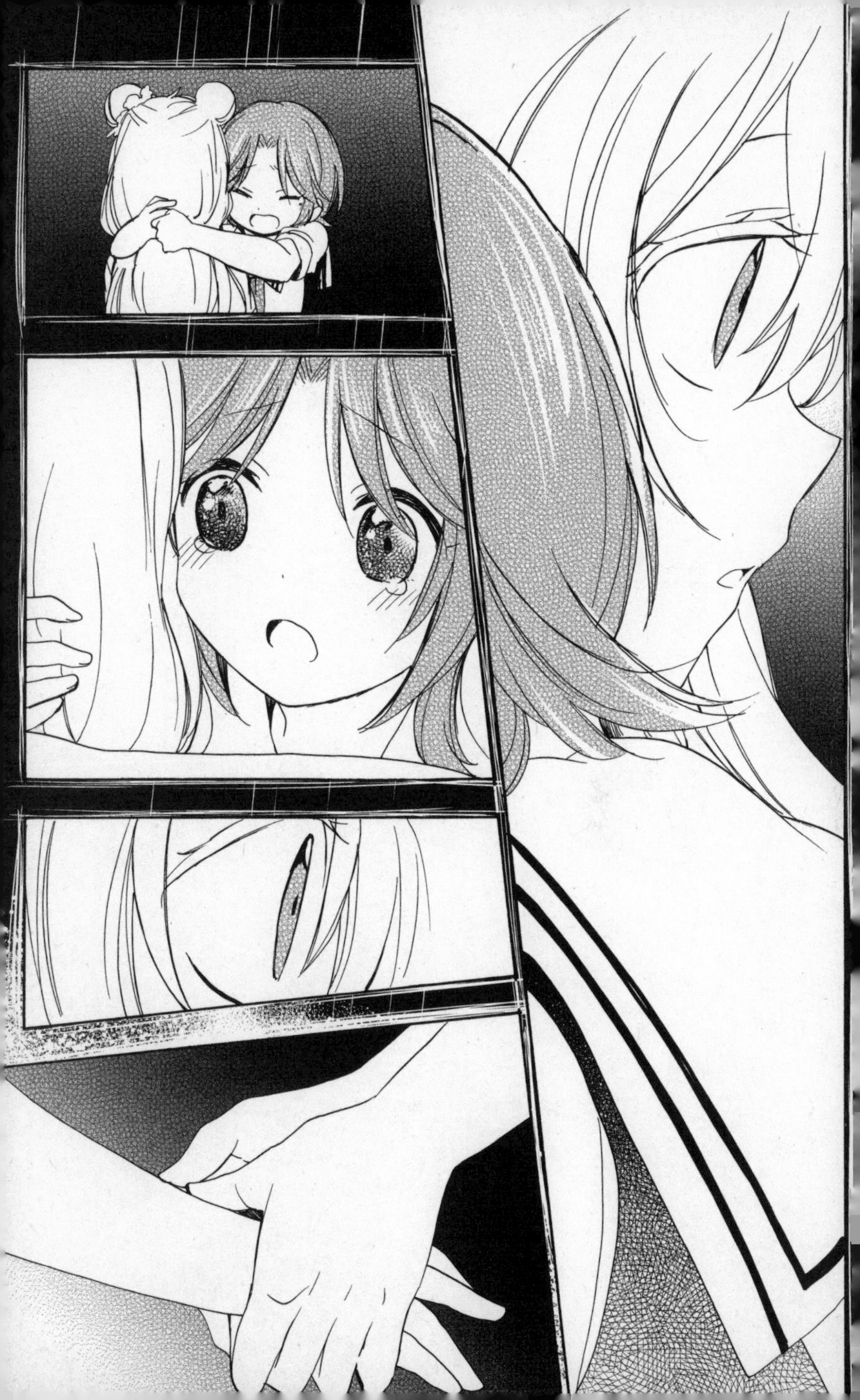

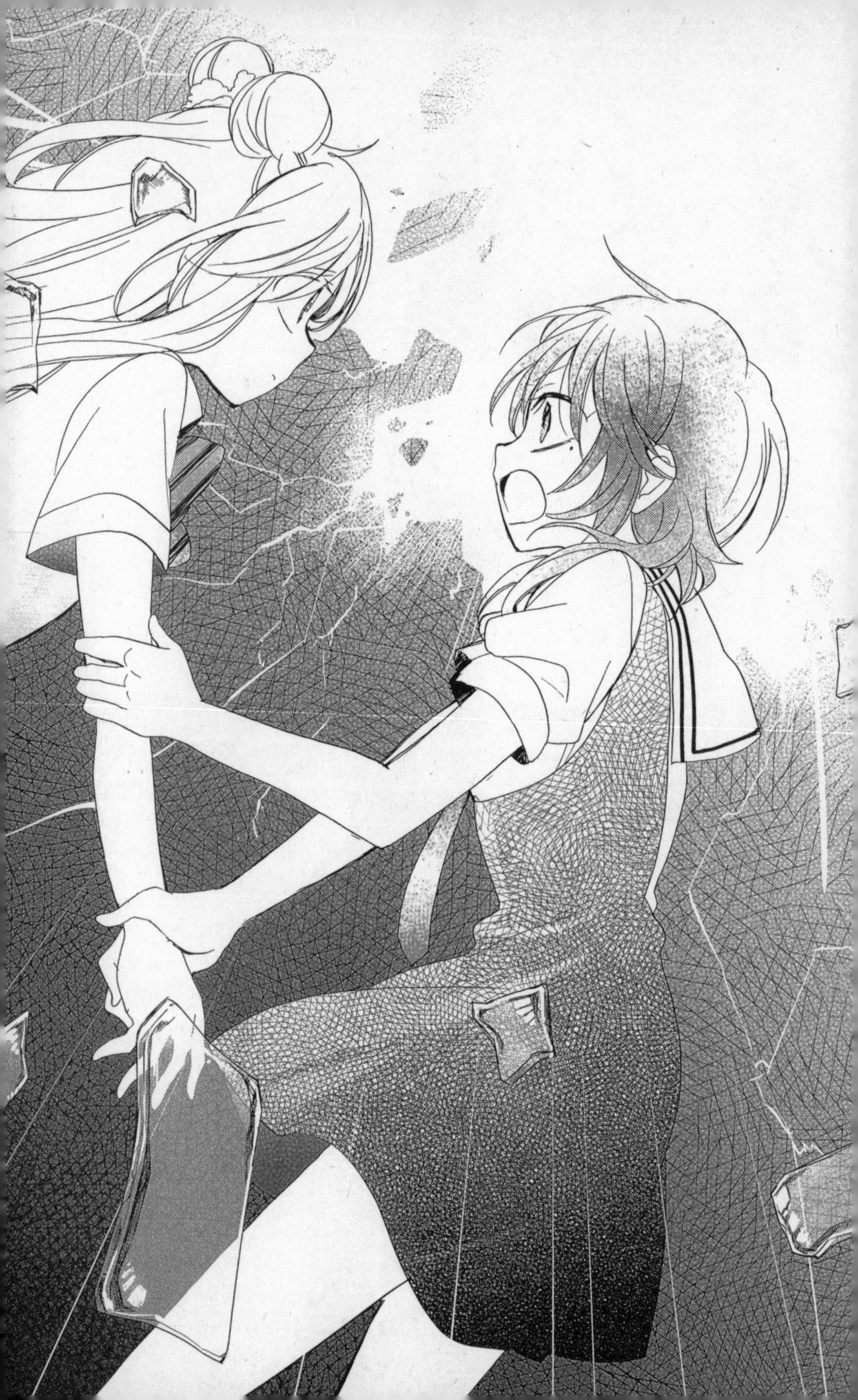

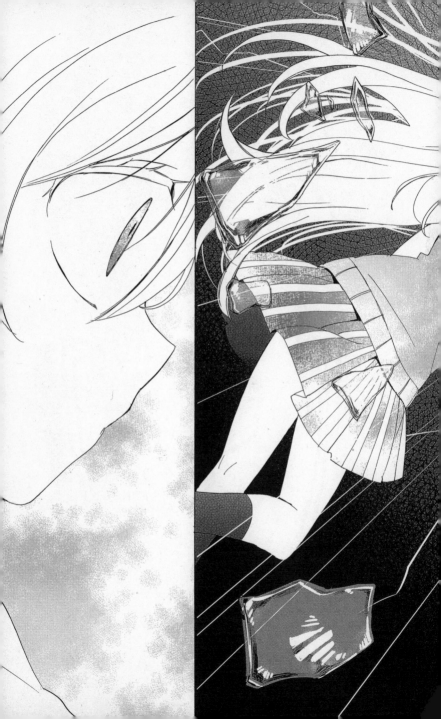

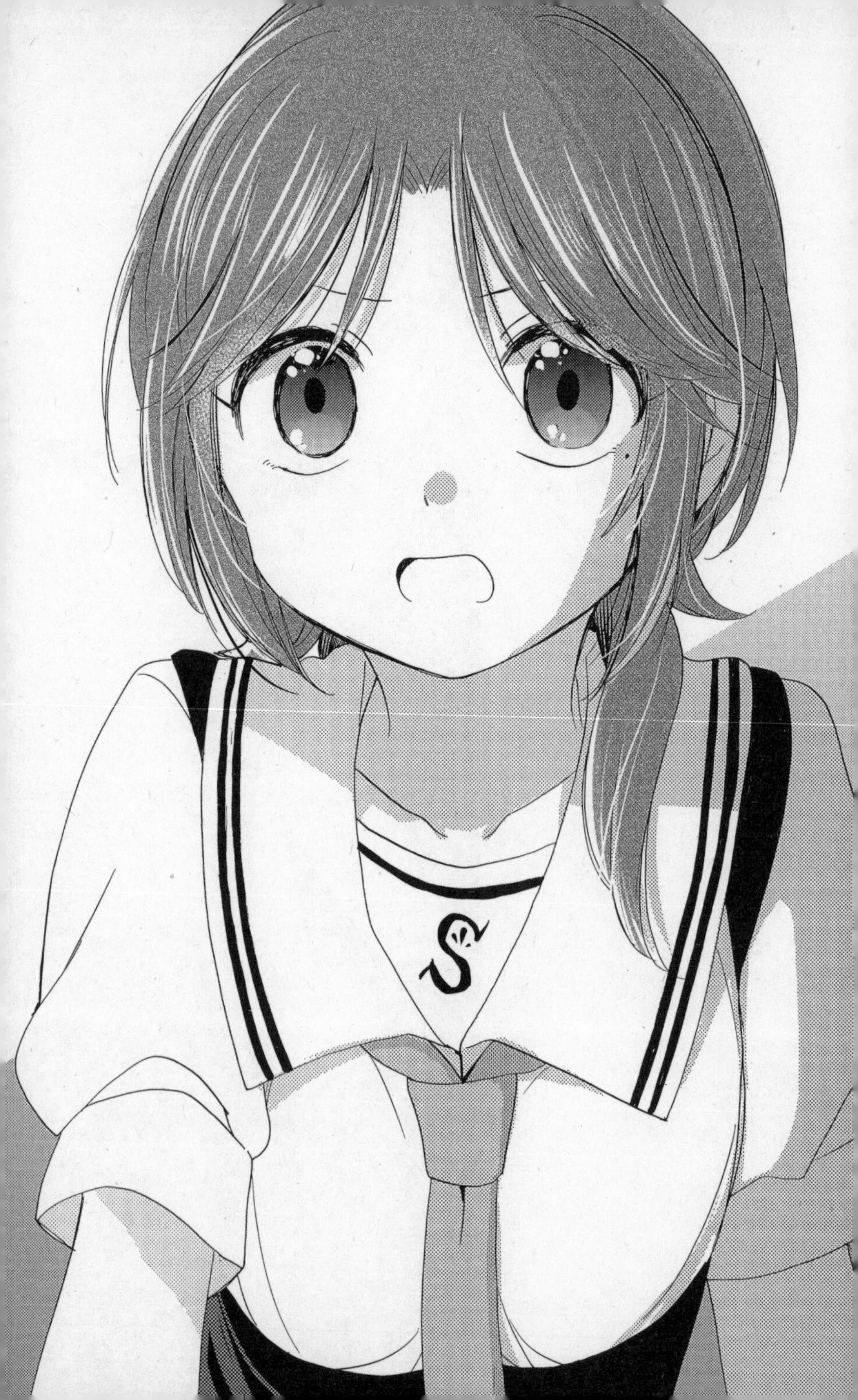

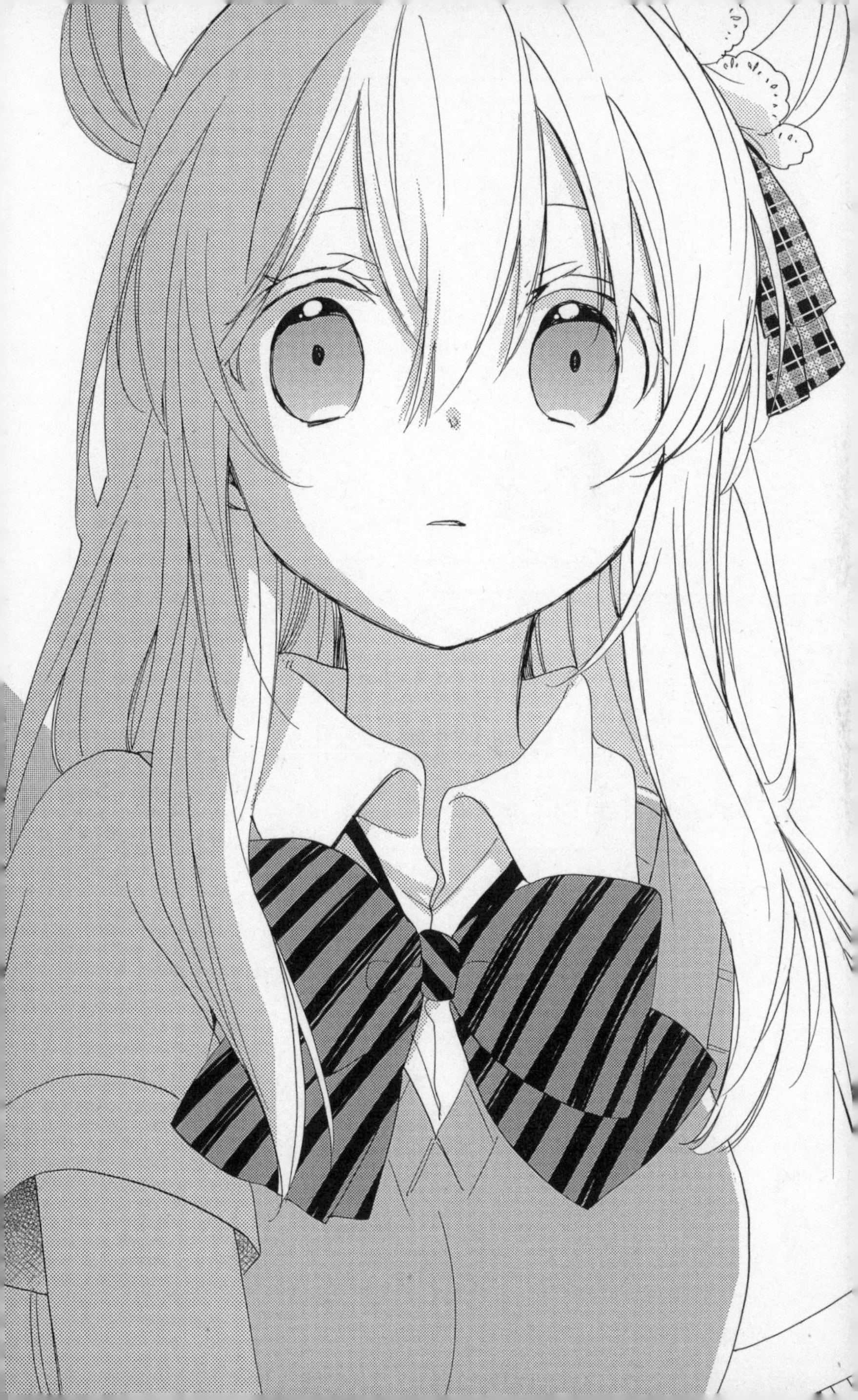

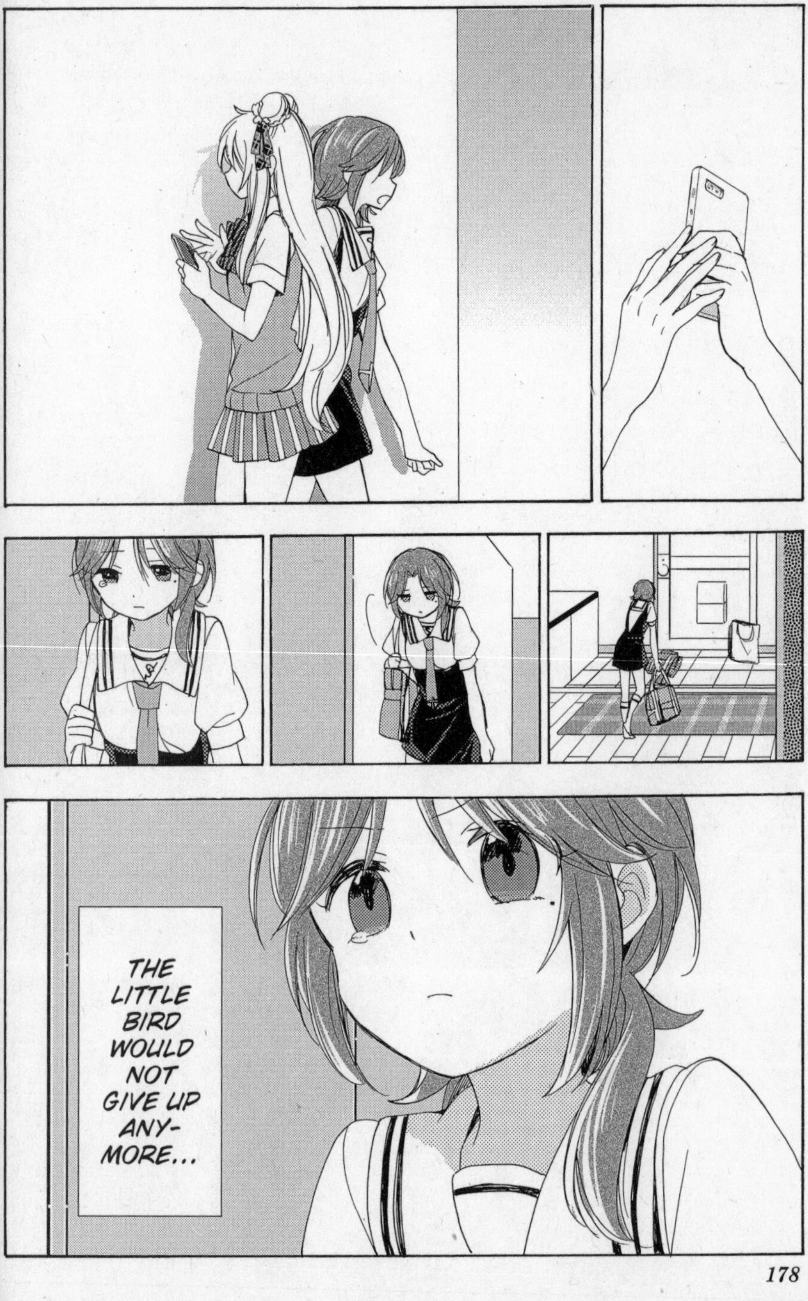
THE LITTLE BIRD WOULD NOT GIVE UP ANY-MORE...

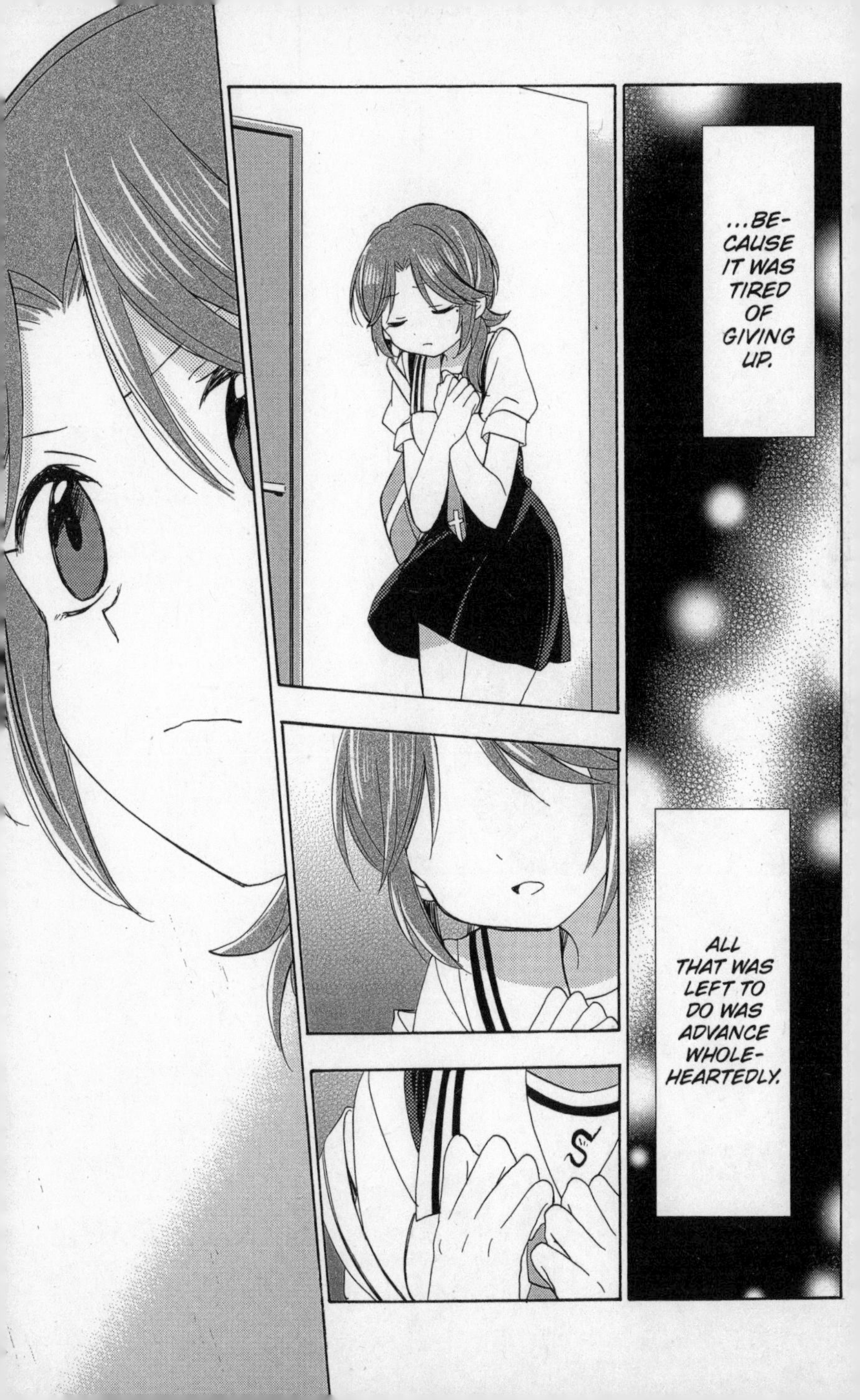
...BE-CAUSE IT WAS TIRED OF GIVING UP.
ALL THAT WAS LEFT TO DO WAS ADVANCE WHOLE-HEARTEDLY.

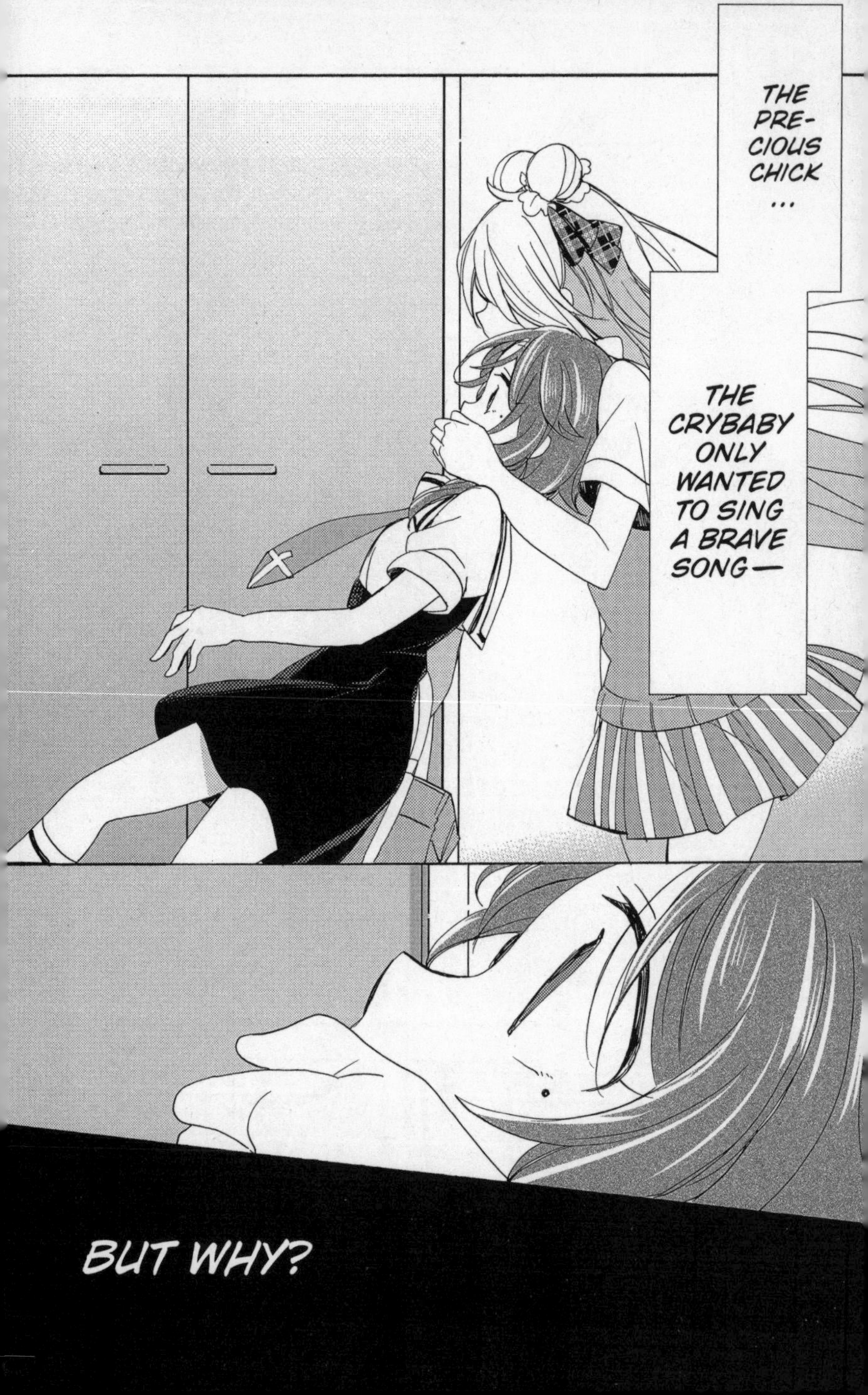
THE PRECIOUS CHICK ...
THE CRYBABY ONLY WANTED TO SING A BRAVE SONG—
BUT WHY?

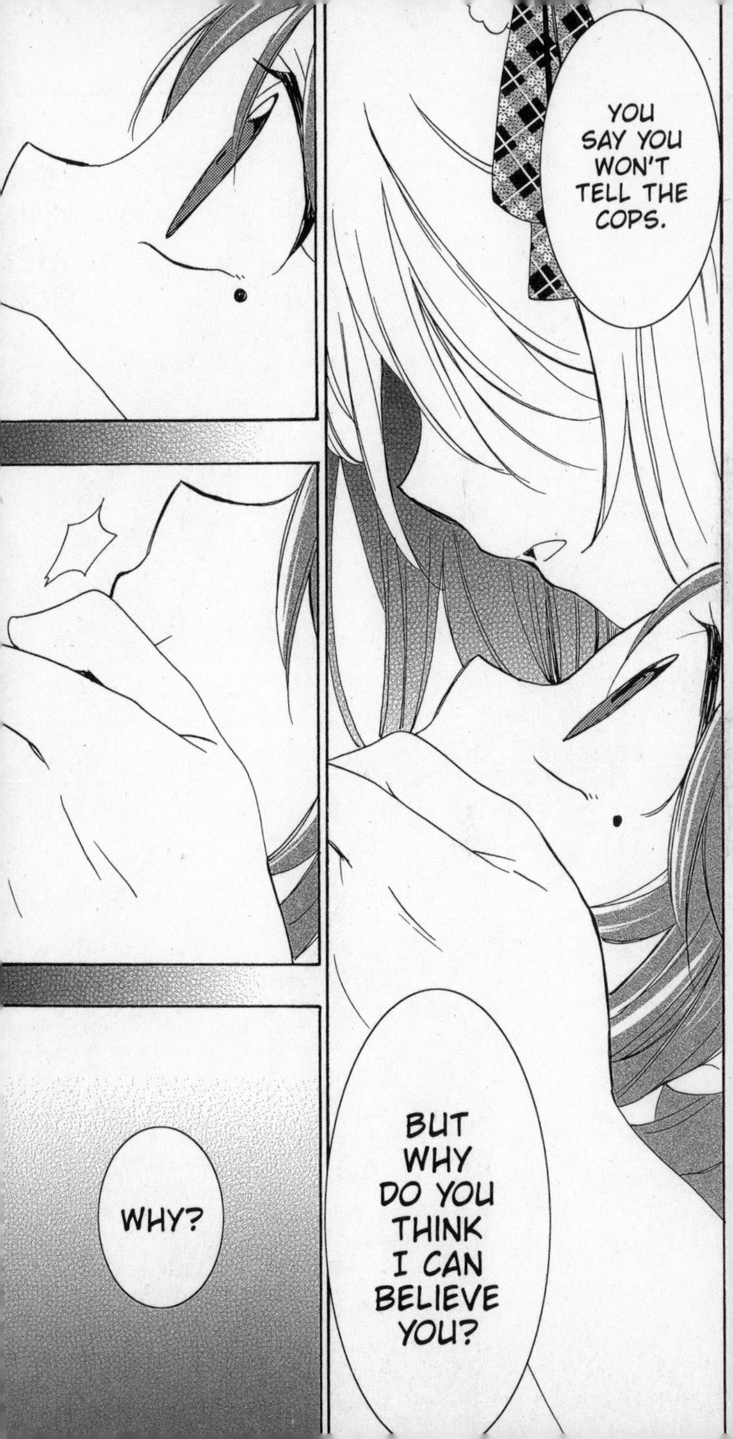
YOU SAY YOU WON'T TELL THE COPS.
BUT WHY DO YOU THINK I CAN BELIEVE YOU?
WHY?

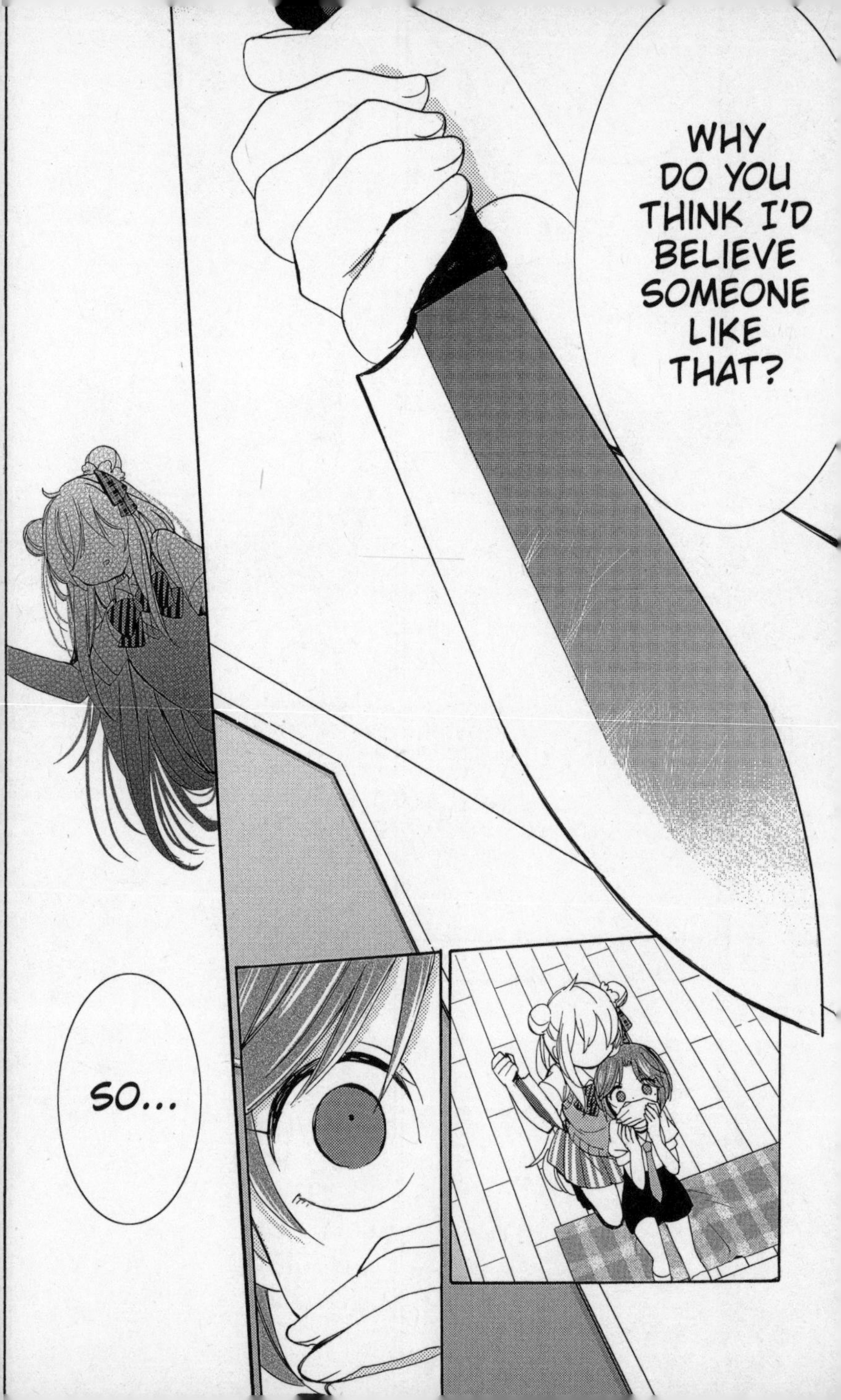
WHY DO YOU THINK I'D BELIEVE SOMEONE LIKE THAT?
SO...

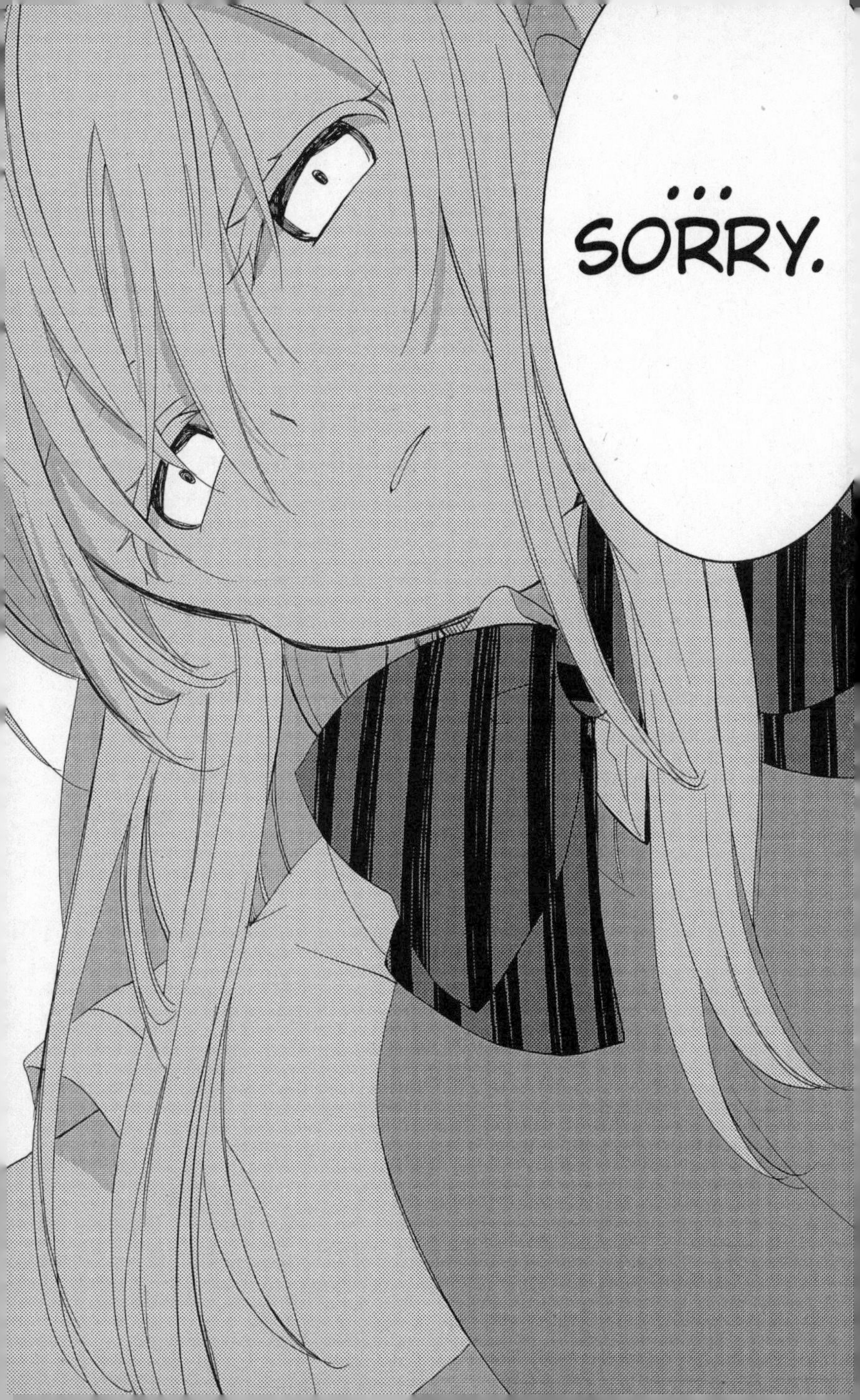
...SORRY.

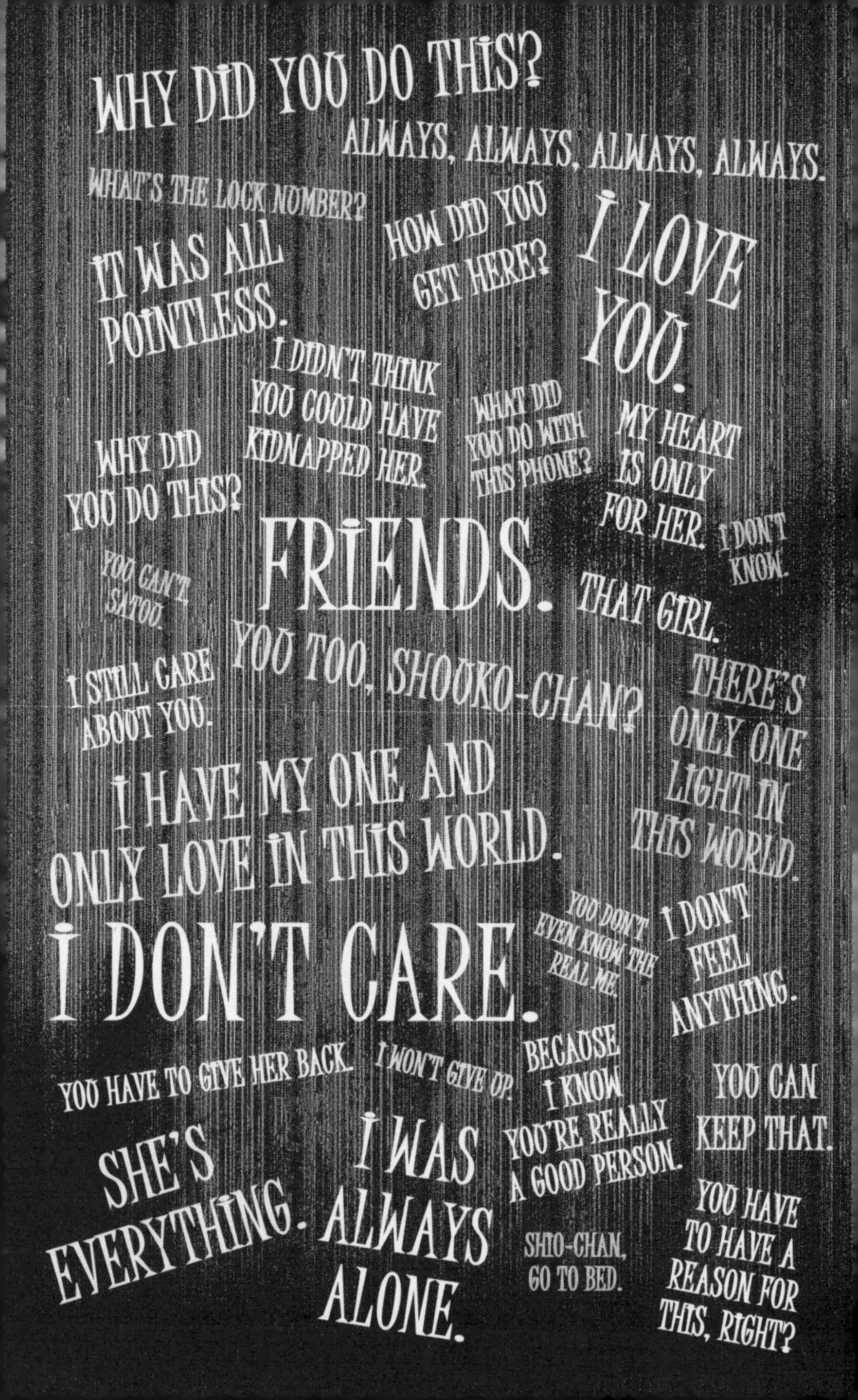
WHY DID YOU DO THIS?
ALWAYS, ALWAYS, ALWAYS, ALWAYS.
WHAT'S THE LOCK NUMBER?
I LOVE YOU.
HOW DID YOU GET HERE?
IT WAS ALL POINTLESS.
MY HEART IS ONLY FOR HER.
WHAT DID YOU DO WITH THIS PHONE?
I DIDN'T THINK YOU COULD HAVE KIDNAPPED HER.
WHY DID YOU DO THIS?
I DON'T KNOW.
THAT GIRL.
FRIENDS.
YOU CAN'T, SATOU.
THERE'S ONLY ONE LIGHT IN THIS WORLD.
YOU TOO, SHOUKO-CHAN?
I STILL CARE ABOUT YOU.
I HAVE MY ONE AND ONLY LOVE IN THIS WORLD.
I DON'T FEEL ANYTHING.
YOU DON'T EVEN KNOW THE REAL ME.
I DON'T CARE.
YOU CAN KEEP THAT.
BECAUSE I KNOW YOU'RE REALLY A GOOD PERSON.
I WON'T GIVE UP.
YOU HAVE TO GIVE HER BACK.
YOU HAVE TO HAVE A REASON FOR THIS, RIGHT?
SHIO-CHAN, GO TO BED.
I WAS ALWAYS ALONE.
SHE'S EVERYTHING.

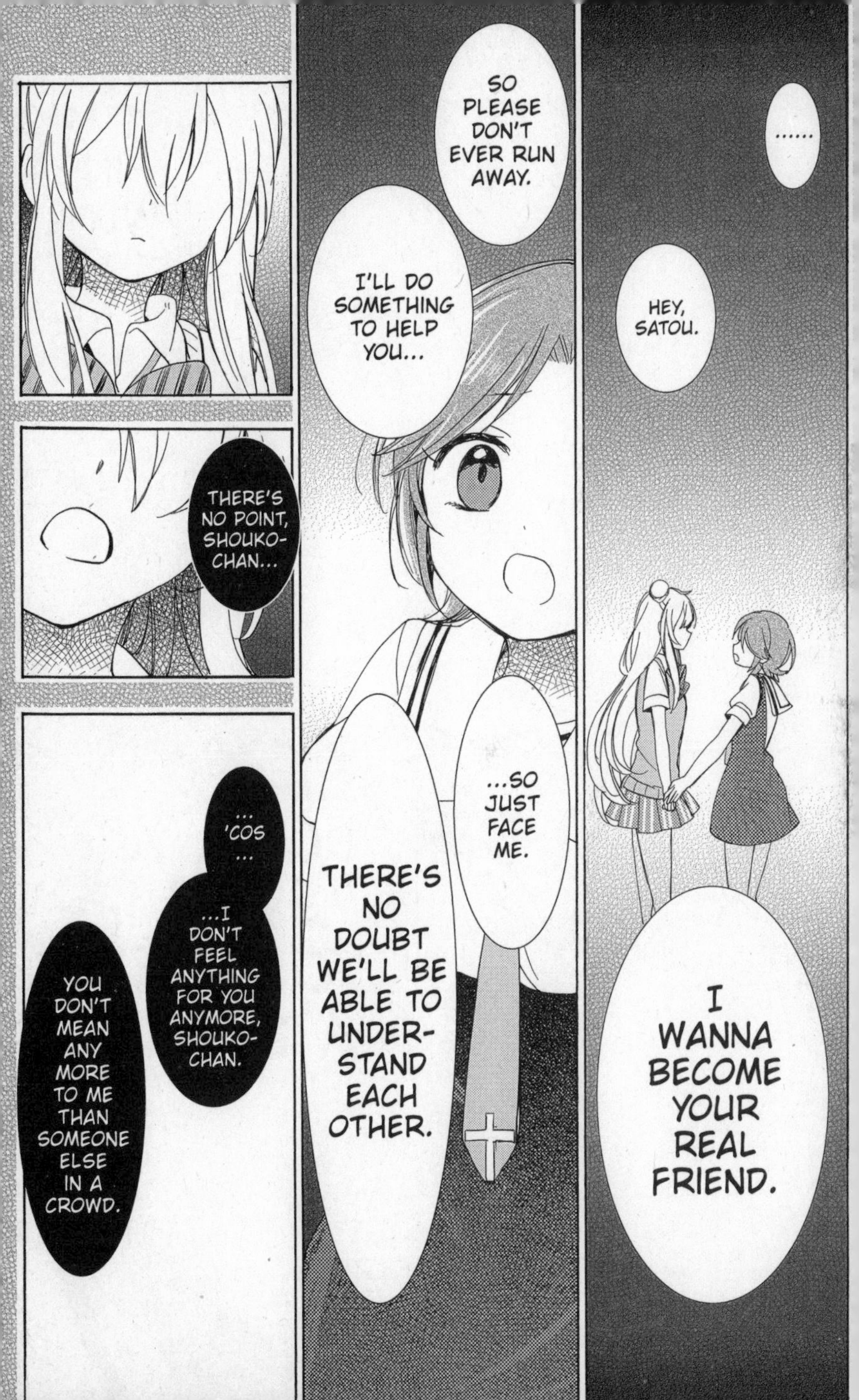
......
HEY, SATOU.
I WANNA BECOME YOUR REAL FRIEND.
SO PLEASE DON'T EVER RUN AWAY.
I'LL DO SOMETHING TO HELP YOU...
...SO JUST FACE ME.
THERE'S NO DOUBT WE'LL BE ABLE TO UNDER-STAND EACH OTHER.
THERE'S NO POINT, SHOUKO-CHAN...
... 'COS ...
...I DON'T FEEL ANYTHING FOR YOU ANYMORE, SHOUKO-CHAN.
YOU DON'T MEAN ANY MORE TO ME THAN SOMEONE ELSE IN A CROWD.

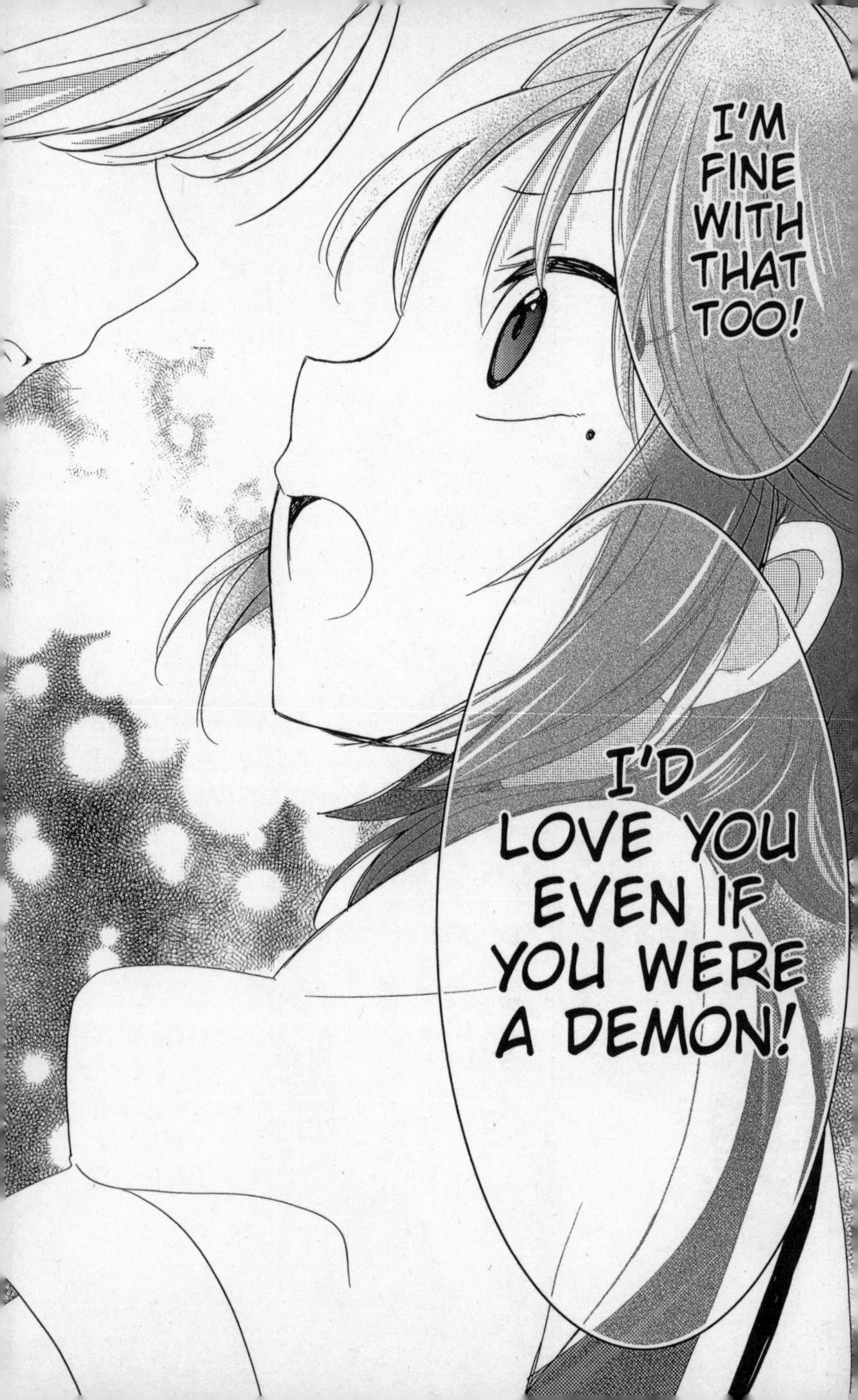
I'M FINE WITH THAT TOO!
I'D LOVE YOU EVEN IF YOU WERE A DEMON!

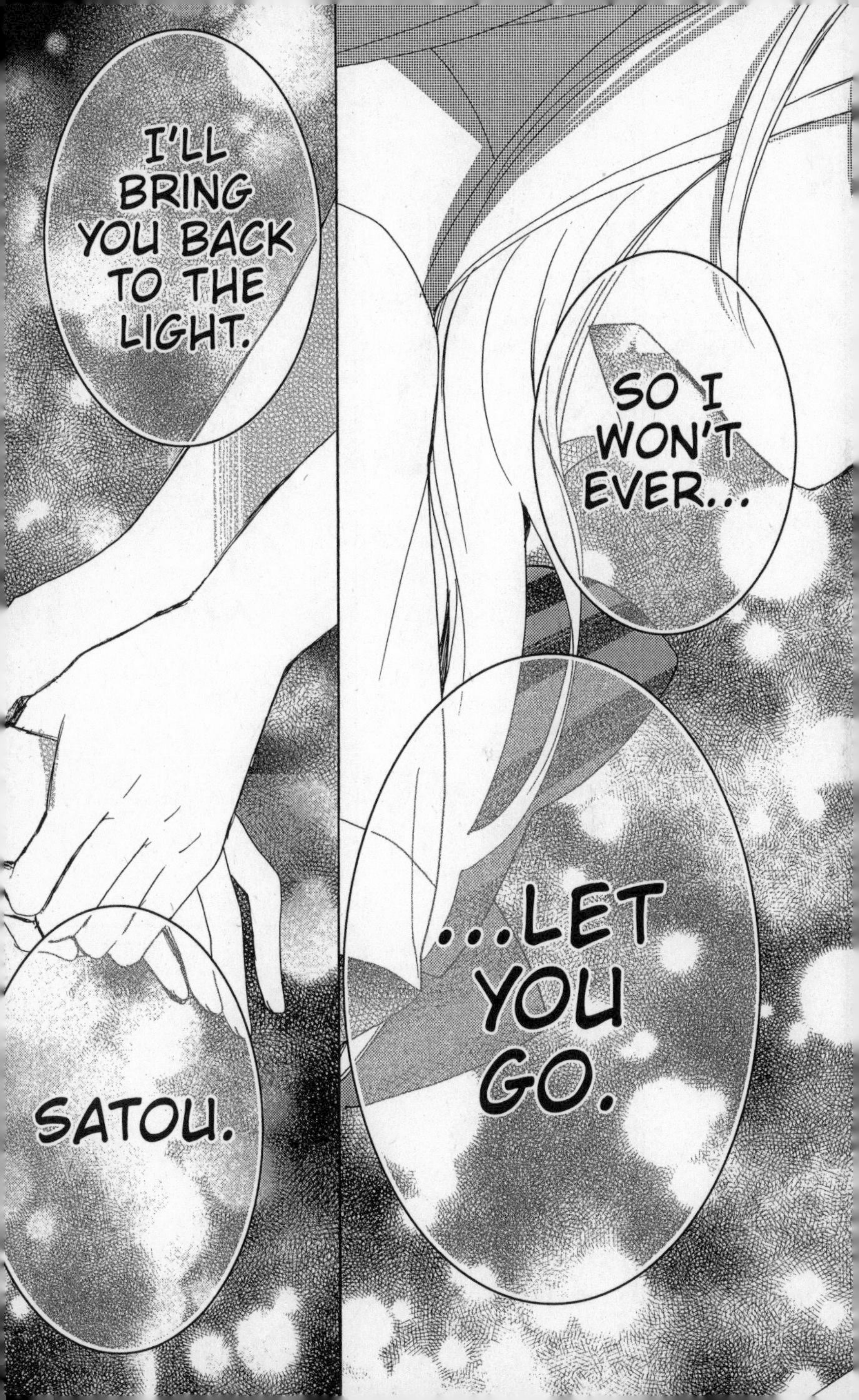
SO I WON'T EVER...
...LET YOU GO.
I'LL BRING YOU BACK TO THE LIGHT.
SATOU.

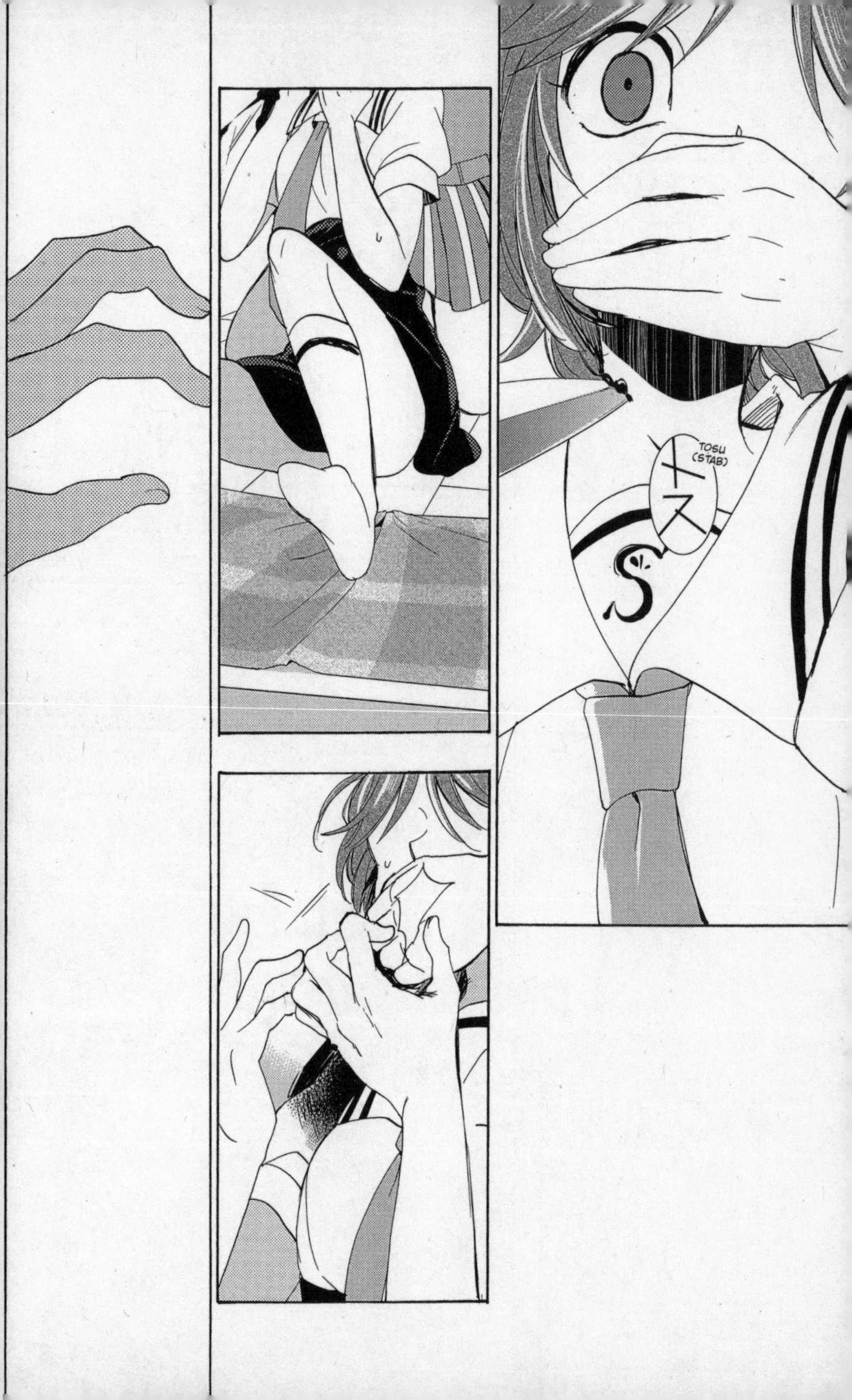
TOSU (STAB)

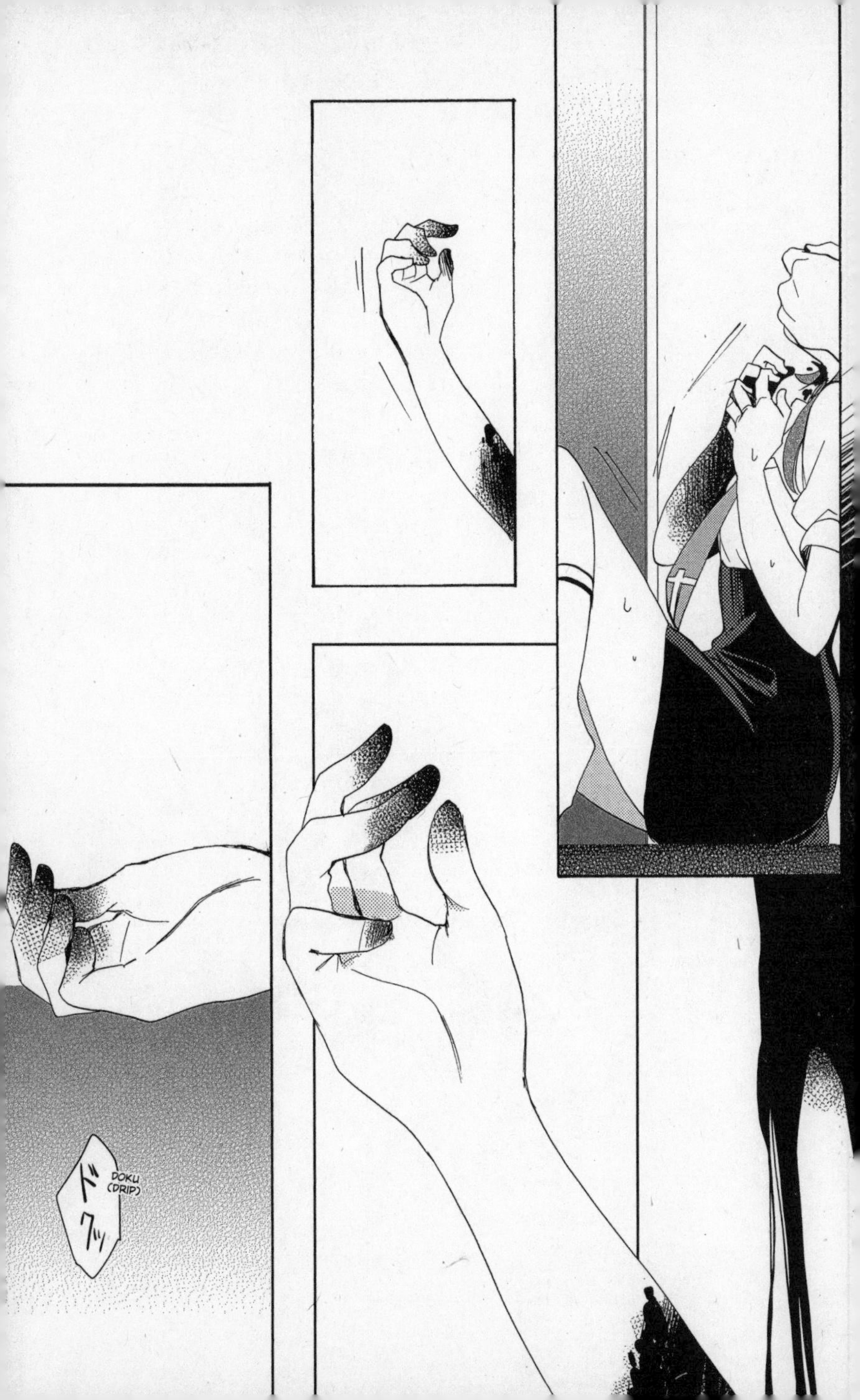
ドクッ
DOKU (DRIP)

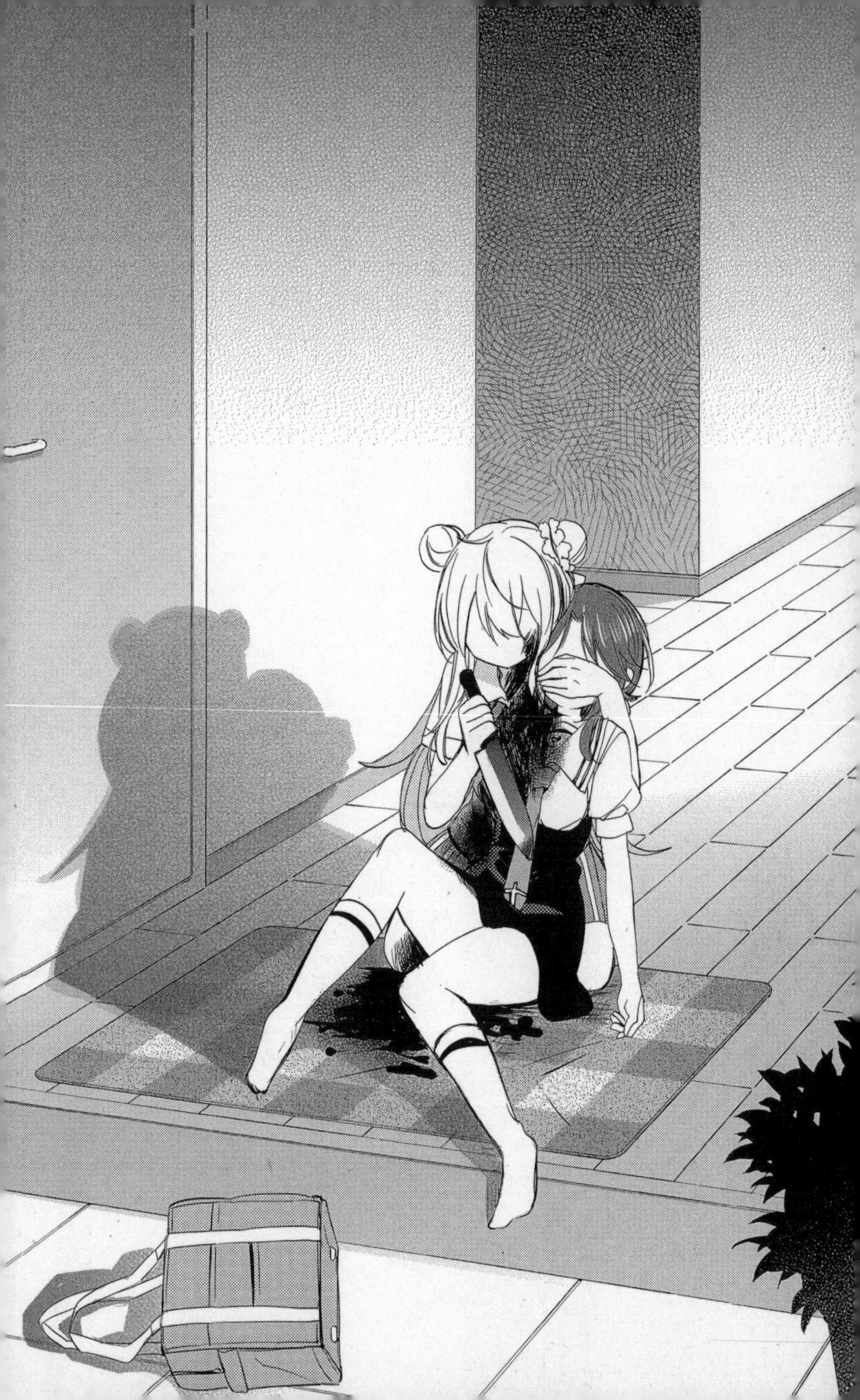

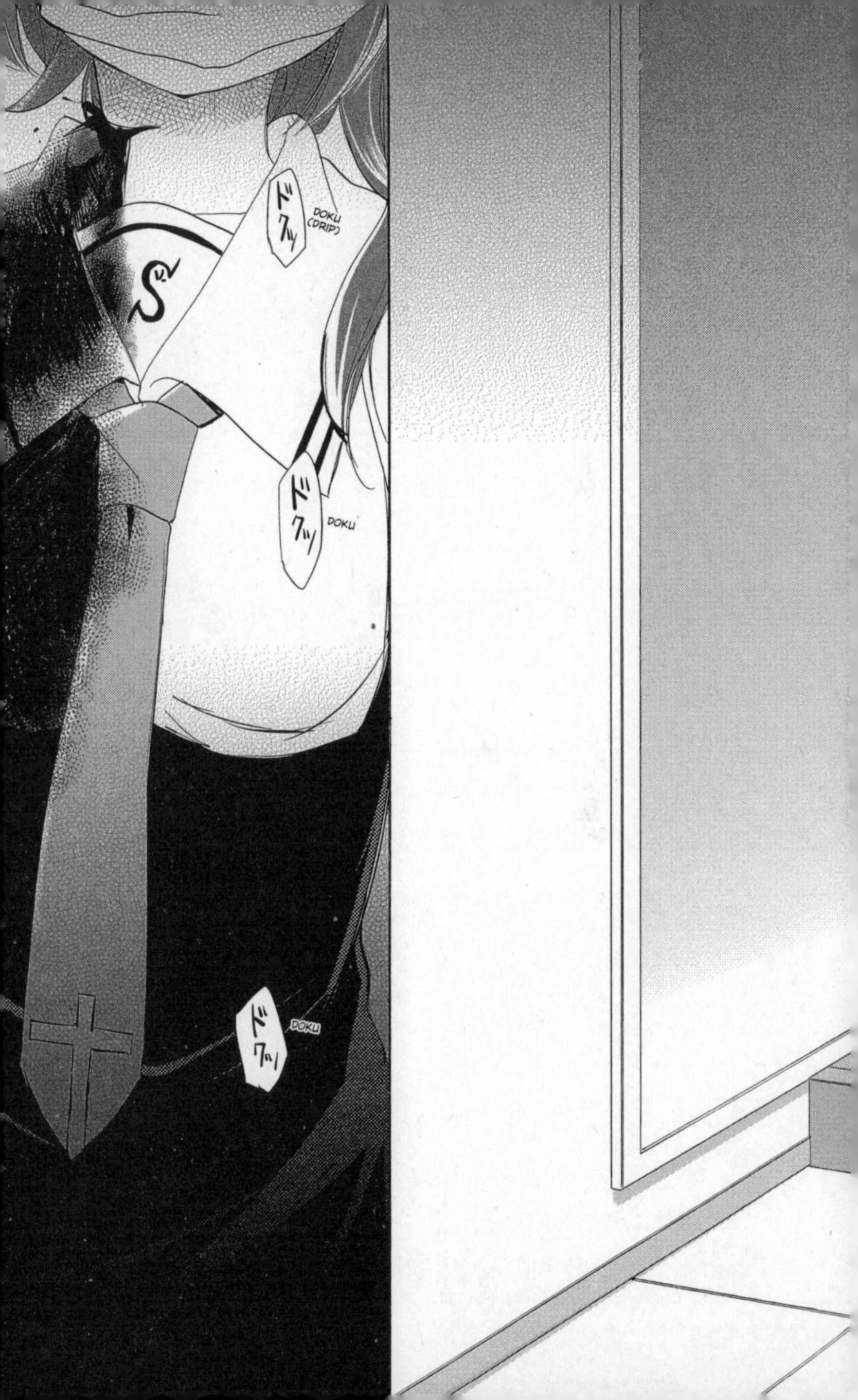
ドクッ
DOKU (DRIP)
ドクッ
DOKU
ドクッ
DOKU

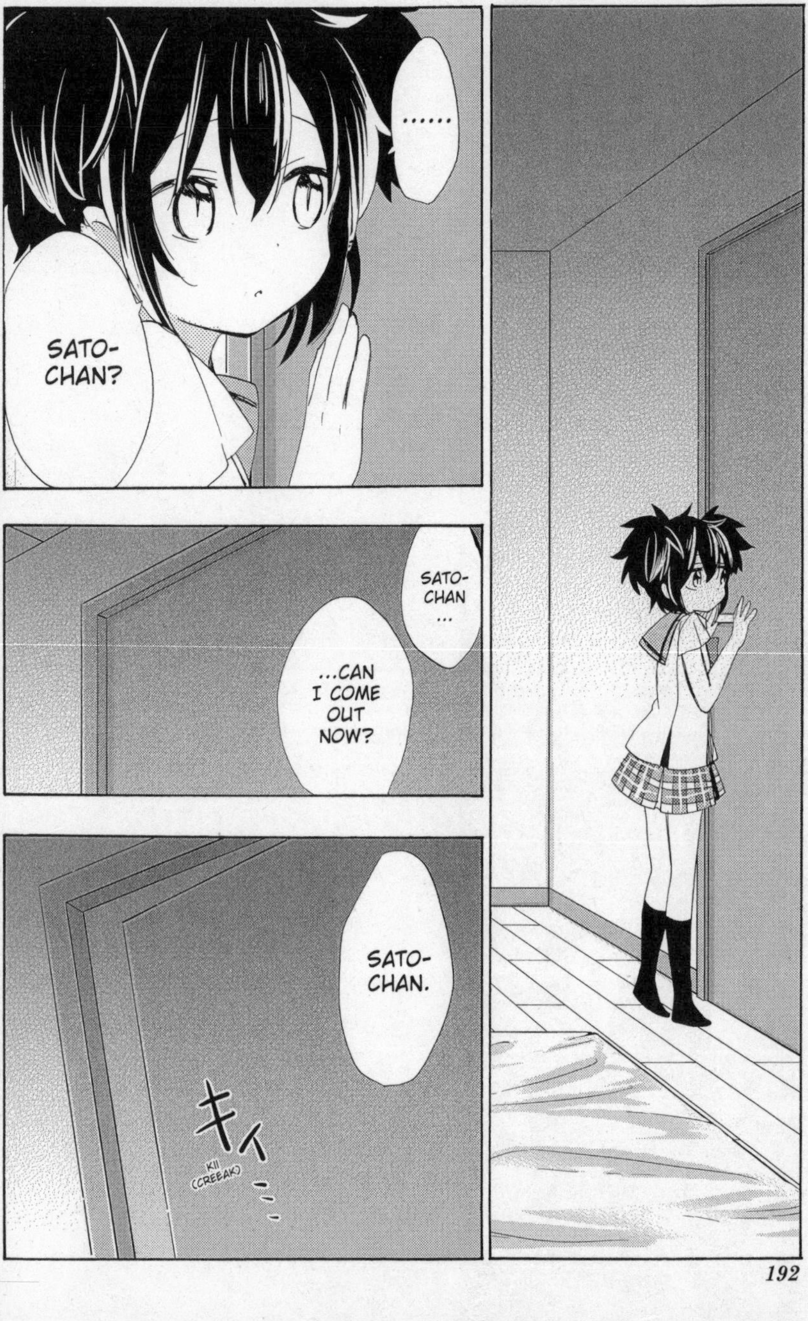
......
SATO-CHAN?
SATO-CHAN ...
...CAN I COME OUT NOW?
SATO-CHAN.
キイ
KII (CREEAK)

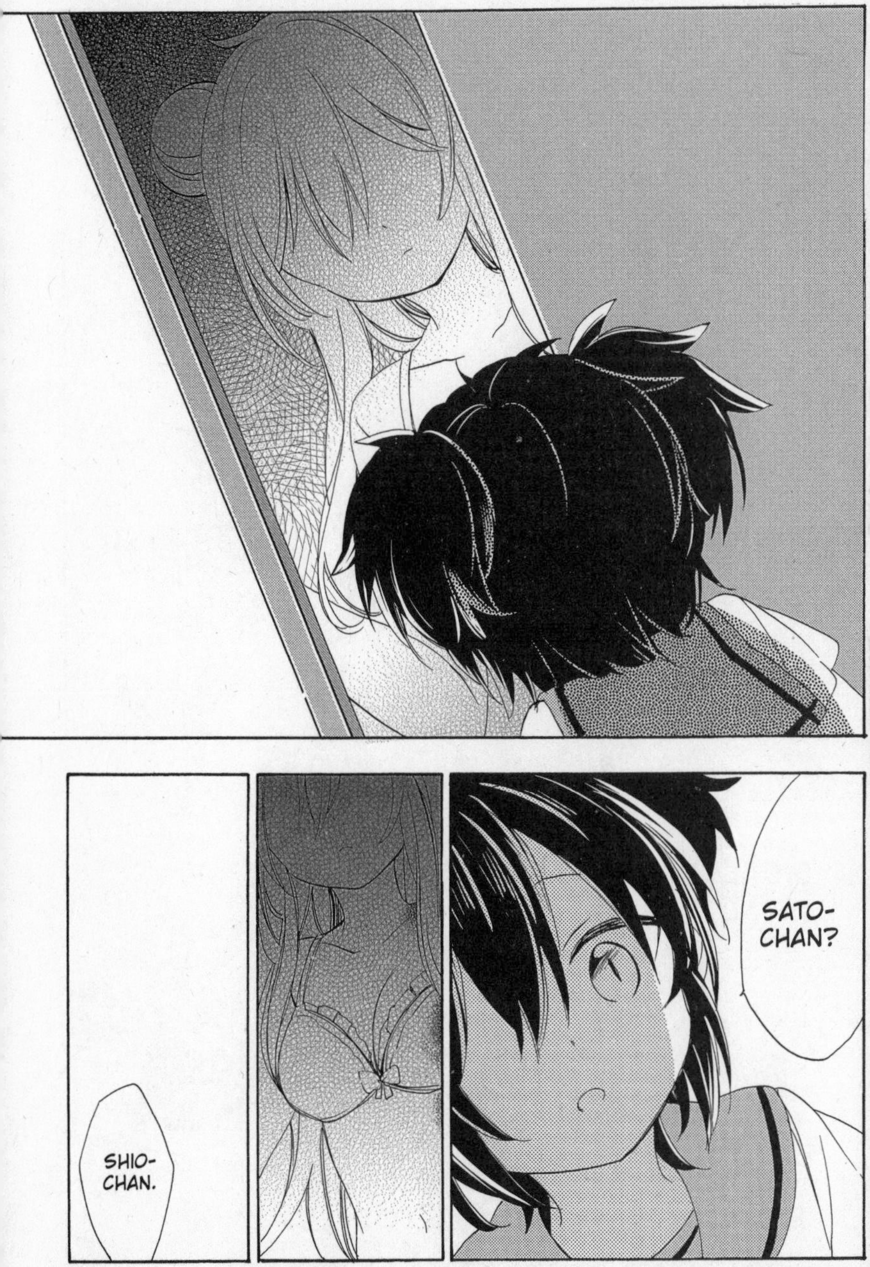
SATO-CHAN?
SHIO-CHAN.

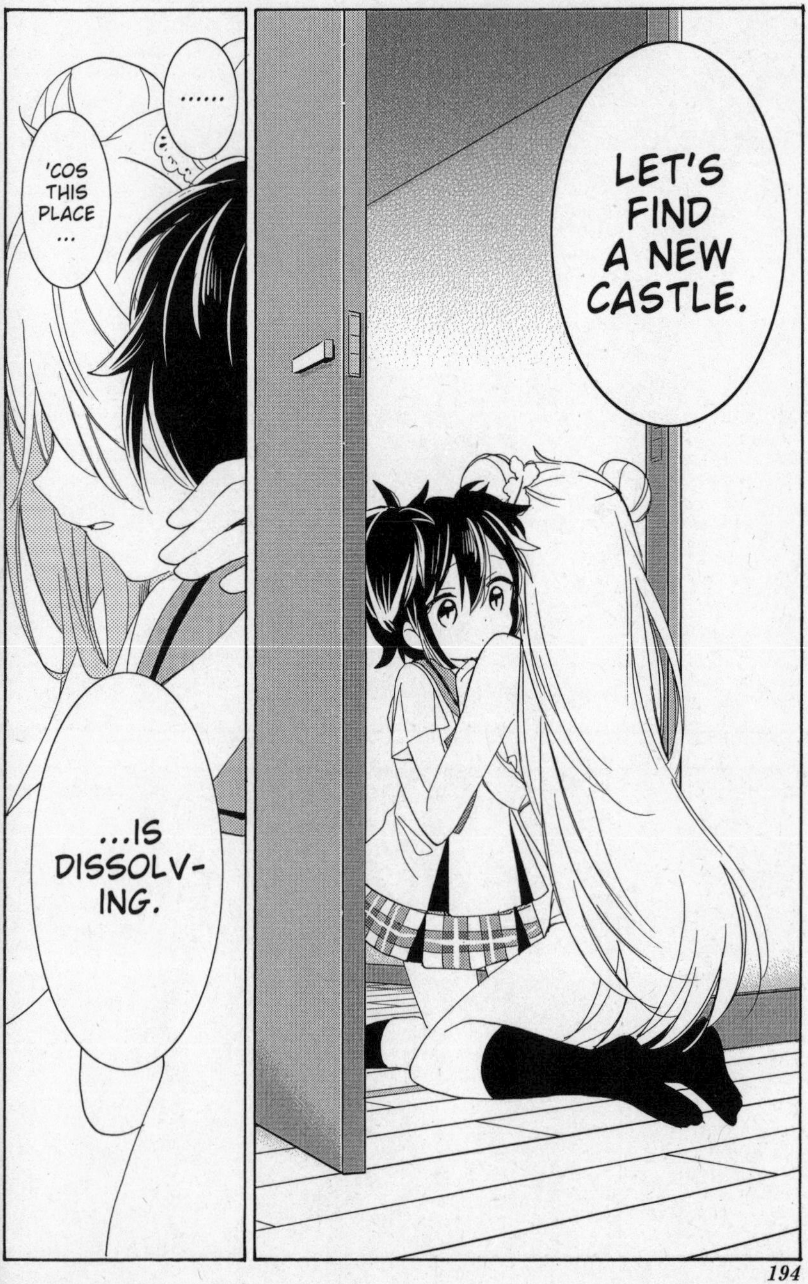
LET'S FIND A NEW CASTLE.
......
'COS THIS PLACE ...
...IS DISSOLV-ING.

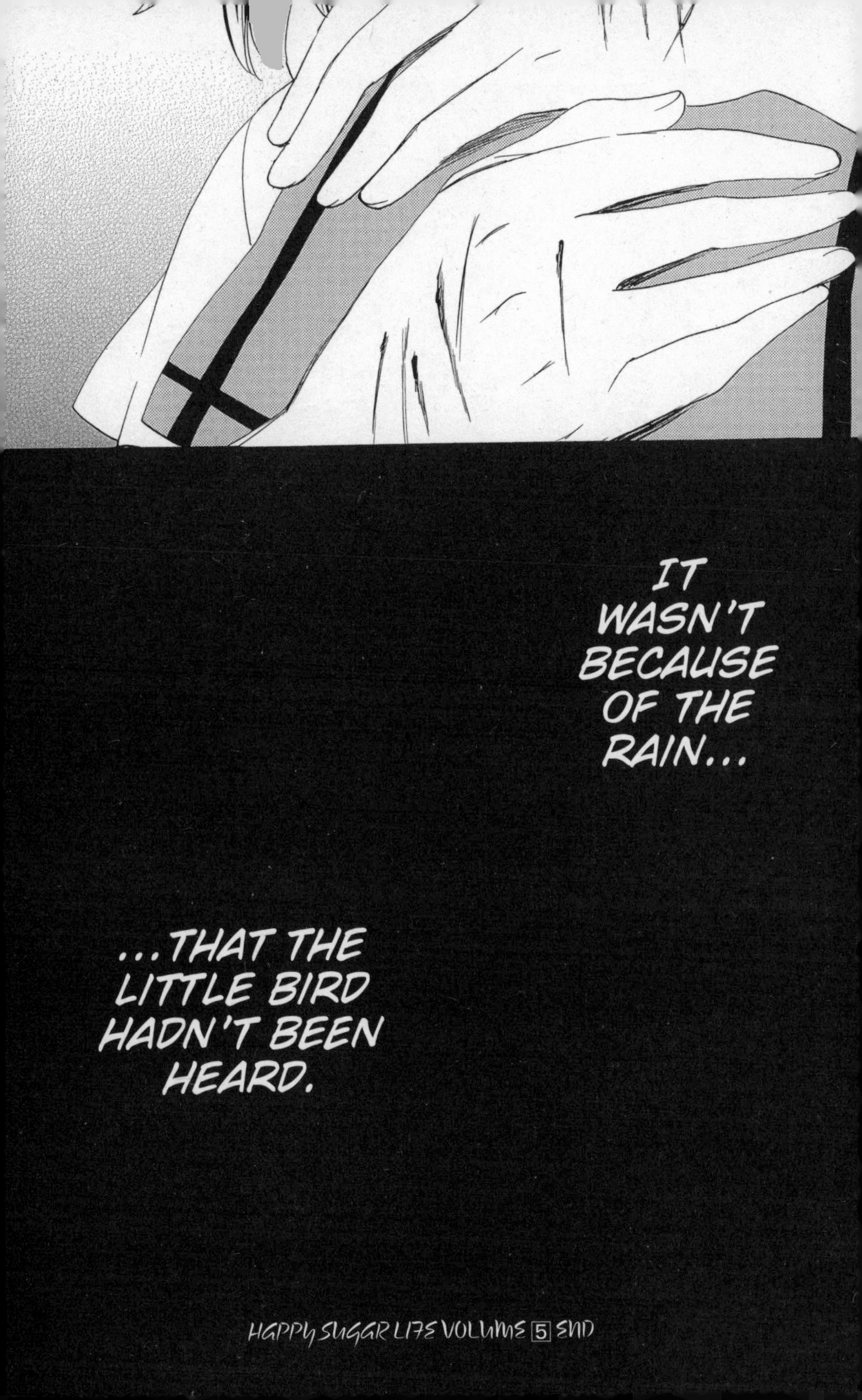
IT WASN'T BECAUSE OF THE RAIN...
...THAT THE LITTLE BIRD HADN'T BEEN HEARD.
HAPPY SUGAR LIFE VOLUME 5 END

es on.

Volume 6 coming Summer 2020!

Life go

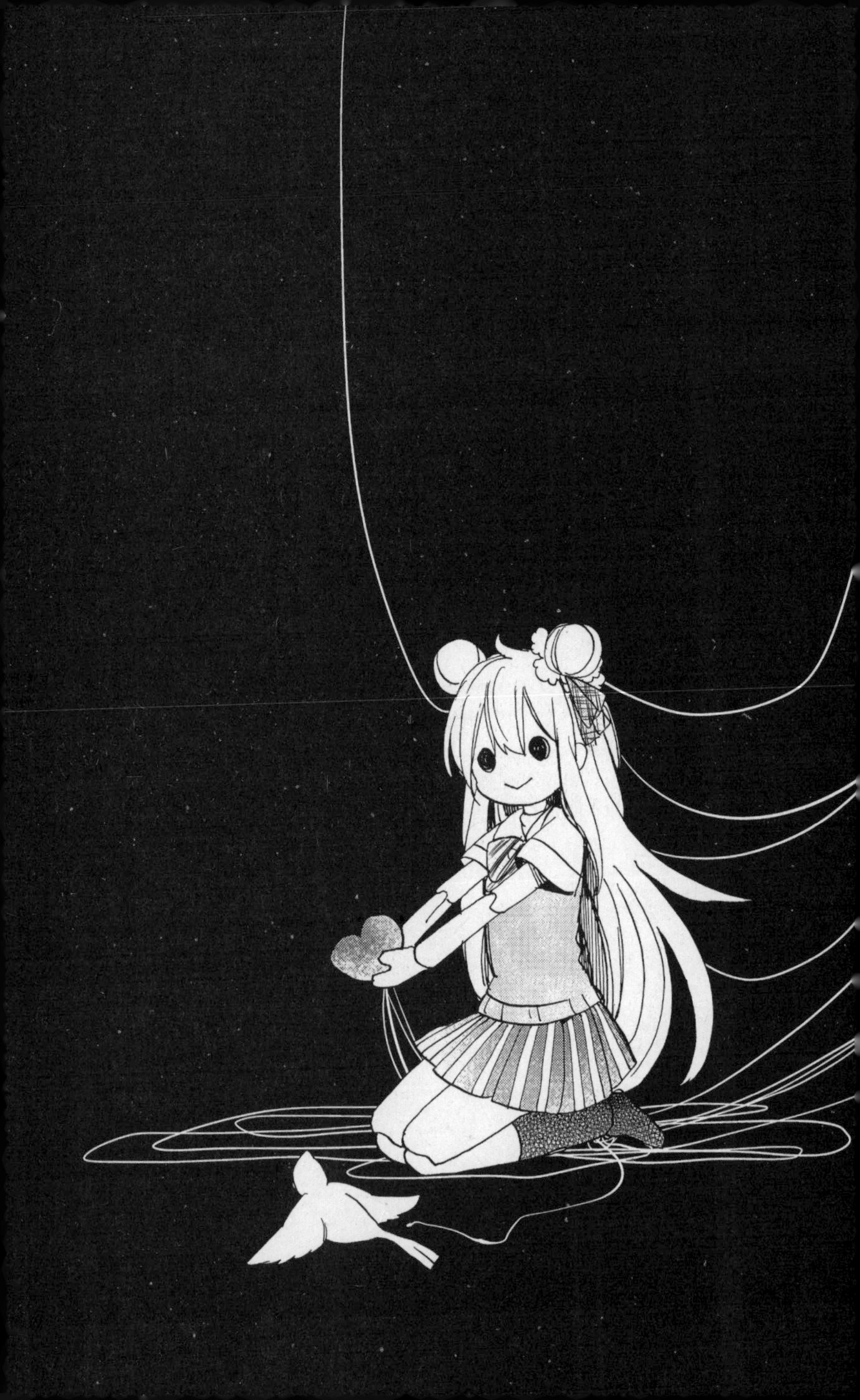

SPECIAL THANKS

TO MY MANAGER.
TO MEGURU-SAMA, TSUNAAGE-SAMA,
TADARAKU HIKARI-SAMA.
TO HARI YOSHITAKA-SAMA,
KIN-SAN, N-SAN.
TO DESIGNER-SAMA.
TO EVERYONE WHO
WAS INVOLVED.
TO THE READERS.

TRANSLATION NOTES

Common Honorifics

no honorific: Indicates familiarity or closeness; if used without permission or reason, addressing someone in this manner would constitute an insult.

-san: The Japanese equivalent of Mr./Mrs./Miss. If a situation calls for politeness, this is the fail-safe honorific.

-sama: Conveys great respect; may also indicate that the social status of the speaker is lower than that of the addressee.

-kun: Used most often when referring to boys, this indicates affection or familiarity. Occasionally used by older men among their peers, but it may also be used by anyone referring to a person of lower standing.

-chan: An affectionate honorific indicating familiarity used mostly in reference to girls; also used in reference to cute persons or animals of either gender.

-senpai: A suffix used to address upperclassmen or more experienced coworkers.

-sensei: A respectful term for teachers, artists, or high-level professionals.

Page 6
Shio is a Japanese girls' name and also the word for "salt."

Page 7
Taiyou is a Japanese boys' name and is also the word for "the sun."

Page 78
Satou is a Japanese girls' name and also the word for "sugar."

Sun Sign Astrology is a form of astrology often associated with newspapers and magazines. This popular form of fortune-telling usually suggests generalized luck based on when a person's sun sign is. Two other terms for sun signs are star signs or the zodiac.

Page 109
Currency exchange rates between Japan and the United States are roughly 100 yen = 1 USD. Satou's cakes cost about $22.

Happy
Sugar
Life

Happy Sugar Life

Volume 6

READ ON FOR A SNEAK
PEEK OF VOLUME 6,
AVAILABLE AUGUST 2020!

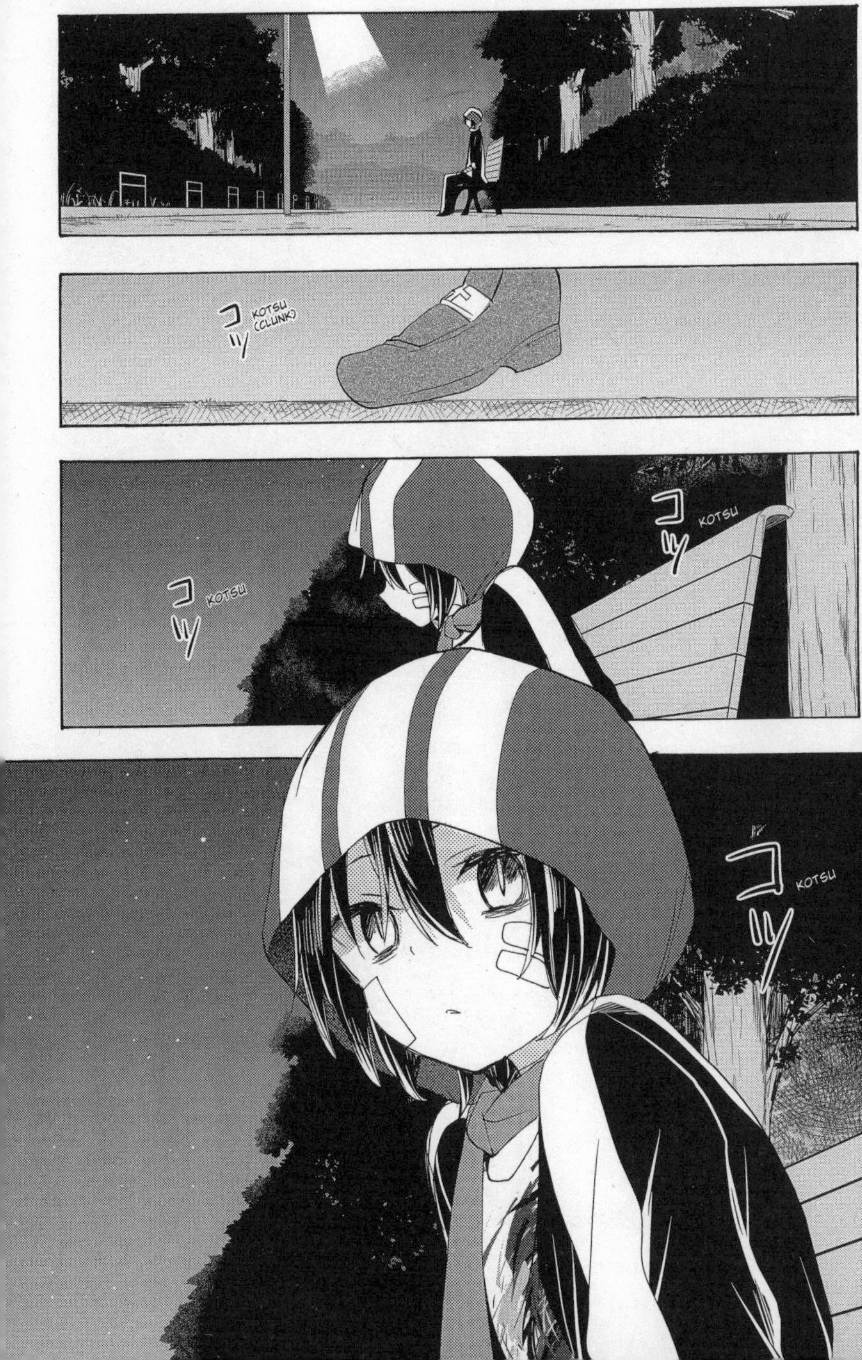
コッ
KOTSU (CLUNK)
コッ
KOTSU
コッ
KOTSU
コッ
KOTSU

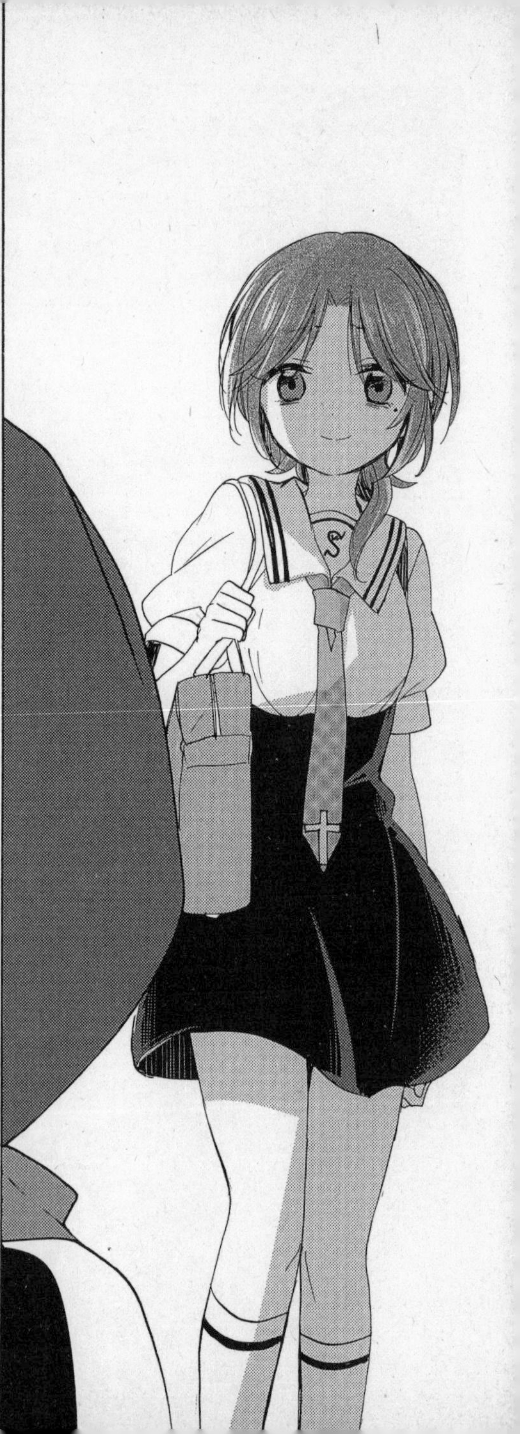

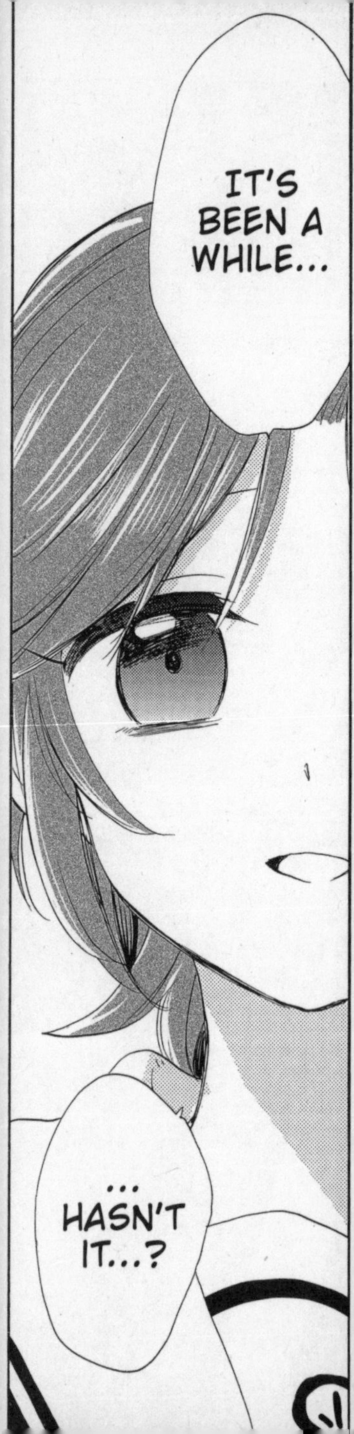
IT'S BEEN A WHILE...
... HASN'T IT...?

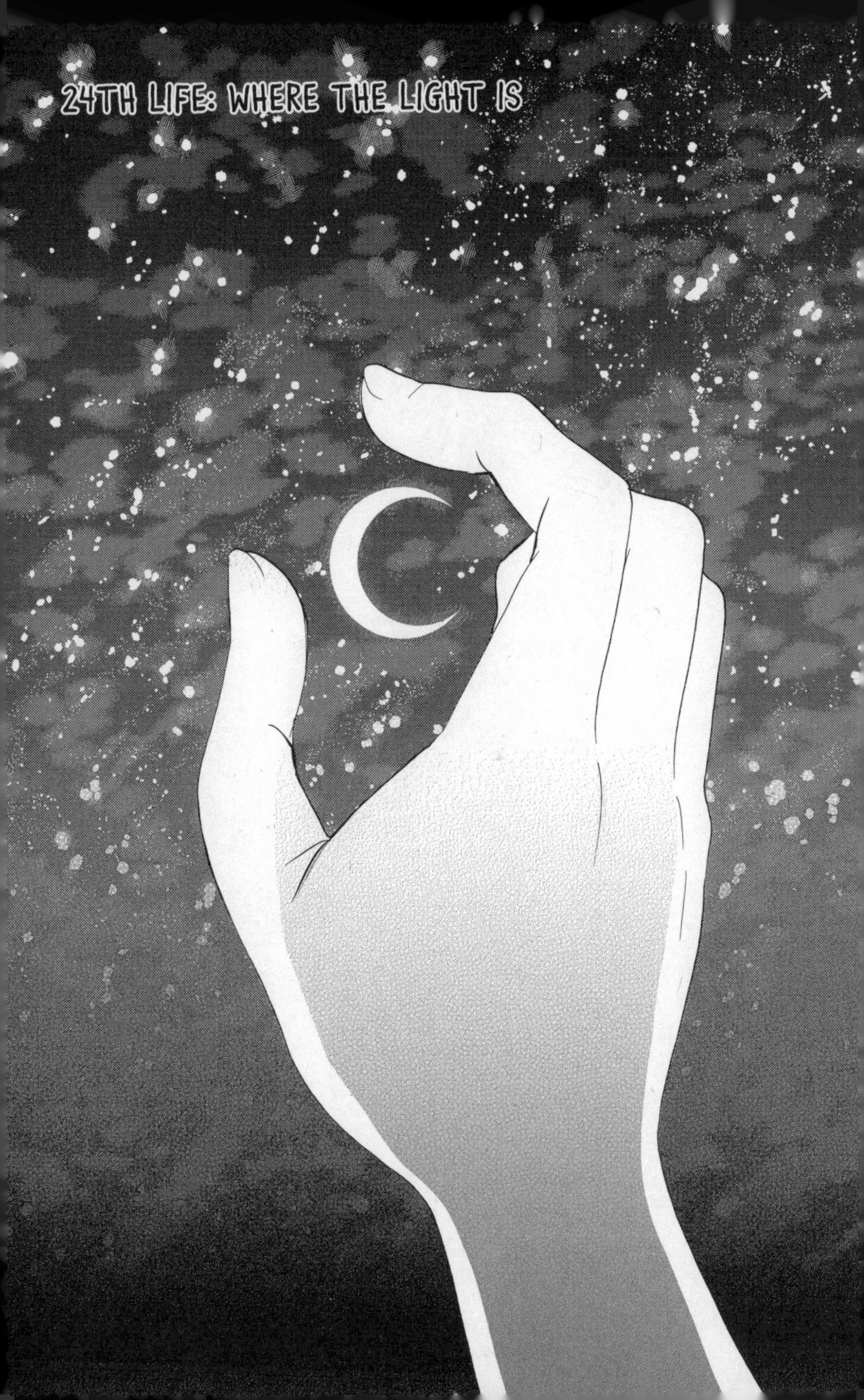
24TH LIFE: WHERE THE LIGHT IS

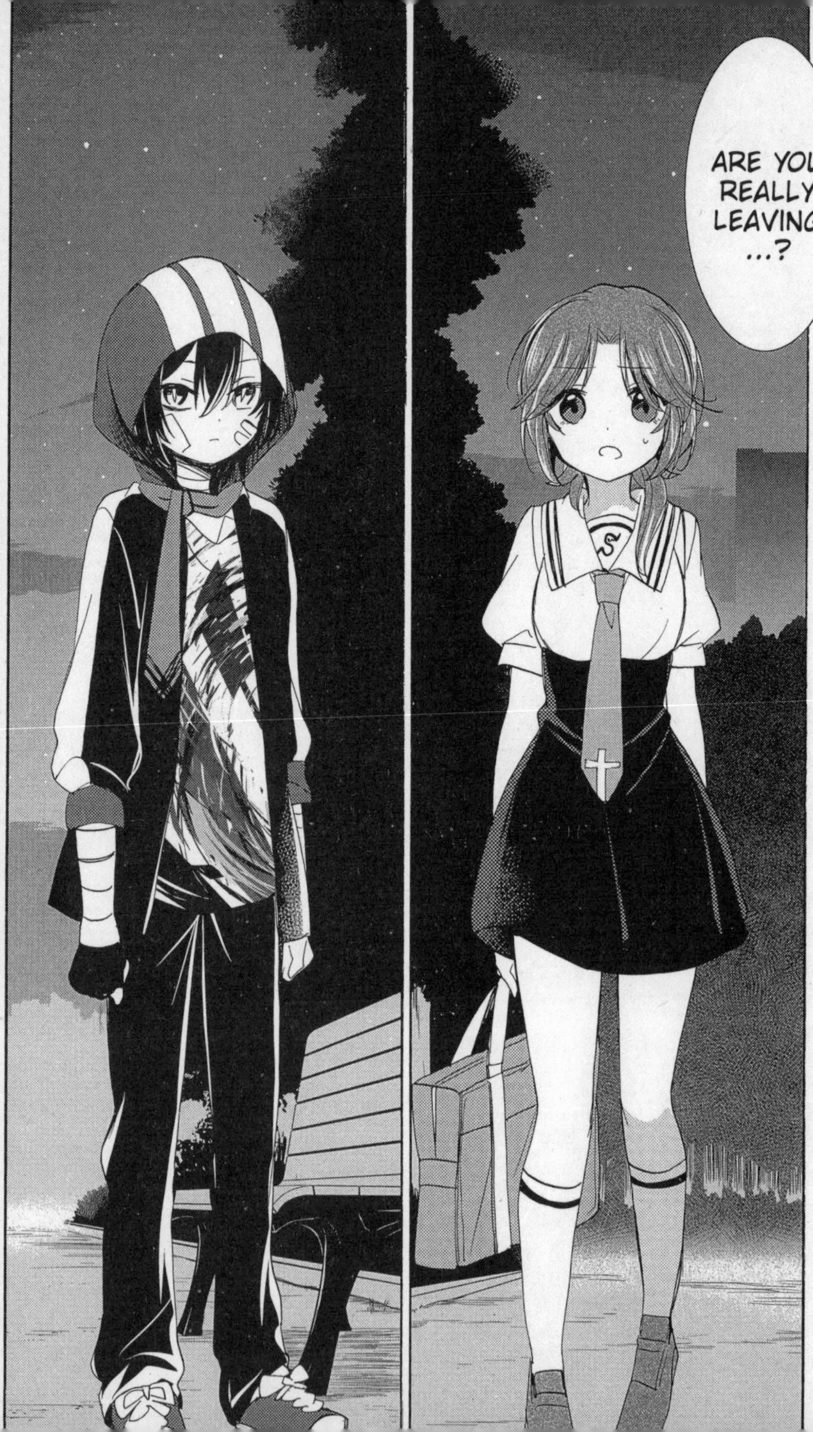
ARE YOU REALLY LEAVING ...?

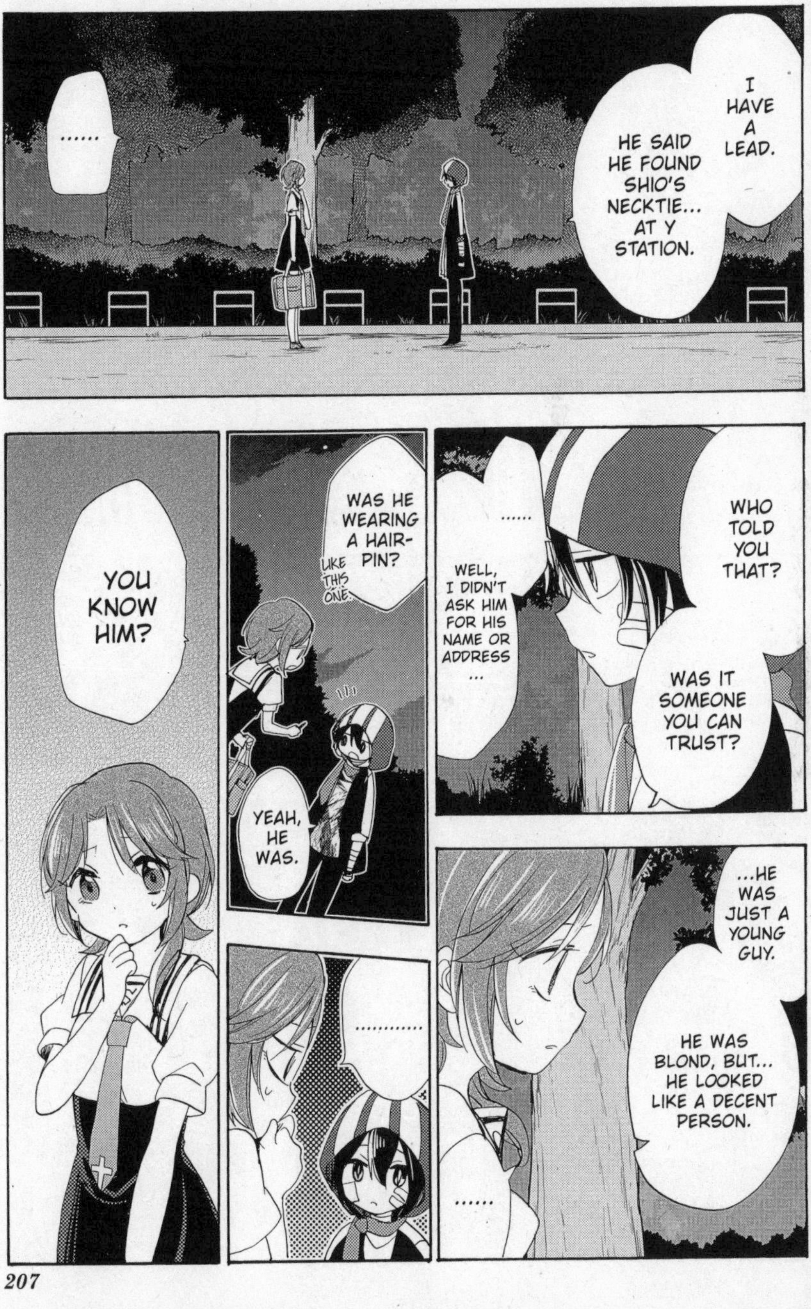
I HAVE A LEAD.
HE SAID HE FOUND SHIO'S NECKTIE... AT Y STATION.
......
WHO TOLD YOU THAT?
WAS IT SOMEONE YOU CAN TRUST?
......
WELL, I DIDN'T ASK HIM FOR HIS NAME OR ADDRESS ...
WAS HE WEARING A HAIR-PIN?
LIKE THIS ONE.
YEAH, HE WAS.
...HE WAS JUST A YOUNG GUY.
HE WAS BLOND, BUT... HE LOOKED LIKE A DECENT PERSON.
......
....
YOU KNOW HIM?

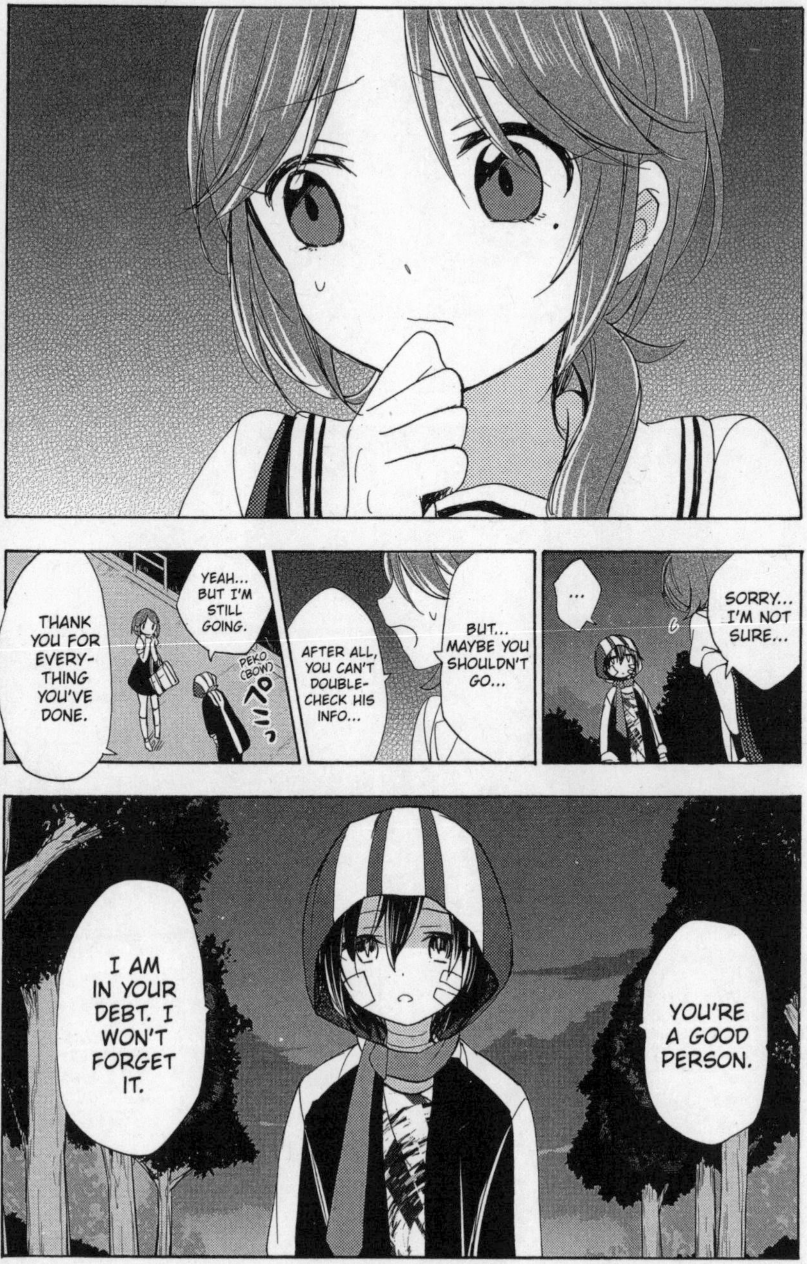
SORRY... I'M NOT SURE...
...
BUT... MAYBE YOU SHOULDN'T GO...
AFTER ALL, YOU CAN'T DOUBLE-CHECK HIS INFO...
YEAH... BUT I'M STILL GOING.
PEKO (BOW)
THANK YOU FOR EVERY-THING YOU'VE DONE.
YOU'RE A GOOD PERSON.
I AM IN YOUR DEBT. I WON'T FORGET IT.

**Find out whether Satou
can protect her**

Happy Sugar Life

in Volume 6!!

Happy Sugar Life 5

Tomiyaki Kagisora

Translation: **JAN MITSUKO CASH**

Lettering: **NICOLE DOCHYCH**

HAPPY SUGAR LIFE vol. 5 ©2017 Tomiyaki Kagisora / SQUARE ENIX CO., LTD. First published in Japan in 2017 by SQUARE ENIX CO., LTD. English translation rights arranged with SQUARE ENIX CO., LTD. and Yen Press, LLC through Tuttle-Mori Agency, Inc.

English translation ©2020 by SQUARE ENIX CO., LTD.

Yen Press
150 West 30th Street, 19th Floor
New York, NY 10001

Visit us at yenpress.com
facebook.com/yenpress
twitter.com/yenpress
yenpress.tumblr.com
instagram.com/yenpress

First Yen Press Edition: May 2020

Yen Press is an imprint of Yen Press, LLC.
The Yen Press name and logo are trademarks of Yen Press, LLC.

The publisher is not responsible for websites (or their content) that are not owned by the publisher.

Library of Congress Control Number: 2019932474

ISBNs: 978-1-9753-0334-1 (paperback)
978-1-9753-8714-3 (ebook)

10 9 8 7 6 5 4 3 2 1

BVG

Printed in the United States of America